CHINA & JAPAN

M. I. SLADKOVSKY

CHINA & JAPAN

PAST AND PRESENT

Edited and Translated

by

Robert F. Price

ACADEMIC INTERNATIONAL PRESS

1975

FORUM ASIATICA / Volume 1

Mikhail I. Sladkovsky *China and Japan—Past and Present.*
Translation of *Kitai i Yaponiia* (Moscow, 1971)

Library of Congress Catalog Card Number: 74-81637
ISBN: 0-87569-062-9

Printed in the United States of America

ACADEMIC INTERNATIONAL PRESS
Box 555 Gulf Breeze FL 32561

CONTENTS

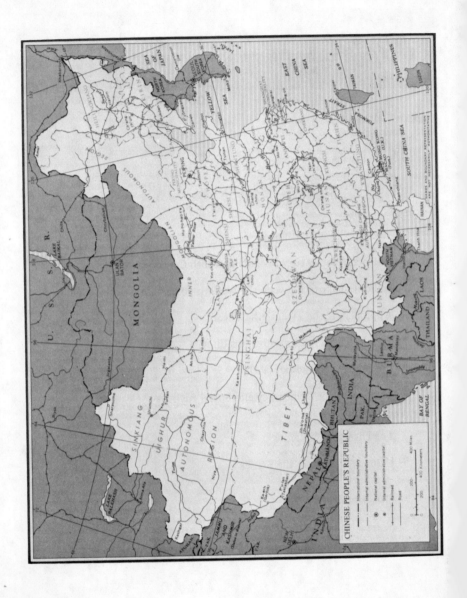

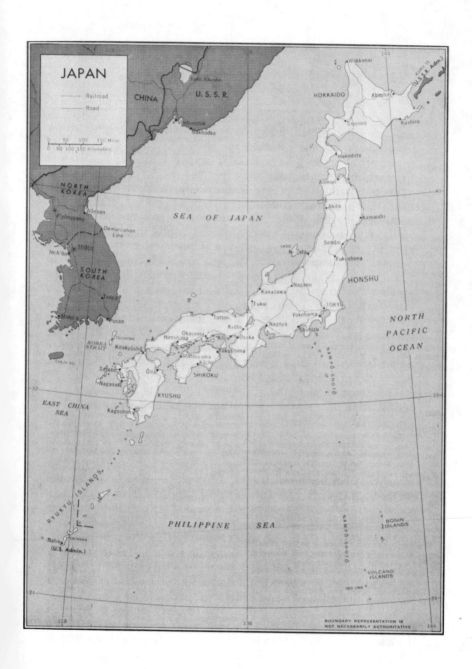

This translation of M.I. Sladkovsky's *China and Japan* is intended for those who do not know Russian but who are interested in the views of an important Soviet scholar about those two lands. Lay readers and specialists may find that the book gives new insights concerning Soviet attitudes toward the Far East. Consequently, the principle aim of the translation is to render the author's ideas into smooth, readable, and transparent English. I did not consider it part of my task to trace Sladkovsky's footnote references back to original sources, or to comment on them except for a very few factual errors. While the text is complete, the footnotes have been condensed and in some cases deleted where it was felt that they contained extraneous details constituting a needless digression rather than a useful explanation of Sladkovsky's main text. The intention was to find a successful compromise that would include all information that is germane and of interest, without distracting readers needlessly by an overabundance of notes. Scholars in the field will be better equipped to compare sources as they delve deeper into the subject. The exception to this rule is that all treaties and international agreements have been found and cited in English versions.

Chinese names and titles have been Anglicized and standardized according to the system used in Wolfram Eberhard's *A History of China* (second edition, University of California Press, 1960). The only departure is that diacritic marks have been left off for simplicity. Biographical and historical facts for the period after World War II were checked in Derek J. Waller's *The Government and Politics of Communist China* (Doubleday Anchor Books, 1971). Geographical names in the text and on the maps are consistent with usage in Albert Hermann's *An Historical Atlas of China* (Aldine Publishing Company, Chicago, 1966). Japanese information was verified in John Whitney Hall's *Japan from Prehistory to Modern Times* (Delacorte World History, 1970), and in Masao Maruyama's *Thought and Behavior in Modern Japanese Politics* (Oxford University Press, 1969). Other useful sources are cited in the notes. Russian names and titles have been transliterated using the Library of Congress system with the following variations: "ya" and "yu" have replaced "ia" and "iu" at beginnings of words, and "y" appears in place of "ii" at the end of surnames such as the author's. Chinese or Japanese names have been used if they differ from Russian variants, or if both appear. Hence,

Ta-lien instead of Dalny. Commonly accepted names such as Port Arthur are used where suitable.

Several considerations influenced the type of notes that have been included. References to works cited by the author are given for readers who may wish to investigate the background of the author's analyses. Frequently repetition has been avoided by combining and abridging notes from the original text into more general form. Finally, persons, places and concepts have been identified and placed in time. The goals were both to streamline Sladkovsky's peripheral information for the intended audience, while providing new details that might be essential for clear understanding of the book. Most of the notes are translations from the author; those provided by the editor are so marked.

Other practices used in translating and editing should be clear in their context. It remains to express my gratitude for the help of my colleagues at the University of Wisconsin-Stevens Point and for the use of special facilities here. Special thanks go to Professor Hugh D. Walker of the History Department for his expert advice on both Chinese and Japanese materials and events, and to Mary Kay Hamilton who voluntarily did much of the typing on the manuscript. Finally, I want to express appreciation to Peter von Wahlde, the publisher, and to my wife Dorothy, for their major contributions toward a smooth English text.

R.F. Price

Stevens Point, Wisconsin

LIST OF TABLES

CHINA
&
JAPAN

PAST
AND
PRESENT

CHAPTER ONE

Ancient China and Japan

The populations of both China and Japan stem primarily from the Pacific Ocean branch of the Mongolian race. Their levels of development through history have differed greatly due to different geographical conditions and varying external factors which have affected progress and modernization. Centralized national government developed earlier in China than in Japan. When this occurred in Japan in the seventh century A.D., China had already completed a long course of historical evolution. Chinese civilization had progressed considerably by the time more or less permanent ties were established with the Japanese islands.

CHINA IN ANTIQUITY

The Han people are the largest on the mainland and form the nucleus of today's Chinese population. Many diverse tribal groups intermingled as they settled on the territory of ancient China. The Chinese historian Fan Wen-lan distinguishes several basic tribes which formed the Han people. The Huang Ti tribe first dwelled in the northwest, then migrated to the territory of modern Ho-nan and Shan-tung provinces. The Yang Ti tribe, which settled the central regions (roughly Ho-pei province), mixed with eastern tribes and the Miao aborigines of the south.[1] Since eventually the Han became the major people of China, Chinese cultural developments are related to Han evolution. Archeological and historical monuments confirm that ancient Han culture formed within the area bordered on the north by the Huang Ho river and on the west by the Hsi Shan mountains. Relatively advanced agriculture and handicrafts were pursued on fertile lands by industrious workers. An advanced culture assured Han ascendance over neighboring peoples who were at a lower level of development.

The Han people included the Chung heritage, which had united thousands of large clans by blood, economic interests and common religion. The economic expansion of the Han and their attacks on neighbors encouraged slavery in China and the emergence of feudal states on its territory. The history of the first feudal states in China is connected with the Shang dynasty, which was later renamed the Yin.

It reigned from the 18th to the 12th century B.C. In the 12th century B.C. a new state arose on the territory of China, the Chou. With the passage of time it disintegrated into a number of principalities only nominally subjugated to the Chou imperial house.

At the end of the Chun-chiu period,[2] from the numerous belligerent petty princedoms the "seven strongest" gradually emerged: the Chu, Chin, Wei, Chao, Han, Chi and Yen. These princedoms engaged in a prolonged civil war seeking to rule all of China, thus laying foundation for the Chang-kuo (fighting kingdoms) period.

The Chang-kuo (403-221 B.C.) occupies a special place in Chinese history. Bitter wars in this period stimulated the production of iron weapons which were more durable than bronze and copper ones. Iron processing was thereby perfected, leading to a significant advance in technology. Various implements and tools also were perfected at this time, such as iron shovels and hoes. High skills emerged in weaving, particularly of silk, as well as in the ceramics, woodcarving and lacquering handicrafts. Building methods developed rapidly, permitting the construction of large imperial palaces, defensive structures, ships and boats. The growth of handicraft and agricultural production fostered Chinese domestic trade, the appearance of large cities and expansion of ties with neighboring peoples. Chinese philosophy flourished, represented by a number of schools: Confucianism founded by Confucius who lived from 552-479 B.C., the Moist begun by Mo-Tsu (478-382), the Tao, founded by Lao-Tsu, the Legist, and so forth. The Chinese material and intellectual culture of the Chang-kuo period laid the foundations for a central government. This development was hastened also by outside factors, chiefly threats from neighboring nomadic peoples.

Around 247 B.C. the Chin kingdom began brutally to subjugate the other six kingdoms and to form the first centralized monarchy, headed by Chang Wan. He proclaimed himself the first emperor of the Chin dynasty—Chin Shi Huang-ti. He added broad territories of the ancient state of Nan-yueh in the south, whose inhabitants were closer ethnically to the peoples of the Indo-Chinese peninsula.[3] Chin Shi Huang-ti forced the nomadic Huns out of the province of Ho-nan. For the protection of his northern borders from nomadic attacks, he constructed the Great Wall of China. This defensive barrier has formed the northern and northwestern border of China proper throughout its entire subsequent history.[4]

The creation of the centralized Chin empire was accompanied by a massive slaughter. Savage force was employed against defeated neighbors, against the Chinese aristocracy and all followers of the ancient Chinese schools of philosophy which had condemned license and tyranny. According to Chinese historians, "all books with the exception of the Chin chronicles, medical, divining and agronomical books, were to be surrendered for burning to district and regional administrations. Those who discussed and debated about the 'Book of Songs' and the 'Historical Documents,'[5] were beheaded, and those who, alluding to the past, criticized the existing order, were executed together with their entire families."[6]

The epoch of Chin Shi Huang-ti left a black mark on the history of China. Especially large numbers of historical and literary monuments were lost. Many original works of outstanding Chinese scholars, poets and philosophers were completely or partially destroyed. On the other hand, the creation of a central authority promoted the rule of law and prepared the way for a more rapid development of China. The territory of the Chinese state was divided into 36 provinces, then subdivided into districts. The provinces were headed by representatives of the central government, under the control of special imperial officials called inspectors. Uniform weights and measures were established, a uniform Chinese calligraphy was introduced, and the monetary system was standardized (the customary turtle shells, seashells and jasper were replaced by gold and copper coins).

The first centralized monarchy, the Chin, lasted only briefly, until 207 B.C. Numerous innovations favorably affected China's progress. At the same time they aggravated the social and national antagonisms which had arisen in the country during the destruction of feudal princedoms and the subjugation of foreign territories on the south and north. The English student of ancient Chinese history, Hawks Pott, wrote that "China annexed and conquered more territory than it was in a position to assimilate."[7] After the death of Emperor Chin Shi Huang-ti and the two-year reign of his younger son Erh Shi Huang-ti, the Chin dynasty collapsed under the blows of popular revolts.

During the revolt against the Chin dynasty, internal conflicts broke out among the rebel forces. A former village elder, Liu Pan, proclaimed himself emperor after eliminating his competitors and it was he who assembled the new Han dynasty. The Han dynasty occupies a major place in Chinese history, ruling from 206 B.C. until 220 A.D. Liu Pan adopted the dynastic title Kao Tsu. He initiated many measures to perfect government administration and to strengthen the nation's economy.

As a result of the internal strife which preceded Kao Tsu and of the struggle with the Huns who invaded China at the beginning of his reign, "the population in the first period of the Han empire was forty percent less than in the period of the six kingdoms."[8] Kao Tsu was forced to disband part of the army and to distribute empty lands to the soldiers. Some cultivated holdings remained under the direct control of the imperial court. Economic endeavors expanded rapidly in the early years of the Han dynasty. The acquisition of salt from sea water became commonplace, iron ore was extracted in larger quantities, and production of iron tools and agricultural implements such as plowshares became common. River dams, canals and irrigation systems were constructed and improved.

Handicraft manufacture expanded, particularly in weaving where Chinese silken fabrics and brocade became known far beyond the reaches of China. Palaces were built, along with temples and enormous underground tombs, attesting to a high level of architectural and mathematical knowledge. Astronomy in this period flourished. A star map was drawn and an eclipse of the sun first was observed in the year 28 B.C. Ancient China's greatest astronomer, Chang Hen (78-139 A.D.), devised a seismograph and the first universal globe, which reproduced the movements of the heavenly bodies. The famous agronomist Fang Shen-chi described methods of land cultivation in detail. Other scholarly disciplines also progressed. The outstanding historian of ancient China, Ssu-ma Chien (146-86 B.C.), in his celebrated "Historical Notes" attempted to recreate the entire course of history from the most ancient times. He restored many chronicles and legends which had been lost at the time of Chin Shi Huang-ti. Ssu-ma Chien commenced the historical scholarship which became the foundation for the "Official History."[9] The Confucian scholar Tung Chung-shu (179-104 B.C.) acquired broad repute as one of the founders of Confucian theology. Confucianism became a part of government ideology and gained followers both within the country and beyond its borders.

The Han empire reached particular heights during the reign of Emperor Wu Ti (140-87 B.C.). The central government was bolstered by the relatively higher levels of culture and technology. This enabled the Han rulers to save China from belittling subservience to the Huns, who from time to time conducted devastating raids on China's western and northern regions. Yet the Han empire itself committed aggression against neighboring peoples. In 110 B.C. Wu Ti's army of 100,000 smashed Turkic-Uighur tribal unions and moved far to the west. Fergana was captured in 102 B.C. Along the routes from Kan-su to

Fergana the Chinese established military posts. Their task was to defend the so-called "Silk Route" which connected China with the Middle East and Central Asia. Simultaneously the Han armies began advances to the south and southwest. In 111-110 B.C. once again they captured Nan-yueh (Kuan-tung province, Kuan-hsi and the northern part of Vietnam), and Tung-yu (the southern part of Che-chiang province and Fu-chien). The southwestern tribes were subdued and in 108 B.C. further campaigns began to the northwest, ending in the capture of Chao-hsien, on the Liao-tung and Korean peninsulas. The arrival of the Han armies on the Korean peninsula fostered permanent ties with Japan. As a consequence of this expansion, the borders of the Han empire approached India, the states of Central Asia, and the Japanese islands. "Wars," Chinese historians remark, "contributed to the enrichment of the Chinese people in geographical knowledge, and to the spread of advanced Chinese culture .... In addition, the physical culture of China benefited from importation of foreign goods including grapes, watermelons, beans, flax, peaches, onions, garlic, black pepper and pomegranates, and such beasts as sturdy Fergana horses and camels. Meanwhile foreign cultural imports improved China's intellectual life, Buddhism from India and Western music and culture being examples."[10]

At the same time war exhausted China. The enormous army, with many foreign mercenaries, lay like a heavy burden on the shoulders of the Chinese. Gradually, resistance to Han rule grew both at home and in captured territories. During Emperor Wu Ti's conquests, a despotic military regime developed. Chinese historians describe it thus: "Applying its special method of tax assessment, the court of Wu Ti took over national wealth by hundreds of millions, acquired tens of thousands of male and female slaves, seized several hundred ching of cultivated land in each large county and over a hundred ching in the small counties, along with homes and estates. The majority of middle and small merchants were ruined financially."[11] Wu Ti's successor employed slave labor and physical coercion, methods which increasingly hampered the development of the country. General unrest spread, bringing large scale rebellions. In the western regions the Turkic-Uighur tribes rose in insurrection, while in the north and northeast the Tunguss-Manchurian tribes revolted.

The sharpening social crisis brought a change of dynasties. In the year 6 A.D. the court minister Wang Mang, having poisoned Emperor Ping Ti in 5 A.D., became the regent for the two-year-old Emperor Ju Chi-yin. In 9 A.D. the child-emperor was removed and Wang Mang proclaimed himself emperor of the Hsin (New) dynasty. Wang Mang intended to solve the problems confronting the country by increased centralization of authority and new military campaigns. His reforms were aimed at strengthening the central government. For example, he laid claim to all land as the property of the emperor, introduced state control over handicrafts and commerce, and established standard prices. Wang Mang also attempted by military force to strengthen the rule of the Han empire over the conquered neighboring nations. His "reforms" and expansionist international policy provoked broad popular revolts by "the dwellers of the green forests" and the "red brows," who brought about his overthrow. In 23 A.D., under the imperial title of Kuang-wu Ti, Liu Hsiu was brought to the throne. He was an aristocrat who belonged to a branch of the Han dynasty.

Threatened inroads by western nomads forced the new emperor to move his capitol from the city of Chang-an (today's Hsi-an) to the city of Lo-yang (in northern Ho-nan). Thereafter the empire became known as the Eastern Empire or the Late Han (23-220 A.D.). It lost the western Uighur tribal territories it had conquered earlier, as well as the northern and northeastern territories which were the ancient homes of the Korean and the Tunguss-Manchurian peoples.

During the reign of the eastern Han dynasty, Buddhism grew in importance throughout China. At the time of Emperor Ming Ti (58-74 A.D.) rulers in some parts of the empire accepted Buddhism. For example, the Chus ruler Tin elevated Buddhism to the rank of official religion. Buddhism gained more followers during the reign of Huang-ti (147-167 A.D.) when translations of the canons and the construction of pagodas and temples were undertaken. The spread of Buddhism accompanied the expanding ties between China and the outside world and acquaintance with the high culture of India and Thailand. Buddhism exerted a great influence on the spiritual life as well as on the material culture of Chinese society. Its legends and rituals became the determining factor for Chinese architecture, applied art, and sculpture. It was adroitly combined in these arts with native Chinese culture.

During the first years of its existence the eastern Han dynasty, by clever manipulation of various western nomadic alliances, preserved relative calm on its borders. This permitted the dynasty to complete a number of undertakings to invigorate the economy and to improve the system of government rule. Significant technological and intellectual advances followed. In the ravaged border regions, former soldiers and landless peasants were sent to inhabit military settlements. State lands and agricultural equipment were rented or simply given to the peasants. Lowered taxes and encouragement of handicraft and commerce stimulated private initiative and assisted production growth. This promoted the development of science and art.

Despite these advances, economic and cultural progress could not continue for long under despotic monarchy. Having just recovered from domestic and international reverses, the imperial court invariably used military terror at home, and further aggression against neighboring peoples. These policies resulted in collapse. Three hostile states emerged as the "Triple Kingdom;" they were called Wei, Shu and Wu. This epoch left a deep mark as a period when the national characteristics of the Chinese people shone in all their diversity, finding expression in the legendary feats of beloved heroes. In very complex situations, China's legendary heroes demonstrated unusual resourcefulness, permitting them to emerge triumphant over treacherous, lying, sometimes strong but always cowardly, stupid enemies. Positive traits predominated in men of the Shu kingdom, whose ruler Liu Pei considered himself the heir to the Han dynasty. The first minister of the kingdom, Chu-ko Liang, is respected in Chinese history even today as a national hero for his patriotism, bravery and military talent. The Shu kingdom stood in sharp contrast to the Wei, ruled by Tsao Tsao, who treacherously usurped the imperial authority. All of his descendants personify falsity, treachery and betrayal.

The idealization of the Triple Kingdom is peculiar to the Chinese historical tradition. In reality, civil wars at that time weakened the Chinese state and promoted its disintegration. The rulers of the Wei kingdom supported the nomadic Huns and Hsiang-pi (Tanguts) against the Shu kingdom, thereby strengthening these tribes in the north and west. China's temporary unity under the western Chin dynasty at the end of the third century did not bring noteworthy, lasting changes. Soon again bloody civil wars sprang up for the imperial throne.

Capitalizing on internal disorder in China, the nomads of the west and north grew aggressive and began to attack the country. They overran western, northern and northeastern regions, and ruled over parts of the Great Plain of China from 304 until 439 A.D.[12] In the last fifty years of this era (390-439 A.D.), a multitude of petty states arose in northern China. Called the period of "the sixteen kingdoms of the five northern tribes," it left a heavy trace in the history of the Chinese state. In their entirety the regions north of the Yangtze were laid waste. The rulers of the western Chin dynasty fled south beyond the Yangtze river; only there did the authority of China's emperors continue in force. The penetration of the nomads reached into the northern Chinese plain. In 317 A.D. the nomads formed a new dynasty, called the eastern Chin, with its capital in the city of Chien-kang (now Nanking). It lasted until 420 A.D. In the south of China four dynasties succeeded each other in quick succession: The Sung (420-479), Chi (479-502), Liang (502-557) and Chen (557-589).

Many agricultural peasants from the northern Chinese plain settled in the south, bringing advanced iron farming implements. Agriculture flourished, as did the handicrafts specializing in iron objects; and textiles, particularly such skills as the production of printed fabrics. A mechanical process for fabric printing was widely employed. Commerce developed, especially in the Yangtze valley. Besides Chien-kang, which had become a mighty commercial center, other commercial towns gained eminence, including Chien-ning, Cheng-tu, Shou-chun, Ching-lo, and Hua-ming. Sea trade with southern countries expanded significantly, largely from the center of Kuang-chou (Canton). The economy of northern China was greatly weakened by destructive wars and the appearance of small hostile states. Gradually, however, as the nomads became settled, they lost their distinctiveness. In 386 A.D., the leader of the Toba tribe (a branch of the Tanguts), Toba Kui, proclaimed himself emperor of the northern Wei dynasty. In 439 Toba Tao, of that dynasty, united all of northern China. The creation of a centralized state in the north hastened the assimilation of the newly settled tribes. After the fall of the northern Wei dynasty and the formation of the northern Chou and northern Chi dynasties, state rule in actuality passed into the hands of the Chinese court aristocracy and feudal lords. These events furthered the homogenization of the nationalities of the north and south, and the two parts of China reestablished economic and cultural ties. This in turn promoted the unification of diverse peoples into a single Chinese national state.

The Sui dynasty became established in the north of China in 581 A.D. Its capital was the city of Chang-an. During the following eight years the Sui dynasty spread its control to southern China. China became united once more, under the Sui emperor Wen Ti. This time as well, peace lasted only a short time. In 604 the second Sui emperor ascended the throne. Yang Ti is known in Chinese history as a cruel despot and a wastrel without measure. He pursued a policy of conquest, continuing defensive wars against the western Turkic tribes and launching aggressive campaigns against Viet Nam, the Ryukyu Islands and Korea. The war with the northern Korean state of Ko-ku-rye proved fateful for Sui China. In 611-612 the Korean army defeated invading Sui forces in several major battles and in 613 they smashed them. According to testimony of Chinese historians, of 350,000 men who crossed the Liao-hsi river, only 2700 survived.[13]

Popular dissatisfaction flooded through the peasantry. It was caused by burdensome taxes and the massive labor conscriptions for construction of luxurious palaces in the new capital of Lo-yang, as well as by destructive military campaigns. In 613, in answer to Yang Ti's attempt to raise another large army for a new campaign to Korea, a mighty peasant rising began in the northern provinces. It spread to the central and southern provinces and led to the overthrow of the Sui dynasty. The vice-regent of the town of Tai-yuan, Li Yuan, headed the rebel army of 200,000 men which captured the ancient capital of Chang-an. In 618 Li Yuan proclaimed himself emperor under the title Kao Tsu, thus beginning the Tang dynasty (618-907). Like the Han dynasty, the Tang dynasty occupies a prominent place in Chinese history. At first, fortunate domestic and foreign circumstances enabled China's economy to develop successfully. The inherent virtues of the Chinese people were instrumental in achieving the highest level of cultural development among the states and peoples of East Asia.

Emperor Kao Tsu received the fertile lands of the south as part of his inheritance from the Sui dynasty. The land area in use reached record proportions, with around 2,000,000 mou[14] under cultivation. Simultaneously, as a result of domestic and foreign wars and ravaging epidemics, the population decreased from 46 million in 606 to 15 million in 627 A.D. The relative abundance of cultivated land in relation to a reduced population forced the Tang rulers to introduce a series of economic measures to increase production in agriculture and handicrafts. An especially positive influence on agricultural yields resulted from a land equalizing system. Landless and small-holding peasants, soldiers, and officials received land from large state reserves composed of newly regained or deserted territories. Every fit adult man received 100 mou (more than 6.6 hectares) of land, of which 20 mou were deeded to him permanently. The aged, invalids and women were granted from 30 to 40 mou, while a woman received an additional 20 if she was head of the household. The eventual purchase of this land became easier when the state waived tax obligations for a period of ten years. Growth in agricultural output was accompanied by an increase in social differentiation. During the second half of the Tang dynasty, land use equalization was discontinued. A system of proprietary holdings became the basic form of land tenure. Landlords and the state became the chief producers.

Handicrafts gradually evolved into an independent branch of the economy. A growing division of labor generated greater output. On the other hand, this process was braked by the concentration of the most fertile lands and basic handicrafts as the property of the imperial court. The court minted coins, produced weapons and agricultural implements, smelted brass and iron, and controlled spinning and weaving, winemaking, sugar production, shipbuilding and papermaking. Despite the lesser efficiency of imperial as compared to private management, the widespread use of slave labor and various forms of coercion enabled the imperial court to be the guiding force in the state's economy. The nation's wealth piled up in the imperial coffers, only to be wasted on frivolities and wars of conquest against neighboring peoples.

The first emperors of the Tang dynasty adroitly maneuvered and exploited the Mongol-Turkic and the Tibetan tribes to strengthen China's borders. Historically, this provided an indispensable service to the country. Then the Tang rulers, relying on the support of various nomadic tribes, turned to conquering other peoples along their borders. Several tribes began massive uprisings against the Turks. Chinese historians record that "the Tang dynasty also attempted to induce them to revolt against each other . . . . In the second year of Chen Kuang (628), a large part of the Tölös tribe revolted against the Turks. Taking advantage of this, the ruler Tai Tsung granted the title of Chen-chu (khan) to the leader of the Seyanto tribe, seeking thereby to encourage him to oppose the Eastern Khanate and to keep him in Tai Tsung's control."[15] After the disintegration of the Eastern Khanate, China began an attack on the Western Khanate which occupied the territory to the west of Yu-men Kuan. Khan Mocho[16] switched to the side of the Tang dynasty and delivered the decisive blow against the Western Khanate, and it ceased to exist near the end of the seventh century. This permitted the Tang dynasty to deal directly with the Arabian Caliphate.

Renewed campaigns started in 644 against the Korean states of Ko-ku-rye and Pekche. By 670 China had won control over all of Korea, including the third state of Silla. The Tang domains were now separated from Japan by nothing more than a narrow strait. The next undertaking sought to subdue Tibet as well, but without success. Campaigns such as these suggested the possibility of advantageous trade with the Arabian East, India, the countries of the Indochina peninsula and the Japanese islands.

In the south, Kuang-chou (Canton) played a large role in Chinese commercial relations with other Asian peoples. Chinese ships sailed from there to the ports of India, Persia and the Arabian Caliphate. Foreign trade through the port of Yang-chou reached quite significant proportions, as it was the main transit point for vessels sailing on the Yangtze river. Also of importance were the ports of Chu-chou and

Ming-chou, which served as terminals for lively trade with Korea and Japan. Commercial relations with India, Persia and the Arabian East gave China the opportunity for acquaintance with these highly developed cultures, thus enabling China to enrich its own national culture.

The Tang epoch enjoyed a blossoming of poetry, painting, sciences such as mathematics, astronomy and history, and applied arts. Radical changes took place in Chinese ideology and social thought. In the outstanding work of Han Yi, "On the Way" (Yuan Tao), invitations to humaneness and love of mankind are heard. "In the very first line of his contemplations," writes N.I. Konrad, "where he presents the central values, Han Yi talks not of heaven, not of the heavenly command, not of the way or the beginning of existence, as had others before and during his time. Rather, he talks of man."[17] The writings of the great Tang poets Li Tai-po, Tu Fu, Wang Wei and Po Chu-i laid the foundations for a new artistic style and original poetic forms. The talented artist Wu Tao-tzu and the sculptor Yan Hoi exalted China in masterpieces of painting and statuary. The historians of the Tang epoch left behind an enormous heritage in the form of chronicles. In part, these relate the history of the dynasties that followed the Han. They are the "encyclopedia" of China's political history. Chinese culture of this period borrowed the best foreign achievements in many intellectual fields. But the flow of culture was not all in one direction, for China exerted a major influence on the architecture, painting, poetry and philosophy of other East Asian nations, particularly Japan.

JAPAN IN ANTIQUITY

Japanese statehood and culture experienced a much slower evolution. Apparently, the country's island status retarded its early development. It would appear that this circumstance slowed the unification of communes and tribes and their transformation to higher forms of social organization. When the Han empire emerged in China and a relatively stable state existed on the Korean peninsula, simple clannish organization still prevailed on the Japanese islands. The ancient population on the islands of Kyushu and Shikoku migrated north to the island of Honshu. As territorial expansion went on, tribal groups formed. In the south the Yamato tribe rose to a dominant position. The leaders of the Yamato tribe began to be called "Mikado," or emperors. Around them the ruling circle formed, composed of the ancestral nobility and the priests. The Yamato group, according to Japanese historians, inaugurated the Japanese state in the second and third centuries A.D. According to the Chinese chronicle "Wei chih," missions were exchanged between the Yamato and the Wei kingdom in China during the reign of Empress Himiko, in 238 A.D.[18]

Japanese statehood arose during the struggle with aborigines in the northern part of Honshu island. Wars with these tribes, called the Ainu or Ebisu, promoted the spread of serfdom. As a result, the class stratification of ancient Japanese society progressed rapidly. Essential changes also took place in technology. Bronze and iron tools appeared almost simultaneously to replace stone implements. Apparently Koreans and Chinese brought these innovations to Japan. Agriculture became one of the chief occupations, and farming advances benefited the physical and spiritual life of the Japanese. Horses were supplied through Korea and China. They served primarily military purposes.

In the third and fourth centuries the communal order decayed and classes developed, forming the basis of the early feudal state in Japan. In the same period the Japanese began activities abroad. Their forces invaded the Korean peninsula several times, and interfered in wars there. When they returned from these campaigns, the Japanese brought back Korean craftsmen, who contributed to the development of domestic handicrafts in Japan. Direct sea communications were established with the Chinese coast, but these had an accidental, episodic character. In the seventh century the Yamato rulers endeavored to stabilize their power with the help of the Sui empire. With this goal the first embassy of the Japanese imperial court, headed by Ono-no Imoko, was sent to China in 607 A.D. Through this embassy the rulers of Japan became acquainted with the state administration of China.[19]

Japanese historiography unanimously accepts the priority of Chinese culture. It exerted a definite influence on the life of the Japanese people as their society was in transition from a barbarian state to civilization. On the other hand, Japanese historians hold the most divergent opinions concerning the nature of Chinese culture and its impact on Japan. Ito, Miyagawa, Maeda and Yosijawa highly value the influence of Chinese culture on Japanese cultural development. They regard the latter as nothing more nor less than "a provincial culture of China."[20] Other Japanese scholars see Chinese culture itself as a part of a general Asian continental culture which absorbed many advanced cultures of the ancient East. The historian Mikami places Chinese culture in fourth place after Egypt, India and Persia.[21] Matsumoto Yoshio declares that not China but Korea played a special role in acquainting Japan with the culture of the peoples of Asia. Through Korea Japan became familiar with the manufacture and use of bronze and iron, with many handicrafts and with the theatrical arts. The Japanese learned the music of the peoples of the Korean peninsula, Manchuria and China, and the more distant peoples of India, Indochina, and the Indonesian archipelago.[22] Gunzi Masakatsu characterizes the Korean Kudara state as "advanced in a cultural sense." It acquainted Japan with a number of artistic genres.[23] Japanese intellectual and material life was shaped largely by Confucianism and Buddhism, which also arrived through Korea and China. Japan's first acquaintance with Confucianism seems to have come in the fifth and sixth centuries. Traditional Japanese historiography, without any sort of documentary evidence, places this event at the end of the third century, and connects it with the arrival from Korea of the Confucian scholar Wang Yi, who supposedly brought to the Japanese emperor gifts consisting of the Confucian work *Lun Yui* and a Chinese language book entitled *A Thousand Hieroglyphs.*[24]

Regardless of the veracity of either date, the teaching of the philosopher and moralist Confucius doubtless lay at the heart of the world view of Japanese leaders during the rise of the Japanese state. Many Japanese scholars assert that Confucianism in Japan achieved incomparably higher levels of development than in China, and that it was only in Japan that these teachings were revealed fully. In combination with the "spirit of Japan" (Yamato-Damashii) and the "Samurai spirit" (bushido), they formed the basis of "the ideal national culture."[25] Relying on the myths and legends in "Kojaki" and "Nihongi," Japanese histories maintain that the spread of Chinese hieroglyphic writing in Japan was closely connected to Confucianism. Actual acquaintance with Chinese literature took place later, on the eve of the Christian era.[26] The adoption by Japan of Chinese ideography is linked to the fourth and fifth centuries. Confucian scholars were the first compilers of the Japanese "Dynastic Chronicles." They played an important role in creating a bureaucratic apparatus for the Japanese emperors. They guided the construction of temples and government storehouses, recorded the census and performed the duties of counselors and scribes. The most numerous and the best prepared among them came from China and Korea.

More dependable data on the spread of Confucianism in Japan, as well as the expansion there of other aspects of Chinese culture, appeared at the beginning of the seventh century. From that time knowledge of Chinese, and mastery of Confucian dogmas, became the obligatory attributes of a genteel, aristocratic education. Science in particular made extensive use of the Chinese language. Nakamura Hajima in his work *Pathways of the Ideas of the Peoples of the East: India, China,*

Tibet, and Japan, published in Honolulu in 1964, remarks: "In the world of science the most educated Japanese in ancient times—Buddhist monks and Confucian scholars—published their works in Chinese. Books with religious and philosophical content appeared in the native language only in the Kamakura period in the 12th—14th centuries. Even the most original thinkers of the 18th century, such as the anti-traditionalist Tominaga Nakamata and Miura Bayen, left works written in the Chinese language." At the same time, Nakamura remarks that "the Japanese frequently interpreted original Chinese texts wrongly. The incorrect reading of sources that transmitted Chinese ideas is one of the most important phenomena in the history of Japanese thought."[27]

In the reign of Emperor Tenji (662-670 A.D.) the first state-supported school was established. Its head was a Confucian scholar who had emigrated from Korea. Under Emperor Temmu (673-686) this institution was transformed into "the emperor's school" and became the center for disseminating Confucianism and Chinese culture. As the ruling ideology of the Japanese aristocracy, Confucianism opened a broad pathway for the diffusion in Japan of the entire Chinese cultural system.

An important feature of Japanese Confucianism was its accessibility only to high aristocratic circles and unavailability to the general population. Confucianism encountered resistance from Japanese feudal lords because it supported imperial power and therefore ran counter to their separatist leanings. The teachings of Confucius thus robbed them of the moral right to dispute decisions of the central authorities. Buddhism, which reached Japan in the sixth century, received greater support from Japanese feudal lords. The Buddhist teaching of rejection of "frail worldly vanity" in order to achieve the state of Nirvana necessary for man's transformation into Buddha,[28] gave the feudal lords a functional ideological weapon in support of their rule over the populace. Buddhist teaching placed all people in an equal position before Buddha. Hence, in contrast to Confucian canons, each feudal lord might claim equal rights with the emperor to rule the people. As Buddhism spread, it was utilized by a single powerful family which was seeking primacy.[29] Imperial authority suffered in the process. Japan's Buddhist teachers began to seek points of contact and harmony with Confucianism on the central political point of the relationship of subject to emperor. They asserted that the Machayanist form of Buddhism, which had achieved the greatest popularity in Japan, did not deny the basic Confucian principles regulating state and society throughout all time, until "the kingdom of Buddha would triumph."[30] Meanwhile, the Buddhist schools adopted rules for students according to which a monk must combine his religious devotion to *bodhisattva* with Confucian service to the state and society.[31]

The Japanese state developed under unique circumstances and these were expressed in a dual authority. While the emperor retained nominal power, in fact the state was ruled by the *Shoguns* (military leaders who had usurped power). In such conditions Buddhism and Confucianism underwent deep changes. In the final reckoning these two contradictory philosophical and religious doctrines were pressed into the service of a single political goal—the education of the people in the spirit of emperor worship and glorification of the Japanese monarchy.

The process of adapting Confucianism and Buddhism to fit Japanese life was speeded in direct relation to the expulsion of Chinese and Korean preachers. Japanese priests replaced them and gradually assumed the direction of temples and schools. Together with these foreign teachings, the ancient Japanese religion of Shintoism maintained considerable influence on Japanese society. This religion was characterized by ancestor worship and submission to the forces of nature. Features of these divergent religio-philosophical doctrines, together with popular traditions generated by socio-historical conditions, formed the ideological foundations of Japanese society.

Additional cultural elements from China, Korea and other continental lands also acquired Japanese features. After absorbing the basic elements of Buddhist architecture and sculpture, and Chinese and Korean painting and handicrafts, the Japanese either changed them fundamentally or used them to create new, more perfected artifacts. In consequence, Japanese material culture acquired unique national forms corresponding to native historical traditions. In writing, with Chinese ideograms as the basis, the Japanese created their own alphabetical writing called *kana,* in two graphic forms called *katakana* and *hiragana.* As a result a mixed hieroglyphic-syllabic writing system evolved. In lexical and grammatical structure, the Japanese language preserved its individuality completely.

Several further factors affected the Japanese state and culture. Major conflicts then in progress caused the disappearance of whole states on the neighboring Asian continent. The rather broad diffusion of continental culture, particularly from China, reached only the privileged classes. The general populace—the peasantry and tradesmen—continued to preserve the national foundations and traditions which influenced the aristocracy and its "Chinified" culture. Furthermore, while Chinese culture was brought into the country by relatively small numbers of Korean and Chinese craftsmen, monks, and artists, it was the Japanese themselves who subsequently spread Chinese culture. Consequently there was no forcible destruction of the national heritage. Two different cultures became established, Chinese and Japanese cultural features influencing each other. In the final synthesis, they blended to form a new culture which preserved most native Japanese features. Finally, in its first attempts to gain footholds on the Asian continent, Japan clashed with China on the Korean peninsula, and suffered a crushing defeat (the Chung-san battle of 663 A.D.). In China, Japan met a fearful adversary and quite naturally grew cautious. Under these circumstances, even in the early stage of state formation, Japanese rulers attempted to limit China's activities in Japanese territories, and to restrict Chinese cultural dissemination.

While turning to account the historical experience of China and Korea, Japan concurrently persisted in developing and strengthening its new national state, invariably preserving its sovereignty. Japan's island location retarded development until a centralized government appeared. Thereafter, isolation positively affected Japanese progress, easing the defense of the country and compensating for economic and cultural weakness in conflicts with stronger continental states.

SUMMARY

Until the formation of the Japanese state, China enjoyed the initiative in establishing and supporting ties between the Chinese and Japanese. The continental state was at a higher level of social development. For several reasons, the Japanese islands held little interest for China at that time. They were off world trade routes. The Japanese people did not participate in major historical events taking place on the Asian continent which were fateful for China. During this era, therefore, Chinese communications with the Japanese islands were not as spirited as with other Asian peoples and states. Occasionally, particularly when China was subjugated by foreign dynasties, communications broke off for centuries.

Despite the episodic nature of Sino-Japanese relations, Chinese cultural influence on Japan did not end. Even before the formation of a centralized state, Chinese colonists frequently lived on the Japanese islands. These included tradesmen, farmers and cult worshipers. They were the first teachers of the Japanese as the latter mastered the more advanced technology and intellectual culture of the continent. Having accepted the Chinese ideographic writing system, the Japanese became bound to the Chinese cultural heritage. Nonetheless, in the course of many centuries they were able to develop their own civilization, basing it primarily on Chinese culture. The conclusion arises that contacts between the peoples of those lands were in fact never interrupted, even when foreign dynasties ruled China. Chinese culture continually influenced Japan and played an important role in the development of Japanese society.

CHAPTER TWO

China and Japan to the Mid-Nineteenth Century

More than a thousand years passed from the establishment of permanent Sino-Japanese relations (the 6th to 7th centuries) until the middle of the 19th century, when active western penetration began in East Asia. The historical development of the two countries took place under different conditions in this period. Specifically, for the entire time Japan remained an independent state and Japanese feudal society evolved to an advanced form. Japan's international position was determined by domestic circumstances and by the ability to support sea communications and conduct foreign trade.

The fate of China took a different turn. From the mid-10th to the mid-19th century, China was controlled by an indigenous dynasty (the Ming) for only 276 years (1368-1644). The entire remaining time the territory of the country was ruled by foreign dynasties. Partial domination was gained by the Kitans (10th-12th centuries), the Churchens (10th-12th centuries), and the Tanguts (11th-12th centuries). The Yuan dynasty (1280-1368) and the Manchurian Chin dynasty (1644-1911) ruled the entire country. Ravaging nomadic attacks and bloody wars interrupted material and intellectual growth, and led to economic and social stagnation. At the same time, China's international position required the preservation of national independence when dealing with neighboring countries.

THE DEVELOPMENT OF CHINA

Under the Tang dynasty the Chinese empire included Turkic and Mongol lands to the north and south of Tien-Shan, and the northeastern part of the Hindustan peninsula. Suzerainty was achieved over Tibet and the northern Korean state of Ko-ku-rye.

After the fall of the Tang dynasty, the Chinese empire disintegrated. The immediate cause was a peasant rising which unfolded in the last quarter of the ninth century, encompassing the territory of today's Ho-nan and Shan-tung provinces. The Tang dynasty then brought in militant Uighur tribes and with their help crushed the uprising. This did not restore the empire's former might. It disintegrated into "five dynasties and ten kingdoms." From that time China became the object of devastating raids by western, northern and northeastern nomads. The history of the subsequent Sung dynasty (960-1279) is marked by protracted battles with attacking nomads. In the vast territories of eastern Turkistan, in the valleys of the Irtysh and the Yenisey, the Orkhon and Kerulen, the Sungari and Liao Ho, states of nomadic herdsmen formed. Among them there were frequent clashes and these led to the destruction of some states and the ascendance of others. Despite their economic and cultural backwardness, many of these states were stronger militarily than China. In the imagination of China's emperors, the Great Wall of China was to protect the country from the mounted nomadic hordes. But it could not fulfill this function, and was even less effective in the western regions where it consisted of nothing more than primitive earthen structures. As historical experience has shown, only the Yangtze river served the Chinese rulers as occasional natural protection. There they might seek cover from attacks from the north, abandoning enormous regions and the capitals of Chang-an, Loyang and Kai-feng.

In the northwest, the Chinese state was subjected to devastating raids by the Tangut state of Hsia. Thus, in 1044 the Chinese emperor was forced to pay the ruler of that state the large "gift of 72,000 liang in silver, 153,000 pieces of silk fabric and 30,000 ching of tea."[1] He was also obliged to recognize Tangut authority.

Toward the end of the ninth century, a nomadic tribal union called the Kitans formed in the north on the territory of Manchuria, Mongolia and northern China. This mighty state was called Liao. The Kitans entered the provinces of Shan-si and Ho-pei and remained a lasting threat for the rest of China. To counter the Liao state, the Sung court entered into a military union with the Tangut-Manchurian state of the Churchens. The Churchens then conducted the battle against the Kitans. Although this union brought about the defeat of the Kitans and their expulsion from the northern provinces, China faced a new threat, this time from the Churchen state of Chin.

The Churchens penetrated the northern and central regions of China, forcing the Sung emperors to move their capital from Kai-feng, south of the Yangtze, to the city of Han-chou. With the fall of Kai-feng, the period of Chinese history known as the time of the northern Sung dynasty drew to a close. The second period of the dynasty, called the time of the southern Sung dynasty, began with the transfer of the capital to Han-chou. The Shao-hsing peace agreement, accepted by Emperor Kao-chung in 1411 from the Churchens, was very difficult for the Chinese people. China agreed to pay the Churchens an annual tribute in the sum of 250,000 lian of silver and 250,000 pieces of silk fabric. Foreign conquerors wrought destruction and insult upon the Chinese people. These sufferings provided the motivation for a crucial struggle to preserve national sovereignty.

The era of the Sung dynasty is studded by heroic feats. On the dynasty's remaining territory physical and intellectual life advanced and national strength consolidated. The goal of reducing political and economic conflicts and creating a defense system resulted in progressive reforms undertaken by Wang An-shih.[2] The economy advanced in many ways. Major projects improved the irrigation system. Government credits were granted to peasants, small merchants, and landlords of small and medium estates (with twenty percent capital return each half-year). The work obligation yielded to a monetary tax. Instead of the monetary tax, the poor could provide the government with recruits. Land surveys ensured proper calculation of the tax (with time payments based on an annual twenty percent installment). Price regulation was accomplished by selling products gathered as taxes at firm state prices. In the realm of defense, the so-called "pao-chia" system was introduced. It required military service by all healthy males. This system also obligated the population to provide horses and various military structures. Moreover, despite the heavy external pressures experienced by China, the Sung epoch was distinguished by new cultural strides. The discovery and practical application of gunpowder, the compass and bookprinting took place in this period. These inventions promoted the diffusion of Chinese influence to other countries.

The humanities and social sciences made large contributions. In the eleventh century the outstanding historical works of Ou-yang Hsiu (1007-1072) and Ssu-ma Kuang (1019-1085) appeared. Ou-yang Hsiu's work *The History of Five Dynasties* exerted a great impact on the establishment of statehood and study of the historical experience of the Chinese people. In Ssu-ma Kuang's work *The General Mirror Which Helps to Rule,* the history of China from the fifth to the eleventh century B.C. is set forth in great detail, filling 294 books. In philosophy, the influence of Confucianism increased once more, although many concepts of that teaching were regarded differently. Chinese philosophy of the period is known as Sung philosophy or neo-Confucianism. It is represented by such mighty thinkers as Chou Tun-i (1017-1073), Chang Tsai (1019-1077), Cheng Hao (1032-1085), Cheng I (1033-1107), and Chu Hsi (1130-1200). Sung philosophy, together with the confirmation of conservative principles of feudal state structure, played a certain developmental role in consolidating national ideology. The conceptions of the most prominent representative of the neo-Confucian school, Chu Hsi, were based on the comprehension of objectively existing reality. They awakened social thought not only in China, but also in nearby lands such as Japan. Chinese artists, particularly painters, created outstanding works in the Sung epoch. The picture scrolls of the Sung artists Ko Hsi, Ma Yuan, Hsia Kui and others are considered masterpieces of Chinese painting.

At the turn of the thirteenth century a new threat hung over China. Toward the end of the twelfth century the Churchen state declined as a result of internal upheaval. Then, in clashes with the Mongol state formed in 1206 by Genghis Khan, it was destroyed. The Mongol capture of the Churchen capital of Yang-ching (now Peking) brought no salvation for China for thereupon a series of new campaigns against China began. Genghis Khan's campaign against the Tangut state of Hsi Hsia in 1226-1227 brought the Mongol conquest of the north and northwest of China. Then, under Genghis Khan's successor Ukete, the Mongols seized a number of central and southern regions of China (1231-1234). In 1280 the Mongol khan Kublai proclaimed his ascension to the Chinese throne, laying the foundation of the Yuan dynasty (1280-1367), with its capital in Yang-ching.

In contrast to the Tanguts, Kitans and Churchens, the Mongol conquerors established their sovereignty throughout China. Mongol rule spread, accompanied by massive terror. The new invaders plundered many cities and their populations and physically exterminated the Chinese population. According to data in the Chinese historical chronicle, after the Mongol invasion and establishment of their power throughout China, the number of peasant households had decreased from 13.6 million to 9.3 million. The rule of the Kitans, Churchens and Mongols delayed Chinese development, particularly in the northern and northwestern regions. These areas endured devastating invasions for many centuries. Foreign conquerors, existing at a lower developmental level than the Chinese, could provide no progressive contributions to Chinese economic life. Moreover, they used China's material and human resources wastefully.

During the Mongol Yuan dynasty, a special Directorate of Handicrafts and Arts was created at the imperial court. It had offices in many Chinese cities. Workshops under the Directorate's jurisdiction employed the labor of Chinese craftsmen. To develop crafts, the Mongol rulers imported master artists from the states of central and western Asia into China. At the same time the Mongols sent many Chinese craftsmen and tradesmen to near-eastern and central Asian settlements. Chinese officials, together with Uighurs and Tibetans, served the Mongolian khans in administrative posts.

Some Chinese officials aided the Mongol conquerors in creating governmental institutions and in strengthening the foundations of the Mongolian feudal empire. Military campaigns and the court whims of the Mongol khans provided many Chinese merchants and pawnbrokers with opportunities to become wealthy together with their foreign captors through speculation and the robbery of enslaved peoples. Thus even in that distant time a particular parasitic stratum of Chinese officials, pawnbrokers and merchants developed. They helped foreign rulers strengthen their authority, filling the functions of special agents or *compradors* in Chinese and other conquered territories. With the help of these agents, the Mongol conquerors created a peculiarly artificial domestic and foreign market, causing China to come into contact with the outside world. This progress took place in unpleasant circumstances, since it was based on trade that discriminated against China. On the other hand, it stimulated the growth of goods production, strengthened commercial connections, and drew China into economic and cultural relations with the foreign world.

During the Mongol conquest Chinese culture suffered a particularly grievous decline. Yet, even in those difficult years Chinese cultural development did not cease altogether. Thus it was during the Yuan dynasty that Chinese literature was distinguished by the appearance of two historical novels which have remained popular until this very day. These were "River Factories" and "The Triple Kingdom."

The Yuan dynasty was weakened by the struggle for succession between the heirs of Shun-ti. Its fall resulted directly from the popular rebellion of "the red bandages," led by the secret "White Lotus" society.[3] The rebels' victory allowed Chinese feudal lords to establish the Ming dynasty (1368-1644).

The expulsion of the Mongol khans promoted the growth of economic and cultural life. Most of the slaves, indentured peasants and tradesmen were given their freedom. The sale or purchase of free people was prohibited. During the reign of the first Ming emperor, Tai-chu, peasants and petty landlords received the lands which had been devastated and deserted under the Mongols. These were in turn exempted from taxes for three years to allow them to place the land in cultivation. Trades and commerce also displayed progress. Silk weaving and cotton cloth production along the right bank of the lower Yangtze developed with particular speed. Porcelain fabrication made notable strides, centered around Ching-te-chen. Rapid growth took place in the towns of Nanking (the southern capital), Peking (northern capital), Hang-chou, Su-chou, Fu-chou, Wu-chiang and Kuang-chou (Canton).[4] Foreign trade waxed. In the second half of the sixteenth century silver money (called the Mexican dollar) was introduced.

As the power of the imperial court grew, so did its inclination toward economic monopoly. The court seized the best lands and the most important craft products, and these resources financed the slave and indentured labor system. Class conflicts became particularly sharp during the reign of the third Ming emperor, Cheng Tsu. China again entered an era of deepening social crisis. Imitating the Mongol khans, the Ming emperors undertook military campaigns to seize former Mongolian lands. They overcame the southern part of Manchuria and established their suzerainty over the northern Manchurian tribes. They also attempted to strengthen their influence over Korea. In the south they launched a series of campaigns against Vietnam. Between 1405 and 1433 Ming China sent seven mighty sea expeditions to the lands of the south seas, attempted to create an alliance with Kokand for joint battle with Timur, and pursued measures for establishing commercial bonds with Persia, Arabia and East Africa.[5]

Exhausting military campaigns and the unbridled waste of the court placed an intolerable burden on the populace. The court, the chief feudal usurer, became the symbol of despotism and oppression. During the reign of Hsiao Tsung (1488-1505) state lands belonging to the Ming dynasty constituted one seventh of all cultivated land, while the numbers of landless peasants reached enormous figures. In the second half of the Ming period, massive discontent spread throughout the country among the landless and the city poor. The position of the dynasty was also complicated by dissatisfaction among national minorities in border regions. These areas had been attached forcibly to China in the first period of Ming rule. Thus, numerous Manchurian tribes, who made their living by hunting, herding and agriculture, endured exploitation by Chinese merchant usurers and the Ming tax officials. State purchase of valuable furs at confiscatory prices, and the growing tax burden, spawned further discontent.

At the turn of the seventeenth century the tribes began to unite around one of their leaders, Nurhatsi, who led an uprising against the Mings in Manchuria. Nurhatsi proclaimed the creation of the Manchurian Chin state and commenced a war with Ming China. From the very first battle against Nurhatsi (at Fu-shung in 1619), the Ming armies revealed the military weakness of the Ming empire. The unsuccessful war in Manchuria deepened the social crisis and "at the end of the Ming dynasty epoch, the people were in a truly untenable position; there remained no alternative but to enter into a struggle for existence itself."[6]

In the third decade of the seventeenth century, peasant uprisings occurred in many provinces. They quickly spread through the country and engulfed major parts of northern and central China. Rebel armies under Li Tzu-cheng took Shan-hsi, Shen-hsi, Ho-pei, Ho-nan, Shan-tung, part of Kan-su, Ching-hai, Hu-pei, An-hui and Chiang-su. At the beginning of 1644 Li Tzu-cheng established a new state on that territory—Ta-shun, with its capital in the city of Hsiang (later renamed Hsi-ching, meaning western capital).[7] Li Tzu-cheng's army took the capital of Ming China, Peking. Emperor Ssu-chung committed suicide. After taking the capital, Li Tzu-cheng attempted to organize resistance to the Manchurians who were advancing from the north. With this purpose Li Tzu-cheng entered into negotiations with General Wu San-kui, the Ming army leader entrusted with protection of the country's northern borders. Li Tzu-cheng suggested that together they continue to resist the Manchurians. However, Wu San-kui betrayed the national good of China by reaching an agreement with the Manchurians and opening China's northern border to the enemy. Another traitor, Hung Chen-kou, helped the Manchurians to "pacify" the south of China.

With the help of the feudal lords, usurers, merchants and the military aristocracy, the relatively small Manchurian army seized China. The Manchurians proclaimed a new dynasty, the Chin. The betrayal by the exploiting classes and their aid to the foreign conquerors had fateful consequences for China. A period of nearly 300 years of Manchurian rule began. The distinguishing feature of Manchurian rule was militarism, especially in its early period. The Manchurian Chin dynasty was buttressed by "the eight-bannered army"[8] and the highest leadership of the government was concentrated in the army ministry, "the Directorate of Military and Political Affairs." The chief provincial leaders were the military governors, while civil authorities, largely Chinese, played a subordinate role. After conquering all of China, the Manchurian rulers systematically prepared the country for ambitious foreign conquests, adapting even internal Chinese life for that purpose. Economic resources were concentrated in the hands of the imperial court, the government seizing the best lands (up to ten percent of total cultivated land) and the chief branches of craft production such as porcelain and mining output. Further measures included the strict regulation of manufacture and trade. A significant portion of economic output reached the government through high taxes and low "official" purchase prices. The remaining production was subject to high provincial and city tariffs. As a result, private enterprise became unprofitable.

The strict control of agriculture and the crafts, and non-economic controls, permitted the Chin rulers to garner great material resources. These were employed chiefly to support the imperial court and military ambitions. Military campaigns, seizure of neighboring territories and enslavement of small nations were the main goals of Chin foreign policy in the sixteenth and seventeenth centuries. "Having conquered China," write Chinese historians, "the Manchurians sought territorial expansion, consolidation of power, and the physical destruction of the Chinese to distract attention from the anti-Manchurian struggle. For these purposes the Manchurians undertook campaigns of conquest in the years of Kang-hsi (1662-1722), Yung-cheng (1723-1735), and Chien-Lung (1736-1795)."[9]

Under Emperor Kang-hsi the Chin court attempted to spread its domain to the north of the Manchurian lands. Manchurian armies made several raids on Russian settlements in the Amur basin, and attacked the Daur, Tungus and other tribes of the Transbaikal, Amur and coastal regions. In 1689 the Nerchinsk agreement was reached between Chin China and Russia. This treaty had the effect of retarding Manchurian expansion to the north. On the other hand, it blocked Russian interests in the Amur region and left the Sino-Russian border in doubt. After the Chin rulers established control over Mongolia in the 1720s, negotiations began between Russian and Chinese representatives on the border question. This was resolved in the Chia-ting agreement of 1727, which laid the basis for state frontiers in the Mongolian region.[10] Later, the Chin empire turned to the subjugation of the small nations northwest, west and southwest of China (Mongolia, Dzungaria, Kashgaria and Tibet). Its attempts at conquest to the north of Manchurian territory ceased. In 1691, capitalizing on internal conflict, armies of Emperor Kang-hsi overran Mongolia. Crushing one Mongolian tribe after another, the Manchurians gradually established their control.

In the mid-18th century Emperor Chien-lung began the conquest of Dzungaria and in 1757 Chin armies captured I-li. Chinese historians remark that "this victory was obtained by the most merciless and nearly total destruction of the populace. At its height Dzungaria contained more than 200,000 families, or more than 600,000 inhabitants; after the military disaster 3/10 of the population were exterminated by the Chin armies, 4/10 died of smallpox and those who escaped death were forced to flee to the Kazakh regions in Russia."[11]

In 1760 Chin armies completed the conquest of Kashgaria, the southern part of contemporary Hsin-chiang province. Since that time the territory to the south and north of Tien Shan has been included in China. The enslaved Uighur populace rose to battle with the Manchurians several times, and in 1764 even enjoyed a temporary victory over the Chin armies. However, they were quickly subdued and once more persecuted and tyrannized.

Throughout the eighteenth century, the Chin emperors sought to establish their control over Tibet. In 1792 they were able to concentrate power in the hands of their resident.[12] Chin influence spread as well to Nepal, Annam, and Burma. These conquests, although they expanded the territorial domains of the Chin empire, did not strengthen China's economic or military power. More important, the captured lands became constant sources of unrest and tension, demanding major military exertions and material costs. Nevertheless, these distant territories served as a unique zone of defense. They formed a barrier separating China from strong and relatively more developed countries. The Manchurian authorities limited the activities of Chinese merchants to these territories, thereby hampering their contacts with the outside world.

The basis of Chinese manufacturing remained the tiny peasant households and cottage industry. The output of larger craft products continued to remain in the hands of the government and for the most part served the imperial court and the army. It exerted no noticeable influence on the economy of the hinterlands, or on the formation of a general Chinese market.

The advance in economic and cultural life, observed in China in the first half of the Chin dynasty, gave way to rapid decline. Middle-sized land holdings grew at the expense of those feudal lords who had resisted the Manchurians. This growth also included the lands left empty by the destruction of the peasant populace during some forty years of war. As a consequence of the catastrophic population decline, the average amount of cultivated land per peasant in China increased from 13.4 mou at the start of the Manchurian wars, to 28.4 mou after the consolidation of Manchurian power.[13] The enhanced size of land holdings permitted greater agricultural productivity, a highly important factor in economic and cultural progress. But due to continued use of primitive agricultural tools, productivity again began to decline as rural population grew. In the mid-19th century, when Chinese population had reached 400 million, and cultivated land totalled no more than one billion mou, the average land per peasant had decreased to 2.5-3 mou, seven to eight times less than at the height of Chin power.

The division of land forced the peasantry to take up cottage industry. Along with this there occurred a process of differentiation in agriculture. Strong feudal lords gathered landed property by dispossessing the poorest peasants. The chief land owner in China continued to be the imperial court. Commercial relations between city and village in Chin China were handled by a small stratum of feudal lords headed by the imperial court, while the millions of working peasants continued to engage in unprotected natural farming. This basic socio-economic disharmony retarded industrial development, limited the sphere of manufacturing's influence on the country as a whole, and predetermined the backwardness of feudal China.

China's backwardness stood out particularly in connection with the appearance in Chinese harbors of ships of economically advanced [Western] countries. These vessels carried modern weapons and brought industrial products. The Chin rulers proved incapable of evaluating the international situation and of placing China's long-term interests in historical perspective. They did not perceive the threat of foreign penetration as a national problem calling for the mobilization of all domestic manpower and physical resources. Rather, the appearance of these foreigners were regarded as affronts to the "omnipotent" monarchy and to the power of the "divine" emperor.

Two tendencies marked Chin policy toward foreign aggression. One was the attempt to shield the Chinese people from progressive foreign influences, even to the extent of avoiding battle with European invaders. The second policy sought compromise with the intruders, the limitation of their penetration to small territories, and their isolation from the Chinese heartland. Complete isolation of the country from the outside world became the basis of Chin foreign policy. One element in this policy was the encouragement of fanaticism and hatred of all things foreign. The Chin rulers depicted the foreigners as incomplete beings, "foreign devils." Contact with them without imperial sanction was punishable by death. The people were instilled with belief in the divinity and grandeur of the emperor, "the son of heaven," and in the infallibility of his every deed. Smugness, conceit and elaborate ceremonies and rituals underscored the Chinese emperor's presumed superiority to foreign rulers. Officials preserved the same tone and style in relations with the Chinese people at large and the ambassadors of foreign governments.[14]

To break the contacts of Chinese merchants with foreigners, the court forbade passage beyond the borders, limited the size of new ocean vessels, and permitted only coastal sailings. In 1757 China closed all sea ports to foreign commerce, except for Canton. In addition, the conduct of trade was allowed only through the King Han guild, which was under the control of an imperial agent. Such passive measures of defense naturally could not limit Western commercial expansion. In fact, they worked to the disadvantage of the Chinese merchantry. The policies established by the Chin court deprived domestic merchants of foreign contacts and placed all foreign trade in the hands of foreign merchants. Chinese merchants were confined to the role of middlemen, serving foreign firms and helping the latter attain maximum profits from exploitation of cheap Chinese labor. The product mix of import and export was determined not by China's needs and abilities, but by the interest of foreign merchants in selling or buying this or that article. As a result, at the beginning of the eighteenth century the main Chinese import became opium, bringing fairytale profits to the foreign dealers. At the same time, silver, silk fabrics, cottage handicraft, tea, and other valuable products were exported from China.

Foreign trade as thus established prohibited China from enjoying the fruits of the industrial revolution and advanced Western accomplishments in science and technology. The Chin emperors declared: "Our empire produces goods in abundance, we have everything we could wish for, and we have never relied on the wares of barbarians (foreigners) to satisfy our needs."[15] The Chin policy of isolation kept the Chinese people in darkness and ignorance, and deprived China of the opportunity to gain acquaintance with advanced ideas and achievements. It contributed to the continued existence of the corrupt and reactionary monarchy. At the same time, this policy inflicted an irreparable loss on China, undermining its international position and condemning it to backwardness and insults. China's first serious clash with the West, the so-called "opium" war with England in 1839-1841 displayed the country's feebleness. "Complete isolation," wrote Karl Marx, "was the first condition for the preservation of ancient China. When with the help of England this isolation was brought to an end, it was unavoidable that decay would begin, just as when a carefully preserved mummy in a hermetically sealed grave is exposed to fresh air."[16]

The Manchurian imperial court thus was the paramount national and social enemy of the Chinese people. China's further development hinged on deposing or preserving the anti-national, decadent and feudal Manchurian dynasty. But the situation in China evolved in an unfortunate direction for the country. The progressive elements in Chinese society at mid-19th century were extremely infirm whereas the reactionary feudal monarchy found support from the Western capitalist states.

THE GROWTH OF JAPAN

The formation of the Japanese state took place in different historical circumstances. In contrast to China, Japan remained an independent state throughout its history. This factor contributed positively to the consolidation of the Japanese nation and the development of a national culture. Learning from China's experience, the Japanese in the second half of the seventh century experienced the "Taika reforms," which received their final formulation in the "Taiho ryo" law codification in 701 A.D. These reforms signaled the creation of an early feudal state with a rather well organized administrative system. Following Chinese examples, the reforms created a central government and a complex hierarchal system of state administration. They also introduced government examinations for officials. A large stratum of aristocracy gathered around the imperial court. In the beginning the court had an important role in establishing centralized statehood and in forming an ideology, based primarily on Confucianism and Buddhism. The centralized state made economic development possible. Irrigation systems sprang up, iron tools became commonplace, wheat, rye, and millet were cultivated as well as rice. Mining and handicrafts developed, commercial warehouses, rice storehouses and roads were built, and in the year 708 minting of coins began. During the Nara (710-794) and the Kyoto periods (795-1186), each named after its capital city, Japanese culture began to flourish under the influence of feudal Chinese culture. The Nara period is distinguished by the composition of the first Japanese chronicles and the famous poetry anthology "Manyoshu." In the Kyoto period,[17] together with the appearance of outstanding new literary works, great achievements sprang forth in painting, woodcarving, metal artifacts, mother-of-pearl and lacquer products.

It was during the Nara monarchy that the cult of emperor worship took root. The populace accepted in totality the belief in the divine origin of the imperial family, and the person of the emperor was proclaimed "sacred and inviolable." The cult of the emperor has left an indelible imprint on all subsequent Japanese history.

As the Japanese state spread to the north from Kyoto, natural forms of husbandry were preserved. Simultaneously the strengthening of local feudal lords tended to isolate the border regions. The process of state decentralization was hastened by the circumstance that the imperial court held but nominal control of land distribution. Land doled out by the emperor as gifts or rewards for military and state service in practice remained private property. Thus strong feudal lords grew to become the foremost landowners and the main sources of national wealth. At the local level they enjoyed an opportunity to gather into their hands not only economic but also political power.

In the tenth and early eleventh centuries a unique situation came into existence. Alongside the ineffective imperial court arose an independent administration composed of feudal lords who were struggling among themselves for control of the country. This situation ended in 1192 with the victory of Yoritomo Minamoto, who was proclaimed Shogun.[18] In Kamakura, which became the second capital, a Shogun government called "bakufu" (military headquarters) was created. This effectively established a military dictatorship in the country. The court aristocracy, headed by the emperor, proved to be isolated, and exercised no governing duties. Land ownership remained in the hands of the strong feudal lords, the Daimyo.

The removal of the aloof aristocracy from power and the transfer of government to strong feudal lords led, on one hand, to the strengthening of the landowners' supremacy. A further sharpening of class conflicts between the feudal lords and the peasantry followed. On the other hand, feudal control exerted a positive influence on agriculture, crafts and commerce. The well-known Japanese historian Hani Goro writes:

In this manner, in the Middle Ages a society based on feudalism arose in Japan. Its productive relationships were those between feudal lords and serfs. A class of strong feudal landowners exploited the populace as serfs, while the serfs were bound to the lands and bore a heavy load of taxes and labor obligation.

It is striking that, although the Japanese people were crushed by these burdens and subjected to cruel exploitation, nonetheless their labor promoted the gradual development of agriculture, labor division and commerce.[19]

In contrast to the despotic rulers of other Eastern nations, the Japanese emperor and the court aristocracy were unable to exploit peasant labor and exhaust domestic manpower in unproductive tasks such as building the Great Wall of China, the Egyptian pyramids and the like. This had a positive effect on the nation's economy, promoted the growth of production, and hastened the employment of better manufacturing techniques.

In the early Middle Ages three varieties of property were found in Japan: the large estates, allotments, and free peasant land vacated by refugees from feudal exploitation. The absolutist imperial authority in Japan was supported by a system of semi-slavery, accompanied by the low labor productivity associated with such a system. The decay of the estate system entailed the establishment of a mode of peasant exploitation based on serfs, which brought an increase in output. This in turn led to increased division of labor and the stimulation of goods exchange. At first trade remained completely in the hands of the feudal lords, who conducted it through merchant middlemen. But with the passing of time, tradesmen and whole merchant organizations materialized. Called "Rakuza," these groups pursued their trading activities independently. As money became the medium of trade exchange, urban settlements and then cities took shape. All this bespeaks a pronounced and spirited economic life in Japan.

The gravest threat to national independence was the attempted invasion of the Japanese islands by the Mongol-Chinese. Even at this date the Kamakura bakufu proved its ability to mobilize human and material resources for defense of the country. After repelling the assault, the Kamakura Shogunate inclined not merely to monopolize political and military authority, but also to gather into its hands enormous land parcels. Such policies provoked the powerful feudal lords to sharp reactions. They joined Emperor Go-Daigo in open armed conflict against the Kamakura Shogunate, which was defeated utterly and its capital burned in 1333.

Emperor Go-Daigo's victory was short-lived. His attempts to expand imperial and aristocratic landholdings to strengthen central political authority ended in failure. After a year and a half of rule, Go-Daigo was removed from power by the strong feudal lords. The aristocracy lost not only the lands it gained during his rule, but their former holdings as well. The civil warring that soon began among individual lords ended with the ascendence of Ashikaga as Shogun. The country was broken into a number of strong fiefs which swallowed the old aristocratic lands and the lands of the ruined small holders. Only monastic estates were preserved.

Japan clearly was not ready for a central government. Although husbandry was promoted by geographical conditions, the insufficient development of goods exchange did not allow the creation of a general market to serve as the basis for formation of a centralized administration. Nor were significant foreign threats present at this period which might have made unification a historical necessity and thereby speeded the extinction of petty fiefdoms.

It was at this time that the peasants and small and middle landowners increased their struggle against the tyranny of the Daimyo. In particular, regional institutions of agricultural self-government (gason-sei) formed to take care of irrigation, trade, and handicrafts. Characterizing the activities of agricultural management of this kind, the Japanese historian Inoue Mitsudo remarks: "When the rulers lost power, the village managements, representing peasant interests, took their privileges on themselves. This occurred in the Kinki region especially. The village management, which existed legally and had the name 'so,' was strictly controlled by a small number of soldiers and influential peasants who managed the settlements autonomously. The 'so' directors called meetings at which they discussed directives for conducting village affairs, and determined regulations for deciding administrative policies."[20]

The conflicts which arose between representatives of the feudal lords and the local village administration led to open peasant uprisings. The peasants demanded reduction of rent payments, annulment of personal indebtedness, and the like. In some provinces, such as Kaga, these uprisings led to the overthrow of local feudal families and the establishment of peasant self-government. This period in Japanese history, despite continuing feuds, is marked by numerous undertakings both at home and in foreign lands. Within the country local markets were created, handicrafts flourished, and fishing expanded. Foreign relations were characterized by piracy and devastating raids on the continental coast. China, which previously gave no thought to the existence of the Japanese empire, now began to feel Japan's growing maritime presence.

Toward the mid-fifteenth century several independent feudal principalities existed in Japan. Around that time changes took place in the country's economy. Large holdings, which constituted the basis of the Daimyos' wealth, had succeeded in increasing productivity. Meanwhile, the impoverished peasantry filled the cities, contributing to handicraft production or becoming homeless wandering crowds. Commerce grew between individual parts of Japan and with the mainland. South of Honshu the port of Hyogo established systematic commerce with China, at first with the Shan-tung peninsula. Trade products included rice and sea produce as well as masterfully produced Japanese weapons, the Japanese having now made first acquaintance with Europeans and their firing weapons.[21]

Japanese military leaders rapidly realized the superiority of firearms. The distinguished Daimyo Oda Nobunaga advocated commerce with Portugal and Spain, and for this purpose he became the patron of Christianization, which he used to counteract the influence of separatist-oriented Buddhist monasteries. His necessary and successful efforts to unite and centralize the government are in large part explained by his ability to judge the circumstances of the day and to harness the elements in Japan seeking progress. "The spread of the Catholic faith," writes a Japanese historian, "was accompanied by acquaintance with Western technology in printing and painting. Trade with the Europeans fostered the development of new tastes in household objects, food and clothing . . . . The attitude of Japan's rulers to Western civilization was to accept it in so far as it served to strengthen their power."[22]

The Japanese regarded the Europeans as representatives of more advanced culture, for mainland Asia was in stagnation at that time. The deep social crisis experienced by China in the last decades of the Ming dynasty convinced the Japanese that in the future the great Asian empire could not be their sole school of cultural and technological advance. Having completed Japan's unification in 1590, the Shogun Toyotomi Hideyoshi, capitalizing on the Ming dynasty's feebleness and waxing unrest in its vassal states, decided to strike China through Korea. His armies were destroyed. In a second campaign, he himself perished. These unavailing campaigns betrayed Japan's weakness and unpreparedness for expansion abroad.

The Tokugawa house, headed by Shogun Tokugawa Ieyasu, ascended to power at the beginning of the seventeenth century. It opened a new period in Japanese history, creating a centralized feudal state with a new capital at the city of Edo, now Tokyo. The new government created by the Shogunate in Edo did not limit its activities to centralizing political and military power. It also endeavored to concentrate landed property in the hands of the Tokugawa family. After defeating his enemies at the battle of Sekigahara on October 20, 1600, Ieyasu confiscated wholly the properties of all his feudal adversaries. As a result the Tokugawa house became the greatest landowners, and owners of the most important mining operations. The emperor, who had remained in Kyoto, became a prisoner, stripped not only of the rights but equally of the means for retaining the throne.

Tokugawa Ieyasu continued Hideyoshi's policies of stimulating trade with the West. In 1600 he attracted the Dutch sea captain Jan Joston and the Englishman William Adams as trade consultants. The bakufu issued trade charters to the Dutch West Indies Company in 1609 and to the British West Indies Company in 1613. Ieyasu restored the interrupted trade with Korea, whereas trade with China was cut sharply thanks to peasant uprisings and violent battles with the Manchurians. The following statistics illustrate the dimensions of Japanese foreign trade:

		Average Import kans *	Vessels
On Japanese vessels (with	1604-1616	15,100	15
government licenses)	1617-1635	9,512	9
On Portuguese ships	1636-1638	18,062	3
On Dutch ships	1634-1637	4,857	9
On Chinese ships	1642-1646	12,244	52**

*1 kan-3.75 kg.

**The author does not list the source of these figures. (Editor)

Thus the quantity of goods imported in Japanese ships surpassed that carried in Dutch and Chinese bottoms, and less was imported in Portuguese vessels. Japan paid for imported goods with silver, the export of which at that time ranged from 130,000 to 165,000 kilograms annually.

Soon, however, the rulers of Japan changed their policies toward the missionaries and merchants of the West. The European colonization of India and the islands of the South Pacific, and the activity of Westerners on the Chinese coast, caused concern among the Japanese. These fears were well founded. Earlier contacts with the Europeans, particularly with the Portuguese and Spaniards, revealed to the Japanese the Westerners' far-reaching plans for Japan. Portugal and Spain intended to subjugate Japan as they had the Phillipines and other South Sea islands. This was to be carried out by the missionaries and merchants, supported by arms. History affords many examples of European intervention in Japan's internal struggles, when representatives of belligerent European colonial powers supported individual feudal lords in their battles with the central government. This intervention was especially pronounced in the affairs of the southwestern clans, whose rulers were not hesitant to accept assistance in pursuing their separatist ambitions. The European threat was perceived as early as the time of Toyotomi Hideyoshi. Despite his interest in trade with Europeans, he was forced to issue a series of decrees which sharply limited or forbade missionary activity in Japan. Such decrees were issued in 1587, 1597, and at other times. But the temptation of European knowledge was too great for Hideyoshi, particularly in military technology, and his decrees were poorly executed.

European interference also increased with the ascension of Tokugawa Ieyasu, compelling the bakufu to adopt a number of harsh measures. In 1614 all missionaries were expelled, and in 1616 Europeans were forbidden to dwell or conduct trade anywhere except Nagasaki and Hirado. Within a six year period (1633-1639) decrees were issued outlawing Christianity, recommending banishment of children of mixed blood and their mothers, forbidding Japanese to travel abroad and refusing entry into Japanese ports to foreign vessels. Only Nagasaki remained open to foreign shipping, and only Dutch and Chinese vessels were permitted there.[23] Korea and the Ryukyu Islands were also excepted, since Japan had established official relations with them. After the ban on Christianity and expulsion of missionaries, the Tokugawa Shogunate began to regulate strictly the hierarchy of Buddhist monasteries. For each sect chief monasteries were selected, and all others subordinated to them. At the same time, Japan witnessed a rejuvenation of Confucianism.

The isolationist policy instituted during the Tokugawa Shogunate aimed at more than the single goal of protecting Japan from the encroachment of Western nations. This policy, the bakufu calculated, would hinder the development of money markets, create obstacles to capitalist development and thereby preserve the feudal serf order. The Japanese historian Fujimura Toru has characterized significance and goals of isolation with these words:

> Closing the country retarded Japan's tempo of economic development in relation to the world historical process. On one hand, the bakufu's policies of isolation sought to hamper territorial pretensions related to the spread of Christianity, which came from various Western European countries as their foreign trade involvement increased. On the other hand, it intended to strengthen the bakufu's power of political domination by using comprehensive feudal control, that is, limiting the free activity of the merchantry and counteracting the growing power of western tribal princes.[24]

In other words, the policy of isolation contained a strongly expressed class orientation.

The policy of closing the country did not mean Japan's complete isolation. In the first place, the bakufu itself strived to keep abreast of all events beyond Japan's borders. For this purpose it used Dutch representatives and seafarers, who came annually to the Japanese islands with political and scientific information. Secondly, despite the bans, the rulers of the southwestern clans continued to receive information on the situation abroad. They employed Western technological achievements rather broadly within their clans. This process accelerated at the end of the eighteenth and beginning of the nineteenth centuries, especially when the power of the central government sharply deteriorated. Thirdly, all groups opposing the bakufu and the feudal regime sought out Western knowledge, using even the slightest opportunity to gain information. Advanced ideas, penetrating from the West, became the special symbols of the anti-Shogun and anti-feudal movement.

In these circumstances, all political groups in Japan, despite their particular goals, cultivated ties with Europe. Regardless of the strict limitations surrounding the sojourn of Dutchmen in Japan,[25] connections with Holland found constant cultivation. They played a large role in acquainting Japan with European science. During the rule of Shogun Tokugawa Yoshimune, permission was granted for translating Dutch books, except those which mentioned Christianity. Dutch medicine, in particular, spread throughout Japan. The Rampo system was adapted by the doctors Maeno Ryotaku, Shugita Henbiku and others.[26] In 1774 German scholarship dealing with astronomy was translated. The teachings of Copernicus and Newton also became known in Japan thanks to the Dutch. A Dutch-Japanese dictionary, compiled through the efforts of Dutchmen and Japanese over many years, made a great contribution to enlightenment.

Acquaintance with Western science promoted domestic learning. Japan developed a new field called Dutch studies, represented by the works *Otsuki Gentaku* (Steps of Dutch Studies) *Genvaku* (The Basis of Dutch Studies), and others. Major domestic scholars made an appearance. Among them Motoori Norinaga stands out notably for attempting to eschew Confucian and Buddhist dogmatism. He exerted a powerful influence on the development of the humanities in Japan. Through Holland Japanese scholars such as Nishi Amane became acquainted with German philosophy; others like Fukuzawa Yukichi studied the European parliamentary system. Such studies worked in beneficial ways to shape ideas in Japan.

The impact of the European industrial revolution may be observed in Japan in the development of natural and technical sciences. Despite the Shogunate's bans, scholars of Dutch studies such as Watababe Kojan, Takano Choei and others created the Shoshikai Society for exchange of information with the West. They openly criticized the bakufu policy of excluding foreign vessels from Japanese ports. There was wide acceptance of the need for trade expansion and introduction of more efficient means of manufacturing. The backward Samurai ideology was subjected to criticism,[27] but at the same time the court aristocracy and its ideologists propagated the "doctrine of emperor worship." Since he supposedly expressed the Japanese national spirit, they demanded the restoration of his power.[28]

At the end of the eighteenth and the beginning of the nineteenth centuries, an internal social crisis was deepening. The peasants, who comprised the bulk of the population and generated most of the national product, continued to use the most primitive implements to cultivate land holdings which had scarcely changed in the course of 150 years. Arable land totalled but 2.8-3 million hectares.[29] At the same time the growth of cities and craft production stimulated the expansion of trade and drew the village into exchange relations based on money. In agriculture, some specialized crops were widely cultivated, especially mulberry trees. Meanwhile, the labor needs of the cities grew, with scant respect for the land utilization patterns which bound the peasants to feudal lords. At the end of the eighteenth century hundreds of craft manufacturers materialized, producing silk and cotton fabrics, porcelain and glazed pottery, sake, and household objects. The natural foundations of the feudal village were weakening, while craft production and commerce were preparing the way for new capitalist social relations.

The Shogunate attempted to preserve territorial divisions among the clans by means of internal tariff barriers and enforced limits on population movements. This merely deepened the social crisis and constrained the growing commercial bourgeoisie, then emerging from within the ranks of the aristocracy and landlords, to follow the change in Japan's social order toward capitalism.

ASPECTS OF SINO-JAPANESE RELATIONS

Relations between China and Japan in the period under consideration were determined by the level of domestic development and the international position of each country. During the first five centuries of centralized government in Japan, that country remained under strong Chinese cultural influence. This dominance resulted from rather extensive Chinese emigration, generally by fleeing members of one or another deposed Chinese dynasty, or of specially invited Chinese philosophers, Buddhist servants, artists, and craftsmen. Together with Koreans, these immigrants filled important functions. They directed the construction of Japanese cities, created universities and temples, and built monuments of ancient Japanese culture which still stand. Yet even in this early development, Japan was not satisfied simply to adopt the experience of the Chinese newcomers. It sent numerous missions of nobles and youths to China to become acquainted with Chinese knowledge. These trained citizens permitted Japan to free itself from its teachers as early as the ninth and tenth centuries. Varying with the degree of Japan's own cultural accomplishments, Chinese culture either blended with the traditional popular culture, or contributed to improved forms while preserving unique native elements.

In the thirteenth and fourteenth centuries, after the Mongolian conquest of China, Sino-Japanese ties were almost completely severed. This is explained partly by the threat of a Mongol-Chinese invasion which forced Japan to look to the organization of national defense. It is also true that the cultural and economic stagnation of China at this time lessened its influence on neighboring countries.

In the fourteenth and fifteenth centuries, when China was freed of the Mongol yoke and the Ming dynasty attempted to spread its influence to Japan, Sino-Japanese relations further deteriorated. Chinese attempts to treat Japan as a vassal and force it to recognize China's hegemony met with staunch resistance as the island nation grew in strength. The Japanese Shogun Yoshimoto, in correspondence with Emperor Cheng-tsu of China relating to raids by Japanese pirates on the Chinese coast, officially rebuffed China's pretensions to domination in East Asia.[30] Now the very opposite occurred as Japan threw down its first challenge to China. Japanese policy toward China became more demanding as the Ming empire weakened. Finally, the rulers of Japan abandoned their defensive posture in favor of a policy of attacking the Asian continent. This new period in Sino-Japanese relations came after Japan was united under the leadership of Oda Nobunaga. His successor Toyotomi Hideyoshi launched ambitious campaigns on the Korean peninsula in 1592 and 1597. Although Hideyoshi's campaigns failed due to Japan's lack of an appropriate economic strength, military skill and experience, they nonetheless proclaimed unmistakably the ambitions of Japan's rulers. They demonstrated that the repeated attempts to conquer the Korean peninsula were not chance episodes, and that the conquest of mainland territories had become one of Japan's most important aims.

Thanks to a worsening domestic social crisis, Ming China began to decline. The Manchurians defeated one Chinese army after another, demonstrating that China clearly was losing hegemony in Asia. More, China now was becoming the prize of Manchurian conquests. In those years communications between China and Japan noticeably lessened.

New forces loomed in the Far East and their influence continued to grow throughout the following centuries. The first Europeans reached China in 1516 and Japan in 1542. On the heels of Portuguese pirates came merchants, and then Christian missionaries. At first their arrival did not provoke serious resistance. In China, the Portuguese even succeeded (not without bribing local officials) in taking the island of Aomen, called Macao by the Portuguese. They turned it into a colonial trade company. In Japan, the first European merchants and missionaries actually enjoyed official protection under Oda Nobunaga and Toyotomi Hideyoshi, who sought superior European firearms and sea vessels in exchange for these privileges.

As European aggression and colonization spread in South and Southeast Asia (India, Indonesia, and the Phillipines), China and Japan altered their attitudes and started to prohibit intercourse with the newcomers. Both countries promulgated decrees strictly regulating the sojourns and activities of Europeans. The protection of national sovereignty became the most important problem for both China and Japan. Their foreign policies sought primarily to limit relations with the European states; the consequence of this policy was isolation from the outside world. Isolationist foreign policy continued in both countries until the middle of the nineteenth century. Isolationism ended in China with the blows of the European states that gained them footholds on China's coasts. (China's hinterlands remained free of Europeans and Americans.) The appearance of the first American squadrons and the demise of the Tokugawa Shogunate ended Japanese isolation.

Behind an outward similarity Japanese and Chinese isolationisms varied quite widely in both aim and content. In China the Manchurian Chin dynasty sought by means of its foreign policy to isolate the Chinese people from progressive Western influences, or from anything that might awaken their consciousness. Guided by these considerations, the Chin rulers concerned themselves not so much with repulsing military attacks and protecting Chinese territory as with erecting ideological barriers to Western revolutionary ideas, which threatened the "divine" imperial throne. They also opposed technological innovations which might change the context of human relationships. By compromise and retreat in detriment of national interests, the imperial court tried to buy its freedom from the West. That very approach furthered China's decline to the status of a semi-colonized state.

In Japan the Tokugawa Shogunate, during the first decades of its existence, expelled Europeans or limited the duration of their sojourns. This policy formed a part of the Tokugawa family's struggle against Christianity, provoked when European and Japanese Christians supported the Shogunate's enemies. The European threat to domestic calm decreased in proportion to the strengthening of the central authority. The policy of isolation had the primary goal of protecting the country from foreign incursions, even though to some degree the Shogunate continued to fear the feudal lords antagonistic to it. It sought to deprive them of European help, particularly weapons.

At the same time, during the period of the Tokugawa Shogunate, relations were preserved with advanced European countries, and with Western science through the Dutch. "Dutch studies" played a definite and positive role in hastening domestic scientific and cultural progress and in acquainting the Japanese with the accomplishments of European philosophy and the natural and technical sciences. To be sure, the Shogunate's isolationist policy held back social and economic transformation. Nevertheless, in contrast to China's policy, it did not attempt to close the country completely to European science.

In the middle of the nineteenth century similar internal conditions prevailed in both China and Japan. Elements of budding capitalism already existed and the economic and political pre-conditions for the displacement of the antiquated feudal manner of production were in place. Large cities arose as centers of crafts and trade. The existence of a monetary exchange system had allowed the internal market to expand. Furthermore, merchants arrived with Western manufactured products, thereby stimulating foreign trade. These forces combined to create the circumstances necessary for the development of capitalism in China and Japan.

The atmosphere which favored this unavoidable historical process evolved differently in the two countries. In China, the fate of the decrepit feudal system depended on the existence of the imperial court. The people as a whole displayed a national hatred of the foreign Manchurian dynasty. The slogan "Ta Chin Fu Ming"—"Topple the Chins and restore the Mings," was the war cry in all of the popular risings during this period. The opponents of the Manchurian monarchy placed the liberation of China above all else. Simultaneously, the growing revolutionary pressures alarmed the Chinese feudal leaders, and other exploiters, who then transferred their loyalties to the imperial court. The lack of patriotism among the exploiting classes weakened the national might of China, so that in a time of decision the strength was not found to meet foreign threats. Consequently, during the 1830s and 1840s the Chinese feudal lords supported the policy of capitulation practiced by the Chin rulers. By so doing, they shared historical responsibility with the Manchurian dynasty for the initial inequitable treaties imposed upon China by the Western nations.

The anti-feudal movement developed differently in Japan. There feudal oppression was connected with the omnipotent Shogunate of the Tokugawas rather than with the ineffectual emperor. The latter was in reality robbed of political power and reduced to an impoverished figurehead. The Tokugawas controlled not only the best lands but the major cities of Japan, including Osaka, the largest city in the south. Unreasonable taxes, heavy, exhausting serf labor, land bondage, limitations on seasonal handicrafts, and other extra-economic forms of coercion in the village prepared the way for peasant uprisings. In the cities, growing resistance to Shogun rule was exacerbated by restrictions on foreign commerce, prohibition of commercial travel abroad, and hindrances to development of commercial centers, ports, and shipping. The peasant struggle against taxes and usury and for equal land use joined that of the craftsmen, merchants, and ruined nobility to form a mighty, united anti-feudal movement. While the impoverished aristocracy enjoyed class privileges, it lacked material resources and therefore made common cause with the merchants and the city bourgeoisie to form a combined force against the feudal despotism of the Tokugawa Shogunate.

The uniqueness of the anti-feudal contest in Japan lay in its advocacy of restoration of the emperor's political rights, which had been usurped by the Shoguns. Restoration was tied to the demand for an end to isolationism, which had condemned the country to backwardness. The emperor was expected to bring a renaissance, along with reform of the state administration, the economy, and national defense. The emperor became the rallying point for the revolting Samurais, the city bourgeoisie and the petty nobility. This lent Japan's struggle against feudalism an organized character and facilitated the overthrow of the Shogunate. Nevertheless these very features, which played such a role in the anti-feudal revolution in Japan and objectively hastened the historical process, constituted a fundamental obstacle to the achievement of the democratic goals of a bourgeois revolution. They preserved certain pre-capitalist forms of relationships in both agriculture and industry, and held back the development of class consciousness in the Japanese people. In the course of Japan's further evolution these features of the anti-feudal movement were to have a decisive impact on the nation's fate.

SUMMARY

The arrival of European colonial powers on Chinese and Japanese shores in the sixteenth century introduced radical changes into both the general East Asian situation and the particular postures of China and Japan. From this point forward the mutual relations of China and Japan became of secondary importance, the paramount foreign policy objective of each country becoming that of averting European advances and of guarding their national independence. For China, the solutions to these problems were made complex by the presence of the alien Manchurian dynasty. Intoxicated by easy victories over feeble neighboring states, the Manchurians displayed extreme animosity toward the outside world and disdain for the accomplishments of world science and technology. They were unprepared for the aggression of the Western powers. Having suffered their first military defeats, the Manchurian rulers began to seek arrangements with the intruders in order to strengthen their power over the Chinese people. The policy of compromise and appeasement toward the advancing capitalist states shaped the diplomatic course of the Manchurian court at midpoint in the nineteenth century and enabled the Chinese reactionary classes to brake social development.

Despite incomparably lesser human and material resources, Japan proved better able to overcome internal social crisis as well as threats to national sovereignty. Japan avoided strangulation by outside forces. It was able, although in limited dimensions, to utilize the experience of world civilizations and thereby to ease its transition to a new form of economic life based on capitalism. Japan overcame the archaic ideology of Confucius and thus liberated itself from the influence of Chinese culture. By the middle of the nineteenth century China had lost its place as Japan's teacher. Now their mutual bond was not so similar a cultural ambience as it was the common and looming threat of incursion by the Western powers.

CHAPTER THREE

China and Japan Between the Western Powers

The cleaving Chinese and Japanese social crises at mid-19th century coincided with the rapid creation of a world-wide colonial system. The policies of isolation practiced by the rulers of both countries over long periods could no longer protect them from the inroads of foreign capital. The epicenter of the contest between the rival powers was in the Far East. As a result, China and Japan were faced with the lurking danger of sinking to colonial status, their fates dependent on the ability of their peoples to unite and to resist Western aggression. Despite their small numbers, the Western armies were equipped with more modern weapons and therefore it was necessary that the rulers of China and Japan display competence in leading their peoples in the struggle for national independence and equal status with other nations.

CONSEQUENCES OF CHINESE ISOLATIONISM

After the Napoleonic Wars, England began aggressive moves in China. In 1833, the English parliament abolished the monopoly of the East India Company and permitted various merchant firms to conduct trade with the East, including China. The English government supported those firms with all means including military force. In November 1839, a new conflict was provoked by the British, who refused to respect the ban on opium trade. An English naval vessel near Hong Kong opened fire on Chinese coast guard junks,[1] thus beginning the "First Opium War." The imperial court proved incapable of organizing the country's defense. After three years of rather minimal military operations, China capitulated, and agreed to sign the first of several demeaning treaties, the Nanking agreement.[2] The "Opium War" of 1839-1842 was the first open military conflict between two social organizations, the vast feudal empire which hitherto had been the mighty colossus of the East, and the advanced capitalist states. China was supported by its vassal neighbors. Yet the Chin empire felt defeat, and the inequitable Nanking treaty entailed far-reaching consequences. The faith of the Chinese people in the divine power of the emperor, long worshipped as "the son of heaven," was destroyed. The emperor's loss of prestige shook the very foundations of the monarchy. Throughout the country numerous secret societies came to life, inciting the people to battle against the Chin dynasty.

The "Opium War" defeat generated similarly unfavorable effects in the economy. The working people were forced to bear the additional burden of military reparations. By means of free ports England followed by the United States, France and other European states, acquired the right to import various industrial commodities without limits, including factory-produced fabrics. The imported products then were sold at lower prices than Chinese handcrafted products, which were subject to high domestic tariffs. Chinese handicraft and domestic production was in no position to compete with the machine products of capitalist Europe and America; it was condemned to ruin. These developments inflicted on the feudal Chin empire a political as well as an economic crisis. Evaluating this period of Chinese history, Karl Marx wrote: "Chinese industry, depending on hand work, could not stand competition with the machine. The unshakable Middle Kingdom endured a social crisis. Taxes ceased coming, the government was on the verge of bankruptcy and masses of the population were pauperized; they began to grow agitated, refused to be subordinated, beat and killed the emperor's Mandarins[3] and Buddhist monks . . . ."[4]

On January 11, 1851, in the village of Chin-chiang, Kuang-hsi province, revolt broke out. Coal workers, joined by local peasants, moved against the Manchurian officials. The Shang Ti (Supreme Lord) religious society, headed by Hung Hsiu-chuan, led the rebellion. In Chinese history this popular rising is known as the "Rebellion of the Tai Ping (Great Peace)." Despite the religious (Christian) nuance of the Tai Ping uprising, as the peasant crowds joined it acquired the character of a peasant revolution against the feudal system itself. The success of the uprising led to rapid consolidation of rebel territories; on August 1, 1851 the state of "Tai Ping Tien-kuo" (The Heavenly State of Great Peace) was established. The next eighteen months brought further victories and the taking of Nanking. It was proclaimed the capital on March 29, 1853, with the designation Tientsin (The Heavenly Seat). Having created a central government, the Tai Ping authorities compiled and published the "Law of the Land of Tai Ping Tien-kuo," which proposed land reform by eliminating imperial and feudal land holdings in favor of equalized land cultivation.[5]

Upholding the mixed political and religious teaching that "the essence under heaven is the single family of God the Father," the Tai Ping gave the peasants land and various other properties. These were not to be privately held, merely privately used. The peasants were formed into communes of 25 families each, headed by elders. The communal land was worked jointly, with all material wealth being divided according to the principle: "If there is land, it is worked jointly; if there is food, it is divided equally among all; if there is clothing, it is equitably distributed to be worn; if there is money, it is spent together."[6] In each such commune a government storehouse was built. Family expenses for weddings, births, and aid to pregnant women were covered by selling supplies from the storehouse.

The Tai Ping leaders devoted great attention to the development of industrial production, including weapons manufacture and construction of highways. They encouraged invention, mineral exploitation, and the establishment of banks. In the realm of finances the Tai Ping policy amounted to placing the basic burden of government financing on the wealthy portion of the population. Of great significance in consolidating the Tai Ping political authority and economic position was the system of democratic elections of army officers and civil servants. Prior to the elections, candidates for these duties underwent complex testing. In addition, each candidate was required to have guarantors who would be responsible for his activities. Various cultural innovations were introduced, among them the use of the vernacular in writing, which gained wide favor. Ancient literary canons and the old calendar were abolished, and the latter replaced by a new calendar starting from the foundation of the Tai Ping state. The Tai Pings exhibited great perception in determining their foreign policy. Their international relations were built on the principle that all countries are "brotherly states which should live together as brothers live." The measures instituted by the Tai Ping rulers in agriculture, handicraft manufacture, trade, and finances undermined the foundations of the feudal order and prepared the way for a new type of social relationship. Despite its religious coloring the Tai Ping revolution clearly contributed to preparing the way for a republican order.

The prospect of destroying the Chin empire and forming a centralized national republic on its remains did not fit into the plans of the Western powers, who were seeking to colonize China. Taking advantage of the Chin's failures against the Tai Ping, England once more provoked conflicts with China. Under this as a pretext a British squadron shelled Canton at the end of 1856, thus beginning the "Second Opium War." Defeated, the Chin government capitulated in June, 1858, whereupon England and France obliged China to sign separate bilateral agreements—

the Tientsin treaties—which granted further rights to foreigners in China.[7] This new capitulation caused a wave of dissatisfaction in China. Fearing loss of its influence at home, the Chin government refused to ratify the treaties. At the end of 1859 the Anglo-French interventionists renewed military operations, marched on Peking and by force of arms compelled the imperial court to surrender. This was the "Third Opium War."

After taking Peking on October 13, 1860, England and France not only thrust upon China the Tientsin treaties, but also concluded the additional "Peking conventions." These greatly broadened the role of foreign commercial capital and limited even further the sovereign rights of the Chinese government. China was deprived of the right to regulate her own import and export tariffs. The foreign states, headed by England as the country carrying the largest trade with China, established control over China's foreign trade, taking into their hands the actual direction of Chinese customs. Moreover, six additional Chinese ports were opened to foreign commerce—Ying-kou, Chih-fu, Taiwan, Swatow, Chiung-chou, and Tientsin. Foreign subjects also gained direct influence on Chinese affairs through diplomatic missions in Peking, openly supporting the feudal Chin monarchy in its struggles with the Tai Ping.[8] Meanwhile, the feudal lords of China more and more turned against the Tai Ping as they recognized the deadly threat it posed to their master. They gathered mighty local armies and gave crucial support to the Chin government. In union with the feudal lords and the western states the monarchy crushed the democratic movement and maintained the feudal order.

The Tai Ping movement, now called the Great Peasant Revolutionary War, lasted fifteen years and left a deep imprint on Chinese history. Evaluating it, Marx and Engels wrote:

> Perhaps Chinese socialism (that is, Tai Ping peasant socialism—M.S.) has no more to do with its European counterpart than Chinese philosophy has with Hegel. It is still gratifying that the most ancient and stable empire in the world, under the blows of England, found itself on the verge of a social upheaval which undoubtedly would have had extraordinary consequence for civilization. When our European reactionaries in the near future reach the Great Wall of China and the gates which lead to the arch-reactionary and arch-conservative citadel, they may perhaps find the inscription: "The Chinese Republic. Freedom, Equality and Fraternity."[9]

The crushing of the Tai Pings could not halt the disintegration of the Chinese feudal order. Even the leading dignitaries of the imperial court were opposed to the traditional policy of seclusion and isolation from the outside world. The most far-sighted members of the Chinese ruling coterie could not fail to see that imperial authority rested on a frail foundation. The Manchurian Chin army, once a feared force which crushed peasant risings and ravaged feeble neighbors, could no longer guarantee the safety of the empire from either popular fury or outside attack.

The modern weapons received by the Chin from England, France and the United States, and the machine equipped factories built at the "free" ports, convincingly demonstrated the advantages of the capitalist system. At the beginning of the 1860s the leaders of the Chin government began to stress a policy of "self-improvement." The nature and goals of this policy were differently understood by various government groups. The group around Prince Kung, representing the "thick-heads" led by the widowed Empress Tzu Hsi, sought to strengthen the monarchy by augmenting the Manchurian "banner" armies, thereby clearly expressing their distrust of the Chinese officer corps.[10] One of the chief principles of this policy was to prevent any foreign participation in training the army and creating military industry. The Manchurian noble Wo Jen wrote to Tzu Hsi: "China is great and there is no need to be concerned of a lack of talent. Why do we need the foreigners? What can they teach us?"[11]

The "thick-heads," like earlier Chin rulers, ignored contemporary international events. On one hand they conducted themselves in a "militant" and "provocative" manner in relations with the foreign states. They attempted to convey "implacability" and played on the Chinese feeling of national insult while inflaming fanaticism and hatred toward everything European. On the other hand, they were ready for further compromise with the European states. They failed to note the danger from Japan, where capitalism was quickly developing. "Their 'self-strengthening,' " writes historian Fan Wen-lan, "was based not on the acceptance of capitalism but on the fear of capitalism."[12]

A band of powerful provincial dignitaries, including Li Hung-chang, Tseng Kuo-fan, and Tso Tsung-tang, believed in other methods of self-improvement. Li Hung-chang sought the road to success in the experience gained by the industrialized countries. He wanted to utilize foreign equipment and steamships and to construct industrial enterprises with the aid of foreign specialists, granting first priority to army needs. "It is a disgrace for China," Li Hung-chang wrote to Tseng Kuo-fan, "that its armament is backward. Every day I urge young and old officers to forget about shame and occupy themselves with serious study of

European secrets in order to profit from them. We will repent our errors if, having spent so much time in Shanghai, we do not adopt their mastery."[13]

The advocates of self-improvement are known in Chinese history as the "Westernizers." On their initiative Chinese officers were sent to study in Europe for the first time. In 1862, with foreign assistance, China began to create arsenals, the first mechanized enterprises in the country. The Westernizers as well as the "thick-heads" strove to preserve the monarchy, but they hoped to achieve this by concentrating already existing industry in the hands of the state, or at least under the control or administration of government offices. Thus, new industry would primarily serve the army. Urging governmental management of military-related industry, Li Hung-chang warned the emperor that "in the high mountains and inaccessible places lean men will gather secretly to adopt foreign methods, and then they will appear with new plans. One fine day they will cease working the fields altogether and will demonstrate the brilliant possibilities of their weapons. Then who will protect the government armies, armed with aged weapons?"[14]

High-placed officials headed the government industrial enterprises and promoted the self-improvement policy. They controlled government resources and were in reality the omnipotent masters of such companies. In this way a specific form of capitalism took shape in China. Legally and formally this capitalism involved state ownership, but actually its control rested in the private hands of government officials. This unusual form of capital, known in modern Chinese history as "bureaucratic capital," found wide application later, particularly in the years of Kuomintang rule.[15] Private Chinese entrepreneurs were not permitted to build factories independently. They might possess only purchased shares in state enterprises and were entirely dependent on bureaucratic capital.

The Westernizers strove to limit industrial development to the direct needs of the army. Nonetheless, it was impossible to avoid creating industries which, while primarily serving the army, by their nature also benefited the entire country. Examples are transportation and coal mining. The Chin administration, however, under the strong influence of Tzu Hsi and her "thick-head" clique, allocated extremely limited resources for the construction and maintenance of state enterprises. From the total income entering the state treasury in 1885-1894 of 815.4 million liang in silver, expenses for maintenance and repair amounted to only 34.7 million liang in silver.[16] Consequently, the wishes of the Chin leaders notwithstanding, including those controlling "bureaucratic capital," a pressing need developed for large amounts of private capital, primarily from domestic merchants and money lenders.

The "thick-heads" rejected the need for adopting foreign technical and scientific achievements. For their part, the Westernizers endeavored to limit industrial development to "bureaucratic capital" and military production. The combination led into a blind alley, since this approach to technology did not correspond to domestic or international circumstances. Machine-type production and transport development lagged. National capital investment in industry and transport from 1872 to 1893 totalled but 18.5 million yuan. This figure included 15 million yuan in "bureaucratic capital" (from both state and private officials' sources); purely private capital amounted to only 3.5 million yuan.[17]

The collapse of the self-improvement policy was finally recognized by its sponsor Li Hung-chang, who by the end of the nineteenth century was the leading figure in Chin foreign policy. In summing up the results of this method, he wrote: "All that was accomplished in this respect serves merely as a model. The supply of industrial materials was insufficient, and resources were wasted senselessly and maliciously."[18]

The retarded development of national capital resources and the preservation of the shaky Chin monarchy served Western interests. The Western powers launched a sharp new campaign against China that demonstrated their dissatisfaction with the inequitable treaties of the 1840s and 1860s which had permitted them to dominate Chinese foreign trade. They objected to the policy which restricted the settlement of foreigners to the "free" ports and to the limitation of commercial undertakings to ship repair and to the processing of exports such as tea, silk, and the like. England occupied the leading position in trade and maritime shipping. Consequently, England also controlled Chinese customs operations. In the 1860s and 1880s France, the United States, Japan, and Russia followed England in actively exploiting China. From 1866 to 1890 China lost control over many neighboring states which had been ruled by the Chin empire in the preceding centuries.

JAPAN DEVELOPS CAPITALISM

Japan's social crisis, which intensified in the mid-19th century, in many respects reflected the Shogunate's isolationist policies.[19] The preeminence of the European countries was clearly apparent in England's "Opium Wars" with China. Japan became concerned and the most progressive circles of Japanese society awakened and began a struggle against isolationism. The few mechanized enterprises then in existence in Japan also demonstrated the superiority of modern technology. Meanwhile, the Western states constantly pursued ways of exploiting Japan. In 1844 and 1847 Holland attempted to establish normal relations with Japan and even offered to act as its agent in establishing contacts with other western European countries. This initiative found no positive response, for the Shogunate continued to seek seclusion from the outside world and to restrain domestic progress. No less than China, backward Japan became the object of Western expansion.

The United States began extensive activities in the Far East. Taking advantage of the involvement of England, France, and Russia in the Crimean War, an American squadron of four naval ships commanded by Commodore Matthew C. Perry entered Tokyo harbor on July 8, 1853. Perry's mission aimed to demonstrate the might of the American fleet and to open Japan to American commerce. During a second visit to Japan, Perry succeeded in forcing the Shogun to make concessions and on March 31, 1854, a treaty "of peace and friendship was signed," Japan's first treaty with a foreign state.[20] Soon Japan signed similar agreements with the other Western countries.

Japan's capitulation further revealed its antiquated feudal structure. The threatened loss of Japan's sovereignty joined domestic social conflicts as problems facing the country. All responsibility for national and social difficulties was attributed to the Shogun, who stood accused of depriving the emperor of his right to power, of disrespect for the dignity of the Mikado, and of destroying national traditions. A massive movement directed against the Shogun spread throughout Japan under the slogan of "respect for the emperor and expulsion of the foreigners." The center of this campaign was the imperial court in Kyoto. The movement grew, gripping all levels of Japanese society and finally exploding into civil war. As adversaries stood the Shogunate and the partisans of bourgeois reform under the imperial flag.

At the beginning of 1868 the civil war ended in the resignation of Tokugawa Yoshinobu and formation of the government of Emperor Mutsimoto on January 3, 1868. Political and socio-economic reforms were instituted with the purpose of internal development based on capitalism, ushering in the period known as the Meiji revolution or the Restoration Epoch. One feature of this uncompleted bourgeois revolution was the bolstering of the imperial order instead of progress toward a democratic bourgeois republic. Central power shifted from Tokugawa's feudal Shogunate to the emperor, a process which suggests a similarity between the historical evolution of Japan and Germany. The preservation of a strong central authority possessed very great significance for the stabilization of Japan's domestic political and economic situation. International events, moreover, proved more favorable for Japan than for China.

The United States, which was the first to have extracted inequitable treaties from Japan, was unable to take full advantages of those agreements. The Civil War of 1861-1865 greatly weakened United States naval power and thereby devastated American foreign policy. England meanwhile was concentrating her attentions on China. At the same time Britain met ever greater competition from other powerful European states, particularly Russia, which had established positions on the shores of the Pacific and began actively to pursue objectives in China. In these circumstances, England's interest in Japan was not that of a conqueror but of a potential ally. According to its diplomats, England was certain to clash with Russia. In the 1890s a rapprochement between Japan and England began, and a treaty of alliance followed in 1902.[21]

The emperor had ascended to power after the Meiji revolution. With his leadership, Japan's rulers were able to take advantage of favorable domestic and foreign events. In the last three decades of the nineteenth century, these conditions were of particular benefit to the newly formed middle class. Japan set out to end its former isolation and to make more intensive use of advanced foreign science and technology. In the words of the Japanese historian Ienaga Saburo, "it is impossible to deny the fact that conversion of Japanese society to modern forms was outwardly a process of borrowing Western culture. We have stated a number of times that in the bosom of Japan a culture was being born which contained features of modern times. But it was nothing more than a basis, a trunk for further growth. Cultural development of something that truly could be called modern culture took place only when the shoots of Western culture grafted onto that trunk."[22]

In 1868 ten model government mines began operation in Japan, conducted along European lines and with the aid of European specialists. A naval arsenal was constructed in Yokosuka, and the first European printing press was brought from Paris. The following years saw rapid construction of textile, metallurgical, metal processing, electrotechnical, shipbuilding, and machine building plants. These were outfitted with the latest English, German, French, and American equipment. In 1872 the first railroad was built between Tokyo and Yokohama, a distance of 29 kilometers. In 1887 electric lighting appeared in Tokyo, and the first hydroelectric power station began operation on Lake Piva in 1891. In 1896 the first electric tramway began operating in Kyoto; 1897 saw the first American automobile in Yokohama.

Japanese historians see the reason for rapid adoption of foreign cultural, scientific and technical achievements in the fact that Japan opened her doors to all progressing nations at once. From France, Japan learned methods for creating and training the army. From England and the United States came models for banks, companies and other business establishments, and a system for building and handling a naval fleet. Germany provided the example for national law and centralized government, and later, army organization. Japan also created a domestic scientific and technical base and started to train numerous qualified specialists. In 1872 the European education system was introduced,[23] in 1877 a university was established in Tokyo, and in 1879 the Academy of Sciences was founded. The 1872 law on conducting land apportionment, and abolition of the ban on land purchase and sale, played an important role in liquidating feudal backwardness and in developing capitalistic economic relationships. On the basis of that law capitalist forms of land ownership were gradually established. The freedom of movement for peasants was granted and the peasant became a legally free producer.

Rapid capitalist development in Japan hastened the growth of cities. Such towns as Tokyo and Osaka, which had 600,000 and 284,000 inhabitants in 1877, were transformed into world metropolises. Their populations respectively were 1,440,000 and 821,000 in 1898. The end of feudalism in the countryside and the growth of industry in cities led generally to rapid increases in childbearing. In the 25 years between 1875 and 1899 the Japanese population grew from 35.1 million to 43.2 million.

At the time of Tokugawa rule large industries, such as mining, shipbuilding, and military arsenals, had been created as state enterprises. After the Meiji revolution the major portion of industry, with the exception of railroads and military suppliers, was in private hands. Indeed, in 1880 many state enterprises were sold to private companies, the Japanese government thereby underscoring its commitment to private capitalism and contributing to the formation of powerful concerns. "In this manner," writes a Japanese specialist, "the sale of those factories and mines became an important event in the formation of so-called 'Zaibatsu,' or financial cliques."[24]

Economic expansion on the basis of modern technology speeded government consolidation and the enhancement of its power. Japan regained customs autonomy in relations with the United States by 1878 through a joint customs treaty. It then denounced inequitable treaties with other countries and concluded new ones, based on complete political and legal equality—with Russia and Germany in 1889 and with England in 1894. Northern Honshu island and Hokkaido island, which had been left untouched until the industrial revolution, were rapidly colonized in the 1870s until, by the 1890s, they had become a part of the general Japanese economic sphere.

Having embarked on capitalist development and opened the country to Western culture, Japan's ruling social groups then sought to adopt certain bourgeois juridical procedures and a parliamentary form of government. At the same time their chief aim was to support the monarchy, to give the emperor unlimited powers. Consequently, the parliament had only an advisory role.

In the economy, the imperfection of Japan's bourgeois revolution was manifested in the preservation of forced labor in manufacturing and in the retention of feudal relations in the countryside. The liquidation of the holdings of the Tokugawa house[25] led merely to division of ownership, not to a change in the feudal basis of agriculture. The peasantry conducted natural or semi-natural farming,[26] renting land on a sharecropping basis and remaining the pawns of landlords and moneylenders. In industry as well, pre-capitalist forms prevailed. Workers contracted through agents for long terms, lived in barracks under near prison conditions, and received wages through foremen.

The Japanese constitution was proclaimed on February 11, 1889. It was a "compromise between the wishes of the national administration to strengthen the authority of the new government headed by the emperor as the central figure, and the popular demand for freedom and normal rights." But the government emerged triumphant, the emperor's power was increased, and the people were imbued with the concept of Japanese superiority and the "Japanese spirit." The determining factors in post-reform Japan became the enhancement of the army's role in political leadership and the militarization of the economy. Declaring their international ambitions as early as the 1870s, Japan's leaders strove to make up for economic weakness through military strength. They realized that the country's economic potential was limited. "In Japan and Russia," wrote Lenin, "military monopoly and vast territory (this applied only to Russia—M.S.), or a special ease in plundering foreigners, partially make up for and partially replace a modern financial monopoly."[27]

Foreign expansion turned out to be the chief purpose of Japanese governmental policy. A rapidly growing middle class, dissatisfied by the limited markets resulting from continuing feudalism, actively searched for foreign trade partners. Wars and armed intervention became the dominant features of Japan's policy of expansion. In 1872 universal military obligations were imposed in Japan, and in 1870 the creation of a modern navy was begun.

SINO-JAPANESE RELATIONS

In the 1870s a new quality distinguished the relations between China and Japan. It was determined by two factors. The first beneficial circumstance for Japan was the Western exploitation of China. This imperiled China's international status and its relations with provincial and island territories as well as with Korea, which was still a dependency. The second factor involved the strained situation between England and Russia, Japan's main rivals in the Far East. Japan did not hesitate to utilize the prevailing animosities, setting as its first objective the annulment of the inequitable provisions of earlier treaties. Secondly, Japan sought equal status with the Western states in attacking China and those of its possessions which were outside established spheres of influence.

At the start of the 1870s Japan began preparing for Korean conquests and for seizing the Ryukyu islands, which had been Chinese vassals. Despite the Sino-Japanese treaty of 1871 which included guarantees of the territorial integrity of each state,[28] the Japanese government moved audaciously. It invited the king of the Ryukyu islands to Japan, and detained him by force. Disregarding Chinese protests, in 1872 Japan proclaimed its possession of the islands and in 1879 they were declared to be a Japanese prefecture. In 1874 Japan attacked Taiwan. Although Japanese armies subsequently withdrew, the Japanese government forced the signing of a treaty calling for payment of 500,000 taels as reparations.

In 1876, in negotiations with the Chinese government, the Japanese representative, Mori Arinori, openly minimized his government's obligation to prevent "violation of or attempts on the rights of either country," as had been guaranteed in the treaty of 1871. He informed Li Hung-chang that international law was "useless" and treaties "undependable," for "great national decisions are based on might, not on right." Also in 1876 the Japanese government forced Korea to agree to terms emphasizing the denial of Chinese suzerainty over Korea, and also to grant Japan unilateral rights to entry and trade in Korea. The following years brought even stronger advances on Korea, finally leading to war with China in 1894-1895. For the first time in its history, Japan defeated its larger neighbor. Japan's defeat of China offered a potent demonstration of the superiority of progressive and capitalistic Japan

over the Chin feudal empire, which possessed far greater natural resources, vast territories, and a population ten times that of Japan.
The Shimonoseki peace treaty forced China to cede to Japan,
Taiwan with the Pescadore islands, southern Manchuria including the
Liao-tung peninsula, and its adjoining district from the port of Ying-
kou to the city of An-tung. China also was required to recognize
Korea's "independence" and to pay Japan the enormous war compensation of 200 million liang in silver, the equivalent of nearly five times
the Japanese state budget of that time. Finally, China had to turn over
the port of Wei-hai-wei to Japan.[29] The unreasonable ambitions of
Japan alarmed Russia, France and Germany. They forced Japan to drop
a number of demands, including those on southern Manchuria. Even so,
the Japanese acquisitions comprised valuable material sources for further development. The consequences of the Shimonoseki treaty for
China went far beyond the territorial and monetary losses. According
to treaty provisions, China was forced to grant to Japan the right to industrial activities in the ports which were open to foreign commerce.

After the Sino-Japanese war Japan moved into the ranks of the most
important imperialist states involved in the division and colonial enslavement of China. It is true that on the eve of the twentieth century
Japan lacked sufficient strength to challenge the largest states—England,
Russia, the United States, and France. At this stage Japan attempted to
play off one hostile group against another. Lacking firm bases on
Chinese territory, Japan in those years supported the American policy
of "open doors and equal opportunities," which contrasted to the
"spheres of influence" advocated by tsarist Russia, Germany, and
France. Just as the United States defended the "open doors" policy,
Japan strove to present itself to Chinese society as the champion of territorial integrity and Chinese state sovereignty.

Japanese diplomatic maneuvers fostered illusions in Chinese liberal
circles. These liberals consoled themselves with hopes that imperial
Japan's activities in international arenas would hinder the encroachments of others against China. Japan was the first powerful modern
state in Asia. Certainly it would help the Chinese people acquire complete independence, equality, progress, and renaissance. Japan had repudiated its aggressive ambitions after the war of 1894-1895, and was preparing openly for battle with tsarist Russia. China interpreted these
policies as proof of Japan's intentions to protect Asia from European
powers. But the leaders of Japan did not miss the chance to capitalize
on the trust of the Chinese liberals. They played quite adroitly on the
national feelings of the Chinese. In 1898, during the "100 days of

reform" in China, the Japanese government dispatched a mission to China headed by Marquis Ito Hirobumi for negotiations with the young Emperor Kuang-hsu. After the reform movement was crushed, one of its leaders, Kang Yo-wei, emigrated to Japan. The Japanese government offered him the opportunity to participate in the movement to unite the nations of East Asia.

All of this attention and patronage accorded by Japanese government officials to Chinese progressives had the sole purpose of finding political support in Chinese society and of using the Chinese to realize their own aims. To achieve these aims, the Japanese rulers were ready to make use of any forces whatsoever in China. Thus, upon the failure of the reform movement, the Japanese with no less politeness began to court Empress Tzu Hsi. Young imperial Japan was gathering its strength and preparing militarily for eventual direct aggression against China.

SUMMARY

China and Japan began the second fifty years of the nineteenth century in approximately similar positions, both dependent on the Western nations. The sovereign rights of both states were limited by treaties granting one-sided financial and legal advantages and privileges to Western countries. By the end of the century, however, as a result of varying internal and external circumstances, the two countries were vastly different. China, which had continued to preserve backward feudal relationships, steadily lost its national sovereignty and was transformed into a semi-colony. Japan, on the other hand, having undertaken a capitalist development, became a progressive state. True, significant vestiges of feudalism remained. Nonetheless, the country won its freedom from inequitable treaties imposed upon it and initiated its own program of aggression.

For the first time in its entire history Japan became the superior force in relations with China. This was not the result of a higher civilization, and was not limited to cultural spheres as in earlier stages of Sino-Japanese affairs. Like other capitalist states in the imperialist stage of development, Japan began to structure its relations with China as if the latter were an object for potential colonial exploitation. Meanwhile, outwardly it attempted to conceal its aggressive intentions behind assurances declaring its "defense of Chinese sovereignty."

CHAPTER FOUR

Approaching the Twentieth Century

The Sino-Japanese War left China greatly weakened and unable to repulse growing threats from abroad. Defeat by Japan caused concern for the country's future, since for many centuries Chinese rulers had considered Japan their vassal. Nourished by Chinese culture Japan, like China, once had endured half a century of insult. Now the Japanese victory proved a heavy blow for all levels of Chinese society, demonstrating as it did the advantages of capitalism even more conclusively than had earlier clashes with the little-known European states. Mechanized industry was shown to be superior to feudal China's methods. The policy of isolation became more obviously disastrous, yet the "thick-head" group[1] around Empress Tzu Hsi and Prince Kung still avoided foreign contacts. The "self-improvement" pro-Western policy of Li Hung-chang was likewise bankrupt. Self-improvement was pursued only to the extent of modernizing weapons; antiquated forms of state administration, scientific and cultural backwardness, ignorance and lack of education all continued. This policy led merely to unproductive waste of already sparse resources.

THE CHINESE REFORM MOVEMENT

The collapse of the self-improvement policy produced confusion among China's ruling circles. Antagonistic groups developed which regarded China's situation and potential development in divergent ways. The Tzu Hsi–Prince Kung group regarded the failure of self-improvement as confirmation of their isolationist course. They attributed all China's misfortunes and disasters to loss of faith in the unshakeable and eternal Chin empire, and to contamination by Western liberal ideas. The isolation of the populace and its continued ignorance and subjection remained paramount need, even were China to lose its sovereignty and territorial integrity. The young Emperor Kuang-hsu (Te Tsung) held different views. Influenced by progressive administrators, and also observing Japan's example of development, Kuang-hsu came to the conclusion that radical modernization of the monarchy was imperative.

By the early 1890s a reform movement had sprung up among scholars and higher officials. Its ideological leader was the respected scholar

Kang Yo-wei, who propounded the theory of the "great unity," according to which a union of the nations of the world was to come. There would be a world state offering social, national, racial and sexual equality. Kang Yo-wei's theory, which was not without Buddhist influence, viewed China as experiencing an "era of chaos," while the European states were in an "era of becoming," remaining as yet far from the "era of unity." Therefore, China should employ progressive knowledge to perfect its national administration and develop the material and intellectual life of the people.

Kang Yo-wei and his close associate Liang Chi-chao were, in sum, proposing that the "Manchurians and the Chinese should not be alienated, and the master and the people should rule together." Rather than toppling the monarchy, they advocated defending and perfecting it. In this they counted on Kuang-hsu's progressive views. Their program of civil rights was limited to free choice of abode, equal opportunities for Manchurians and Chinese, and abolition of economic restrictions. "Our people," wrote Liang Chi-chao, "still lack consciousness, and few understand the true meaning of freedom. Should events lead to revolution, it would be as successful as in America. Hence revolution is the most dangerous and the most extreme measure.[2] As the Chinese historian Fan Wen-lan stresses, Kang Yo-wei and Liang Chi-chao "were concerned about preserving the yellow race and not about the people." Therefore, in their foreign policy plans they counted on Japanese support, and regarded Japanese aggression in Korea and the occupation of Taiwan as merely a manifestation of the "fate" awaiting Japan. These conquests did not represent expansion but, rather, Japan's destiny to "cross the Yellow Sea and the Bay of Po-Hai (Chih-li) and revitalize China." He goes on: "They stood for the union of China and Japan in joint resistance to the Europeans."[3]

Scholars and journalists were not the sole participants in the reform movement. Representatives from commerce and industry joined together with prestigious government dignitaries in reform efforts, but caused a breakdown in the unity of the movement. Tan Hsi-tung led the left wing, which insisted on innovations and blamed China's backwardness and weakness on the reactionary imperial regime. "Even now," wrote Tan Hsi-tung, "China can expect a renaissance only after rivers of blood flow in battle between the old and new parties. Today it remains only to see who is bolder and more stubborn." But the left wing limited its radicalism to "stalwart support" of Kuang-hsu's progressive reforms, that is, it advocated the preservation of the monarchy.

The reformers acquired added strength as the result of the death of Prince Kung on May 29, 1898. He had exercised great influence on state affairs as president of the supreme imperial council. Kuang-hsu now had the opportunity to attach Kang Yo-wei to the court, together with other leaders of the reform movement, and with their help he formulated and carried out reform programs. The "hundred days of reforms," which began with an imperial decree published on June 11, 1891, etched deep impressions on Chinese history. The decree presented a new course in politics and announced the founding of China's first university in Peking. The nearly one hundred decrees published by the middle of September, 1898, foresaw radical changes in education, culture, economics, military and government administration. For example, according to the decree of June 11th—

> The methods of state administration instituted during the Sung and Ming dynasties bring no benefit to the country under present circumstances. Hereby we announce to the general public that henceforward officials and dignitaries in the capital and the provinces, from princes and members of the imperial clan to scholars and the common people, are obliged to dedicate their whole strength to the throne, to inspire and display heroism, to make the holy principles of Confucius the basis of all their actions and thoughts, and to western sciences which relate to contemporary conditions.[4]

Kuang-hsu's decrees reflected the views of Kang Yo-wei and other reformist theoreticians. At the same time, they contained suggestions made by commercial and industrial circles, and military and civil officials, dealing with such concrete problems as industrial and railroad construction, publishing, and censorship. Kang Yo-wei's conclusions and recommendations were based in the main on the study of Japan's bourgeois transformation. His "Research on the Reforms in Japan" described Japanese innovations and made recommendations for their application in China, and became a handbook for Emperor Kuang-hsu. "Every day I would work on composing the successive chapters of my book," recalled Kang Yo-wei. "In issuing this or that decree, the emperor would employ my remarks and commentaries on the Japanese reforms."[5] Chinese reformers also counted on receiving military and political assistance from Japan. They looked with sympathy on the activities of "The Society for Asian Renaissance" in Japan, which aimed at aiding the yellow race in protecting East Asia, and preventing Germany, Russia and other states from dismembering it. In February 1898, Tan Hsi-tung, leader of the left reformers, conducted negotiations with representatives of the Japanese general staff on creation of a Sino-Japanese alliance.

Kuang-hsu's decrees recommended the study of the experience of the Western nations. To accomplish reforms, Englishmen, Americans and other Western citizens were invited to China as advisors and directors. However, different approaches governed the relationships with the Western nations and with Japan. The reformers eagerly utilized England's progressive scientific and technical knowledge, and even sought closer relations. At the same time, they looked solely to Japan for military and political support. As Tang Tsai-chang rhetorically asked: "How can alliance be achieved with England? Through the aid of Japan." It was Tan Hsi-tung who most definitively and completely voiced the reformers' policy with regard to England and the other Western countries. In a proposal to enlist the aid of the English consul in Han-chou to reestablish the reformers' secret society under the guise of a Christian commune, he wrote:

> A secret agreement will be made (with the English consul Karles— M.S.)[6] and its text will have to be carefully rendered so that in the form of a Christian society a Confucian essence will be preserved. In this manner we will protect ourselves in the present and fortify the way for later endeavors. We do not intend to give the Europeans the slightest benefit or the least rights. Let there be many words with little said. As soon as the agreement is completed, we can rejuvenate the society at any given moment. Who then will dare not to submit to us.[7]

Leaving aside racial prejudices, the caution displayed by the reformers in relations with the Western nations was justified by numerous factors relating to spreading aggression against China. In 1898, the reform movement reached its apogee and a domestic commercial and industrial bourgeoisie was forming. At that very moment the imperialist states began an attack on China's sovereign rights, with the aim of dividing China into "spheres of influence."[8] The "thick-head" group centering on dowager Empress Tzu Hsi took advantage of the situation to lay complete blame for unpunished Western banditry on the reformers and their patron, Emperor Kuang-hsu. On September 21, 1898, as a result of deputy war minister Yuan Shih-kai's treachery, the emperor was removed from power and incarcerated in the imperial summer palace. Under the pretext that Kuang-hsu "had requested she take political guardianship over him," Tzu Hsi assumed absolute command of the government. The reform movement was crushed, its leaders Kang Yo-wei and Liang Chi-chao fleeing to Japan, and within a month all of Kuang-hsu's innovations had been abolished. Empress Tzu Hsi, finding support from Western nations, was able to avoid the collapse of the Chin monarchy for several more years.

But the defeat of the reformers could not halt unrest in China. A new and more radical movement already was forming, proclaiming the need for China's renewal not through "self-improvement" or "perfection" of the monarchy, but by toppling it and forming a democratic republic. The new order would then destroy the artificial isolation created by the Chin court. The head of the movement was Dr. Sun Yat-sen, who struck away the illusions of the reformers and laid bare the guilt of some members of the Manchurian dynasty for domestic backwardness and military defeats, and determined to wage an all-out struggle against the dynasty. With that purpose, in 1894 he had formed the "League of Renaissance" among Chinese immigrants in the Hawaiian islands. Notwithstanding small numbers and separation from the mass of the Chinese people, the League and Sun Yat-sen launched preparations for an armed rising in south China against the Manchurians. In 1895, the first attempt ended in failure. Sun Yat-sen and his closest allies were declared outlaws by the Manchurian authorities and expelled from China for many years. Nonetheless, this abortive uprising had broad repercussions in China.

Now the overthrow of the Manchurian Chin dynasty became the overriding goal of Sun Yat-sen's movement. Yet he still preserved illusions concerning England and Japan, hoping that they would support Chinese patriots in their struggle against Manchurian despotism. The League of Renaissance made no effort to force an anti-imperialist struggle upon the Chinese, although the society's resistance to foreign conquerors grew. The success of the campaign against the Manchurians depended in large part on thwarting imperialism. Sun Yat-sen's personal authority and the influence of the League of Chinese Renaissance continued to grow as branches of the society formed in many Chinese cities. Meanwhile large-scale anti-imperialist demonstrations swept through China spontaneously. In some instances leadership fell to adherents of the Chin court, particularly at the time of the Ichetuan or "Boxer" rebellion.

The impoverishment of the Chinese peasant went on, aggravated by the flooding of the Huang Ho (Yellow) river valley and crop failure in provinces along the lower Yangtze. Widespread peasant unrest sprang up in various regions, including An-hui, Chiang-su, Ho-nan, Sze-chwan, Kan-su and Hsin-chiang. In northern China, especially in Shan-tung province, the peasants labored under the oppression of landlords and office-holders. Further pressures came from German colonists who drove the populace from fertile land in order to use it for railroads, mines, and industrial development. The Chinese people were agitated also by the activities of European and American missionaries who had penetrated into the furthest regions of China. As a result of all these pressures, in 1899 a large portion of northern China, led by the society known as "A fist in the name of peace and justice," was swept by the "Boxer" rebellion, as it is popularly known.

The rebellion began with anti-Manchurian and anti-feudal motives, but soon acquired an anti-imperial coloring as well. The imperial government, headed by Tzu Hsi, labored to turn the popular hatred of foreigners against them and thereby to deflect this hostility away from the throne. Falsely declaring its sympathy with the struggle against imperialism, the regime won control of the Boxer detachments and united them with reactionary government troops. The old peasant slogan "Down with the Chin, restore the Ming dynasty" under which the Boxer movement had started, was now replaced with "Support the Chin, destroy the foreigners." Fanatical hatred was fanned against foreigners and those Chinese who advocated national renewal. The anger of the fanatics' also was manipulated against the incarcerated Emperor Kuang Hsu, who was declared a "follower of the foreign devils."

When the foreign powers brought their armies against northern China "to protect their interests," the Chin authorities sent the Boxer detachments directly into battle, hoping to demoralize them. They were told that the foreigners were so weak and incompetent that "application of the art of boxing alone was enough to drive out the devils without any particular difficulty." Meanwhile, the Chinese regular army, which was equipped with firearms, with proper organization and popular support, would have been able to resist foreign intervention effectively. The Boxer movement, which spread throughout the northern provinces, found no support among the southern rebels who were influenced by the League of Chinese Renaissance. Since his primary aim was to topple the Chin monarchy, Sun Yat-sen declined to support the northern rebellion. He advocated aloofness from the north, where Tzu Hsi controlled the Boxer movement, and with this in mind he was inclined to accept aid from England and Japan.

The Boxer rebellion was brutally crushed by the armies of Germany, Japan, England, France, Russia, the United States, Italy and Austria-Hungary. Japan played an especially active role in the intervention, providing one of the largest contingents—8,000 men—commanded by Marshal Yamaguchi.[9] Such active participation in a joint attack on China should have revealed Japan's policy of expansion quite clearly. But even after this, progress-minded Chinese, including Sun Yat-sen, continued to idealize Japan in the hope that common Asian interests would prevail in its policies. When the Boxer rebellion ended, the Chin government accepted fresh and demeaning terms from the imperialist states. The "Final Protocol" signed September 7, 1901, obliged China during the succeeding 39 years to pay the enormous reparations of 450 million exchange taels, with four percent annual interest on the unpaid balance. (By 1940 the total would have reached 982 million exchange taels.)[10] To assure payment, the foreign governments established their control over China's most important income sources. The Final Protocol also called for destruction of the military forts in Ta-ku, and banned the import of weapons, military supplies and strategic raw materials into China for two years. This ban might be extended to subsequent years "if the states found it necessary." In addition, foreign states were to be permitted to maintain guard forces in the Peking diplomatic quarter.[11]

It was under these extremely unpleasant circumstances that China began the twentieth century. Empress Tzu Hsi's group established an even harsher regime in attempting to shore up the monarchy on an old and dilapidated foundation. The foreign policies of China relied on concessions and compromises, and resulted in foreign control of all major river and sea ports, the bulk of industry, and railroad transportation.

JAPAN'S SPHERES OF INFLUENCE IN CHINA

After the Sino-Japanese war of 1894-1895, Japan enjoyed a rapid rise. In a period of ten years (1894-1903) invested capital in industrial and transport companies increased fourfold, from 232 to 888 million yen. Shipbuilding grew with particular speed. In 1898 the Mitsubishi shipyards launched a vessel capable of carrying 6000 registered gross tons. Japan began the construction of even larger vessels, including naval ships. On the other hand, the easy victory over China did not satisfy Japan, for that triumph could not be exploited as hoped. Under pressure Japan was forced to relinquish Port Arthur and Wei-hai-wei, which were quickly occupied by Russia and France respectively. With Russian support, the Korean royal court frustrated Japan's hopes for complete control of Korea.[12] Japan's expansion plans for Korea and China thus foundered on the resistance of their intended victims and on the might of Japan's rivals for empire. Russia in particular hindered Japan from enjoying the fruits of victory over China.

In the prevailing circumstances it was necessary for Japan to weaken Russia's position in China in order to clear the way for its own expansion. China had to be neutralized, or else attracted to Japan's side. On

October 31, 1898, a new government headed by the militarist party leader Marshal Yamagata Aritomo took power in Japan. Yamagata's administration began preparations for a major war. He greatly increased allocations for the army and navy, allowing army strength to treble between 1896 and 1903 while naval tonnage more than quadrupled—from 60,000 to 278,900 tons. However, Japan still remained significantly weaker than the leading imperial states in the Far East, and therefore could not risk confrontations with them. Consequently, a major feature of Japanese foreign policy became the exploitation of conflicts between England and the United States, and between these powers and Russia. Japan also participated with America and England in actions against the other European powers (mainly Russia, but also France and Germany). The developing rapprochement of England and the United States gave Japan cause to expect the aid of these powers in a war with Russia. At the same time, the rapprochement forced the Japanese government to reckon with the interests of its future allies, and to coordinate its China policy with them.

Lacking permanent bases on the Chinese mainland, Japan actively supported the "open doors" policy proclaimed by the United States. This was directed against the exclusive rights enjoyed by the states which maintained "spheres of influence" in China. In protecting "open doors and equal opportunities," the rulers of Japan undertook to present themselves as supporters of China's sovereignty and territorial integrity and guardians of the common interests of the Asian peoples. Under the guise of concern for the territorial integrity of Fu-chien province, which was closest to the island of Taiwan, the Japanese government demanded in April, 1898, that China declare that "it would not cede nor lease any part of its territory in the province of Fu-chien."[13]

The rulers of Japan, concealing their true intentions, adroitly maneuvering and playing on the national sentiments of the Chinese people, tried to win the favor of Chinese public opinion. They acted openly as patrons of anti-Manchurian progressive movements, granting them haven and cooperating with their activities. They permitted anti-Manchurian organizations, publishing houses, and intensive training of Chinese youths in Japan. The influx of young revolutionary Chinese into Japan waxed because of other factors as well. Despite growing militarist influences, Western progressive ideas were making their way into Japan. Together with rapidly developing industry, the proletariat also expanded, and social conflicts were aggravated. In 1897, under the leadership of Katayama Sen, the first trade unions emerged, and in 1901 the Social Democratic Party came into being.

In Japan the revolutionary democrat Sun Yat-sen created militant revolutionary organizations and prepared to overthrow the Chin monarchy. Here as well appeared the first Chinese Marxists, Chen Tu-hsiu, and Li Ta-chao, trained by Japanese socialists educated in the West. For many years Japan remained the political school for the peoples of Asia. These developments, despite the patently aggressive intent of Japan's rulers, allowed forward-looking Chinese to continue to hope for Japan's help in gaining national and social liberation. They hoped that Japanese military incursions onto Chinese territory during the crushing of the Boxer rebellion represented not expansion but a Japanese desire to assist the Chinese in repelling Western aggression.

Although it gained no new territory as a result of the eight-nation intervention in China, Japan nevertheless became a recognized force among the imperial rivals. Its active military participation in the intervention demonstrated the growing competence of the Japanese armies. Now Japan finally concluded that in order to accomplish its aims in China it would have to clash with its rivals. At that time the chief competitor was Russia. In any conflict with Russia Japan expected aid from some of the other countries, particularly England. On January 30, 1902, in London, an Anglo-Japanese agreement laid the basis for strong cooperative bonds between these countries. In making this agreement England hoped to bring about a Russo-Japanese conflict, calculating that no matter what the outcome, Russia would be distracted from the Chinese interior. Consequently the English might extend their control to China's northern provinces. English, then American support assisted Japan in preparations for war with Russia. During the night of February 8, 1904, the Japanese attacked the Russian squadron anchored at the outer roads of Port Arthur, thus igniting the Russo-Japanese War of 1904–1905.

Japan commenced military operations against Russia on Chinese territory without the agreement and against the interests of China. Nonetheless Japan justified its actions by cloaking them in the guise of a unique "liberating" mission in Asia whereas in reality it longed to destroy the Russian "sphere of influence" and shield the "open door" policy in China. The leaders of England and the United States and even some Chinese middle class nationalists encouraged this Japanese propaganda. Russia's lease rights were transferred to Japan under provisions of the Portsmouth Peace Treaty of 1905. These included Port Arthur, "Dalnyi" (Ta-lien), and southern divisions of the Chinese Domestic Railroad. Japan also began to create a military and economic base in southern Manchuria. Nevertheless, Sun Yat-sen, who was then in Japan, maintained his faith in the positive contribution of bourgeois Japan to the fate of China. Evaluating the period of the Russo-Japanese War, he wrote: "The powers leaned very much toward the division of China, and Tsarist Russia had already taken steps toward the colonization of Manchuria. But then a disturbed Japan began war with Russia, and thereby saved China from perishing."[14]

Following the Russo-Japanese War, when Japan became the actual master of southern Manchuria, Japanese ruling circles no longer wished to support without qualifications the American doctrine of "open doors and equal opportunities." Having captured one of China's richest regions, they certainly did not care to open to their rivals the same opportunities given Japanese monopolies. At the same time they were not averse to enjoying equal opportunities in other regions of China, where none of Japan's competitors had as yet established monopolistic control. Thus, while insisting on recognition of its special interests in southern Manchuria, Japan continued to support the "open doors" policy for other regions of China. The policy of "recognition and denial" of the "open doors" doctrine allowed Japanese diplomacy to maneuver and to conceal its strategic goals in China and thus win concessions from its rivals. This policy found its best reflection in the Root-Takahira agreement of 1908, between Japan and the United States.[15] Confirming the existing *status quo* in the area, the agreement enabled Japanese diplomats to insist on preservation of the "special" regime the Japanese had set up in southern Manchuria. On the other hand it recognized "China's independence and integrity and the principle of equal opportunities for trade and industry of all peoples in that empire."

A short time previously, on July 30, 1907, Japan and Russia had concluded an essentially similar agreement. In the form of a convention, it contained open and secret articles. The open articles proclaimed the "open door" policy in China while the secret ones called for the division of Manchuria into Japanese (southern) and Russian (northern) spheres of influence.[16] On the territory of southern Manchuria, without China's agreement and against its interests, Japan began to create a powerful military and economic base. Japanese monopolies invested significant capital in industry, transport and commerce in southern Manchuria while practically closing off the area to other foreign investors. Taking advantage elsewhere of "equal opportunities," Japan became active in the Yangtze valley. On the eve of World War I, direct Japanese capital investments in China amounted to 132.6 million dollars in Manchuria, or 68.9 percent, and 59.9 million dollars, or 31.1

percent, in the rest of China. In Manchuria about 55 percent of Japanese investment went to the South Manchurian Railroad Company (SMRC), created in 1906 using Russian railroad property, where rail repair and construction shops began to appear. The port of Ta-lien was expanded, the Fu-shun coal mines and various other auxiliary enterprises sprang up.

The distribution of direct Japanese capital in China as a whole by 1914 was as follows:[17]

	Yen (millions)	Dollars (millions)	Percent of Total
Transportation	136.7	68.3	35.5
Municipal Enterprises	6.8	3.4	1.8
Mining Operations	58.3	29.2	15.1
Manufacturing	21.2	10.6	5.5
Banks and Finances	12.6	6.3	3.3
Land Ownership	17.0	8.5	4.4
Foreign Trade	85.2	42.6	22.1
Other	47.3	23.6	12.3
	385.1	192.5	100.0

Along with direct capital investments, Japan devoted considerable resources to loans, which it granted formally to the Chinese government. In reality they were utilized by Japanese monopolies for their own purposes. A characteristic feature of Japanese policy in China was that Japan did not participate in collective capital loans, but functioned independently. Toward the end of 1913, the Chinese government's debt to Japan was the following (in thousands of dollars):

Mukden—Hsin-min-tung railroad construction loans	125
Kirin—Chang-chun railroad construction loans	1,125
Debt service loans on the Peking—Han-kou loan	1,100
Loan to the Chinese Ministry of Communications for railroad construction	5,000
Loan for financing copper processing in Shen-hsi province	1,500
Loan for guaranteeing the paper currency of the Nanking Government	750
	9,600

In addition, the debt of the Chinese government to Japan under the "Final Boxer Protocol" amounted to $23,891,000.

Besides direct investments and loans to the Chinese government, Japan endeavored to gain holdings in Chinese companies. The story of the Han-yeh-ping iron works in the Yangtze valley serves as an example. By 1899 Japanese capital had begun to finance that company, and required that it deliver iron ore to Japan. In 1908, after Chinese government participation in the company ended, a Chinese imperial decree granted Japanese the right to own the company's stock. In 1913 the "Yokohama Specie Bank" and the Yawata metallurgical factories gained control of the Han-yeh-ping company. The cast iron produced by the company and part of the iron ore it mined was exported to Japan. Japanese investments in the company in 1914 amounted to 15 million dollars. In addition, Japanese banks provided capital for the Chiang-hsi railroad company, in the amount of 2.5 million dollars. In this way Japanese capital on the eve of World War I reached beyond Manchuria and was moving into the "spheres of influence" of other imperial nations, particularly England, in the Yangtze valley.

THE HSING-HUI REVOLUTION AND JAPAN'S CHINA POLICY

After the Russo-Japanese War and the Russian revolution of 1905 the Chinese people's struggle for national renaissance took a new direction. The slogan of past generations calling for overthrow of the Chin and restoration of the Ming dynasty no longer satisfied the wants of the progressive elements in Chinese society. Among the tasks confronting the Chinese was not merely the overthrow of the Chin dynasty but also the destruction of the monarchical order. The Chin monarchy and its imperial patrons were unable to protect China from the influence of Western democratic ideas. V.I. Lenin, in characterizing that period in the Chinese revolutionary movement, wrote: "The mighty growth of a 'new spirit' and 'European currents' in China, especially after the Russo-Japanese War, is beyond doubt. Consequently, the transformation of the old Chinese rebellions into a conscious democratic movement was also unavoidable."[18]

In 1905 under the leadership of Sun Yat-sen, the "United League" (Tung-meng-hui) was created, with the task of toppling the monarchy and creating a republican order. Its declaration stated: "The simple people will make a revolution, in order to establish a national government. The president will be elected by all the people. Parliament will consist of popularly elected deputies. It will prepare a constitution for the Chinese Republic, and all will be obliged to observe it. Whoever tries to restore the monarchical order will be struck down by a vengeful arm."[19]

"Three popular principles" suggested by Sun Yat-sen formed the basis of the United League's activities. Presented as a program for revolutionary democratic action, these were "nationalism," "popular rule" and "the popular welfare." Carrying into life the principle of nationalism—the consolidation of national strength to overthrow the alien (Manchurian) monarchy and assure Chinese sovereignty—was to Sun Yat-sen the most important and the primary task of the Chinese revolution. Together with this he asserted that true national liberation could be realized only "by the power of the simple people." Therefore, the principle of nationalism must be linked firmly with the principle of popular rule. Citing Chinese history, Sun Yat-sen remarked that dictators, even when they were native Chinese, always had aimed to divide the country and weaken the nation for their own benefit and power. "It should be stressed," wrote Sun Yat-sen, "that with the current political regime in China, a revolution is unavoidable even were the monarch to be a Han."[20]

To Sun Yat-sen the third principle of "popular welfare" depended upon the solution of the social problem. However, as he asserted, "the social problem is not so sharp for us as the national question or the problem of popular rule." The accomplishment of the principle of popular welfare was dependent upon establishment of a popular government, which in Sun Yat-sen's conception should be "not simply popular, but socialist." However, he based his theory of popular government not on principles of social development, but on his own subjective aspirations. His dreams idealized the Chinese people and gave no notice to evolving social processes and class differentiation. He believed that China could avoid the development of capitalism by means of government control of the powerful, chiefly foreign capital monopolies. Consequently, the social purposes of the Chinese revolution should be limited to destruction of feudal exploitation and establishment of "equalized" land tenure. Sun Yat-sen surmised that, due to the unique qualities of the Chinese people, it would be possible to create popular rule and a peaceful society which would include the bourgeoisie and the proletariat.

In 1912 V.I. Lenin, in his article "Democracy and Populism in China," noted the noble subjective socialist aspirations of Sun Yat-sen, and his implacable stance against oppression and exploitation. Lenin also pointed out the historical limitations of his program: "Sun Yat-sen, with an inimitable, one might say virginal naïveté, smashed to dust his own reactionary populist theory, admitting that which life forces one to admit,—that 'China stands on the threshold of gigantic industrial (capitalist) development', that . . . there would be many Shanghais, metropolises of capitalist wealth and proletarian need and poverty."[21]

Along with the rapid growth of foreign industrial enterprises, domestic capital ventured into industry. By 1911 some 521 domestic companies capitalized at 160 million yuan existed in China. (This number included 36 mixed companies with a capital of 27 million yuan.) There were 72 mining and metallurgy companies with 41.3 million yuan in capital, three machine tool companies with 757,000 yuan, 193 textile enterprises with 40.8 million, 100 food industries with 17.6 million, and 153 others with 59 million yuan in capital.[22] Naturally the working class grew along with this industrialization, and the status of the Chinese middle class also consolidated. Conditions in China became such that the imperial court could no longer rule by the old despotic methods. It was forced to make concessions to public opinion, and to accept a modified form of absolutism.

The situation became even more critical after the almost simultaneous deaths of Emperor Kuang-hsu and the dowager Tzu Hsi. Prince Chung, who became regent for the two-year-old emperor and the actual ruler, replaced Chinese with Manchurian nobles in all high government posts. By this act the imperial court alienated powerful Chinese dignitaries and generals, who formerly had served as the throne's bulwarks. The anti-Manchurian mood proliferated widely among differing levels of Chinese society, and was fueled further by the failure of the Chin dynasty to act purposefully to counter intensifying foreign encroachments. The overthrow of the Chin monarchy, which the Chinese people blamed for all their woes at home and abroad, became a general demand. The Chin government's attempt to secure support from foreign governments and thereby delay the collapse of the empire bore no results.

The Hsing-hai revolution began with the rebellion of the military garrison at Wu-chang on October 10, 1911.[23] On October 27 the Chin court named General Yuan Shih-kai premier and accepted one of the reform leaders, Liang Chi-chao, into the government. However, the imperial regime continued to lose control over the situation in the country. On November 3 a provisional revolutionary government was formed in Shang-hai, and similar institutions sprang up in several southern provinces. Then, on November 28, the Chin government proclaimed a constitutional order—too late to save the monarchy. On February 12, 1912, Emperor Pu Yi abdicated and was placed on a state pension. As the dimensions of the popular rising and of worker and peasant participation in it grew, the revolution inevitably expanded beyond demands for merely a change in the form of national authority. Especially in the southern regions, the peasants rose to fight for an end to the landowner system and establishment of equal land rights. These developments threatened the vested interests of Chinese feudal lords, and equally affected the liberal bourgeoisie, which was linked closely to feudal land exploitation. The fear of a large national movement contributed to a consolidation of reactionary forces, headed by General Yuan Shih-kai, who had been selected even before the emperor's abdication. Meanwhile, uncertainty swept through the United League, where many representatives had come from the liberal bourgeoisie and the landowners.

Once more two opposed camps formed in China. In the north, in Peking, the forces of reaction gathered around Yuan Shih-kai in support of the monarchy and preservation of the feudal land system. Revolutionary forces concentrated in the south and looked to Sun Yat-sen who had returned from exile on December 24, 1911. Five days later, on December 29, he was elected the provisional president of the Chinese Republic by an assembly of representatives of the southern provinces.

And now, once more, just as fifty years earlier, the fate of China was decided by intervention. The scale of the national movement, particularly in the south and in the Yangtze basin, aroused the imperial powers to worry about their large investments, and about the future of the "spheres of influence" and "open door" policies in China. The general policy of the six imperial states was set forth on December 20, 1911, in separate messages to the plenipotentiaries of the Peking government and the southern provisional governments, who were conducting negotiations. The six countries declared unambiguously that "continuation of conflict in China affects not only that country but the material interests and security of foreigners." Stressing their interest in Chinese affairs, the imperial powers sent landing parties into Shang-hai, Hankou, Chih-fu and Canton the very moment the Hsing-hui revolution broke out, and made plain their resolve to turn to armed intervention if necessary. Under the direction of Japanese Vice Admiral Kawashima, an amphibious landing was mounted at Han-kou, the strong point of the revolutionary forces.

While cooperating to protect their common interests, the imperial powers approached the impending battle between the northern and southern groups in separate ways. Japan and England displayed the greatest political activity. Japanese policy sought to prevent the spread of revolutionary unrest to Manchuria and northern China, its chief "spheres of influence." Japan also hoped to weaken China generally and to hinder the formation of a stable, unified Chinese government.

The Japanese authorities pursued these goals by suggesting the dispatch of an international expeditionary force to protect China's emperor, Japanese troops to form the bulk of this force. When this plan found no support from other nations, Japan decided to take unilateral measures as a means of buttressing previous conquests in China and creating favorable conditions for further expansion in Asia. Beginning at the end of 1911 Japan concentrated powerful naval forces at Chemulpo and strengthened garrisons on the Liao-tung peninsula. Making use of the Peking regime's frailty, and assured of support from tsarist Russia, Japan spread its influence to Inner Mongolia.[24] At the same time, not wishing to lose sight of China's southern regions, Japan sought reconciliation with England. The rulers of Japan partially supported England's policy of separating southern and central China from the north at the same time that Japanese progressives welcomed Sun Yat-sen's southern democratic republican movement. Influential members of the middle class also supported contacts with Sun Yat-sen, searching for ways to solidify Japan's influence in the south by means of a democratic republican regime. This ambiguity in policy toward China reflected the diverse opinions prevalent among Japanese leaders. Whereas the military bureaucracy (including General Tanaka and war minister Uehara Yusaku) demanded military intervention in Chinese affairs, moderates (such as premier Saionji) considered that the time had not arrived for Japan to be drawn into open conflict with the United States and other Western states over China.

On the eve of the Hsing-hui revolution Japan assumed that relations with the United States would worsen after its attempts to advance into Manchuria. It undertook several steps designed to improve poor relations with England negotiating the new Anglo-Japanese treaty of alliance, signed June 13, 1911 in London, which effectively neutralized England. The two countries agreed to preserve mutual special interests in the Far East and India and to consult with each other before "entering into special agreements with any state to the detriment of the goals of this treaty."[25] The Anglo-Japanese rapprochement strengthened Japan's position in northern and northeastern China. It also provided an opportunity for political activities in the central and southern regions. Following England's example, statesmen in Tokyo sought ways to maintain connections with the revolutionary south of China.

Sun Yat-sen and his adherents attributed particular significance to the policies of Japan and England concerning the Chinese Republic. Before returning to his homeland, Sun Yat-sen characterized the positions of these states at the start of the Wu-chang rising as follows: "In Japan the people regard us with sympathy and the government regards us with enmity. In England the people are on our side, while the government has not yet determined its position. Therefore, the crucial question in my negotiations, upon which the success of our revolution and the fate of our people depends, was the policy of England. For if England were to side with us, Japan could do us no harm.[26]

Japan's first steps for the "protection" of the Chin emperor gave clear evidence of the anti-revolutionary position of the Japanese rulers. Nevertheless, because of favorable Japanese public opinion, Sun Yat-sen did not lose hope that he might sway Japan to support the revolution in southern China, or at least obtain a promise of neutrality. When entering into negotiations with official English representatives, Sun Yat-sen set forth three conditions: cessation of loans to the Chin court, prevention of Japanese aid to the Chin court, and assistance for his return to China. Sun Yat-sen received assurances on these points, and he did not doubt the honesty of English policy. He believed that the English government, which had just concluded a treaty of alliance with Tokyo, would be able to influence Japan. Consequently, the revolutionary south might count on both nations for aid in its struggle with the reactionary north.

Sun Yat-sen failed in his first efforts to obtain credits for his government in England, France and the United States. A bank consortium of four nations also rejected his plea that it cease financing the Chin government (through earlier loans) and instead grant support to Sun's revolutionary government. Then England, which in fact operated Chinese customs, began keeping all customs income in the southern and central regions "to secure foreign loans." This action deprived the revolutionary authorities of an important source of foreign exchange. In violating promises made to Sun Yat-sen, England and the United States supported Yuan Shih-kai, whom they considered a strong man able to control the revolution and protect the interests of foreign states. Moreover, the influence of the United States in Peking was growing. Jealously watching the actions of its rivals, Japan openly violated the neutrality which the foreign nations had declared and together with Germany, assiduously supplied Yuan Shih-kai's army with weapons.

Notwithstanding these developments, Sun Yat-sen continued to ignore the real threat posed to the revolution by the very states upon which he counted for aid. He adhered to a policy of establishing "friendship" with the European nations and the United States. In a declaration issued on becoming the provisional president of the republic, he stated: "After establishing a provisional government we will assume all functions of a civilized state in order to take advantage of all privileges enjoyed by one. The shameful actions of the rule of the Manchurian Chin dynasty, and the anti-foreign spirit, should be ended forever. We will adhere to the principle of maintaining peace and we will build bonds of cordiality with friendly governments.[27] In the first official act of the republic, the provisional president's message to foreign states, the revolutionary government announced that it would respect all international agreements made by China before the Hsing-hui revolution. China recognized its foreign debts and the rights of foreign states and individual foreigners, along with all other obligations. Undoubtedly Sun Yat-sen, in making such concessions, was guided solely by noble aspirations, by the desire to strengthen the Chinese Republic and direct its development in harmony with his three popular principles. In an objective sense, however, his anticipation of assistance from world imperialism smothered the anti-imperial feelings of the Chinese people. It ignored the aspirations of the democratic-republican movement, when workers at many foreign enterprises felt the burden of foreign capital on their shoulders.

It is true that quite radical notes may be discerned in Sun Yat-sen's statements, which left no doubt of his national, democratic hopes and his rejection of exploitation. Ignoring the inborn vices of capitalism and deferring the solution of social problems to the future (the chief fault of his United League program), Sun Yat-sen remarked: "The capitalists, in league with new forms of oppression, are perhaps even more cruel than they were under an absolute monarchy. We must wage bloody battle for the revolution." From this he drew the conclusion that China's development should be guided in the direction of state socialism. The land and large enterprises should be nationalized and profits should "become the social property of the people."[28] Sun Yat-sen's radical views were supported by only a small group of his associates and did not become a practicable program for the United League among the Chinese people. Most of Sun Yat-sen's associates were from middle class, landowning, liberal circles. His ideas of popular rule failed to please the generals who had joined the movement and who held leading posts in the revolutionary government and armies. In the end these generals fell into the arms of the reactionary north. Thereupon Yuan Shih-kai, counting on support from England and other imperial states, bloodlessly forced the emperor's abdication, a maneuver which also brought Sun's resignation of the provisional presidency of the republic. Yuan Shih-kai replaced him.

A new party was created by compromise between various democratic, republican political factions, including the United League and various bourgeois, landowning, liberal parties. Called the Kuomintang, or National Party, its program was considerably more moderate than that of the United League. The creation of the Kuomintang only quickened the decline of the revolutionary forces, which had begun after Sun Yat-sen's voluntary resignation of the presidency and replacement by Yuan Shih-kai. Because it offered no concrete agrarian program, the bourgeois democratic block, riddled by internal contradictions, could not count for support on the main progressive element of the anti-feudal revolution, the working peasantry. Furthermore, its compromising attitude toward the inequitable treaties, and its attempts to conclude alliances with the imperial nations, drew the hostility of some of the city populations who opposed imperialism—workers, some merchants and the industrial middle class.

After Yuan Shih-kai was selected provisional president, the imperial states immediately took steps to gain control of the new Chinese government. They seized upon a loan application made to the international bank consortium, a proposal which provoked a severe conflict among the foreign states concerned. Unsuccessful in efforts to control China's finances, the United States left the consortium and refused to participate in the loan, basing its policy on the disparity between the loan conditions and the declared policy of "Chinese independence." China received the reorganizational loan, as it was termed, in April 1913, from an international bank consortium consisting of England, France, Germany, Russia and Japan. It amounted to 25 million pounds sterling (121.66 million dollars), and was earmarked in large part for payment of indebtedness to those same nations, as well as for "reorganizing" the army and funding other needs of the Peking government. "The new Chinese loan," wrote V.I. Lenin, "was concluded against Chinese democracy: 'Europe' is *for* Yuan Shih-kai, who is preparing for military dictatorship. Why is it for him? For the sake of a good business deal. The loan was concluded for a sum of about 150 million rubles at a rate of 84 per 100. This means that the bourgeois of 'Europe' will pay China 210 million and take 225 million rubles from the public."[29]

The reorganizational loan transaction, which was opposed in the parliament by the Kuomintang majority, aroused real indignation in democratic public opinion. Sun Yat-sen delivered a categorical protest against the unconstitutional and terroristic actions of Yuan Shih-kai. "After the murder of Sun Chao-jen,"[30] he wrote, "everything became clear to me. Until now I never imagined that your actions could contradict your words, but the death of Sun Chao-jen disillusioned me. Besides that unheard-of crime, you concluded a five-fold loan agreement, ignoring the constitution, to build your own treasury. You removed those governors who were displeased by your lawlessness . . . . The people feel such hate for you that they are prepared to sacrifice thousands of lives for your downfall."[31]

Sun Yat-sen's appeal evoked a large response from the people. On May 11, 1913, a rising in Su-chou ignited the "second revolution," which swept through southern and central provinces. The impressive dimensions of the new revolutionary movement had their effects on foreign countries such as Japan. Despite unquestionable diplomatic successes in "peaceful" competition with the United States, the rulers of Japan were not content with the role of a mere "participant" in the general concert of nations. Moreover, they distrusted Yuan Shih-kai. Therefore, Japan anxiously searched for another foothold in China, or at least a chance to weaken the Peking government. During the second revolution, the "Mitsui" firm, with Japanese government knowledge, provided weapons and military supplies to the rebelling southern provinces, totalling about 300,000 yuan. However, since Japan in fact was participating already in the reorganizational loan, and the balance between the north and south was clearly swinging to the north, the Japanese authorities preferred to wait. The second revolution was crushed, the Kuomintang dispersed and Yuan Shih-kai "elected" as president. Subsequently, the Japanese authorities displayed the greatest activity during the general policy reversal of the imperial powers, who now demanded that the president of the Chinese Republic give unconditional guarantees for the preservation of all previously established rights and privileges of foreign states and their subjects on Chinese territory. The terror which fell upon the Kuomintang forced its leaders to seek refuge abroad. After the English government refused him permission to live in Hong Kong, Sun Yat-sen left for Japan.

SINO-JAPANESE RELATIONS DURING WORLD WAR I

The war begun in Europe brought fundamental changes to the Far East. England, France, and Russia were forced temporarily to cease activities in the Far East, and Germany was completely cut off. Only two imperial contenders remained—the United States and Japan. Japan enjoyed a major advantage over the United States due to its geographical nearness and its powerful strategic bases in southern Manchuria and on Taiwan. The United States had not established any permanent military or economic presence in China by the time World War I began. Also, President Wilson's "peace loving" declarations and demagogic statements on preserving China's national sovereignty and territorial integrity had produced a noticeable impact. As a result, the United States possessed definite ideological advantages, particularly in Chinese bourgeois, democratic circles.

During the first days of the war Japan revealed its true goals in China. As early as August 3, 1914, the Chinese government had requested that the belligerents not carry their military operations to Chinese territory, and on August 6 it declared its neutrality. Without declaring war on Germany, Japan sent its fleet into Chinese territorial waters. Within a week, on August 15, Japan presented Germany with an ultimatum "without conditions or compensation" to turn over the leased territory of Chiao-chou. Japan hypocritically declared that it was doing this to protect China and would return the leased territory to China. Brief military activities ended with the capitulation of the German garrison at fortified Ching-tao. Japan failed to seek Chinese participation in administering the former German lease territory, and in addition overran a significant part of Shan-tung province, and set up an occupation regime there.

By January 7, 1915, German resistance had ceased. Nevertheless, the Japanese government rejected the request of the Chinese government that Japanese troops be removed from Shan-tung. On January 18, the Japanese ambassador Hyoki on behalf of his government presented 21 demands, conditions which ultimately would strip China of sovereign rights and transform it into a Japanese colony. The essence of the document follows:

(1) *The Province of Shan-tung* The Chinese government is to give complete agreement to all conditions that the Japanese government may make in the future (at the time of a peace treaty) with the German government regarding rights, interests, and concessions which Germany had enjoyed in Shan-tung province.

(2) *Southern Manchuria and Inner Mongolia* The lease period for Port Arthur, Ta-lien, the south Manchurian and An-tung–Mukden railroads is to be changed from 25 to 99 years (from 1898), and Japan is to be granted exclusive rights in southern Manchuria and Inner Mongolia.

(3) *The Han-Yeh-Ping Company* The Chinese Han-Yeh-Ping mining and metallurgy company, located in the Yangtze valley (at that time the first and only such company in the Chinese interior) is to become a mixed Sino-Japanese enterprise. China shall not dispose of the company's property without Japan's agreement.

(4) *Leases along the Chinese Coast* The Chinese government is to assume the obligation of not conceding or leasing to a third state any harbors, bays or islands along the shores of China.

(5) *General Political Demands* The Chinese government should "invite" the Japanese in the capacity of advisors on political, financial, and military matters; police institutions in major Chinese cities should be directed jointly by Japanese and Chinese; China should purchase fifty percent of its military weapons in Japan, create Sino-Japanese arsenals, and grant Japan the right to equip the railroads in central China.

The Japanese administration ignored the protests of foreign states and the irritation of the Chinese people. It agreed merely to remove some of the demands in the fifth group and to soften several demands concerning Inner Mongolia and railroad construction in central China. On May 7, 1915, the Japanese government sent an ultimatum demanding that, by six p.m. on May 9, China give a satisfactory reply. Otherwise Japan threatened to take "such measures as it might consider necessary." On May 8, 1915, Yuan Shih-kai's government capitulated and accepted the Japanese "demands." On May 25 this betrayal was formalized legally by the signing of the appropriate treaties.

The 25th of May has been called the "day of national shame" by the Chinese people. A large-scale anti-Japanese movement began to take shape throughout the country. Many members of the middle class intelligentsia who earlier had held illusions about Japan's "special liberating role for the nations of Asia" now finally glimpsed reality. Japanese imperialism stood revealed before the Chinese people as its most frightening and dangerous enemy, one which had pushed China to the brink of national catastrophe.

Having legally formulated its "rights," Japan now set about enslaving China. The weak link in Japanese industry was its insecure supply of raw material, primarily the iron ore and coking coal needed for the new naval fleet and for further rapid expansion of war industry. In Manchuria, Japan concentrated its attention on iron ore deposits in the Pen-hsi-hu and An-shan regions and on the coal mines of Fu-shun, Pen-hsi-hu and Yang Ti. It also began the creation of a metallurgical industry in Manchuria itself for the purpose of exporting iron and steel. In 1915 in Pen-hsi-hu the first blast furnace was built, with a capacity of 130 tons per day. It was followed by a similar one in 1918. To develop the An-shan mines, a formal mixed Sino-Japanese company was created, controlled by the South Manchurian Railroad. During World War I the Japanese took from southern Manchuria up to three million tons of coal, 177,000 tons of iron ore, and as much as 45,000 tons of smelted iron.

In central China, Japan devoted great attention to the Han-Yeh-Ping company, which it controlled through long-term treaties. The Yokohama Specie Bank and the Japanese Yawata steel foundries granted the company a loan of 7.5 million dollars, earmarked to cover the company's debts of three million dollars and to expand coal and ore mining and smelting of iron and steel (4.5 million dollars). The Han-Yeh-Ping company operated ironworking and steel foundry plants in the city of Han-yang, iron mines in Ping-hsiang, iron mines and blast furnaces in Tai. By 1917 the company had produced 150,000 tons of iron, 43,000 tons of steel, 946,000 tons of coal, 240,000 tons of coke, and 542,000 tons of iron ore. In acquiring this firm Japan took over China's entire metallurgy capacity and much of its coal industry. Exploiting the reduced European competition and the mercenary opportunism of the Peking government, Japanese monopolies strove to penetrate other branches of Chinese industry. Thus, World War I provided to Japan the opportunity to acquire for the moment key positions in the Chinese economy.

Japanese expansion in China evoked deep concern in other world capitals. England, Russia, and France embroiled in a European War possessed no realistic means to hinder Japanese aggrandizement. In this situation the United States determined to counteract Japanese ambitions as much as possible and simultaneously to shore up its own position in China. Prior to the signing of the Sino-Japanese agreements, the United States had protested to the Japanese government concerning violations of international agreements, insisting on the "open doors and equal opportunities" policy. The American note stated: "The United States government respectfully informs the imperial Japanese government that it cannot recognize any agreement or obligation which has been concluded or might be concluded between the governments of Japan and China, which violate the treaty rights of the United States and its citizens in China."[32] Thereafter America undertook several diplomatic steps aimed at demonstrating its "peaceloving" policy, but these moves did not represent realistic measures to counteract Japanese expansion. The Americans could not as yet dare openly to provoke the Japanese, although it was at this time that the conflict between American and Japanese goals in China became quite obvious. A clash between the United States and Japan appeared inevitable.

Contemplating their military advantages, the Japanese authorities hastened to solidify their position in China before the war ended in Europe and the other interested nations could renew their activities. The United States was not prepared for a Far Eastern war, and the Japanese tried to convince the Americans to recognize Japan's rights to the former German holdings in China. Such recognition would strengthen Japan's position in the Chinese interior and offer an opportunity to fulfill the terms of the agreements made with the Yuan Shih-kai regime on May 25, 1915. These Japanese plans were completed behind China's back, the Japanese government basing its policy on adherence to the capitulative agreements obtained from the Yuan Shih-kai government. Further negotiations with other Chinese governments could only diminish the results already garnered.

Diplomatic negotiations continued between February 16 and March 1, 1917. Japan received English, French, and Russian agreement that during the peace conference they would support the Japanese claims concerning the disposition of German rights in Shan-tung and German island holdings north of the equator. Counting on Entente support, Japan next searched for an understanding with the United States. The negotiations, between the special plenipotentiary of Japan Ishii and U.S. Secretary of State Robert Lansing, lasted two months. On November 2, 1917, Japan and the United States confirmed by an exchange of notes that "the government of the United States recognizes Japan's special interests in China, especially in that part which borders its possessions."[33] Doubtless this declaration posed a major diplomatic triumph for Japan since, on the eve of the Versailles peace conference, it had won public recognition for its territories in China. Apparently Japan also made concessions to the United States. It repeated assurances that "the territorial integrity of China would nonetheless remain undiminished." Given the circumstances then existing, Japan had reinforced its position with the military bases it had established in wide areas of China. Japan's confirmation of Chinese sovereignty was purely for the sake of appearances.

To broaden their claims in China and to lend them substance as the peace conference neared, the imperialistic leaders of Japan publicized the "major Japanese loans" supposedly granted to China in 1918. To confirm this, the Japanese press widely reported the journey to China of a bank agent, Nishihara, representing the semi-official Chosen and Taiwan banks. He represented himself as a representative of private businessmen who had sent him to China to offer commercial loans to the Chinese government. The Japanese press carried stories that Nishihara had concluded agreements for railroad construction. His sojourn in China coincided with the completion (on March 25, 1918) of a military agreement between Japan and the Peking administration of Tuan Chi-jui. This agreement was openly anti-Soviet in character and had the purpose of organizing intervention against the Soviet Far East. It is likely that the "Nishihara loans" were intended primarily to arm an anti-Soviet Japanese expeditionary corps, in which the Chinese armies of Tuan Chi-jui would participate.

At first Japanese public announcements insisted on the private character of the "Nishihara loans," but on October 2, 1918, an official communique was published which stated that the former Terauchi government[34] before resigning "had agreed to the following loans with the Chinese government":

1. Four loans for construction of four railways in Manchuria and Mongolia (linking Tao-nan-fu and Jehol, Chang-chun and Tao-nan-fu, Kirin, and Kai-yuan via Hai-lun, and a junction on the Tao-nan-fu-Jehol line with a sea port). The overall length of these railways would be 1000 miles, and the estimated cost 150 million yen.

2. Loans for construction of railways in Shan-tung, Chih-li, and Chiang-su provinces. The total length of these railways would be 460 miles, and the estimated cost 70 million yen.

3. A loan for construction of a metallurgical plant (evidently in the Yangtze valley). Supposedly the loan would be negotiated by the Chinese government and a Japanese syndicate. The estimated amount was 100 million yen. Besides these loans, the communique indicated that the Terauchi cabinet had granted China supplementary loans for establishing a telegraph system, building the Kirin–Hui-ning railway and for developing forest resources and gold reserves in Kirin and Hei-lung Chiang provinces.

This Japanese government communique on the "Nishihara loans" was intended to convince world public opinion, on the eve of the peace conference, that the agreements extracted from China in 1915 were not empty declarations. It was directed especially at the victors in the war against Germany, demonstrating that the treaty provisions were being transformed into reality. Clearly, Japan's special interests in China had been buttressed by major capital investments.

JAPANESE IMPERIALISM AND CHINA'S QUEST FOR NATIONAL REBIRTH

The revolution of 1911-1913 did not start China on the road of independent capitalist development. Nevertheless, it was an important event in the struggle to create a republican system to aid in national liberation. Yuan Shih-kai's attempt in November and December of 1915 to restore the Chinese monarchy and proclaim himself emperor met resistance even among his closest associates, and produced a new upsurge in the democratic republican movement. After Yuan Shih-kai's sudden death, the new president, Li Yuan-hung, was forced to restore the constitution of 1912 and the rights of the parliament. Actual power was concentrated in the hands of Tuan Chi-jui, Japan's puppet, who attempted to establish a military dictatorship. This ambiguous situation furthered the political disintegration of China and the separatism of the provinces under the administration of governors-general, usually local generals. In the south, the governors supported the democratic republican movement (in Yun-yang, Kuei-chou, Kuang-tung, Che-chiang, and certain other provinces). As a result, on September 6, 1917, a government was formed in Canton, headed by Sun Yat-sen. In the north, contests continued between various militarists, including those who advocated a restoration. (On July 1, 1917 General Chang Hsi-un attempted to restore the overthrown Emperor Pu Yi.)

Despite political cleavages and the aggression of the Japanese, which retarded industrial development, China entered international commerce. China enjoyed the aid of foreign capital, and benefited from the departure of England, France, Germany, and other European states from Chinese markets. Circumstances favored Chinese industrial expansion, even though handicraft and cottage industry still formed the basis of the country's manufacturing. Between 1915 and 1919 Chinese business built eleven cotton textile mills as well as oil and flour mills and other mechanized plants. Though at a slower pace, foreign industry continued to expand. The growth of basic industries during the war years is shown in the following table:[35]

	1913	1920
Factories employing more than 30 workers	245	673
Cotton mills in the above figure	28	54
Cloth spindles in thousands	1210	1650
Milling enterprises	57	141
Iron ore mining (thousands of tons)	959	1865
Iron production (thousands of tons)	150	258
Coal mining (millions of tons)	14	21
Railroads (kilometers)	8688	10440

The number of workers also waxed. By the end of the world war there were about 2.5 million workers employed in factories and transport, and from eight to twelve million men in handicrafts and cottage industries. At this point in Chinese industrial development, however, the workers lacked professional and political organizations, and their participation in the democratic republican movement was sporadic and unorganized in character.

The Chinese middle class was poorly developed. Its weakness and the absence of an organized national mass movement forced middle class Chinese democrats to seek support from foreign countries. China's entry into the war on the side of the Entente[36] fostered illusions in liberal circles and in their most prominent representative, Sun Yat-sen. They believed in the possibility of the restoration of complete independence with the help of the Allies, particularly the United States. Inspired by President Wilson's call for international cooperation and peace conditions "making new wars impossible," Sun Yat-sen suggested that the great powers establish an international organization to plan industrial development in China. He wrote: "If President Wilson suggested formation of a League of Nations to prevent the occurrence of armed conflicts, then I suggest to countries interested in China's development that they take the path of collaboration and mutual assistance, to put an end to trade wars forever."[37]

The industrial plan prepared by Sun Yat-sen envisaged large industrial, transportation, housing, and other construction, to be carried out for the most part with resources supplied by the major powers. Private and public enterprises would be created under Chinese governmental control. Sun Yat-sen assured the great powers that they would enjoy access to the huge Chinese market for many years, and suggested that the restoration of the prewar economic levels of their countries could not be achieved without development of China's natural resources. The economic development of China on the basis of international collaboration "could not fail to help fortify brotherhood; and the latter, in my conviction, should become the cornerstone of the League of Nations." Surveying the historical development of China and remembering that in the past "it had held the leading position in the East," Sun Yat-sen remarked that "China itself had exaggerated its own accomplishments and belittled those of other nations. This had become a custom and had been considered completely natural. As a result, China consciously sought its own isolation . . . . China's isolationism and its haughtiness have an extensive history." The great democrat believed that the adoption of progressive social and economic experiences from all the world would alter the spiritual life of his people. For this purpose Sun emphasized the need to analyse the psychological traditions and way of life of the Chinese people, suggesting that "today neither nations nor people can get along without mutual services and assistance."

Sun Yat-sen's illusions about aid from the great powers for restoring a sovereign and flourishing China were soon dispelled. China had fulfilled her military obligations to the Allies and spent around 220 million Chinese dollars on the war against Germany. It sent 130,000 workers and prepared 100,000 soldiers for the European front. Despite these contributions, the allied nations completely ignored China's rights. The peace talks conducted in Paris showed that the Entente continued to regard China as an object of exploitation. China's delegation attempted to demonstrate that China's entry into the war entitled it to an equal position with the others. Therefore, all agreements which had been made concerning China without her participation should be annulled. This received no support. As in the past, the most aggressive stance was taken by Japan. The Japanese strove to use the Paris Peace Conference to legitimize their conquests in China. Japanese claims to the German holdings in China provoked hot debates among rival imperial nations. Threatening to leave the conference, and citing earlier agreements with the Entente nations and the United States, Japan insisted on recognition of its "rights" to the German lease territories in Shan-tung (articles 156, 157, and 158 of the Versailles Peace Treaty).

The decisions of the Paris Peace Conference smashed Sun Yat-sen's hopes for collaboration with the imperial powers "in the name of peace and progress." They destroyed at last his faith in "racially and culturally kindred" Japan. That nation had been transformed into the most dangerous and cruel enemy of the Chinese people. The Chinese must find new means of salvation from the imperial nations, from the chains of feudalism and capitalist exploitation, from the pestilence of militarism, in order to build a rationally unified, democratic China.

CHINA'S ROAD TO REVOLUTION

The demeaning provisions of the Paris Peace Conference incited stormy indignation in China. On May 4, 1919, a protest meeting took place in Peking, led by students of Peking University. The participants in the demonstration destroyed the homes of Chao Ju-ling and Lu Chung-yu, ministers known to favor Japan. A powerful anti-imperial wave rolled through the country. A boycott of Japanese products began, and workers struck against Japanese factories in Shang-hai, Ching-tao, and other cities. The acts of the Entente against China demonstrated once more to the Chinese people that China's renaissance could be achieved only through battle with imperialism.

The October Revolution in Russia had a deep effect on progress-minded members of the Chinese intelligentsia and on the Chinese conscience. The first Marxist cells appeared under the leadership of Li Ta-Chao, Cheng Tu-hsiu, and other progressive social activists in Shang-hai and Peking. From university lecturns and from the pages of newspapers and journals, public figures unfurled the ideas of October and the experience of Soviet Russia. Students, intellectuals and workers came forward with systematically developed, politically consistent declarations. The conditions were being created for the founding of a communist party in China.

Formation of the first worker-peasant government in Russia had great significance for China's international status. The Soviet government suggested negotiations with Chinese authorities to annul the Sino-Russian Treaty of 1896, the Peking (Boxer) Protocol of 1901, and the Russo-Japanese agreements of 1907-1916 that concerned China. New agreements would then be made between equals. The situation grew unfavorable for those foreign powers that had stood together against a half-colonized China, for in the north China now bordered on the new socialist state.

Recognition of Soviet Russia and conclusion of new and equitable treaties became the most important issues in China. Under the leadership of Li Ta-chao, the Association of Sino-Russian Friendship was created. It played an important role in the mobilization of public opinion in support of China's rapprochement with Soviet Russia. In southern China the government, led by Sun Yat-sen, warmly supported the idea of friendship with Soviet Russia, and took concrete measures in that direction. Sun Yat-sen wrote to Chicherin:[38] "I would like to meet you and other comrades personally in Moscow. I am extraordinarily interested in your cause, particularly in the organization of your Soviets, your army and education . . . . Like Moscow, I would like to lay the foundations of the Chinese Republic deep in the minds of my generation, the laborers of tomorrow. With best wishes to you and my friend Lenin and all those who have done so much for the cause of human freedom."[39] In the north the Peking government, under pressure from the imperial powers, did everything possible to delay the establishment of normal relations between China and Soviet Russia.

Meanwhile, the capitalist threat to China's sovereign rights increased even more. The conflict between the capitalist states also worsened. Japan's position was complicated by the return of England, France, and other Western European countries to the Far East. American interests in the area were stimulated by the opening of the Panama Canal in July, 1921. Together with a serious deterioration in Japanese-American relations, Japan had to take account of Anglo-American cooperation. English interests in central and southern China had been harmed seriously by Japanese monopolies during the war. Overlooking Anglo-American disagreements, England did not undertake to renew the Anglo Japanese treaty of alliance which had expired in 1921.

The newly established quadripartite consortium, initiated by the United States and including England, France, and Japan, demonstrated Western solidarity. These powers forced Japan to make important concessions, as compared to the first such consortium. Notwithstanding its persistent demands, Japan proved unable to have Manchuria and Inner Mongolia excluded from the consortium's zone of operations. On this occasion England and France joined the United States in insisting that the operations of the consortium be carried on within the Japanese sphere of influence. An English government memorandum declared on August 11, 1920: "Manchuria and Mongolia are important Chinese provinces, and any attempt to exclude them from the sphere of activity of the consortium would be a direct denial of the very principle upon which this consortium is created."[40]

Japan had to be content with a provision confirming its "special interests" and the exemption from control of the South Manchurian Railroad and other railroads, as well as industrial enterprises built by Japan in southern Manchuria and the eastern part of Inner Mongolia. In accepting such apparently fundamental concessions, Japanese officials were planning in advance to violate their obligation to waive their special interests. As later events showed, this they successfully accomplished: the new consortium never actually functioned. Nonetheless, the very fact that Japan relinquished special interests as part of the consortium agreement demonstrated that it appreciated the altered international situation and had resorted to tactical maneuvers. Japan also experienced difficulties at home. Opposition took hold among the Japanese people, particularly after the highly unpopular intervention against Soviet Russia. Moreover, the general economic crisis which struck in 1920-1921 took its toll. The reduction in Japanese textile exports and the consequent decrease in shipping activities led to a 30-40 percent fall in production: of 57 major shipyards, only 27 continued to work. Unemployment spread, and with it the strike movement. In mid-1921 35,000 shipworkers in Kobe struck, and they were supported by workers in other towns.

In these conditions Japanese leaders were forced to resort to complex maneuvers, particularly since the adventurism of the premier, Hara, and the war minister, Tanaka Giichi,[41] met with opposition even in high government spheres. At the Washington Conference, which began on October 12, 1921, Japan had to encounter even firmer American and English opposition. These powers weakened Japan's military strength in the Far East and deprived it of advantages gained during the war. Japan was forced to accept recommendations calling for a ratio of 5:5:3 for major naval ships to be maintained by England, the United States and Japan, instead of the Japanese proposal of a ratio of 10:10:7. The three powers and France agreed to guarantee the inviolability of their island possessions in the Pacific, and the Anglo-Japanese agreement of July 13, 1911 was voided, thus officially ending the Japanese military alliance with Britain.

Japan also encountered a united Western front during the consideration of the Chinese question at the Washington Conference. The eight participants unanimously rejected China's legitimate demands, presented by Peking's representative in highly abridged form and containing only the most essential conditions for restoring Chinese national sovereignty. Instead, they reaffirmed the policy of "open doors and equal opportunities." Further, the imperial powers, despite demagogic assurances "to respect the sovereignty, independence, and territorial and administrative inviolability of China," refused to take any real measures. The elimination of exterritorial rights was basic to restoration of Chinese sovereignty. On December 10, 1921, the Washington Conference declared that the eight nations "were prepared to renounce the exterritorial right after they were convinced that Chinese law, measures concerning its administration, and other circumstances, protected them in the required manner."[42] The question of restoring China's customs autonomy was treated with even less ceremony. Postponing this issue for consideration by a "special conference," the eight nations decided that duty levels should not exceed a rate of five percent ad valorum (in addition to 2.5-5 percent to replace local collections). This deprived the Chinese of the right to determine for themselves their own customs income. Further, the Chinese government was enjoined not to make changes "which might destroy Chinese maritime customs in their present form," that is, China must leave customs administration in the hands of the English and other foreigners.

The policy of open doors and equal opportunities, which left China an unprotected "free" market, was calculated also to destroy Japan's spheres of influence, and to eject it from the Chinese market which for years it had dominated. On February 6, 1922, Japan signed the Washington treaty "concerning principles and policies to be observed in relation to China." Thereby it agreed to refrain from "utilizing the situation currently found in China for seeking special rights and advantages which could harm the rights of subjects or citizens of friendly nations" (Article 1, Paragraph 3). Japan as well as the other eight nations would not seek nor "support their citizens in seeking a) agreements which could bring any sort of general superiority in commercial or economic development of any particular region of China; b) such monopolies or advantages which could deprive citizens of any other country of the right to engage in legal commerce or industry in China . . . or that could be calculated to paralyze the practical application of the principle of equal opportunities" (Article 3). Under pressure from the United States, England, and other Western states, Japan and China signed a separate accord on February 4, 1922. Within six months of the conclusion of the treaty Japan was to return the lands which had been German lease territories in Shan-tung. Japanese armies were to be removed. Completely abandoning its "21st demand," Japan agreed to relinquish to the consortium all rights acquired in the treaty of 1915 with China concerning railroad loans for southern Manchuria and Inner Mongolia.

Japanese concessions at the Washington Conference had no practical significance for China inasmuch as their implementation was postponed. Nonetheless, they reflected Japan's weakness. It feared to jeopardize relations with its rivals and did not wish to decide Chinese problems without the participation of the other nations. The decisions of the Washington Conference again showed the Chinese people that restoration of their sovereign rights could be accomplished only through determined struggle with imperialism and with the domestic militarists who had torn the country to shreds. The Chinese revolution needed the help of international progressive forces. Having taken the lead in the revolution, Sun Yat-sen's southern government launched a widespread campaign for renewing relations with the Soviet Union in order to learn from its experience. On December 1, 1923, Sun Yat-sen declared: "The Russians are of great experience and broad acquaintance. Therefore they know how to develop correct methods. If we want to conduct a revolution successfully, it is necessary that we study with them."[43]

The friendly attitude of Soviet Russia and its readiness to treat China as an equal contrasted sharply with the policy of the imperial powers. With wide support the revolutionary wing of the Koumintang in the south, and the communist party in central and northern China, compelled the Peking government to renew negotiations with the Soviets. On May 31, 1924, the two powers signed an accord "On General Principles for Regulating Questions Between the USSR and the Chinese Republic," the first agreement made by China on equal terms. It pointed the way to new forms in international relations based on full equality, respect for national sovereignty and mutual interests.[44]

Under pressure of the imperial powers, the Peking government began to violate the Sino-Soviet agreement soon after its signing. It refused to conduct the Sino-Soviet conference called for in the agreement (Article 2), and it failed to take any measures to disperse bands of White Russian emigres on Chinese territory, as provided for in Article 6. Indeed, the Peking government even supported their activities. By contrast, the government of south China supported the Sino-Soviet accord. Sun Yat-sen searched for ways to promote friendly relations with the Soviet Union. In the name of the southern government, he directed a request to the Soviet people for aid for China's revolution. In answer, hundreds of Soviet military and civilian specialists went to China, including the outstanding Soviet commander V.K. Bluecher and the famous figure of the international communist movement M. Borodin.[45] In 1925, counting on Soviet support, the southern government undertook a revolutionary campaign against the northern militarists. The revolutionary fight was bolstered by the working classes, particularly the city proletariat. The Chinese militarists, feudal lords and the bourgeoisie were backed by the imperial powers, forming a united reactionary front to oppose the Chinese revolutionary movement. The Chinese revolution thus became an inherent part of the international proletarian revolution. The allies of the workers and peasants of China, fighting for their national and social liberation, were the world's first socialist state—the Soviet Union—and the international proletariat.

SUMMARY

At the beginning of the twentieth century radical changes occurred in Sino-Japanese relations. They reflected the varying levels of socio-economic and political development and the differing international positions of the two countries. For China, then a semi-colonial and semi-feudal state, Japan exemplified the progress and rapid development capable of transforming a backward and dependent Asian country into a flourishing industrial world power. Those Chinese who desired progress strove to imitate Japan in remaking their socio-economic system, assimilating the achievements of world civilization, and applying advanced industrial experience to their own economy. They also hoped to find sympathy and support in Japan since in the recent past it too had been oppressed by the Western countries.

Even after the overthrow of the Chin monarchy, China was unable to accomplish a bourgeois democratic reformation, end backward feudal relationships, or restore national independence. China's progressives received no assistance from Japan in satisfying these aspirations. They became convinced that Japanese officials intended to keep China undeveloped and to dismember it. While Japan's advanced intelligentsia sympathized with Chinese ambitions, its rulers thought only of establishing political and economic control over separate regions and gradually over wider Chinese territory.

In the years immediately preceding World War I, and during that war, imperial Japan revealed the true extent of its expansionist policy.

Monopolistic capital, which had become "an international power," searched for markets to capture and peoples to enslave, particularly those of backward countries. If anything distinguished Japanese policy in the first quarter of the century from that of the United States, England, and other imperial powers, it was that because of its weaker economic muscle Japan was forced more frequently and in greater scale to use military force and armed intervention. Consequently Japanese policy grew ever more militant and cruel. Racial similarity and cultural and environmental closeness merely fed Japanese imperial ambitions.

The activities of the United States in the Far East and the return of England, France, and other European states to the arena forced Japan into temporary retreat. In this atmosphere Chinese progressive public opinion, still not grasping the true nature of imperialism, hoped for assistance from the United States and other Western powers for China's economic and political renaissance. However, the Versailles Peace Treaty and the Washington treaty finally dispelled these illusions. Notwithstanding their struggle with one another for hegemony, the imperial powers remained unified in contriving to keep China backward, weak, and incapable of resistance.

The Chinese people were choosing a new way for solving social and national problems. The ideas of the Great October Socialist Revolution, the experience of creating the first workers and peasants' government, Lenin's foreign policies based on equality, liberty, and independence of all nations and peoples, exerted a decisive influence on the development of the Chinese revolutionary movement. Revolutionary China found new friends and allies in the Soviet Union and the world proletariat. The Chinese revolution became an integral part of the world revolutionary movement. The anti-imperial and anti-feudal struggle which unfolded in China in 1924-1925 created real conditions for establishing a national popular democratic government. This prospect ran counter to the calculations of the imperial powers, who had major "interests" in China. Japan already controlled China's richest region of southern Manchuria; in deepest secrecy Japan's rulers now began preparations for a general assault on China.

CHAPTER FIVE

Japanese Imperialism Threatens China

The Chinese revolution of 1925-1927 had a powerful impact on the general situation in the Far East. It led to a sharp deterioration both in relations between the imperial powers and in Sino-Japanese relations. At the beginning of the 1920s two autonomous political centers were to be found in China. The Peking government was China's official representative in the outside world while the southern or Canton government was headed by Sun Yat-sen. In addition, various provinces were ruled by individual war lords who accepted neither northern nor southern authority. Among these, the most powerful were Chen Chiung-ming in the south, Chang Tso-lin in Manchuria, Wu Pei-fu in northern and central China, and Sun Chang-fang in the east.

After the Kuomintang alliance with the communist party was formed, the southern government became the center of all Chinese revolutionary activity. The executive committee of the Kuomintang was located in Canton, and the All-China Trade Union conferences of May 1, 1922 and May 1, 1925 were held there. At the first conference of peasant unions in Kuan-tung province a decision was made to create the Whampoa military-political school, which became the main center for preparing military personnel for the National Revolutionary Army. With the active participation of the communists, the Canton government adopted a manifesto at the first Kuomintang congress in January 1924. It set forth the tasks of the Chinese anti-feudal and anti-imperialist revolution:[1] "The militarists, whose interests are opposed to those of the people, cannot exist independently. They enter into relations with the foreign imperialists . . . . Consequently, disorders in our country are created by the great powers, who use the militarists to destroy our people as they pursue their own conflicting goals in China."

Having adopted the "three principles of the people" of Sun Yat-sen as its program, the first Kuomintang congress gave them a new revolutionary interpretation. The "principle of nationalism" was tied directly to the national liberation struggle against imperialism. As the manifesto declared: "In confirming the anti-imperialistic impulse of the principle of nationalism, we will lend energetic aid to popular organizations to enable growth of national might. Only through close contact between the Kuomintang and the popular masses can we hope for true victory and independence." The manifesto called for pursuing the "principle of popular rule" by granting the people complete lawmaking and executive powers: "Power should belong to the whole people, and not to a small group . . . . It is inconceivable that these rights be granted carelessly to the enemies of the Republic." Ways for achieving the "principle of popular welfare" also were suggested in the manifesto. Large monopolies were to be limited "so that private capital would not be able to hold the means of peoples' existence in its hands." The government was obliged to provide land and help in working it for "peasants who because of land scarcity had become renters." Briefly, the agrarian program adopted by the congress was expressed in the slogan offered by Sun Yat-sen: "A field for every plowman."[2]

To achieve these goals Sun Yat-sen proposed three political principles: "Alliance with Russia, alliance with the communist party, and peasant and worker support." The Canton government supported the unfolding strike movements in Shang-hai, Canton, Tsingtao and other cities. The southern regime gained dependable allies among the people by encouraging the working peasantry against the landlords. It could count on spreading its influence rapidly throughout China. Canton's foreign policy, based on friendship with Soviet Russia, also enjoyed widespread approval.

The southern government's progressive policies even found adherents among northern generals. General Feng Yu-hsiang, who commanded a group of Wu Pei-fu's armies, regarded Sun Yat-sen's national liberation ideas sympathetically. He led the fight against the reactionary Peking government of Tsao Kun and Wu Pei-fu. With the support of generals Ho Chien-yi and Chang Tso-lin, he took Peking on October 23, 1924. For a time Feng Yu-hsiang was the commander-in-chief of the armies in the Peking region. However, such palace coups could not change the political situation in the north. Furthermore, Feng Yu-hsiang's allies proved to be no less reactionary than the generals they had deposed. Within a month Peking was in the hands of the Japanese puppet Chang Tso-lin, the head of state was the Japanophile Tuan Chi-jui, and Feng Yu-hsiang was transferred to command an army group in Kalgan. "The Peking coup," as the short reign of Feng Yu-hsiang has been called, led to no fundamental changes in the Peking government. Nevertheless, it exposed the instability of the Peking regime and produced greater activity among Sun Yat-sen's followers. Public pressure compelled Tuan

Chi-jui to confirm the invitation sent to Sun Yat-sen by Feng Yu-hsiang to visit Peking for a conference to seek agreements. The movement spread for unifying the country, calling a national assembly and establishing a national democratic government. At the end of 1924, in Peking and Shang-hai committees were formed for cooperation in calling a national assembly, and the communists participated actively in them. The assembly was to create popular rule, eliminate the war lords' mastery over the country, and annul inequitable treaties.

Before the Peking conference began its deliberations, Sun Yat-sen presented the revolutionary democratic platform for future domestic and foreign policies. "In deciding Chinese problems this time," he stated, "in domestic affairs we will liquidate the militarists, while in foreign policy we will end intervention by foreign powers so that the Chinese people will become the complete master." Concerning the relations of the southern government with the USSR, Sun Yat-sen explained: "The goals of the Chinese revolution and the goals of the Russian revolution coincide . . . . The Chinese and Russian revolutions are following the same paths. Thus China and Russia not only have close relations, but in their revolutionary bonds they truly form a single family."[3]

However, in Peking at the time of Sun Yat-sen's arrival an unhospitable atmosphere existed. On December 11, 1924, diplomatic representatives of the powers had given the Chinese government a joint note warning that they would recognize the new regime only if it adhered to treaties and guaranteed foreign privileges. In other words, prior even to the opening of the conference, the note demanded rejection of the revolutionaries' anti-imperialist program.

In answer to domestic and foreign intrigues, the communist party organized massive popular demonstrations in support of Sun Yat-sen's position. In January, the clandestine fourth congress of the Chinese Communist Party adopted a manifesto in Shang-hai. The document analyzed the domestic and international situation and portrayed the reactionary intentions of the militarists who were conspiring with the imperialist powers against the Chinese people. The statement appealed for action to revoke the inequitable treaties; it called also for a national assembly to include representatives of the workers, intelligentsia and social organizations. Tuan Chi-jui's Japanophile group rejected the demands of the Chinese Communist Party and Sun Yat-sen, whereupon the Kuomintang refused to participate in the conference. On February 1, 1925, the "restoration conference" opened, attended solely by the reactionary forces of China. A wave of protest, abetted by the newly-created Committee for Calling a National Assembly in Peking, led by the communists, insured the failure of the "restoration conference." Joint discussions on the problems of China's reunion on democratic principles collapsed, and the sudden death of Sun Yat-sen generated renewed hostility between the Peking and Canton governments.

A further wave of revolutionary activity burst into the open and spread to the major industrial cities of central and northern China. The beastly murder of the Shang-hai textile worker Ku Cheng-hung aroused public anger and provoked organized demonstrations by workers, students, the intelligentsia and other city dwellers. Historians term these developments "the events of May 30;" they prepared the way for the bourgeois democratic and anti-feudal revolution of 1925-1927.

Canton became the revolutionary focal point. The Canton government gathered much strength after the dispersion of the counter-revolutionary "paper tiger"[4] group in October 1924. Further gains followed the successful conclusion of the first eastern expedition against the southern warlord Chen Chiung-ming in February-May 1925, and the crushing of revolts by warlords in Yun-nan and Kuang-hsi. On July 1, 1925, the government was reorganized as the "National Government of China" and the southern armed forces united into the "National Revolutionary Army." The Chinese nationalist government contained several factions. The leftist Kuomintang members played an important part, headed by Liao Chung-kai, the minister of finance and commissar of the Whampoa school. The communists relied on support from anti-imperialists of the industrial cities and peasants who were rising against their landlords; it was these groups which became the main guiding force of the Chinese revolution.

The scale of the revolutionary movement threatened the status of the imperial powers and the warlords of China. It forced them to resort to more vigorous measures. The main buttress of the counterrevolutionaries in the south and center of China was England, while in the north Japan supplied the most plentiful aid. The policies of these countries and other imperial states consisted of dividing and weakening the revolutionary front, while simultaneously providing material and political sustenance to the Peking government and individual warlords. Subsequent reactionary acts included the murder of the leader of the Kuomintang left, Liao Chung-kai, an attempted counterrevolutionary coup in Canton on March 20, 1926, and terrorism and reprisals against communist and union activists in Shang-hai and Peking. All were calculated to break the strength of the revolution. Meanwhile England and Japan began direct military intervention in the Chinese civil war. In the south, England rearmed a defeated general, Chen Chiung-ming, and assisted his new campaign against Canton; after the defeat of his army, during the second eastern campaign of October-November 1925, the English organized a naval blockade of Canton (February 1926).

Japanese military intervention reached even greater dimensions. The Mukden clique headed by Chang Tso-lin permitted Japan to control Manchuria and also regions of northern and eastern China. It was Chang Tso-lin, thus, who headed the main elements offering resistance to the revolutionary south. For this reason Japan's rulers strove to preserve the leading role of this group in the Chinese government. In November 1925, General Feng Yu-hsiang declared his sympathy with the revolutionaries and began to attack Chang Tso-lin, taking Peking on November 26. General Kuo Sung-ling joined him and they threatened Mukden. At this point Japan hastened to rescue its puppets. With the tacit approval of the imperial powers, Japanese armies moved openly against Feng Yu-hsiang's forces. The Japanese fleet sailed into waters near Tientsin in March 1926 and thereby shifted the military balance in favor of the armies of Mukden and Chih-li, which once more took Peking and regions of northern China.

In tandem with direct military intervention in China's internal affairs, the imperial states set about a campaign of ideological warfare, with Japan in the lead. A variety of demagogic declarations were issued for the purpose of quelling the anti-imperialist movement among the Chinese people, and promises made to use peaceful means to solve the problem of restoring Chinese customs autonomy and removing the extraterritorial right of foreigners. For this purpose the nine participants of the Washington conference gathered for a customs conference on October 26, 1925. Actually, according to the Washington agreements of 1922, this meeting was to have taken place three months after the signing of that agreement. In January 1926 the signatory nations formed a commission to consider abolition of extraterritorial rights in China. The chief of the Japanese delegation, Eki Hyoki, attempted to convince the Chinese delegation (and thereby Chinese public opinion) that in the past Japan itself had been deprived of customs autonomy thanks to unequal treaties. Therefore the Japanese delegation would approach the problems before the conference with sympathy and perception, and with friendly understanding of the Chinese position. Despite these "friendly assurances," Japan sponsored some of the obstacles put in the way of adoption of concrete responses to the problems in question. When the Peking government, wishing to still public opinion, unilaterally announced increases in customs duties, the Japanese government compelled the Chinese authorities to exempt the Japanese lease territory of Liao-tung. For the moment, the Japanese government chose not to undertake a more comprehensive intervention in China. This is explained in part by a desire to avoid further damage to relations with Japan's imperial rivals. Even so, social antagonisms in Japan were escalating, as was its financial dependency on American and English banks, particularly for reconstruction after the catastrophic earthquakes of 1923. Thus the Japanese were forced to reckon and to act in agreement with these nations in China. This "negative policy" of the Shidehara cabinet,[5] as it was labeled by the bourgeois press, provoked sharp opposition from military circles sympathetic to General Tanaka,[6] who in 1925 had become the president of the Seiyu Kai, the party of the powerful monopolies. Japanese militarism viewed the accomplishments of the Chinese revolution and the movements of the nationalist revolutionary armies in the Chinese interior as threats to its strategic plans. Before long military extremists took over government leadership, and Japan set about preparation for new attacks on China.

JAPAN AND THE KUOMINTANG GOVERNMENT IN NANKING

The northern campaign of the nationalist revolutionary army, which stirred the peasantry and the city poor alike, bared the deep social cleavages of Chinese society. The large and embittered middle class resisted from the outset and joined forces with the imperial powers (in such events as the "paper tiger" rebellion and General Chen Chiung-ming's advance on Canton). The Kuomintang left wing and the communists joined forces with the peasants who were dispossessing landlords, and with workers demonstrating in the cities. Jointly they demanded social equality and political freedom from the imperialists and the Chinese middle class, calls which produced the wholesale hostility of the middle class and the bourgeois intelligentsia to the revolution, and their union with the counterrevolutionary forces.

This development found reflection in the military and political leadership of the northern campaign. The commander-in-chief, Chiang Kai-shek, represented the extreme right wing of the Kuomintang. He looked at first at concentrating his authority while neutralizing the communists and the Kuomintang left wing, while isolating the Soviet advisors M.M. Borodin and V.K. Bluecher.[7] The leftists failed in attempts to limit Chiang Kai-shek's dictatorship and to transfer military and political leadership to a collective of generals. At the conference of the Kuomintang left wing on February 7 and at the third plenum of the Kuomintang central executive committee, on March 10, 1927, nine names were nominated for a permanent executive committee. But Chiang Kai-shek violated the agreement to transfer government, party and military authorities to the regime in Wu-han. Instead he endeavored to separate the bulk of the military forces from the Wu-han government, and thus forced an advance toward Nanking and Shang-hai. The Kuomintang right wing brazenly revealed its attitudes by its reprisals against trade union organizations in Canton, Nan-chang, An-ching, and other cities, reprisals which had the added purpose of "soothing" the imperial governments. Nationalist army units entered Shang-hai, where rebelling workers had already expelled warlord armies. Then Chiang Kai-shek initiated official contacts with foreign consuls to assure them that their interests were safe. In turn, the imperial powers promised him political support.

They hurried to demonstrate this. On March 24, 1927, English and United States naval vessels shelled Nanking under the pretext that units of the Nationalist army had violated the property rights of their citizens. This was followed by troop landings in Shang-hai. These actions were intended to terrorize and intimidate those Chinese leaders who opposed imperialism as well as to provide direct support to Kuomintang rightists for a counterrevolutionary coup. On April 12, 1927, the foreign military forces arrested numerous communists, trade unionists and workers in the international settlements. These unfortunates were turned over to Chiang Kai-shek's punitive forces for reprisals. The coup led by Chiang Kai-shek, with the support of domestic and foreign reactionaries, sought to smash the united Kuomintang and Chinese Communist Party front, to make an end to worker and peasant unions and to crush all organized opposition within the country. Chiang Kai-shek's forces carried out massive terrorism in Shang-hai after the coup of April 12, 1927. Subsequently, a broad wave of repression swept the territories controlled by Chiang Kai-shek's armies. Next it spread to the region under the jurisdiction of the Kuomintang government in Wu-han.

On July 15, 1927, with the preliminary agreement of Chiang Kai-shek and Wang Ching-wei, the Kuomintang central executive committee in Wu-han officially banned communist activity. A new stage of the Chinese civil war began. Chiang Kai-shek's ascension to power brought a fundamental foreign policy change by the rightist Kuomintang government in Nanking, which wished to break relations with the Soviet Union, and demanded recall of Soviet political and military advisors. After these diplomats left southern, central and northern regions of China, official representatives of the USSR in Shang-hai and Canton became the targets of provocations. Like the previous militarists, the Nanking authorities tied their fate to the imperial powers and pursued anti-communist policies. As it turned out, even the unification of the forces of reaction in China failed to eliminate the mutual antagonisms of the imperial powers, and it even sharpened their animosities. As the separatists were eliminated the problem of political union and creation of a unified Chinese government gained special urgency, and each rival thought of assuring the leading position for himself.

Prior even to the official formation of the rightist Kuomintang government, the imperial nations launched their struggle to influence the new Chinese authorities. In winter 1926 Chiang Kai-shek sent a prestigious envoy, Tai Chi-tao, to Japan with instructions to negotiate for political support with the Japanese government and American representatives. Since Japan continued to control provinces in northeast and central China (north of the Yangtze), it did not hurry to support the claims of the rightist administration to rule all of China. Furthermore, Japan was interested in limiting the power of the rightist Kuomintang, and attempted to prevent nationalist expansion to the north. The United States reacted differently to the Chiang Kai-shek regime. Its government was extremely dissatisfied with its secondary role in Chinese affairs. The spheres of influence established by old treaties limited the zone where American capital might expand and created an uncertain situation for it. Hence the United States was interested in a change in Chinese rulers, and searched for a new treaty system allowing equal opportunities to it. In a secret agreement, concluded in Japan with Chiang Kai-shek, the United States accepted an obligation to aid the rightist government, which in turn agreed to accept American advisors.

After Chiang Kai-shek's return from Japan and the formation of the Kuomintang government on January 7, 1928, the United States became its chief political tutor. The declaration of July 7, 1928, called for renegotiation of treaties which had expired or would expire soon. China had agreements with France, Japan, Belgium, Spain, Portugal, Italy and Denmark. The United States was quick to reply to the declaration; it completed and signed a new treaty with China on July 25, 1928, before the other nations had even replied. In essence, the new Sino-American treaty gave China no advantages. The formal recognition of customs autonomy did not change much. It granted the Americans the same privileges enjoyed by citizens of other countries, but in fact Americans already enjoyed these rights. Until it concluded treaties with the leading trading countries, China would have no customs autonomy.[8] Nonetheless, even this agreement held a definite political significance for China.

It upset the unity of the imperial powers and complicated English and particularly Japanese maneuvers to preserve the inequitable treaties. Chinese bourgeois and intellectual circles regarded it to be a success of Kuomintang diplomacy and a manifestation of American good will. As later events showed, the United States government made excellent use of this evaluation of its treaty with China.

Fearing for its large investments in the southern and central regions of China, England sought a compromise as a means of maintaining its leading position. Following the American lead, English authorities agreed to reconsider the agreement then in effect. On December 20, 1928, England signed a new customs treaty with the Nanking government.

The situation took an unfavorable turn for Japan. The Chinese military leaders Chang Tso-lin and Chang Tsun-chiang had helped Japan gain control of the Peking government, and had halted the Nationalist advance in the lower Yangtze valley. Now they suffered defeat. The strengthened pro-American Nanking government threatened to weaken Japan's position in China even further. Chiang Kai-shek's rise to power and increased American influence led to a political crisis in Japan. On April 17, 1927, the Wakatsuki government resigned.[9] According to Japanese extremists, it had taken an insufficiently strong stance. The formation of a new cabinet was entrusted to General Tanaka, the leader of the Seiyu Kai party, whose ascent to power was followed by extremely reactionary domestic and foreign policies. Hoping to bolster the Chinese generals in Manchuria, the Japanese military establishment employed "pacification troops" to spread terror against the communists and Kuomintang leftists, to crush worker organizations and carry out anti-Soviet provocations. In April 1927, 28 communists led by Li Ta-chao were arrested in Peking. On the 28th, they were executed. At the same time the Soviet Embassy in Peking was attacked, Soviet diplomats were thrown into prison and anti-Soviet harrassment plagued the Chinese Domestic Railroad. Although joining Chiang Kai-shek's anti-Soviet stance the Japanese government still did not want a unified Chinese government, something particularly true inasmuch as pro-American factions might win control.

In the middle of 1927 Premier Tanaka developed a broad program of expansion, which he presented to the emperor in the form of a secret memorandum on July 25. Tanaka suggested that Japan seize Chinese territories. The memorandum stated: "If we are able to conquer China, all the other small Asian countries, the Indian and also the oceanic countries will fear us and capitulate to us. Then the world will understand that eastern Asia is ours, and it will not dare to dispute our rights."[10] Tanaka's initial assumption was that conquests in China would lead unavoidably to a clash with the United States. Hence he recommended the acquisition of Manchuria and Mongolia as the primary task, in order to "utilize that region as a base for penetration into China proper." "But grasping control of Manchuria and Mongolia," wrote Tanaka, "is only the first step if the nation of Yamato wishes to play the leading role on the Asian continent."

In his memorandum, Tanaka declared that Manchuria and Mongolia were "non-Chinese territories." With the aid of massive Korean immigration into Manchuria, Japan would be able to increase the non-Chinese population and "if the need arose, incite them to military action." With cynical candor, Tanaka recommended that the emperor " . . . use a million yen 'from secret funds' of the war ministry to send 400 retired officers to Outer and Inner Mongolia without delay. These officers, dressed like Chinese citizens or pretending to be teachers, should mix with the population, gain the trust of Mongolian princes, acquire permission to engage in animal husbandry and mining and thereby lay foundations for our national welfare for the next hundred years." Tanaka considered war with "Red Russia" to be unavoidable. He declared that it was essential for Japan to " . . . cross swords with Russia in the fields of southern Manchuria in order to gain the riches of northern Manchuria. Until this underwater reef is broken, we will not be able to move forward rapidly along the path to penetration of Manchuria and Mongolia." On the basis of this plan the Japanese government considered it "mortally essential," within the context of the continuing Chinese civil war, to prevent advances by the northern forces toward Peking. The nationalist armies of the Kuomintang must not take northern China and Manchuria. At the same time, Japan must speed the preparation of a military base in southern Manchuria in the zone of the Japanese "protective" army.

Within Japan, the Tanaka cabinet pressed development of heavy and military industry, employing government subsidies and other forms of monopolistic capital assistance. Simultaneously, the Seiyu Kai party continued to build its power, causing even the limited parliamentary democracy which existed gradually to wither, and permitting a military fascist regime to become established in Japan. These measures were to insure "national preparedness" for accomplishing the plans of the notorious Tanaka memorandum.

A more decisive and militant policy toward China was signalled by the so-called Chi-nan conflict. In April 1928, the Nanking authorities declared that they would continue the northern campaign against the Japanese puppet Chang Tso-lin. The Tanaka government sent additional troops to Shan-tung province to resist the Nanking armies. The Japanese took the city of Chi-nan and clashed with Chinese forces on May 3-10, 1928. Even so, Japanese attacks on Kuomintang troops followed by temporary cessation of fighting, failed to improve Japan's position. Anti-Japanese sentiment in China waxed. Generals Feng Yu-hsiang and Yan Hsi-shan now joined the northern campaign and began advancing on Chang Tso-lin's armies in Peking. The Japanese ultimatum to the Nanking government to withdraw from Shan-tung was not answered. On June 5, 1928, Chang Tso-lin, the main supporter of the Japanese militarists in northern China and Manchuria, was driven from Peking by General Yan Hsi-shan's soldiers.

As it had done in 1915, Japanese imperialism chose armed intervention as the primary means of guarding its interests in China. Thereby Japan became the chief direct threat to China's national sovereignty. Censuring earlier cabinets for their compromising and inconsistency, Tanaka insisted on a policy of "blood and iron" toward China, thinking it impossible to avoid difficulties in East Asia. The Japanese government rejected Nanking's proposal for reexamination of the Sino-Japanese treaty,[11] even though three years before, during the Peking customs conference (in August 1925), the Japanese delegation had strongly advocated customs autonomy for China. Then Chang Tso-lin, who had accepted Japanese military assistance in the battles against the Nanking government, contrary to the expectations of Japanese military circles, proved incorruptible. When the Nanking armies approached Peking, which had been taken by Chang Tso-lin, the Japanese command proposed that he withdraw his forces to the north, thereby strengthening Japan in Manchuria. Chang Tso-lin instead called for the union of the Nanking and Peking governments. This did not coincide with the plans of the Japanese, and they decided to dispose of the insubordinate Chinese general. On June 4, 1928, as Chang Tso-lin was travelling to Manchuria at Japanese insistence, the train he was riding was blown up and the general himself was killed.

Japan's status in China was impeded even more by other factors. It refused to negotiate with the Nanking government, and there were difficulties in settling the Chi-nan conflict. Japan tried to restrain the new Manchurian leader Chang Hsueh-liang (who had replaced Chang Tso-lin) from recognizing the Nanking authorities as the central government. Meanwhile, heightened disagreement with the United States and England complicated Japan's international situation. Once again Japan was forced to back away, and the "uncompromising" Tanaka cabinet gave way to a new one led by Hamaguchi Osachi, the leader of the Minsei To party.[12] As later events demonstrated, the Minsei To party cabinets were no less prepared actively to seek conquest. However, they followed a more flexible policy, choosing methods and means with an eye to the actual international situation and the level of Japanese military preparedness. Japanese leaders strove to convince the United States, England and other imperial powers that the Chinese revolution was spreading and that the "Red peril" loomed over the interests of all imperial nations. Japan was summoned to carry out its "special mission" by actively intervening in Chinese affairs.

Meanwhile the new Japanese cabinet projected a spirit of compromise toward China as well as toward other nations. On June 3, 1929, Japan officially recognized the Nanking government, and on May 3, 1930 signed an agreement on Chinese customs autonomy. At the end of November, 1929, Japan accepted England's proposal for renewal of the interrupted negotiations concerning naval armaments (broken off in 1927). At the tripartite London naval conference (the United States, England and Japan), Japan dropped its demand for adjustment of the ratio of ships of the line in its favor. This evoked stormy displeasure among rightists, even though the Japanese delegation gained some concessions concerning smaller ships and submarines. At the same time that Japan attempted to compromise with the reactionary Kuomintang and with American and English imperialism, the authorities also practised anti-Soviet policies and at home employed fascist methods.

IMPERIAL JAPAN'S CONQUEST OF MANCHURIA

The Nanking authorities made use of terrorism and force, and banned all democratic organizations. These measures spawned a swelling resistance among the Chinese people. Under communist leadership, revolutionary forces in some regions went to the attack. In ferocious battle with the reactionaries, the Chinese Red Army was born, and the first Chinese Soviet regions were formed. During 1930 and 1931 the Nanking government dispatched three punitive expeditions against Soviet areas in central and southern China, unsuccessfully trying to quell the popular democratic movement by force of arms.

In foreign policy, Nanking took a consistent anti-Soviet position. In October 1927 Kuomintang forces attacked the Soviet consulate in Shang-hai. In December of the same year the Soviet consulate in Canton was sacked and five Soviet consular officials killed. During 1928 and the early part of 1929, at the instigation of Kuomintang authorities, systematic harassments were launched against Soviet workers in Manchuria. On July 15, 1929, at a session of the central executive committee of the Kuomintang, Chiang Kai-shek gave a slanderous speech against the Soviet Union. He attempted to convince the Chinese people that it was not the imperial powers that threatened China, but the USSR. " 'Red' imperialism," he stated, "is more dangerous than 'white' imperialism, for the nature of the former is more difficult to establish."[13] This speech served as a signal for further harassment of Soviet citizens. The Nanking authorities ignored a Soviet proposal for an urgent conference to consider all questions relating to the Chinese Domestic Railroad. In collusion with international imperialists, Nanking next sought a break in diplomatic relations with the Soviet Union by provoking hostilities on the Soviet far-eastern border.

The civil war and worsening relations with the Soviet Union dissipated China's democratic forces and their capability for resisting imperialist aggression. Steadily the Nanking government lost popular support. Consequently, in the early 1930s the ruling circles of Japan reached the conclusion that the time had come to serve "Yamato's historical mission" in Asia. Meanwhile the United States and England became convinced that the Nanking leaders were not living up to expectations. They had failed utterly to crush the Chinese revolutionary movement and had failed to guarantee imperial interests. For this reason American and English relations with Japan underwent a change. The Atlantic powers began to interpret the Japanese ambition to police China in a different way; now they hoped that by limiting Japanese expansion roughly to the "sphere of influence" in Manchuria, they might utilize Japan to preserve "order" in China.

Japan undertook aggression in Manchuria knowing that the area's southern part lay already under its complete military and economic hold. Thus communications stood open to Korea and the Japanese islands. Manchuria as an initial object of aggression interested Japanese planners for political reasons in addition to the military and strategic advantages it offered. They assumed that Manchuria's population of Manchurians, Mongols, Koreans and other national minorities knew at first hand the usurous Chinese commercial bourgeoisie and therefore might readily be persuaded to oppose the Chinese. Moreover, for 268 years the Manchurians had ruled, and the last heir of the Manchurian Chin dynasty, the overthrown emperor Pu Yi, was living in Japan. Thus the Japanese plan was to exploit anti-Chinese nationalism in Manchuria and, cloaked with the banner of a Chin restoration, to win control of Manchuria, and then of all China.

To accomplish this design at the beginning of July 1931 in the village of Wan-pao-shan, thirty kilometers from the city of Chiang-chung, the Japanese provoked an incident between Chinese peasants and Korean colonists who had been sent especially into the region. The Japanese authorities attempted to manipulate the provocation into a "general Korean disturbance" and thereby artificially to kindle "anti-Chinese" actions in Korea. To fire chauvinistic flames in Japan itself, the Japanese propaganda apparatus spread rumors that Chinese soldiers had murdered a Japanese "geological researcher" near the city of Tao-nan. According to impartial foreign observers, the Japanese could present no evidence to support their version of the story.

Next the Japanese undertook substantial military actions. During the night of September 18-19, with no prior demands made of the Chinese administration in Manchuria and claiming that Chinese soldiers had destroyed railroad roadbed near Mukden, Japanese troops shelled Chinese barracks and the Mukden arsenal. On September 19 they took control of Mukden, Chiang-chung and other important centers in southern Manchuria. For the next three months the Japanese met no organized resistance from Chang Hsueh-liang's armies, who strictly followed Chiang Kai-shek's directives. The Japanese forces conquered important areas of southern Manchuria and the southeastern Manchurian provinces. This was followed by the arrival of substantial new contingents of soldiers and arms in Manchuria, along with economic advisors, engineers and various other specialists. A carefully devised plan, followed minutely, aimed at military takeover and the establishment of administrative and economic control of Manchuria.

The methods and tactics of the Japanese militarists in penetrating Manchuria reveal that Japanese leaders anticipated no support for their actions even from the exploiters among the Chinese population. They endeavored to play on the national feelings of the Manchurians, Mongols and other nationalities. With this purpose the Japanese stirred up anti-Chinese demonstrations among the local Manchurian inhabitants, attempting to create the impression of a broad movement for independence from China. They dismissed the local Chinese administrations and replaced them either with their own local agents or with officials from Japan. Nevertheless, the Japanese declared that all changes in Manchurian administration resulted from actions by the local populace. Furthermore, during the early days of Manchurian occupation, the Japanese authorities dragged "emperor" Pu Yi onto the political arena.[14]

Japanese anti-communist policies in China exerted a growing influence on the United States, England and other imperial powers. These countries made no move to stop Japan's aggression; China's protests to the League of Nations produced no results. The Anglo-American stand on Japanese actions rendered the Nanking government powerless. On October 25, 1931, Nanking's representative officially informed the League of Nations that because Japanese troops were approaching Chinchou, Chinese armies had been ordered to retreat to Shang-hai-huan, beyond the Great Wall of China. The Nanking government requested that the League of Nations create a demilitarized zone on Manchuria's border with China proper, with English, French and Italian troops to police the zone. Chinese soldiers and citizens were instructed not to resist the advancing Japanese armies. Chiang Kai-shek tried to appease Japan by conceding Manchuria to it. Meeting no resistance from the Kuomintang armies, with the tacit consent of the League of Nations and the United States, Japan occupied all Manchuria in February 1932.

MANCHURIA BECOMES A JAPANESE COLONY

On February 29, 1932, the Japanese military authorities staged an "All-Manchurian conference" in Mukden. On March 1 this conclave published a "Declaration of the Formation of Manchukuo" and on March 3 "elected" Pu Yi the provisional ruling regent of the puppet Manchurian state. The creation of Manchukuo aimed at soothing world public opinion. On December 10, 1931, the League of Nations resolved to send a special commission to Manchuria, led by Lord Lytton,[15] to acquaint itself with the prevailing situation. To intensify pressure on the League of Nations and the Nanking government and divert their attention from Manchuria, Japan unleashed an attack on Shang-hai at the end of January, 1932. Major naval and infantry forces concentrated in the region containing the greatest capital investments of England, the United States, and France. The resistance of government army units stiffened, and found the determined support of the Shang-hai workers, thereby creating a new and complex situation for the United States, England and other imperial nations as well as for the Kuomintang authorities. The direct threat posed by Japan carried new dangers against the strengthened national front of the Chinese people.

British and American diplomats served as the active intermediaries for settling the Shang-hai "incident." As proposed by the League of Nations on March 3, 1932, Japan agreed to cease military actions in the Shang-hai region and begin peace negotiations with the Nanking authorities. As a result, on May 5 a Sino-Japanese agreement settled the Shang-hai conflict. In essence, it amounted to a deal between the Western nations and Japan at the expense of China's interests. While accepting the League of Nations' proposal for the peaceful settlement of the Shang-hai hostilities, the Japanese government nevertheless proclaimed that it did not and could not recognize China as an "organized" nation. Japan blamed China for all that had taken place in order to justify its own perfidy and arrogate to it the right to interfere in internal Chinese affairs in the future.

Settlement of the Shang-hai conflict and the subsequent evacuation of Japanese armies from the region represented a real concession by imperial Japan. These actions reflected a desire to avoid direct conflict with the United States and England, as well as fear of a prolonged war with the Chinese while the situation in Manchuria remained unsettled. At the same time, Japan received the basic acceptance of Anglo-American diplomacy for its ambition to act as "the preserver of order in China." Japanese militarism thereby gained a pretext for demanding support from the two Western powers as a form of recompense for the "obligations" it shouldered. At minimum Japan felt it might count on Anglo-American neutrality in the Sino-Japanese conflict. In this way the Shang-hai incident again demonstrated to Japan that England and the United States were unprepared to act resolutely to counteract Japan's expansion in China. Events seemed to indicate that the Western nations feared Japan less than "Red China" and the increasingly powerful Soviet Union. England and the United States were ready to cooperate in strengthening the Japanese position in Manchuria, for this would push Japan into a clash with the Soviet Union. They regarded Japanese advances into northern Manchuria as an open violation of the Portsmouth Treaty of 1905,[16] which had been confirmed by the Soviet-Japanese Convention of 1925.[17] Consequently, the Japanese push might damage relations between Japan and the Soviet Union. The Japanese government rejected the Soviet proposal of December 31, 1931 for a Soviet-Japanese non-aggression pact, and the Japanese continually violated Soviet property rights on the Chinese Domestic Railroad. Apparently the calculations of the West proved correct. However, the peaceful policies of the Soviet government made no contribution to deterioration of Soviet-Japanese relations, and the military strength of the Soviet Union exerted a growing deterrent effect on Japanese leaders.

In Japan the fever of great-power chauvinism continued to rise. Fascist groups created a war psychosis and threatened progressive groups, in particular the communist party. On May 15, 1932, army and naval officers organized a fascist putsch in which Premier Inukai Tsuyoshi[18] was fatally wounded. The non-partisan "national" cabinet of Admiral Saito[19] which now took over the government continued to pursue the policy of conquest in China. The basic conceptions of that policy were presented clearly in the "Declaration of the Formation of Manchukuo." On the presumption that "in the past Manchuria and Mongolia were separate states, distinct from China," the Japanese authors of the declaration proclaimed Manchurian "independence" in the name of "the All-Manchurian Conference." They also offered proof of the legitimacy of Mongolian independence, while also portraying China proper as a disorganized country which had been thrown into chaos by the 1911 revolution and had not recovered: "Twenty years have passed since the revolution took place, but in the course of that time the militarists (of China-M.S.) who took control have completely ignored the well-being of the people and permitted themselves greed, extravagance and license."[20]

Thus while focusing their attention chiefly on Manchuria, Japanese rulers still felt no need to conceal their plans for conquering all of China. The puppet state of Manchukuo was to be the prototype for future "independent" states on the territory of a dismembered China. Relations between Japan and Manchukuo were defined by a protocol signed on September 9, 1932. The agreement legalized Japan's military intervention and granted it unlimited rights in Manchuria. The Declaration of the Formation of Manchukuo claimed all inhabitants of that "state," including the local Japanese, as subjects. Thereby many military and civil officials became "Manchukuo citizens," eligible to hold any official position in government institutions. In this way was legalized the transfer of the entire administration of political, economic, cultural and military affairs in the puppet state into Japanese hands.

The Japanese undertook large-scale economic measures in Manchukuo. These included open expropriation of Chinese property, and physical destruction or expulsion of Chinese entrepreneurs and technicians. Numerous laws and regulations of the Manchukuo government had the purpose of establishing state monopolies in particular branches of the industrial economy, including mining, transport, and certain manufactures. Besides that, Japanese companies created "local" concerns which received state monopolies from the Manchukuo authorities. For example, with the participation of the Nissan firm and the aid of Japanese militarism, a company was formed to develop heavy industry in Manchuria. Named Mangio, it assumed a leading position in strategic

military, industrial and transport construction. Mangio became one of
the largest concerns in Japan as well as Manchuria, as witnessed by the
following figures on capitalization of the three largest Japanese corporations:

> Mangio . . . . 1963 million yen
> Mitsui . . . . 1822 million yen
> Mitsubishi . . . . . . 1463 million yen

Mangio gained control over the six most important Japanese companies in Manchuria: the Manchurian Coal Company, the Shiowa Steel
Foundries Company, the Manchurian Non-Ferrous Metals Company,
the Manchurian Coal Industry Company, the Dowa Auto Plant, and the
Manchurian Mining Company. Since all Manchuria's railroads and transportation enterprises, with the exception of the Chinese Domestic Railroad, already were controlled by the Japanese South Manchurian Railroad, Japanese monopolies obviously had taken over all industry and
transportation in northeastern China. To facilitate the penetration of
Japanese capital into Manchukuo, free circulation of the Japanese yen
was permitted on Manchurian territory. A new monetary unit also was
introduced, the gobi, which was valued at par with the yen. Somewhat
later, in February 1935, Japan concluded a customs agreement which
placed Japanese merchants in a privileged position not only in relation
to other foreigners but also to Manchukuo citizens.

The policy of imperial Japan toward Manchuria ruled out any independent development of Manchukuo or its conversion into a true
national state. Members of the Manchukuo "government" who were not
Japanese, including Emperor Pu Yi, were not even permitted to work.
As Pu Yi recalls: "I discovered that I was isolated in a hotel. What
particularly struck me was that they would not even permit us to come
down to the first floor."[21]

The Japanese government did not stop at insuring that basic production and transport were in Japanese hands and served Japan's needs.
It proceeded to link the Manchukuo economy and the Japanese economy indivisibly. This policy found expression first in the unification of
the railroads in Manchukuo and northern Korea in 1933. The South
Manchurian Railroad Company, which held control, represented the
interests of the most powerful Japanese concerns. Energy, mining and
other resources of Manchuria and Korea were also combined. In July
1935, an agreement was signed between Japan and Manchukuo forming
a joint economic commission. If necessary, the commission enjoyed the

right to "make recommendations to the governments of Japan and Manchukuo concerning all matters relating to the efficient coordination of the economies of the two countries."[22] The economic commission became the chief Japanese instrument for colonization of Manchuria. Without its approval, not a single commercial or industrial enterprise might function; the Manchukuo government was obliged to accept its recommendations without question.

Agriculture won a great deal of attention in Japanese plans for Manchurian colonization. At the time of occupation the Manchurian population amounted to some thirty million, of whom about eighty percent lived in the villages. Manchuria provided substantial quantities of China's agricultural exports, particularly soy beans, cotton-oil cakes and vegetable oils. Japan intended to convert Manchuria into its chief source of foodstuffs and agricultural raw materials. As Japanese armies won control of agricultural regions deep in Manchuria, the Japanese government instituted massive population resettlements, moving Japanese and Koreans, in particular, into the regions of Mu-tan-chiang, Harbin, Chang-chun and Tu-men. It was planned that Japanese colonists would form the population nucleus in agricultural districts. They manned what were termed state agricultural stations created by the Manchukuo government throughout Manchurian territory. Strict government control was established over agriculture. The peasants were obliged to cultivate only those crops designated by the government, and to deliver quotas of produce to state processing organizations at low official prices. The cruel colonization system created by Japanese occupational authorities in the agricultural sphere found official formulation in the government decision, published April 21, 1936, under the title "The Basis of Manchukuo Government Policy on Agricultural Development."

Having launched extensive colonization in Manchuria, Japan adopted an uncompromising stance in Sino-Japanese disputes before the League of Nations. Japan demanded that member governments of the League of Nations unconditionally recognize the independence of Manchukuo. Failing in this, Japan announced its resignation from the League of Nations on March 27, 1933. This move accorded Japan an opportunity to legalize its severance of Manchuria from China. On March 1, 1934, the Japanese occupiers proclaimed Pu Yi the "emperor" of Manchukuo, and changed the country's name from the Manchurian State to the Manchurian Empire, Manchutsikuo. This step was meant to signify the "salvation" of Manchuria from dependency on China and to confirm the "new state of Manchuria," which during its two years of existence

. . . "had strengthened mightily, and the well-being of the nation had greatly improved thanks to the patronage of Heaven and the concentrated exertions of the people, and thanks to brotherly cooperation with its friendly neighbor, the Japanese Empire."[23] Japanese diplomacy felt no need to conceal the fact that Manchukuo's independence meant, more correctly, its separation from China. This "independence" necessarily must be "supported" by Japan, the brotherly and friendly neighbor. In other words, the new state was maintained at Japanese bayonet-point. The conquest of Manchuria and its conversion into a subjugated colony under the banner of an "independent" national state completed the first stage of Japanese conquest in East Asia.

JAPAN IN NORTH CHINA AND INNER MONGOLIA

The next stage in Japan's aggressive plans was an advance into northern China and Inner Mongolia. Just as in Manchuria, Japanese government officials provoked incidents to justify this new aggression, creating chaos and anarchy. Next, they claimed the role of peacemaker and upholder of order. But in pursuing its established strategy for dismembering China, Japan now employed a different tactic than in Manchuria. The situation differed, for in the areas in question Japan had neither prepared bases nor previously billeted army units, as had been the case in Manchuria. Therefore the Japanese military leaders temporarily abandoned rapid military maneuvers.

After concentrating superior and much better equipped forces, the Japanese armies delivered a short but mighty blow and conquered important strategic points, which were converted into fortified bases. It was hoped that this move would demoralize the Chinese forces by demonstrating military superiority, and crush the Chinese people's will to resist. At the beginning of 1933 the Japanese took Shang-hai-huan, thereby gaining a mountain approach into north China. In the second half of February of the same year, they entered Jehol province in Inner Mongolia. As March began, meeting no significant resistance from Kuomintang forces, they conquered that province. Jehol province was made part of Manchukuo for the purpose of demonstrating Japanese assertions concerning the historical uniqueness and distinctness of both Manchuria and Mongolia in relation to China. Next, Japanese armies began the planned conquest of the mountain passes along the Great Wall of China, thereby threatening Peking and the Tientsin region.

Some Nanking army units and partisan detachments resisted the Japanese invaders heroically, but they received no support from the

Kuomintang authorities. Chiang Kai-shek considered the primary enemy to be the national liberation movement of the Chinese people, and therefore directed his main forces against the Soviet regions which had been formed in Fu-chien, Chiang-hsi, Ho-pei and Ho-nan provinces under the leadership of the Chinese Communist Party. When the Japanese began incursions south of the Great Wall of China in April 1933, the Nanking government instructed its armies to abandon these regions. On May 31, 1933, it entered a capitulation agreement with Japan known as the "Agreement in Tanku,"[24] the provisions of which demilitarized extensive territories in northwestern Ho-pei province. After signing the agree-ment, Japanese ruling circles labored to set up a puppet government in northern China called "Hoapeikuo" (The North China State), including the five provinces of Ho-pei, Chahar, Sui-yuan, Shan-tung and Shan-hsi. The concept of separating the northern Chinese provinces was expressed openly in a speech by the commander of Japanese forces in northern China, and was confirmed publicly by Japan's foreign minister, Hirota,[25] on October 7, 1935. With the help of its agents, the Japanese command unfolded a sweeping campaign for creation of an "independent Hoapei-kuo" which would establish an "alliance" with Manchukuo and Japan. Meeting stubborn resistance from patriotic Chinese forces, the Japanese militarists fell back in retreat. Japan was obliged to be content with the Nanking government's agreement to form an eastern anti-communist au-tonomous government and a Hopei-Chahar political council under Chi-nese control. The effect of the signing of the Agreement in Tanku was to sanction the Japanese occupation of Jehol. This acquisition allowed Japan to control the approaches to the province of Ho-pei, the location of northern China's capital, and to open the way to a complete conquest of Inner Mongolia.

The planning of the seizure of Inner Mongolia was carefully prepared by the Japanese long before the occupation of Manchuria. As was the case in Manchuria the Japanese thought to bribe and attract Mongolian princes by exploiting their feelings of national injury after years of Chi-nese feudal and commercial domination. The Japanese guardians of Pu Yi also deployed the "Chin emperor" to stimulate the anti-Chinese movement among the Mongolians. Recalling that time, Pu Yi writes: "I issued several 'imperial edicts' and sent two of my nephews, Hsian Yuan and Hsian Tsi, to the northeast, to bring certain Mongol princes to our side and make them obedient to Chang Hai-peng and Kui Fu, who were among the first to submit to Japanese occupation forces. At the demand of a Japanese officer, I signed letters to the resisting Ma Chiang-shan and some other patriotic Mongol princes, advising them to surrender."[26]

The principal puppets of Japan were the Mongol prince, Devan, and the Chinese militarist Li Shou-hsin, who had gone over to the service of Japan. Devan's campaign for Inner Mongolia's "autonomy" was crowned by the conference of Mongolian princes called in July 1933 in Pai-lien-miao. The conference demanded that the Nanking government grant autonomy to Inner Mongolia. At the second conference of Mongolian princes in October 1933, the "Organizational Law on Inner Mongolian Autonomy" was drafted and forwarded to the Nanking government. Nanking, continuing its policy of capitulation, on March 7, 1934, recognized the "autonomous" government of Inner Mongolia. In April 1934, Japan's *protégés* announced the creation of the Political Council of Inner Mongolia in Pai-lien-miao as a provisional government, thus laying the basis of the official political and administrative separation of Inner Mongolia from China. After establishing control in Inner Mongolia, the Japanese began to publicize the "national liberation movement" among other national minorities, principally the Moslem Dungans, Tanguts and Uighurs who inhabited the provinces of Shen-hsi, Kan-su, Ching Hai and Hsin-chiang.

Japanese military penetration into north China and Inner Mongolia created a real threat to the rest of China. Kuomintang policy, encouraged and supported by American and English imperialists, was calculated to appease the Japanese aggressors and to deflect them against the Soviet Union. It failed. The Japanese authorities feared a conflict with the Soviet Union at a moment when Japan was already deeply engaged in China. They understood that lengthy preparations would be needed for war against the Soviet Union and therefore assigned priority to further aggression against China. Japan also weighed the growth of the economic and military might of the USSR. Further, the peaceful and conscientious policies of the Soviet Union gave Japan no excuse for accelerated war preparations against the USSR. The sale of the Chinese Domestic Railroad by the Soviet Union in 1935 was eloquent proof of the firm Soviet decision to avoid a clash with Japan. This step put a definite end to anti-Soviet plans, which visualized the provoking of a confrontation, entertained by certain warlike factions in Japan. On the other hand, the firm Japanese commitment to pursue its aggressive intent south of the Great Wall of China evoked the anxiety of the United States and England for their interests in China. Japan made no secret of its wish to avoid restrictive international obligations.

The next move of the Japanese was to demand the renegotiation of the terms of the Washington Treaty relating to naval ratios. Talks began between Japan, England and the United States in London in June 1934, and continued until October. The impossibility of reaching agreement soon became evident; in December 1934 negotiations were broken off permanently. Simultaneously, Japan made clear to the United States and England that it did not intend to permit them advantages in central and southern China.

In Japan a decision was reached that the time had come to reveal its plans concerning China as a whole. The government would "clarify" to the United States and England its position that, given the prevailing circumstances of growing "Red danger" and continuing "internal chaos" in China, Japan was concerned for the fate of China as a whole. Consequently, it must play a "special" leading role in all the affairs of that country. On April 17, 1933, the Japanese Ministry of Foreign Affairs made the following declaration of its China policy.

1. Japan's position in China is determined by its "special responsibility in East Asia," and it "cannot agree in all cases with the policies of foreign states." "Japan is responsible for the maintenance of peace in East Asia."

2. Japan will "resist any attempt by China to employ the influence of any foreign state against Japan."

3. "Japan will resist the protection of China by foreign military aircraft, construction of airports on China's territory, assignment of foreign instructors and military advisors, or loans to China for political purposes which would clearly interfere with friendly Sino-Japanese relations or relations with other nations, and would lead to violations of peace and order in East Asia."[27]

In this manner Japan publicly decided the destiny of East Asia and declared its intention of disregarding Chinese sovereignty and the interests of Japan's competitors in China. Preparations for further aggression in China were accompanied by increased militarization and by fascist trends in the Japanese government. Monopoly capital endeavored to place the entire burden for the arms race and warmaking on the shoulders of the workers. Exploitation worsened and wages declined. Japan's limited raw materials were allocated chiefly for war production, while the output of consumer goods underwent a crisis and employment dropped in consumer industries. The situation in agriculture, particularly after the major crop failure of 1934, became extremely difficult.

The financial offensive met with resistance from Japanese workers. In 1935 the strike movement spread among city workers and the number of "lease conflicts" increased in the countryside. In autumn 1935, Japanese trade unions joined in a demonstration at elections for the district assemblies with the result that worker parties gained 39 deputies, while many other workers' candidates were elected in village districts. At parliamentary elections on February 10, 1936, the leftist parties succeeded in increasing their mandates. The inflating activity of Japanese workers disturbed the militarists, who demanded the total mobilization of all material and human resources for the realization of their ambitious plans for expansion abroad. On February 26, 1936, the most extreme militarists organized a fascist-military coup, intending to remove all "vacillators" from the government and army leadership. Disputes in the army, inspired by quarreling "old" and "new" factions, centered merely on the selection of methods of establishing a fascist dictatorship, for the army leaders agreed on the central principle that Japan should become "the great empire" and the ruler of East Asia. To accomplish this goal, all material and human resources of the country must be mobilized.

The Hirota government which took control after the putsch, supported by the "Tosei Ha" (Control Faction), prepared the "Basic Principles of National Policy" which turned Japan's development in the following directions:

1. The large-scale expansion of arms production and the equipment of the army with modern weaponry as insurance of Japan's "stabilizing force in East Asia."
2. Intensification of "Japan's national defense in Manchuria."
3. Comprehensive "reformation" within the country as a means of "creating suitable conditions for unifying public opinion, for rapid armament and acquisition of the resources and materials needed for war industry."[28]

With the purpose of "unifying public opinion" in Japan, a propaganda campaign emphasized the "exceptional and divine" Yamato race which was called to accomplish an historical mission in Asia. The Japanese were instilled with scorn for the Chinese, Koreans and other "inferior" Asian peoples, who must submissively recognize imperial Japan's right to rule them.

The unrestrained propaganda of Japanese racial supremacy, in combination with appeals for Samurai sacrifice and the elaboration of the "spirit of bushido,"[29] promoted chauvinism and prepared the way for collaboration with the fascist regimes of Hitler and Mussolini. In the sphere of foreign policy, the military dictatorship in Japan led initially to deterioration of relations with the Soviet Union, the supposed source of all social upheavals in Asia. The leaders of Japan calculated that the time was approaching for a clash with the Soviet Union. Preparations for war with the USSR thus occupied an important place in imperial Japan's foreign relations. Yet at the same time the Japanese recognized the serious consequences of such a clash. Even the successful outcome of such a war and conquest of Soviet coastal territories would not solve the problem of raw material sources for the Japanese economy, an essential factor for any further conquests. War with the USSR would emaciate Japan and it would be inconceivable that the United States and England would not take advantage of this. Cautious Japanese politicians felt that without dependable allies Japan dared not enter a large-scale war with the Soviet Union. In their view, under the prevailing circumstances it would be more productive to focus Japan's efforts towards the political isolation of the Soviet Union from China. An anti-Soviet ideological front should be created which, under certain conditions, would bring about an armed conflict of China with the USSR.

Japan could not count on effective support from the United States, England or France. Its policy in China had been directly opposed to their interests and sooner or later would have led to hostilities with them. More probable and ideologically more desirable for Japan would be an alliance with fascist Germany. Hitler's Germany, which had concentrated its full efforts on preparation for war and establishment of its rule in Europe, entertained no serious interests in East Asia. Japanese aggression in Manchuria and China involved the USSR, England, France and the United States, and distracted the attention of these powers away from Europe. Consequently it gained the undisguised sympathy of fascist Germany.

Japan's expectations were equally great. Tokyo's rulers were convinced that fascism would lead inexorably to war in Europe. Consequently, as had happened during World War I, Japan would gain a free hand in the Far East. Japanese politicians believed an alliance with fascist Germany would be of particular importance in determining Germany's policy concerning the USSR. The character of Japan's policy toward Germany was influenced also by the stance of England, the United States and other Western nations. Their notorious "policy of appeasement" was calculated to turn fascist aggression against the Soviet Union, to destroy the Soviet government and through such a conflict to weaken their imperialist rivals in Europe and the Far East. This would permit these powers to establish their undivided supremacy in those areas of the world. A rapprochement with Germany, Japan hoped, would end its international isolation which had begun when Tokyo left the League of Nations. The predictable outcome of the political and ideological friendship of Japan and Germany was the Anti-Comintern Pact which they signed on November 25, 1936.[30] Japan accorded this agreement great significance and did not conceal its anti-Soviet intent. A session of the privy council was devoted to the conclusion of the pact, at which Foreign Minister Arita stated: "Henceforward, Soviet Russia must take into account the fact that it will be obliged to come face to face with Germany and Japan."[31]

The nature of the struggle between the imperial powers was such that the pact between Japan and Germany intensified the anti-American and anti-English impulse of Japanese foreign policy. That circumstance particularly disturbed pro-English and pro-American Japanese leaders, who still hoped to deal with the United States and England at the expense of China. The conclusion of the German-Japanese pact was preceded by stormy discussion and dissension, the lack of decision exerting a considerable impact on the entire preparatory period for war in the Pacific, until the Japanese imperialists agreed on aggression in a southerly direction to strengthen Japan's position for a coming conflict with the Soviet Union.

With the promise of German support, Japan set out to isolate the Soviet Union in the Far East. After completing the occupation of Manchuria and forming puppet regimes in northern China and Inner Mongolia, Japan attempted to attack the Mongolian Peoples Republic. Relations between the Soviet Union and the Mongolian Peoples Republic, based on equality, independence and mutual assistance, constituted a new form of relationship between large and small nations in different stages of social development. This relationship had rescued the Mongolian people forever from the threat of enslavement and forced assimilation by reactionary China and imperial Japan. The Mongolian example demonstrated that even small backward nations, with the aid of international socialist powers, could achieve national and social liberation and successful socialist development. Therefore, during the late 1930s the Japanese assigned to the battle against the Mongolian Republic, and Soviet political and cultural influence in that country, a prominent place as an important political and military objective. They attempted to capture territories of the Mongolian Peoples Republic and then the northwestern provinces of China (Kan-su, Ching Hai and Hsin-chiang), populated by Dungans, Uighurs, and Kazakhs. For several years Japanese agents there had engaged in diversionary and subversive activities. This policy foresaw the creation by imperial Japan of buffer "independent national" states bordering the Soviet Union, useful against the Soviet Union as well as China. A chain of such satellites, calculated Japanese strategists, would create a barrier against the USSR and isolate it from China. This concept formed part of the general strategic plan of overwhelming China piecemeal by carving it into pro-Japanese states.

After organizing border incidents near Lake Buir Nor (in the Halhin-miao region), the Japanese demanded that Mongolia open its borders to Japanese subjects and grant Japan the right to station representatives there. On July 4, 1935, the Japanese command delivered an ultimatum to the Mongolian delegation sent to discuss the border dispute. It included the admission of Japanese "military advisors" and permission for extension of Japanese military telegraph lines "for better communications with Japan and Manchukuo." When the Mongolian government refused these brash demands, the Japanese multiplied border provocations, leading in the spring of 1935 to a clash between Mongolian border troops and Japanese forces in Manchuria. The Soviet Union could not remain disinterested in these incidents, and sent a stern warning to the Japanese government. On March 12, 1936, the USSR signed a protocol with the Mongolian Republic obligating both countries to offer each other various assistance, including arms. The firm position of the Soviet government had its effect. Japanese leaders were not yet willing to start a major war with the Soviet Union. Even the militant Kuan-tung Army command, quartered in Manchuria, preferred a campaign against China. These circumstances compelled Japan to turn away from the Mongolian Peoples Republic. Japan proved unable to isolate the Soviet Union from China and excise its revolutionary influence in East Asia. Such a major defeat of Japanese aggression exerted a decisive influence on the outcome of the struggle that was to follow.

JAPAN'S ADVANCE INTO CHINA AND THE SINO-JAPANESE WAR

With the decision made to continue the advance into China, the rulers of Japan began preparations by 1) consolidating Japan's domestic forces and mustering army contingents to invade the Chinese interior; 2) weakening the Anglo-American position in China while preserving direct economic ties, important for Japan's military preparations; and 3) undermining Chinese morale by shows of armed strength and terror, subversion of the ruling Kuomintang group and creation of separatist puppet regimes. Immediately prior to the invasion, a cabinet change took place in Japan. On March 31, 1937, the Hayashi cabinet[32] failed to gain support in the elections, and formation of a new cabinet was entrusted to Prince Konoe Fumimaro.[33] Japan's rulers thought that Prince Konoe, a flexible and experienced diplomat, would be able to unite rival groups in the country and combat growing foreign resistance to Japanese aggression. In Manchuria, Korea and several northern regions of China, Japanese armed forces continued to assemble. They had been brought to battle readiness and awaited only a suitable incident. A month after the formation of the Konoe cabinet, in the night of July 7-8, 1937, this incident occurred in Lu-kou-chiao (at the Marco Polo bridge), giving Japan a pretext to move supplementary military contingents into northern China.

Twenty days later, on July 27, Japanese armies began a broad advance which signalled the beginning of the prolonged, eight-year Sino-Japanese War. Using to advantage concessions made by the Kuomintang government and by the United States, England and France, which still hoped to localize Japanese aggression, Japan's armies took Shang-hai in November. By the end of 1937 they had captured Nanking and the capitals of Chahar, Ho-pei, Sui-yuan, Shan-hsi, Che-chiang and Shan-tung provinces. Meanwhile the Japanese navy blockaded the sea coast.

Early successes did not blind the Japanese to the difficulties which awaited them. The taking of Shang-hai, Tientsin and other cities threatened to cause a clash with the United States and England too soon. Therefore Japanese diplomacy continued to veil Japan's real aims, trying to deny its territorial ambitions in central and southern China and insisting that Japan would respect the rights and interests of foreign powers in China. Meanwhile, Japan continued to build its military forces in occupied territories and pre-empted preferences in customs, currency and other spheres of the Chinese economy. The governments of the United States and England delayed breaking relations with Japan, although they could not fail to see the real threats to their interests in China. They limited themselves to "condemning" Japanese aggression, still hoping that an economically weak Japan would remain dependent on Anglo-American capital and would at some point be forced to turn to its old creditors for help. Thereupon it would be possible to restrict Japan while assigning to it the role of "preserver of order" in China. The provocative Anglo-American policies stood revealed clearly at the Brussels conference,[34] where the United States and Britain continued to encourage Japanese aggression and push Japan into war with the USSR while they functioned as the "chief commissariat" of the Japanese army.

American and English neutrality in the Sino-Japanese War, which they termed an "incident," created a certain balance in the relations between these countries. This did not mean that Japan's leaders really wished a compromise and would abandon their chief strategic purpose of expelling the Western nations and establishing Japan's undivided hegemony in China. Japanese occupation forces utilized all possible means to discredit American and English policy, attempting to direct the anti-imperialist movement among the Chinese people against "white imperialism." Thus the force and merciless terror employed by the Japanese in occupied territories were characterized in Japanese propaganda as Samurai heroism and sacrifice in the name of establishing "legality" and "order" in China. The popular democratic movement in China, a "communist danger" and a "threat to the system of private property," was caused by American and English incompetence in managing their affairs in China, and their lack of understanding of the "spirit of the peoples of Asia."

The standard-bearer of the Asiatic "order" was to become Manchukuo, created at the point of Japanese bayonets. In early November 1937, the Japanese announced the conclusion of peace between Japan and Manchukuo, on terms which included Japan's "denial" of extraterritorial rights received in old treaties with China. Manchukuo acquired all administrative rights, including those in the zones of the South Manchurian Railroad. The Japanese publicized this treaty as a document of "great principial significance," supposedly restoring the sovereignty of an Asian state. The treaty stated that Manchukuo would "introduce improvements in lawmaking and various government functions" which would "completely do away with the right of extraterritoriality." This, claimed the Japanese, should serve as unquestionable proof of the superiority of the "order" they had established. Japan's "denial" of extraterritoriality moderated the anti-Japanese mood of the Chinese bourgeoisie and turned them against the United States and England, who were continuing to enjoy special advantages.

These developments generated resistance among the Chinese. The aroused patriotism of the Chinese compelled Chiang Kai-shek to meet the demands of the Chinese Communist Party for a united popular front against the Japanese. As it overcame factionalism and left deviations in the early 1930s, the Chinese Communist Party stubbornly worked for a unified effort to counter Japanese aggression and to create international solidarity in the struggle against fascism and war. In August 1935, the Party central committee published "an appeal to the people for resistance to the Japanese and salvation of the homeland." It called for an end to the civil war in order to mobilize the country's entire strength for the sacred cause of resisting Japan. Human reserves, military and financial resources as well as the armed forces, were needed. The Communist Party of China expressed willingness to enter into negotiations on the question of a government including all parties, groups, political and military figures who "wished to take part in the cause of resisting Japan and saving the homeland."[35] This resolution assessed the Chinese political situation and defined the party's tasks:

> The chief feature of the current situation is that Japanese imperialism, after seizing the four northeastern provinces of China, has set out to seize north China, and then to occupy all of China and change it from a semi-colony of various imperialist states into (Japan's) private colony. In the counter-revolutionary camp, indecision and factionalism have increased. A part of the national bourgeoisie, many prosperous peasants, small landlords and even some militarists adopt a position of benevolent neutrality. They even take part in the national movement now beginning. The popular revolutionary front has expanded.[36]

The appeals of the Communist Party of China found broad support. Even among the Kuomintang leadership voices began to join the communists' plea for a united anti-Japanese national front. At the fifth session of the Kuomintang in November 1935 a number of important leaders (Sun Ching-ling, Fen Yu-hsiang, and others) demanded the consolidation of national forces for the struggle with the Japanese intervention. In June 1936 a conference of students and social organizations was called. There the All-Chinese Association of National Salvation was formed. Nevertheless, Chiang Kai-shek continued to avoid cooperation with the communists. He attempted a major new assault on the Chinese Red Army and on the Kuomintang generals in the north Chang Hsueh-liang and Yen Hsi-shan, who supported a united front. Chiang Kai-shek's attack provoked great dissatisfaction even among his own Kuomintang leadership, and led to the Sian incident, as it was called, when Chang Hsueh-liang and Yen Hsi-shan arrested Chiang Kai-shek.

The danger arose of a new flare-up in the civil war, which would undoubtedly benefit Japan. At this critical juncture in Chinese history, the communists overcame the vacillation caused by factionalization (of Mao Tse-tung and others), whereupon the Party central committee called for a "peaceful solution to the Sian incident." Chiang Kai-shek's group, under broad public pressure, discontinued the civil war which had waged since 1927. In April 1937 the Kuomintang leadership sent a delegation to Yen-an, headed by Chang Chiu-nem, for negotiations with the communists, the first step toward a peaceful solution of the problems stirred by the Japanese invasion. Unofficially, the Kuomintang representatives agreed to halt combat operations in regions held by the Chinese Red Army and to end demands for that army's dissolution. In turn the Chinese Communist Party representatives agreed to abolish the Central Workers and Peasants Government, and also to consider the Red Army as a component part of the National Revolutionary Army, abolishing the very name "Red Army." Collaboration between the communists and the Kuomintang was to be based on the "three popular principles" of Sun Yat-sen, which both groups had accepted in 1924.

On the basis of these preliminary accords, a meeting was held between communist and Kuomintang representatives at Lo-shan in August, 1937. They agreed on legal status for the governments of the border provinces of Shen-hsi, Kan-su and Ning-hsia, and on transformation of the Red Army into the Eighth National Army of China, commanded by Chu Teh and his deputy Peng Teh-huai. The official agreement was confirmed by a resolution published by the Chun-yang agency on September 22, 1937, laying the foundation for a united national front.[37]

The end of the civil war and formation of a united front created a new situation in China. The populace demanded that Chiang Kai-shek promise "to seek cooperation between the countries which sympathize with China's struggles against Japan." This meant, primarily, the Soviet Union. Even during the first negotiations the government of the USSR had signed a "non-aggression pact" with the national government of China (on August 21, 1937),[38] wherein both nations rejected war as an instrument of national policy. The Sino-Soviet treaty of non-aggression was recognized by the Chinese public to be of enormous moral support at a moment of greatest tribulation. The Soviet and Chinese governments now began negotiations on military and financial aid to China.

Subsequently the Soviet Union granted China two loans in 1938 of fifty million dollars each and one in 1939 of 150 million dollars. They included credits for arms, vehicles, fuel and various materials and supplies. Soviet military deliveries to the northern regions of Indochina, occupied by the Japanese, were accomplished through the Vietnamese port of Haiphong, then via the railway to Yun-nan province. Beginning July 6, 1940, all deliveries went through Hsin-chiang province along a highway stretching for 3,500 kilometers from the Soviet Central Asian border to the city of Lan-chou. To help the Chinese master aircraft, tank and artillery technology, the Soviet Union sent instructors and advisors. Not only did they instruct Chinese officers, they participated directly in military operations against the Japanese invaders at Wu-han,

Chungking and in other regions of China. At Kuldja in Hsin-chiang province an aviation school was organized where Soviet specialists trained Chinese flight crews. Near the city of Urumchi an aircraft assembly plant was built with Soviet aid; the Soviet Union supplied all necessary airplane parts, machinery, and materials.

Soviet aid secured China's defense capability and made possible the consolidation of Chinese national forces for the struggle with Japan. It also strengthened the position of the Chinese Communist Party. On July 1, 1938, a national political council was attached to the nationalist government of China, which included a number of communist members such as Tun Pi-wu, Wang Ming, Mao Tse-tung, and Lin Tsu-han. The Chinese Communist Party highly appreciated Soviet assistance in those difficult years.

JAPANESE POLICY IN THE CHINA WAR

The situation in the Far East at the beginning of 1938 revealed the frustration of Japanese calculations for a lightning victory. The war in China had become a war of attrition which demanded further militarization of the Japanese economy. In March 1938, the Japanese parliament passed a law "On the General Mobilization of the Nation." It provided for complete control of industry and permitted the Japanese government to spend two thirds of the national budget on war needs.

In 1938 Japan expanded its anti-Soviet policies. The increased resistance of the Chinese and Japan's waxing international isolation were blamed on the Soviet Union. Accordingly the Japanese government proclaimed its "resolution to fight China and the Soviet Union to the finish." The circumstances of the time seemed to "be moving rapidly toward war with the Soviet Union." The main goal of Japanese politicians became that of forcing the Soviet Union out of the Far East and isolating it from the peoples of East Asia. In the battle with the USSR, Japanese ruling circles counted on the support of their Western partners in the anti-communist pact. For this purpose, during the first half of 1938, Japan, Germany and Italy initiated new talks for strengthening the "Anti-Comintern Pact." In March 1939, the Hiranuma cabinet[39] proposed a military alliance with Germany against the USSR. Convinced of inevitable war between fascist Germany and the Soviet Union, Japanese leaders believed that even limited military actions against the USSR in the Far East would hasten a German attack on the Soviet Union.

With this hope the Japanese decided to invade the southern coastal territory of the Soviet Union. At the end of July 1938 the Japanese government, acting in the name of Manchukuo, presented an ultimatum for surrender of the heights at Zaozernoe (Beyond the Lake), near Lake Hasan, and threatened military action should there be a refusal. On receipt of a well-documented refusal, the Japanese attempted to take the strategically important territory by force of arms on July 31, 1938. This first armed provocation was intended by the militarists in Tokyo to force the Soviet government to yield a vitally important concession, one which would open the way to greater conquests. The crushing resistance of the Soviet forces encountered by the Japanese at Lake Hasan forced the latter to retreat temporarily and to request "a peaceful solution to the conflict."

Notwithstanding this lesson, the Japanese government did not alter its anti-Soviet policies. On Manchurian territory they quickly built strong fortifications directed against Vladivostok, Nikolsk-Ussurisk, Khabarovsk, Blagoveshschensk and Chita. New strategic railroads were built from Tsitsikar to Kei-ho, Mu-tan-chiang to Chia-mu-ssu and elsewhere. Along the Soviet-Manchurian borders strong contingents of Japanese troops were deployed and other measures adopted in preparation for large-scale aggression against the Soviet Union. A new attempt to test Soviet war readiness followed in May, 1939, with the goal of driving through the Mongolian Peoples Republic to separate the Soviet Far East from Siberia. Between May and September 1939, along the Khalkhyn-Gol river which separates the Mongolian People's Republic from Manchuria, Soviet and Mongolian troops fought the Japanese in fierce battles, encircled the Japanese Sixth Army and destroyed it. The defeat at the Khalkhyn-Gol had far-reaching consequences. The Japanese general staff grew convinced that it had overestimated its war readiness and the military hardware of its army. War with the Soviet Union proved much more dangerous than previously supposed. Further, the Japanese government was compelled to assess the conduct of its allies in the Anti-Comintern Pact. Germany was not inclined to subordinate its plans for the conduct of war. Not yet ready to attack the USSR, Germany wanted Japan to commence military operations against the United States and the western European nations.

In influential Japanese quarters, as a consequence, the opponents of aggression against the Soviet Union gained the upper hand. They argued that war with the USSR would be very risky for Japan without the active support of its allies, that is, a German attack on the Soviet Union from the west. Otherwise, Japanese military forces would be expended dangerously, risking the collapse of already shaky positions in China. The general plan of achieving mastery of East and Southeastern Asia was shelved indefinitely.

THE "GREAT EAST ASIAN CO-PROSPERITY SPHERE"

The war begun by Hitler in western Europe meant a weakening of the British, French and then the United States' position in China and other Far Eastern countries. Japanese imperial quarters hoped with good cause that German aggression would not bypass the Soviet Union and that the USSR thereby would be neutralized in the Far East and rendered incapable of interfering with Japanese plans there. Japan took advantage of domestic Chinese difficulties, exacerbated by the Kuomintang attack on the liberated regions late in 1939. These areas had been controlled by the communist Eighth and Fourth armies. With control established over the most important industrial centers and ports in China, the Japanese occupation forces in effect stopped military operations against the Kuomintang, which throughout had offered no serious resistance. Instead, the Japanese began to seek a compromise, meanwhile turning their efforts to their main strategic goal, the creation of a "Great East Asian Co-Prosperity Sphere." Beginning late in 1939 the Japanese government publicly advertised this program, making no haste prematurely to set the boundaries of this sphere, although diplomatic and military experience demonstrated clearly enough that Japan would not be content with Manchukuo and China. A shift in Japanese aggression in the direction of Southeast Asia was under way. In negotiations with its European allies the Japanese government won agreement for its ambitions. Article 2 of the Triple Alliance Pact of September 27, 1939 stated: "Germany and Italy recognize and respect Japanese leadership in the creation of a new order in the Great East Asian domain."[40] In their effort to create "a sphere of co-prosperity," Japanese leaders needed to offer some general concept of the proposed union by way of demonstrating East Asia's unity of purpose. This common purpose was declared to be the struggle against communism and "white imperialism." The Japanese rulers considered everyone a communist who, in resisting Japanese aggression, had collaborated with the Soviet Union or who had supported the anti-Japanese national front. Japanese propaganda in China urged the overthrow of the Chungking government, which still included a nucleus of implacable foes of Japan, and the strengthening of the puppet regimes.

In March 1940, the Japanese authorities formed a "government" in Nanking led by Wang Ching-wei as the "executor of the duties of president." His assignment was to work for the capitulation of the nationalist government. As the decree of the Imperial Japanese Conference stated in November 1940: "Japan should enable the Chinese side to take measures on its own initiative for the purpose of developing cooperation between Nanking and Chungking; the imperial government should offer indirect help in that direction."[41] To create the appearance of "independence" of the Wang Ching-wei government and represent it as a "truly national" institution to the Chinese people, the Japanese occupation authorities granted apparent concessions to China. They also showed "friendly understanding" for the aspirations of the Chinese for liberation from demeaning inequitable treaties forced upon China by "white imperialism." On November 30, 1940, the Japanese government signed in Nanking with the Wang Ching-wei government a "Mutual Assistance Treaty Between Japan and the Chinese Republic." Under the banner of "mutual defense against communism," Japan received the right to maintain its armies in China "for the amount of time necessary for the joint preservation of social calm" (Article 4), to "deploy naval forces for the necessary period" (Article 5), and to "enjoy the privileges of working mines and in commerce" (Article 6).

After Japan was accorded the right to occupation and control of the resources of China, the earlier inequitable treaties no longer possessed any meaning whatsoever. Even more, Japan was interested in the annulment of those treaties in order to remove the legal basis of the special privileges enjoyed by its foreign rivals. These considerations caused Japan to include in the treaty with the regime of Wang Ching-wei a provision (Article 7) which stipulated: "In the interests of developing new relations between Japan and China, and based on the present treaty, the government of Japan repudiates the right of extraterritoriality which it had enjoyed in the Chinese Republic, and returns its settlements to the Chinese government. The government of the Chinese Republic opens its territory for the sojourns and economic activities of Japanese subjects."[42]

Japan placed England and the United States in a disadvantageous position through this action, for these Western nations upheld their extraterritorial rights as granted by previous treaties. However the real privileges of the Japanese occupation authorities were incomparably greater. Japanese monopolies became the masters of occupied Chinese territory. They acquired Chinese enterprises and certain equipment at low prices, with the aid of the occupation forces, and created branches of their own concerns under the guise of mixed Sino-Japanese companies.

"The North China Development Company" had operated since 1938. It controlled transportation, port installations, communications, production and distribution of electrical power, mining industries, all salt transactions, and other branches of industry. Japanese economic control in north China was supplemented by the operations of the federated bank created by Japanese occupation authorities. The federated bank enjoyed the right to issue banknotes called *fabi*, which replaced the Chinese and foreign currency previously in circulation. These measures separated north China from other regions of the country and promoted the steady dismemberment of China by imperial Japan.

In central China, the Japanese "created conditions" for the formation of a mixed Sino-Japanese "Company for the Development of Central China," with the same total control of that region's economy. By 1941 the Japanese monopolies controlled many branches of industry in occupied China. However, the largest enterprises continued to be the property of England, the United States, France and other Western countries. Japan still delayed the direct expropriation of European capital assets for several reasons. Following the repudiation of the Japanese-American trade treaty on July 27, 1939, the U.S. government declared a "moral embargo" on export of strategic materials to Japan. Even so, Anglo-American firms in China (factories and trade companies) remained a legal channel for supplying the Japanese occupation forces with provisions, oil products, vehicles and other strategic materials. Japan gained advantages in return for allowing the operation of Anglo-American companies in occupied areas, a temporary policy in the Japanese view. Meanwhile Japan made preparations for a decisive clash with its rivals in furtherance of its goal of establishing unchallenged hegemony in East Asia.

In the looming battle with the United States and England, Japanese leaders still hoped to utilize the Chinese nationalists. With this in mind, in 1941 they launched a broad campaign calling for an end to extraterritorial rights, renunciation of foreign concessions and settlements, and other inequitable privileges. The campaign was "against the white race" in "defense" of the yellow race. It is impossible to deny that this racist propaganda had an effect among the influential levels of Chinese society and their representatives in the nationalist government, who feared the growing influence of the Chinese Communist Party. Assisted by Japanese agents, the nationalists began to speak of the possibility of a mighty Asian empire which would fortify national independence while preserving capitalist and feudal relationships.

The racist and defeatist tendencies among certain segments of the Kuomintang leadership flowered as Japan easily and with impunity escalated its aggression in the direction of Southeast Asia. The Chinese became convinced of the viability of the "Great East Asian Co-Prosperity

Sphere" thanks to the successful landing of Japanese forces in northern Indochina. Japan's press toward the south seas spawned hope in the Chinese nationalists that the Japanese army and Japanese capital would be spread more thinly and that the Japanese occupation of China would be softened. This mood among Chinese reactionaries was reflected in the theory of "a curved line for saving the homeland," which found many adherents in the territory held by the Kuomintang. In 1941 many units of the Kuomintang army switched to the side of the puppet regimes. This trend continued in subsequent years and resulted in the replenishment of the puppet forces at the expense of the Kuomintang. The latter ceased to resist the Japanese in favor of accelerated operations against the Eighth and Fourth (communist-dominated) armies.

At this point a schism developed in the anti-Japanese nationalist front, occurring at a time of peaceful interlude on the battlefronts held by Kuomintang armies. Meanwhile the Soviet Union was experiencing difficulties in the first months after the treacherous attack by Hitler's Germany. These factors allowed the Japanese command to concentrate powerful forces against north China. They unleashed an attack on the liberated regions of Shan-hsi, Chahar and Ho-pei, accompanied by cruel reprisals on the peaceful populace. The Japanese militarists calculated that with the help of terror they might undermine China's will to resist and discourage a growing communist military activity. Thus demonstrating their solidarity with the Kuomintang in the anti-communist battle, the Japanese believed that Chiang Kai-shek's government would be swayed in the direction of capitulation based on Konoe's "three principles."

Although the Chinese resisted heroically and won some victories over the Japanese occupiers, the conditions of the moment did not favor lasting success. The nationalist Chinese armed forces, with better weapons and with a developed command system, halted its participation in the struggle against the Japanese, allowing the war to assume a difficult and protracted character. With limited forces imperial Japan was able to occupy the most important regions of China. The elite and best equipped forces of the Japanese army, numbering as many as a million men, remained in reserve positions oriented against the Soviet Far East. Only strong regular armies with modern military equipment and technology might withstand them. China needed a dependable and strong ally. The United States and Britain, though seriously affected by the Japanese occupation, continued to maneuver. Their opposition to Japan was limited to political declarations and ineffective commercial restrictions such as blocking of Japanese funds and the like.

At the same time the American and English leadership did not lose hope that they might maneuver Japanese aggression against the Soviet Union. The German attack on the Soviet Union encouraged them, and they were prepared to compromise with Japan, particularly at China's expense. The Japanese-American talks which began in February 1941 were largely devoted to bargaining over China. On May 13, 1941, Japan presented the following ultimatum to the United States: recognize Manchukuo; refrain from supporting the government of Chiang Kai-shek; develop a common policy for "the battle against communism"; grant Japan unlimited rights to necessary strategic raw materials in the southwestern Pacific Ocean; restore mutual trade; and recognize the principle of Philippine "independence." On May 16, 1941, Secretary of State Cordell Hull replied to the Japanese Ambassador Nomura.[43] He expressed his thinking on the possibility of accepting the three principles proposed by Konoe "with certain corrections." The official American answer of June 21 rejected Japan's continued occupation of China and designs for economic advantages in China and the western Pacific. On the other hand, the United States government expressed its willingness to discuss the proposal concerning "mutual defense against communism." The remainder of the Japanese-American negotiations in October and November, 1941, confirm that the United States along with England displayed no interest in halting Japanese aggression in China until the very onset of war in the Pacific Ocean. Although it formally demanded Japanese withdrawal from China, the plan which Secretary Hull presented to the Japanese on November 26, when the Japanese fleet was already steaming toward Pearl Harbor, contained no provisions for the defense of China.

This English and American position served merely to encourage Japan. Imperial circles in Japan considered their preparations sufficiently advanced, and the situation completely favorable, for asserting their leadership in East Asia by force of arms. In deep secrecy from the Japanese people and international observers, a conference of Japan's highest political and military leaders took place in Tokyo on September 6. In the presence of the emperor, the decision was made to begin war against the United States, England and the Netherlands. On October 18, 1941, a new cabinet took over, representing the most militant fascist group and headed by General Tojo.[44] Japanese armed forces were concentrated at staging points for a decisive confrontation with Nippon's chief imperial rivals, the United States and England. The victory won by the Japanese armed forces inexorably led to the complete enslavement of China.

SUMMARY

At the outset of the 1930s imperial Japan began systematically to carry out its program of conquest in East Asia. The central focus of this program was China, the largest neighboring Asian country and the richest in material resources. In the minds of Japanese strategists, gaining control of China would guarantee Japan's leading role in East Asia. Japanese ruling quarters recognized the difficulties posed by their plans. In China they would meet the resistance of millions of Chinese who were already struggling for national and social liberation. They would also meet opposition from imperial rivals, primarily the United States and Britain, which had major interests in China. They were equally wary of the Soviet Union, which exercised a growing revolutionizing influence in the East, both in China and in Japan itself. The successful industrialization of the Soviet economy was transforming the USSR into a modern, powerful state. Under these circumstances, the Japanese government was impelled to conduct a multifaceted policy in order to avoid unifying its opponents into a single front.

Japanese policy toward China was constructed with consideration of national animosities and anti-Chinese sentiments among national minorities in China (Manchurians, Mongolians, Uighurs, Tibetans, and others). These peoples had suffered centuries of oppression by Chinese feudal lords, merchants and moneylenders. Starting with the conquest of Manchuria, Japan propagated the slogan of protecting the Manchurians, Koreans, and Mongols from Chinese military despotism, "which had thrown the country into prolonged chaos." Under the pretext of "self-determination" and with acquiescence of other imperial powers and the Kuomintang, Japan quite easily overran Manchuria and Inner Mongolia. These were separated from China as "independent" Manchukuo and Autonomous Mongolia. During preparations for penetration into central China, anti-Soviet sentiments began to prevail among Japanese leaders. These feelings originated in the assumption of inevitable war with the Soviet Union, since it would be impossible to establish Japanese rule in East Asia so long as a Soviet presence existed there. Influential Japanese military leaders pushed Japan toward war with the USSR as a primary precondition of success in the entire East Asian program of conquest. The Japanese setback at Lake Hasan and in the attempt to invade the Mongolian People's Republic compelled its rulers to postpone their anti-Soviet plans temporarily and limit their efforts to isolate China from the Soviet Union. The anti-communist impulse of Japanese policy was shared by the major imperial powers. They were ready to grant Japan the role of "keeper of order in Asia" and even to aid Japan in becoming the principal anti-Soviet, anti-communist force in the Far East, at the price of appeasement and recognition of Japan's "special interests." This American and English attitude provided to Japan the opportunity, at the end of 1938, to seize all the important industrial and rail communications centers of China.

In these difficult conditions for China, the Soviet Union provided military, material and technical assistance. This had a decisive role in bolstering the anti-Japanese popular front in China, and in establishing the leading position of the Chinese Communist Party in containing Japanese aggression. As a result of Western encouragement of Japanese aggression and the capitulation of the leaders of the Kuomintang right, Japan achieved various successes in undermining the anti-Japanese national front. Japan then turned to the creation of "a sphere of co-prosperity of East Asia," founded on the alliance of the three states of Japan, China and Manchukuo, led by Japan.

The unfolding war in Europe created favorable circumstances in the Far East for realization of imperial Japan's aggressive program. Under the demagogic slogan of battle "against white imperialism" and shelter against "the communist threat," Japanese imperial circles developed a broad political campaign in 1939-1941. Supported by military measures, it sought an alliance of East Asian nations based on racial foundations. With the aid of the puppet regimes in China and neighboring countries, Japanese occupation authorities attempted to attract the peoples of those countries to their side as they asserted Japanese imperial supremacy. These policies would result in the concept of the "Sphere of East Asian Co-Prosperity." As the decade of the 1940s opened, a real threat of enslavement by Japanese imperialism hung over China.

CHAPTER SIX

The War in the Pacific, 1941-1945

ORIGINS AND JAPAN'S SUCCESSES

In the spring of 1941 important talks took place between the "Axis" powers of Germany, Japan, and Italy. Preparing for the attack on the Soviet Union, Hitler's Germany urged wider Japanese operations in the Far East. In a directive to the German armed forces, Hitler declared: "The aim of collaboration in the Triple Alliance is to draw Japan as quickly as possible into active steps in the Far East. This will attract powerful English forces there and shift the center of gravity of United States' interests to the Pacific. The sooner Japan intervenes, the better will be the prospects for success, given the lack of preparedness of her rivals. Operations according to "Barbarossa" will create favorable political and military conditions for Japan."[1] During the visit of Japanese Foreign Minister Matsuoka Yosuke to Berlin in March and April, 1941, Hitler and Ribbentrop informed him of the impending attack on the Soviet Union. They demanded that Japan expand warfare in the Far East to include the USSR as well as the United States and England.

Japanese leaders did not wish to follow Hitler's will blindly, recalling that at the time of the "Khalkhyn-Gol incident"[2] Hitler had not been especially faithful to the "spirit of the Axis." While not rejecting the idea of an inevitable conflict with the Soviet Union, the Japanese government for the moment did not hasten to complicate relations with the USSR. Japan considered it more to the point to neutralize this opponent temporarily. On April 13, 1941, Japan signed a pact of neutrality with the USSR, thereby demonstrating to Hitler that national, not allied interests came first.[3] The essence of Japanese foreign policy as concerned the USSR was revealed starkly by the resolution of the secret conference of Japanese military and political leaders of July 2, ten days after Hitler's attack on the USSR: "Although our relationship to the Soviet-German war is determined by the spirit of the Rome-Berlin-Tokyo axis, nevertheless for a certain period we will not interfere in it, but will begin secret arming for war against the Soviet Union on our own initiative. During this time we will continue diplomatic talks with great precautions. Should the Soviet-German war take a favorable turn for Japan, we will apply force for the solution of the northern problems, thereby assuring a stable situation in the northern regions."[4]

While continuing to prepare for war with the Soviet Union, Japan concentrated on completing preparations against the United States and Britain. The military clique headed by General Tojo Hideki, which took over the government on October 18, 1941, finally set the time for the start of the war. By November 1, Military Operational Plan No. 1 was formulated for the attack on American, English and Dutch naval and air bases in the Pacific theater. In deepest secrecy, under cover of a diplomatic diversion,[5] Japanese naval forces began gathering on their targets. Japan employed its favorite tactic of surprise attack on an opponent without declaring war. Japanese aircraft carriers, which stealthily approached the Hawaiian islands, on the night of December 7 launched 50 bombers, 40 torpedo planes and 81 dive bombers for a sudden blow on the American base at Pearl Harbor. Eight ships of the line were taken out of commission (of which four sank), along with three cruisers, three squadron minelayers, and other ships. An attack was also made on the British fleet in the south seas, resulting in the sinking of two of the largest English naval vessels, the battleships "Prince of Wales" and "Repulse."

The launching of Japanese military operations in the Pacific was coordinated with the approach of German armies to Moscow. It was believed that after the fall of Moscow, fascist Germany would be able to tie down large British and American forces in Europe, thereby weakening these powers in the Pacific theater of operations. Germany quickly declared war on the United States; on December 11, 1941, the Tripartite Pact was signed between Italy, Germany, and Japan for combined war against the United States and England.[6]

The American and British high commands knew as early as July that the Japanese command had begun to concentrate forces for a mighty strike after taking southern Indochina. Nonetheless, Japan's first attacks in the Pacific revealed the lack of preparation of these powers for a large-scale conflict there. As a result, within a short time the Japanese armed forces overran strategic Western bases and sources of raw materials (oil, rubber, lead) and provisions (rice, vegetable oil, and others). Within six months the Philippines, French Indochina, Thailand, Burma, Malaya, and Indonesia were taken. Together with the occupied parts of China, Japanese conquests now totaled six million square kilometers with a population of about 400 million. The Japanese held the greatest part of world production of rubber (60 percent), lead (75 percent), and several other valuable raw materials. Japan could almost completely satisfy its needs for important commodities such as oil, tungsten, nickel, manganese, jute, chrome, and rice. Japan now propagated the idea of "liberation" from the yoke of "white" imperialism and the creation of "independent" national Asiatic states in the "great sphere of co-prosperity." Meanwhile Japan counted on placing under its flag the enormous human reserves of the region, which would assure victory over its rivals.

THE "GREAT EAST ASIAN CO-PROSPERITY SPHERE"

The Axis powers, in keeping with the Tripartite Pact of September 27, 1940, recognized "Japan's leadership in the cause of creating a new order in the great expanses of East Asia" which were populated by the yellow race, even though the treaty did not define any boundaries. According to Japanese planning, the East Asian region should grow in proportion to the successes of the Japanese armed forces and the solidification of Japan's position in the occupied territories. In a speech at the privy council session of October 12, 1942, Premier Tojo reiterated that the "sphere" would include only those countries which first had been subjected to Japanese aggression; "the sphere would expand in relation to the increase in occupied territories."[7]

Consideration of the plans for a prosperity sphere in the Japanese parliament and in the press laid forth three successive stages in its creation. In the first stage a small association was envisioned, based on Manchukuo, Outer Mongolia, and occupied regions of China, in addition to Japan proper. In the future would be added Soviet territories southeast of Nerchinsk (including most of the Coastal [Primorskaya] and Khabarovsk territories), the eastern territories of the Mongolian Peoples Republic, and part of the Philippines (Luzon Island). The middle-size sphere would hold part of the Chinese interior, part of Hsin-chiang, Ching-hai, and Tibet, northern Sakhalin and eastern Siberia to Lake Baikal, central Mongolia, eastern India, Burma, Thailand, Indochina, Malaya, Indonesia, New Guinea, and the rest of the Philippines. The "large sphere" would swallow the remainder of China up to the Great Wall of China, eastern and western Siberia (to Omsk), Kamchatka, western regions of Mongolia, and would even extend beyond the limits of the territories populated by the yellow race. It would include Afghanistan, eastern Iran, Nepal, India, Australia, New Zealand, and the Hawaiian islands. Thus Japan would establish its "sway" over a "space" which would encompass no less than one third of the earth's surface with a population including more than half of mankind. This would significantly exceed the "space" to which Hitler and Mussolini aspired.

Imperial circles in Japan added that the Asian peoples recognized the superiority of the Japanese nation and that the "sphere of co-prosperity" would be built on racial community, on the principle of Asia for Asians under Japanese leadership. Such was the factual content of the political appeal offered by Japanese strategists to "free one billion people from the handcuffs of Anglo-Saxon supremacy, create a new order and establish the 'Great East Asian Co-Prosperity Sphere' "[8] which would unite the Asian peoples under the Japanese flag. Japan's leaders did not hide the fact that their model for the political organization and economic structure of the co-prosperity sphere would be the new order established by them in Manchuria and on occupied Chinese territory. There, Japanese propaganda asserted, the first stage was already completed. A "moral union of three nations"—Japan, Manchukuo, and China—had been achieved.

Even prior to the war in the Pacific, in September, 1941, a special committee had been formed in Japan to prepare a system of administration for these territories. The committee was called the "research society for state policy." On February 13, 1942, under Premier Tojo's direction a committee on the "construction of Great East Asia" was formed, with 37 members. The committee included government officials and the directors of all major concerns and banks representing the monopolies active in Manchuria, central and northern China. Directors of the major firms controlling oil, metallurgy and other branches of industry in Japan itself were also members.

Next, the Japanese authorities turned to creation of a special ministry for the affairs of East Asia. After examining this question on September 1, 1942, the Tojo cabinet decided to dissolve the existing colonial ministry which managed the affairs of Korea, Formosa, and other colonies already in the Japanese Empire. These duties were transferred to the ministry of internal affairs, and a ministry for "Great East Asia" was formed. The ruling quarters of Japan made no effort to hide the purpose of this new state institution. Premier Tojo explained: "With complete openness Japan has proclaimed the creation of Great East Asia, so there is no need now to conceal the use of the term 'the Ministry of Great East Asia'." The chief function delegated to the new ministry by the government was to "convert all East Asia into a monolithic organism." From the outset it worked to centralize the economy of the "co-prosperity sphere" and to define the regional distribution of the most important industries for the purpose of maximum utilization of resources.

At the "East Asian Economic Conference" in Tokyo on November 26-28, 1942, the Ministry of East Asia announced its plan for industrial development. The major centers of metallurgy and coal production were to be Manchuria and Sakhalin, and of aluminum—Korea and Manchuria. On Japanese territory was foreseen the development of machine building, instrument production, electrical energy, and the major branches of military production. It is not difficult to perceive that the fundamental purpose of the sphere's economic plan was to assert Japan's leading role in East Asia. Japan would become the outstanding industrial center of Asia and would hold the most vital and economically most viable branches. These colonizing plans called for "efficient and essential" collaboration in order "by common exertions to eliminate Anglo-American influence."

The advertising of Japan's "liberating mission" enjoyed definite, if transitory, success among the national bourgeoisie and the feudal lords of Southeast Asia. The Japanese paid special attention to Indonesia and announced, in April, 1942, the "Three A" movement, which was based on the slogan "Asia for the Asians" and on recognition of Japan's leading role in the liberation of Asia.[9] To bolster pro-Japanese sentiments in Indonesia, in July, 1942 the Japanese occupation forces freed from Dutch prisons the leaders of the national liberation movement, including one leader of the Partindra Party—Sukarno.[10] The Japanese also tried to employ the influence of feudal sultans among the populace by granting them nominal power in their former realms and striving with their help to crush the Indonesian liberation movement. In reality, of course, the Japanese had no intention of sharing power with local nationalist organizations. By the fall of 1942 an occupation administration had taken control in Indonesia. Its major officials were Japanese, while the lower echelons of government were manipulated by Japanese advisors.

In some captured territories the Japanese command did not even disguise the occupation regime and made no attempt to include national representatives in the administration. In Indochina, for example, the struggle of "racial brothers" against "white imperialism" was not stressed inasmuch as French colonial authorities helped the Japanese exploit the richest resources of the region.[11] Elsewhere, the Japanese harnessed Burmese national aspirations against England's colonial rule, permitting the Army of Independent Burma, created in Thailand by Aung San, to join the Japanese army in Burma and even to participate in the "Free Burma Committee."[12] This was short-lived. In July of 1942 Japan vetoed any proclamation of Burma's independence and broke up the Army of Independent Burma and the Free Burma Committee. On August 1, 1942, in keeping with the decree of the Japanese occupation commander-in-chief, a "civil administration" was established under the leadership of Ba Maw.[13] This administration remained completely under Japanese control; in essence it was a section of the Japanese Ministry of East Asia for the affairs of colonial Burma. Thus, prior to the end of 1942, Japan had established colonial administrations and puppet regimes throughout the occupied territories. Now Japanese imperialism had demonstrated what lay behind the screen of the "Great East Asia Co-Prosperity Sphere," had shown the peoples of Asia that it did not differ essentially from "white imperialism," and that its methods of administration were even more cruel.

CHINA'S STRUGGLE AGAINST JAPANESE IMPERIALISM

The military situation in Europe and in the Pacific at the end of 1941 impacted noticeably on China. The initial successes of Hitler's armies on the eastern front, together with fascist claims of the total defeat of the Soviet armies and the impending fall of Moscow, revived anti-Soviet sentiments among Chinese leaders. Furthermore, the European military situation strengthened the puppet governments in the territories under Japanese occupation. On July 1, 1941, Germany recognized Wang Ching-wei's regime as the central government of the Chinese Republic. Then, in November, 1941, that regime, along with Manchukuo, joined the "anti-Comintern pact."[14]

Although Chiang Kai-shek's government continued to support "normal" official relations with the Soviet Union, his foreign policy reflected anti-Soviet tendencies to an increasing degree. Contrary to Chinese national interests, Chiang Kai-shek began curtailing economic ties with the USSR. Official representatives of the Chungking government did not hesitate to express their sympathies with Germany and hoped for an early appearance of Germany on China's borders in Central Asia.[15] Reactionary Kuomintang leaders saw in Germany a mighty anti-communist force which they would use willingly to crush the Chinese nationalist liberation movement. Anti-communism, which in the foreign policy of the Axis nations took the form of anti-Sovietism, became the ideological foundations for Hitler, the Japanese militarists, and the Chinese reactionaries. The mood of surrender among the Chinese ruling classes and higher military circles, together with their anti-Soviet posture, strengthened after Japan's first successes in the Pacific war.

The anti-Soviet attitude also penetrated the leftist forces in China. Mao Tse-tung's campaign, announced on February 1, 1942, "to correct the work style in the party" ("Cheng Feng"), developed into a broad attack on internationalist communism and on the friends of the Soviet

Union with the purpose of disrupting international communications between communists. Mao had broken away from the large industrial centers and lost connection with the Chinese working class. Now he sought support elsewhere, not from brotherly communist parties or from the Soviet Union, but from the wealthy and petty bourgeoisie. He adopted a nationalist point of view and anticipated prolonged partisan warfare. During these difficult days for the USSR, when Hitler's forces were not far from Moscow and Japan was making broad advances in the Pacific, Mao and his supporters failed to take real measures to engage Japanese armies in China, and openly put off tying China's fate with that of the beleaguered Soviet Union.

The united anti-Japanese national front collapsed due to the policies of Chiang Kai-shek and the democratic left. This, together with the anti-Soviet attitude of the Kuomintang, weakened the Chinese will to resist, allowing the warmakers of Japan to control the key centers of China with relatively small forces. For this purpose they employed the million men composing the armies of the puppet regimes, enjoying as an added benefit, the ready availability of the resources of the occupied territories. In 1942 and early 1943 Japanese and puppet troops advanced into north China against the liberated regions,[16] constructing numerous fortifications along the railroads and around towns and garrisons. During 1943 they extracted some 50 million tons of coal, 1.8 million tons of iron, and 900,000 tons of steel from Manchuria and north China. Metallurgy plants were built or reconstructed at Tai-yuan, Shih-chin-shan, and Tientsin.

China's difficult position further deteriorated when its allies in the Pacific war, the United States and England, failed to afford sufficient support. Early in the war American strategy was simply to conserve strength and gather reserves for a coming counterattack, while the war was waged by its allies. In the south, China played the key role among the Allies, its armies finding employment in Southeast Asia while in the north the Soviet Union would hold in check the million-man Japanese army on the Manchurian frontier. President Roosevelt defined American military policy in that period as follows: "At the present moment the fundamental players are the Russians, Chinese and, to a lesser degree, the English. Our role is destined to be that of the players who enter at the decisive moment. Before our forwards spend themselves, we will come with fresh forces. If we choose the right moment, our forwards will not be too tired."[17] Of course, while they observed, American strategists were anxious lest their allies suddenly be knocked out of "the game," lest they too soon exhaust their strength to the point that the United

States would have to "protect its goal" before "the deciding score." Guided by these considerations, the American government granted the Chinese nationalist government a loan of 500 million dollars in February, 1942. This was to pay for war materials, to bolster Chinese currency, and to guarantee issuance of internal loans. To keep track of the "correct" use of the loan, General Joseph W. Stilwell was sent to China as a military advisor to Chiang Kai-shek. Earlier Stilwell had been the U.S. military attache in China and knew the Chinese language well. On March 10, 1942, he was appointed chief of the Chinese General Staff.

Stilwell's main assignment was to preserve the Chungking government's alliance with the United States. To accomplish this he had to prevent the spread of defeatism among the Kuomintang. The American command did not feel bound by "the relationship of alliance" to participate in joint battle against Japanese occupation forces in China, or to support the re-establishment of state sovereignty and democratization of China. Rather, it was important that circumstances prevail in China whereby Japan would not become fully entrenched, nor would China gain true independence of foreign capital. In waging war in the Pacific, Washington intended primarily to crush belligerent Japan, but at the same time also hoped to weaken their imperial rivals in the Far East. In contrast to Japan's racist slogan of "Asia for Asians," American officials on October 9, 1942 declared their readiness to fight for the "complete equality" of the peoples of the yellow race. To confirm this, on October 24, 1942 Washington began talks with the Chinese ambassador on rescinding extraterritorial rights. The conversations culminated in a Sino-American agreement which was signed on November 11, 1943.[18] The United States did not hesitate to assume the role of "defender" of independence for other Asian peoples as well. To inspire the Chinese armies sent to Burma under the command of American generals, the United States demanded that England grant Burma "independence" after the war. Generous American aid to the Chungking government in the form of loans and materials on lend-lease was far from altruistic. It was intended to assure favorable conditions for American capital in China after the war, and to guarantee an advantage over defeated Japan and America's ally, England. United States relations with China, thus, were determined not so much by alliance in the war against Japan as by aspiration to solidify American hegemony in East Asia.

The English alliance with China possessed an even more conditional character. With the exception of Manchuria, England owned most of the foreign property located in zones occupied by the Japanese. Hoping to expel Japan from China, England feared with good cause that after victory over the Japanese, English property might fall into American or Chinese hands. These fears compelled England to concentrate on defense of its Pacific colonial possessions and, as far as possible, to avoid active military operations against Japan in other sectors of the Pacific theater. The rescue of Asian nations from Japanese enslavement was not England's chief goal in the Pacific. Nevertheless, the British government could not fail to consider the growth of national liberation movements among colonized peoples. These circumstances required the English government to take action, with the result that England and the United States initialed the Atlantic Charter declaration on August 14, 1941.[19] In it they demagogically proclaimed "respect for the right of all nations to choose for themselves the form of government under which they want to live." If only outwardly, England was constrained to support American and Chinese policies. The British government, simultaneously with United States authorities, signed the agreement renouncing extraterritorial rights on January 11, 1943, agreeing as well to return concessions—which in any case remained in Japanese hands—to Chinese administration. England did, however, receive "agreement" from the Chungking authorities for maintaining its rule over Hong Kong and the Kowloon peninsula, China accepting the obligation to protect British real property on its territory.

Massive war material and financial help received from the United States strengthened the Chungking government's position and to some extent neutralized pro-Japanese sentiments within the Kuomintang. The Kuomintang leadership believed that a propitious time had arrived for consolidating its dictatorship in China. Accordingly, it denied its obligations to preserve a unified anti-Japanese national front and set out to destroy the liberated regions. Such a course was eased by Japan's policy of favoring the Chungking government. Indeed, for all purposes Japan had ceased military operations against the Kuomintang armies, for by the beginning of 1943 the anti-Japanese front was in disarray. The Japanese occupation authorities then found it possible to concentrate their troops for operations against the isolated liberated regions, which had been visibly weakened by the divisive activities of Mao Tsetung and his associates.

The American and English policies consisted of avoiding active military involvement in China and rendering aid solely in the form of military supplies to Chungking. This amounted to cooperation with the Chungking government's anti-democratic plans; it promoted the collapse of the unified anti-Japanese front which was offering the chief resistance to the Japanese invaders. Thus, by early 1943, the domestic and international support of the battle of the Chinese people against the Japanese invaders had dwindled. China's national unity had been destroyed by reactionary Kuomintang circles and extremists of the left, and victory postponed to the distant future. Only the restoration of national unity and the support of progressive international forces could hasten the expulsion of Japanese occupation troops from Chinese soil and hurry the hour of final victory.

JAPAN IN STRATEGIC DEFENSE

The successful outcome of the battle on the Volga (at Stalingrad) for Soviet armies on February 2, 1943 exerted a decisive influence on the entire course of the Second World War both in the West and in the Pacific. No longer might Japan count on a German victory over the Soviet Union. Japanese strategic plans foresaw that a German attack on the British Isles would cause a shift of English and American forces from the Pacific to Europe. These plans now collapsed. The battle of the Kursk salient during the summer of 1943 hastened the rout of fascist Germany, forcing Japan to reexamine its strategic plans for the war. It was necessary to reckon with the possibility of an English and American counterattack in the Pacific theater, for now their reserves could mount rapidly due to changed circumstances in the European theater. Growing convinced that the war would be prolonged in character, Japanese troops switched to strategic defensive preparations. But the dispersion of Japanese forces throughout the South Pacific islands hampered the defense of captured territories as well as of matériel and supply lines. As a result, during the second half of 1943 Japanese units began to evacuate the most distant islands, thereby shortening the lines of defense. The unfavorable circumstances developing for Japan stirred growing anxiety in the country. The Japanese press published calls for the mobilization of all resources in order to change the course of the war. "The Japanese people is enduring the greatest difficulties," wrote the newspaper "Mainichi," "that it has ever endured since the very founding of the empire."[20]

Some sentiments favoring Japan had spread among bourgeois nationalists in the occupied territories of Southeast Asia during the first days of the Pacific war. This generated hope in the Japanese command of drawing the peoples of these countries under their flag. But with the change of Japanese fortunes, these hopes disappeared. The openly terrorist regime of the Japanese occupation administration had spawned popular hatred. Instead of support, the Japanese army began to meet increasing resistance from the local populace, further complicating the already difficult situation. The impending crisis compelled Japanese leaders to seek political means of insuring the new military plans for strategic defense. Confronted by growing American and English forces and amid open local hostility, defense of occupied territories was beyond the strength of the Japanese army. Therefore, Japan's rulers attempted once again to play on Asian nationalist feelings. An extensive campaign was publicized for establishing new "equal" relations among the countries of the "co-prosperity sphere," with the aim of popularizing the ideas of a common destiny and unity of purpose. Japanese historiography would provide foundations for the "unique" mission of Japan in the war of "liberation" in the Pacific Ocean area. In the spring of 1943, Dr. Kohsara Timura wrote an article "The Genesis of the Pacific War." In it he mentioned Japan's unequal status in the past and the demeaning treaties forced on Japan by the United States and other Western countries in the middle of the 19th century. He labored to include Japan among the oppressed nations and to show that its salvation from inequitable treaties and conversion into a progressive "civilized" nation proved possible solely because of the "special qualities" of the Japanese nation, the uniqueness of which determined its "historical mission" in East Asia.[21]

To confirm its "good" intentions and "understanding" of the humiliating position of the Asian nations, particularly China, the Japanese government announced a "new" policy toward occupied countries. Accordingly, after the Nanking government declared war on the United States and England on January 9, 1943, together with Japan it signed a declaration concerning "return of concessions and revocation of extraterritorial rights." A series of concrete steps to implement the declaration followed. On February 9 the Japanese government "transferred" to the puppet Chinese authorities more than a thousand structures representing "enemy" property which had been captured during the war. On March 22 the sovereignty of puppet governments was "restored" in the Peking diplomatic quarter. On June 30 an agreement was signed with China "restoring its administrative rights" to the international settlement in Shanghai. For the future, the Japanese press reported, "the extraordinary status of China's territorial composition will be completely eliminated."[22] Premier Tojo remarked, addressing a special session of the Japanese parliament on June 16, 1943: "On our part, we warmly welcome the development of China and we are more than ever resolved to help it by all possible means. In this spirit we intend to make a fundamental reexamination of agreements between Japan and China, having in mind further expansion of active collaboration between our two countries."[23]

After negotiations in Tokyo, "president" Wang Ching-wei spoke on the radio to the people of unoccupied China on September 23, 1943. He called for an end to resistance to Japan. The national traitors surrounding him strove to convince the Chinese public that, with Japanese aid, the basic problems of the national liberation revolution might be solved. Wang Ching-wei's followers endeavored to cover their criminal ties to Japan by invoking Sun Yat-sen's name, citing his speeches at an earlier time when Japan had not revealed its territorial ambitions in China. They ignored Sun's later conclusions, made when the Japanese were actively pillaging China.[24]

The propaganda campaign culminated in the signing of a "Treaty of Alliance Between Japan and China" on October 30, 1943. It was signed in Nanking by Japanese "ambassador" Masayuki Tani and the "foreign minister" of the nationalist government, Chu Ming-yu. As interpreted by Japanese diplomacy, this "treaty marked a new epoch in Sino-Japanese diplomatic relations, built on the foundation of eternal friendship and respect for China's sovereignty and independence."[25] The Japanese government tried to convey the impression that this treaty would serve as the basis for complete transfer of powers to "the Chinese government." Relations between the countries then would be conducted through normal diplomatic channels, as between sovereign states. While continuing to exert pressure on the Chungking authorities, the Japanese government worked to convince them that Japanese military operations in China had but a single purpose—counteracting the aggressive intentions of Britain and the United States. Military activities were "not directed against the Chinese people" and "the Japanese government would not treat Chungking's soldiers as enemies if they avoided cooperation with America and Britain."[26]

The Japanese administration demonstrated its "new policy" in relations with other Asian nations as well. On August 1, 1943, it recognized Burma's "independence," after which Burma concluded an alliance with Japan and declared war on the United States. On October 14, Japan recognized Philippine independence and a Japanese-Philippine "treaty of alliance" was concluded. On July 4, a Japanese-Thai communique on increased cooperation was issued. Through these acts Japan strove to unite the Asian countries for a struggle of the yellow race against white "aggression."

On November 5, 1943, an assembly of East Asian nations took place in Tokyo. Attending were Japan, Wang Ching-wei's China, Thailand,

Manchukuo, Burma, and the Philippines. The representatives of these six "independent" countries were joined by an observer from the provisional government of India.[27] At the suggestion of Tojo, the assembly adopted a "joint declaration" on November 5, 1943, laying forth the purposes of the war: "The United States of America and the British Empire, in striving to assure their own prosperity, are oppressing other nations and peoples. Particularly in East Asia they surrender to pleasures and insatiable appetites; they attack, exploit and procure means to satisfy their boundless ambitions, enslaving whole regions. In the final analysis this creates a serious threat to the stability of East Asia. Herein are concealed the causes of the present war." The assembly's participants accepted responsibility "for taking joint actions for the satisfactory conclusion of war in East Asia, for liberation of their territories from the yoke of Anglo-American mastery . . . ."[28]

The Tokyo assembly of East Asian nations was Japan's last attempt to harness its oppressed Asian neighbors to its own further expansionist aims. It had hoped to force these peoples to join Japan's armies in fighting for a "new order" in the "East Asian Co-Prosperity Sphere." Following China's lead, the occupied nations of East Asia resolutely rose in battle against imperial Japan. It became clear to them that Japanese policy was not based on the common culture, way of life or historical destiny of the yellow race. Rather, it was determined solely by imperial goals, aspirations to hold the peoples of East Asia in Japan's colonial sway. In the war with the United States and Britain the goal was not liberation of oppressed Asian peoples from "white imperialism." Rather, Japan wished to expel its imperial rivals and take their place.

The Chinese people, who more than others had suffered under imperial Japan, increased their resistance to the Japanese occupation forces and their puppets. This contributed to Soviet victories over the Germans, while inspiring the Chinese people as prospects of defeating imperial Japan appeared. Even the Kuomintang nationalist press admitted that the "battle for Stalingrad must be considered to be the focus of the general world war. Soviet armed forces protect not only the USSR, but also the peoples of all allied countries."[29] Meanwhile, the progressive elements in Chinese society gathered force, as did the internationalists within the Chinese Communist Party. These internationalists consistently advocated solidarity with the Soviet Union and the world communist movement. The growing authority of the Soviet Union in international affairs helped to neutralize expansionist ambitions in the United States and England, particularly where China was concerned. At the Moscow foreign ministers conference in the fall of

1943, attended by Great Britain, the United States, and the USSR, the Western powers were constrained to accept a series of obligations confirming the principle of the "sovereign equality of all peaceloving states . . . ." They also declared that after the conclusion of the war they "would not employ their armed forces on the territories of other nations without prior consultation."[30]

Nevertheless, the United States and Britain had no intention of renouncing their goals. Even in those years American monopolies sought China's promise not to develop local heavy industry, particularly in machinery production. China was advised to rely on American "assistance." American experts hoped to direct capital investments in China into railroad construction during the first postwar decade for the purpose of linking the country's hinterlands with sea ports. Given the lack of indigenous industry, China would have to import rails, rolling stock, and various other railroad equipment to accomplish this plan. The value of these imports, according to American calculations, would amount to no less than three billion dollars annually. Viewed differently, this approximately tripled China's imports and quadrupled exports over prewar years. This economic plan would bind China for many years to the United States as its chief supplier and would place basic Chinese exports in the hands of American firms, which would expand materially by exploiting distant underdeveloped regions.

In questions of the conduct of the war and the creation of a democratic and sovereign China thereafter, American and English political figures also disregarded the spirit of Allied declarations.[31] American and British forces undertook no direct military action against Japan on Chinese soil. Although Kuomintang armies had been defeated during Japanese campaigns in the Heng-yang valley in the summer of 1944, the American command in central and south China continued to transfer Chinese troops to Burma for battles in that region. They sought to draw the Soviet Union into the war with Japan as soon as possible. In these circumstances, the United States and England needed to seek certain compromises. For example, in China the Americans were forced to make official declarations against civil war and for the establishment of a democratic republic. Guided strictly by practical military considerations, Chiang Kai-shek's chief of staff, General Stilwell, urged the settlement of the conflict between the Kuomintang and the Chinese Communist Party. Stilwell could not fail to recognize the military qualities of the armies led by the communists. He willingly used those armies in the fight with Japan, which placed them under American control. In the fall of 1944 negotiations were renewed between communist representatives and the Kuomintang on joint actions against the Japanese.

The alliance with the Soviet Union obligated the United States and England to exert a certain influence on the Chiang Kai-shek government. At least they proved unable to block a Sino-Soviet rapprochement. In this regard the Yalta conference of the three powers had particular importance. On February 11, 1945, an agreement was signed which called for Soviet entry into the war against Japan two or three months after the capitulation of Germany. The Soviet Union expressed willingness to conclude "a treaty of friendship and alliance between the USSR and China and to aid the latter with armed forces for the purpose of freeing China from the Japanese yoke."[32] In China a united anti-Japanese national front was possible again, based on organization of the country's democratic forces and friendly relations with the world's progressive powers, primarily with the Soviet Union.

THE SOVIET DEFEAT OF JAPAN IN CHINA

The loss of real hope for German assistance, and Anglo-American strength in Southeast Asia, compelled Japan to retreat. Its armies were evacuated from distant theaters of war and concentrated at the approaches to the Japanese islands. The Japanese command counted on American and English inability to gather superior forces at bases on the Asian mainalnd, particularly in China. Therefore, Japan must strengthen its defensive positions in China. In holding China the Japanese still hoped for a respectable way out of the war by making concessions to the United States and England, including ones at the expense of China. In the summer of 1944 the Japanese command concentrated military contingents in central, north, and northeast China, and launched a massive assault on Ho-nan province. Then they drove in the direction of the Vietnamese border. Meeting no serious resistance from the Kuomintang armies, the Japanese captured strongholds along the entire length of the Peking—Han-kou—Canton railroad, then broke out into districts bordering Vietnam. They blockaded all the lightly populated points on the southeast China coast which still remained in Kuomintang control and might provide landing places for future Anglo-American invasions.

These advances in China in 1944 possessed major significance for the Japanese. First, they led to control over new and rich agricultural regions. Second and even more important, they gave Japan main lines of communication behind the battle lines. This permitted more reliable ties with Indochina and Indonesia, thereby easing Japan's growing economic crisis at home. By the beginning of 1945 Japanese troops controlled the territories where seventy percent of the Chinese population lived. Kuomintang losses during 1944 amounted to no less than 600-700,000 men killed, wounded or (the majority) captured. Japanese armies had snatched the ten largest American airbases and 36 airports. Before them lay the poorly defended path to Kuei-yang and Chungking. However, Japanese ruling circles did not consider it purposeful to defeat the Chiang Kai-shek group by force of arms. Halting the offensive, they pursued "peaceful" means of settling relations with Chungking. The Chiang Kai-shek government was in no condition to organize serious resistance. It placed reliance on the might of its allies, while trying to preserve the battered nationalist armies to bolster Kuomintang authority after the war's end.

The corruption and venality of the Chiang Kai-shek regime convinced the American military command in China that it could not count on Chungking's armies in a war with Japan. At the same time the American command could not fail to notice the growing combat readiness of the Eighth and Fourth National Liberation Armies under communist control. Therefore, Washington considered it timely to seek unification of these two forces under Chiang Kai-shek's command. Such a unification supposedly would strengthen the Chungking leader and weaken Chinese communist forces. While pursuing this course, the United States as before provided military supplies only to Chiang Kai-shek's armies. The United States and Britain took no real measures to regain territories held by the Japanese, even though influential American commanders believed that Japan could be beaten only from Chinese bases.[33] American bombing of Japanese cities had increased since the beginning of 1945, causing mainly civilian losses, but failing to hasten the end of the war. Japan still maintained an army of about five million men at its command, of which two million were in Japan itself. In the opinion of the American command, invasion of the islands of Kyushu and Honshu would require the concentration of no less than five million officers and men, and losses during the operation might reach more than a million men.[34] These factors led President Truman to the conclusion that "Russia's entry into the war has become ever more imperative. It would mean saving the lives of hundreds of thousands of Americans."[35] Soviet aid was also expected by democratic Chinese, who once more faced civil war fanned by the reactionary Kuomintang with the help of American arms.[36]

True to its obligation to the Allies made in the Crimea Declaration,[37] precisely three months after the German capitulation the Soviet Union declared war on Japan. On August 9, 1945, Soviet armies attacked Manchuria, clashing with the elite, technically well-equipped Kuan-tung army counting (with reserves) 1.2 million men. Despite lengthy preparations, the Japanese command clearly underestimated the military might of the USSR. The first massive blows by bombing aircraft, artillery and armored divisions, accompanied by landings of commando units deep in the Manchurian rear, proved to be a complete surprise. During the first two days of the war, Soviet armies attacked the enemy on land, sea, and air along the entire Manchurian border and the northern Korean coast. Bombardment rained upon the most important military targets of Harbin, Chang-shun, and Chi-lin, and on the northern Korean ports of Yuki, Najin (Tasin), and Chongjin (Seishin). The "unapproachable" stacked-echelon Japanese defenses along the Soviet-Manchurian border, contiguous to Greater and Lesser Hing-gan, were overrun and crushed. Soviet armies broke through to open operating spaces.

The breaking of the fortified lines upset Japanese hopes that these defenses would protect Manchuria from invasion and provide staging areas for offensive operations. The strategic plans of the Kuan-tung army were thus destroyed. It became clear to the Japanese government that it could not count on a prolonged war.[38] After two days of Soviet advances, the Japanese government felt obligated to announce its readiness to capitulate on condition that the emperor's prerogatives be preserved. Yet four more days of bitter combat followed, during which Soviet armies crushed the main pockets of Japanese resistance in Manchuria. Emperor Hirohito accepted the repeated Allied demand for unconditional surrender on August 14. Even after the official announcement of capitulation, Japanese armies continued to resist the Soviet Army, counterattacking in a number of sectors. On August 19, Soviet armies were approaching Chang-chun, Mukden, Tsitsihar, Chang-pai, and Jehol, while paratroops were landing at Harbin, Chi-lin, and Mukden. Moving in the direction of Chang-chia-kou (Kalgan), Soviet armies smashed strong Japanese units that were blockading part of the Eighth National Liberation Army. The Eighth Army could then begin a broad offensive in north China. In the Ping-chuang region the commanding general, Chao Wen-tien, wrote the Soviet Seventeenth Army command: "We are particularly grateful to the Army of the Soviet Union. We were in an extraordinarily difficult position. Far superior forces were concentrated against us; they had encircled us, cut off retreat routes and restricted our maneuvering possibilities. On the evening of August 9 we were racking our brains for a way out of this predicament. The arrival of the Red Army on Manchurian territory that day completely shifted the balance of power. We went from the defensive to the offense. Thus the Red Army saved us from perishing, and we are especially thankful."[39] The Kuomintang government demanded that the Eighth army refuse to accept Japanese capitulation and that it refrain from using captured weapons. The Soviet command could not agree to this. Therefore Soviet armies turned Japanese weapons over to the Eighth army and helped it become supplied with modern armaments.

By September 1, Soviet armies had completely disarmed the Kuantung army, the Manchukuo army, and troops in Inner Mongolia. They had liberated all of northeastern China (Manchuria, and the Liao-tung peninsula) and northern Korea to the 38th parallel. The Asian nations and particularly China warmly greeted Soviet entrance into the war against imperial Japan. The leaders of the "Committee to Save the Homeland" and "the North-East Army of China" wrote: "We approve and thank the Soviet Army with our whole hearts for entering Manchuria to free its people. The people of Manchuria will do everything to aid the Soviet Army in destroying the Japanese aggressors and their toadies in China."[40]

On September 2, 1945, on the American battleship *Missouri* in Tokyo harbor, the documents of Japan's unconditional surrender were signed. The Japanese were represented by Foreign Minister Shigemitsu and Chief of Staff Umezu Yoshijiro. General Douglas MacArthur represented the United States, Lieutenant-General K.N. Derevyanko the Soviet Union, and Admiral Fraser, England. Also signing the acts were representatives of China, Australia, Canada, France, Holland, and New Zealand.[41]

The Japanese empire was crushed. It had attempted to establish rule over East Asia as the "chosen" nation among peoples of the yellow race. Its defeat convincingly showed the failure of racist policy and the utter bankruptcy of efforts by Japan's rulers to create a "league of nations" or a "co-prosperity sphere" on a racial foundation. At the same time, concord among various peoples during the war against fascist Germany and imperial Japan convinced Asia's oppressed nations of their common interests and goals, common friends, and enemies. They learned that true friendship and alliance must be based, not on racial kindred, but on social and national equality. The freedom and independence of small and large nations and peoples must be recognized. The Soviet contribution to Japan's defeat promoted national liberation movements in dependent and colonial areas, strengthened progressive democratic tendencies, and encouraged establishment of people's democracies in East Asia.

SUMMARY

The signing of the unconditional surrender brought an end to a long period of Japanese expansion in East Asia. Like Germany, Japan espoused the reactionary idea of "racial supremacy" as the foundation for hegemony in Asia. Japan's rapid economic development, permitting it to join the industrially advanced countries of the world, was attributed not to historically determined domestic and foreign circumstances, but to the special qualities of the Japanese people. They were supposedly called to fulfill a leading "historical mission" in Asia. In keeping with their foreign policy plans, leaders in Tokyo transformed the country into an obedient war machine directed by fanatic militarists. Japan intended to achieve its plans by war with the United States and England, its chief imperial rivals, and the USSR, the "saver" of communism in China and other Asian countries. Japan's rulers hoped that after eliminating Anglo-American control and the Soviet Union's ideological influence, they would be able to bring the countries of Asia under their banner. They would utilize them in the battle to end the mastery of the "white race" and to remove the "communist threat." On that basis they would create an East Asian empire.

Significant military successes early in the war and demagogic racist propaganda were accompanied by showy gestures with no practical meaning. The latter included the liquidation of inequitable treaties and special concessions for Europeans. English, American, and Dutch colonies declared their independence. As a result, the Japanese experienced early successes. They were able to set up puppet regimes and to gather quite numerous armies which frequently they used to deal with national liberation movements. This was the case, for example, in China. Yet even in the first stage of occupation, the Japanese interventionists were unable to conceal their true goals, reflected in haughty, scornful treatment of local populations, in mockery of local culture and customs, and in establishment of terroristic regimes in those countries. Japanese monopolies usurped key industries and whole sectors of the national economies. Domestically owned enterprises were confiscated along with those belonging to European and American capitalists.

Japanese rule convinced East Asians that their new conqueror was no less greedy and cruel than its predecessors from Europe and America. Appeals for union of the yellow race to support Japan against the

United States and England only disguised Japan's imperial strivings to rule Asia. It is true that there were essential differences in methods and forms of administration. Since they knew local conditions and customs better, the Japanese could set up direct ties with local entrepreneurs and cultural and educational institutions. They exerted direct influence on production, cultural affairs, and daily life. Meanwhile they excluded native middlemen and agents, and rarely employed the services of the local intelligentsia. Herein lay imperial Japan's superiority. It was able to utilize local resources and establish control more quickly, completely and effectively. The Japanese made up for their economic weakness by brute military force, terror, and expropriation. Policies were carried out by the occupation government apparatus, freely using armed might. Yet it was these very advantages which spawned Japan's weaknesses. The Japanese interventionists quickly lost the support of the workers and the bourgeoisie in occupied territories. Open brutality met with growing resistance as Asian peoples rose to relentless struggle against the occupation forces.

Germany's defeat on the eastern front changed the Pacific war radically. Prospects seemed better to the East Asian peoples for expulsion of the Japanese conquerors and an end to colonial dependency as well. The peoples of these countries, having experienced colonial rule by both white and yellow masters, realized that true national independence could not be achieved without social liberation. They needed the support of world progressive opinion based on class solidarity rather than racial solidarity. Imperial Japan's defeat dealt a heavy blow to the colonial system. Japanese leaders had failed to remove the foreign "tint" of colonialism by hoisting the banner of racism, which might have lengthened its existence. Japan had undergone a long process of development from its debut in the world arena to its final defeat in the war. Its experience proved clearly that, in the imperial epoch, international relations were determined by the interests of the ruling classes and not by a racial community of interests. The latter reflected only superficial similarities, not vital interests.

CHAPTER SEVEN

The Search for Democracy and Social Rights, 1945-1949

CHINA AND JAPAN AFTER WORLD WAR II

During World War II the principles of postwar democratic transformation were defined by the heads of the three chief nations of the coalition against Hitler, the USSR, the United States and England. At the Teheran conference in 1943 the allies declared: "We will strive for collaboration and active participation by all countries, large and small, whose peoples, like our poeples, have dedicated heart and mind to the elimination of tyranny, slavery, oppression and intolerance. We will welcome their entry into the world family of democratic countries, when they wish to do this."[1] The problem of governmental democratization related chiefly to Kuomintang China. President Roosevelt had been forced to express his disapproval of the government's character to Chiang Kai-shek as early as the Cairo conference in December, 1943.[2] At the Teheran conference, Roosevelt revealed Chiang Kai-shek's promise to "bring the Chinese communists into the government prior to general elections, and to conduct those elections as soon as possible after victory."[3]

Japan's defeat and the Soviet liberation of Manchuria generated great impact on the growth of popular democracy in China. Communist internationalists gained stronger positions in the Chinese Communist Party, while splinter groups and bourgeois nationalists were eliminated from the Party leadership. The Party once again took the initiative in peace negotiations with the Kuomintang to bring an end to the civil war. On August 25, 1945, the central committee published a "Declaration on the Current Situation," presenting conditions for agreement with the Kuomintang and expressing readiness for immediate negotiations.[4] Chiang Kai-shek was forced to negotiate with the communist party by prevailing international and domestic circumstances. On August 28, Mao Tse-tung, Chou En-lai and Wang Jo-fei arrived in Chungking, and on October 10, representatives of the Chinese Communist Party and the Kuomintang signed a joint communique in which both parties agreed:

> unequivocally to avoid civil war with the hope of building a new, independent, free and flourishing China and of completely achieving the three national principles.

They further recognized that:

for the realization of peaceful national development, it is absolutely essential to have political democracy, to transfer all armies to the government's control and to recognize equal legal status for all political parties and groups.[5]

A consultative political conference was to be called which would determine basic national policies and decide the question of calling a national assembly.

To implement the agreement of October 10, the Party leadership issued an order on October 18 to the New Fourth Army to withdraw from territories south of the Yangtze. The leadership was prepared to abide by other decisions of the agreement. Democratic public opinion warmly welcomed the accord, and a movement spread throughout the country calling for the quick convening of the consultative political conference. Thus favorable political circumstances developed in China for the peaceful formation of a democratic government including all progressive parties and groups. By the end of 1945, Soviet and American armies had fulfilled their responsibilities for disarming the Japanese army. They were to leave all Chinese territories except those specified in treaties and agreements. Northeastern Chinese territory freed by Soviet armies saw the establishment of popular-democratic governing institutions, which assumed political and administrative functions, and nationalized heavy industry, transportation, communications and banking, which previously had been operated by Japanese capital.

Favorable conditions also existed for democratization in Japan. The defeat undermined the foundations of the military fascist regime, opening prospects of peaceful development to the Japanese people. The Potsdam declaration, signed on July 26, 1945 by the United States, England and China, joined by the Soviet Union on August 8, determined basic policy toward Japan. The main provisions were as follows:

In Japan "those who had deceived and deluded the Japanese people, and forced the country to seek world conquest, were to be stripped of power and influence forever;

Japan was to be demilitarized and deprived of the ability "to make war;"

Japanese sovereignty was to be limited to "the islands of Honshu, Hokkaido, Kyushu, Shikoku and lesser islands" determined by the allies;

"The Japanese government was to eliminate all obstacles to the renaissance and strengthening of democratic tendencies among the Japanese people" and "freedom of speech, religion and thought, and also respect for fundamental human rights, were to be established;"

There were to be "no branches of industry which would permit Japan to rearm itself again for warmaking."[6]
The Potsdam declaration reflected the peace-loving hopes of democratic people throughout the world, who demanded an end once and for all to Japanese militarism, which had brought woe and unhappiness to Asian peoples. Now conditions should be created for democratic development in Japan.

For American leaders, the Potsdam declaration constituted a compromise, a concession to the democratic world. Demilitarization of the Japanese economy and liquidation of monopolies corresponded to U.S. interests at the end of the war. Hence the American occupation administration consistently acted in that direction. On October 31, before the formation of Allied institutions, the headquarters of the American occupation forces, headed by General MacArthur, proposed to the Japanese government that the powerful monopolies be dismantled. No firms using assets of those monopolies received American sanction. At this stage the U.S. government agreed in part to coordinate its policy with its allies. In December 1945, foreign ministers of the USSR, United States and England adopted a decision calling for creation of a Far East Commission, to meet in Washington, with representatives of eleven nations as the directorate. It would be called upon to determine fundamental policies toward Japan. An Allied Council for Japan, located in Tokyo, made up of Soviet, American, English and Chinese emissaries, would monitor the fulfillment of Allied policies by Japan.

From the outset the United States occupational administration restricted the Far East Commission and the Allied Council for Japan. Administration of the country was concentrated in the hands of the American army. The American government unilaterally granted unlimited power to the commander-in-chief of U.S. forces in Japan. He was directed to operate "within such bounds as would satisfactorily achieve American goals." In case of disagreement with Allied representatives, "United States policy would prevail."[7] Despite the obstacles presented by MacArthur's headquarters, the Far East Commission and the Allied Council for Japan still managed to serve a useful function in democratizing the country. This goal was also insisted upon by the Japanese public. Late in 1945 an amnesty freed political prisoners from prison, many of whom were veteran members of the Japanese Communist Party, and it was they who led the struggle of the working class for political and social rights. The legalized communist party set to work with appeals calling for popular government and agrarian reform, taking active part in creating trade unions and other large worker organizations.

The first postwar years were characterized by rapid growth of Japanese political consciousness. The collapse of Japanese militarism disgraced those racist theories which had justified Japanese imperial aspirations for the mastery of Asia, including a "philosophy of world history" and a "philosophy of the imperial path." At the same time, progressive ideas began to gain favor. Philosophers connected with the "Society for Study of Marxism," which had appeared in 1932 only to be disbanded during the world war, promoted the idea of scientific socialism. Scientific societies of materialist philosophers sprang up—The Institute for Study of Materialism, for example—and journals appeared, including "Studies in Materialism" and "Theory." These exerted a positive influence on the formation of a new democratic ideology.

A strike movement spread through the country, accompanied by demonstrations by intellectuals and political activists. Demands were advanced for worker control of production and establishment of a popular government. The developing situation forced the occupation authorities to reckon with popular demands and to institute certain democratizing measures. Of importance for the Japanese was the appeal of the Far East Commission for new labor legislation to allow workers and employees to organize trade unions, bargain collectively, and strike. At the insistence of the Soviet representative, the Allied Council adopted a much improved proposal for agrarian reform. The original recommendation had been condemned in the Japanese parliament. This agrarian reform legislation dealt a serious blow to remnants of feudalism in Japanese villages.

Japanese democratic hopes found full expression in the discussions concerning the forthcoming constitution. On May 18, 1946, the Far East Commission called for public participation in these deliberations, which were to reflect "the freely expressed will of the Japanese people." Under the leadership of the Japanese Communist Party, large worker organizations demonstrated for a republican form of government. The demonstrations aroused the concern both of the ruling classes and of the American occupation authorities. On May 20, MacArthur published a "warning to the Japanese people" which ran counter to the decision of the Far East Commission. The warning threatened punitive action if "lower elements of society" did not "manifest the self-restraint and self-respect demanded by the situation." This stand of the American occupation authorities stand prevented democratic public leaders from effectively helping to prepare the new constitution.

The Japanese constitution, which took effect on May 3, 1947, preserved the monarchy. However, according to the new constitution, the emperor no longer possessed legislative functions. He might fulfill his duties only "with the advice and consent of the cabinet," and his status depended "on the will of the Japanese people, which possessed sovereign authority." Universal suffrage for both men and women, and the freedoms of speech, the press, and assembly, were important steps forward in comparison with the earlier constitution of 1889. The most important victory of the Japanese democratic public was expressed in article nine of the constitution. It stated Japan's "eternal renunciation of war as an expression of state sovereignty, and of application or threatened application of force as a means for settling international disputes." It added that, in order to achieve the stated goals, Japan "would not maintain army, navy or air forces, or other military forces."[8] This important decision facilitated the restoration and development of Japan's peacetime economy. The transformation of Japan into a peace-loving democratic nation corresponded to the interests of all freedom-loving nations, especially those in Asia.

CHINA, JAPAN AND AMERICAN IMPERIALISM

The Chinese struggle for a democratic and popular republican govern-ment, together with growing democratization in Japan, upset American plans for expansion. With good cause, American leaders reached the conclusion that democratic developments would bring greater national independence as well, and thereby deprive U.S. monopolies of the opportunity for controlling these leading Asian nations. Establishment of popular democracy also thwarted the Chinese and Japanese rulers, for they saw it as a threat to their own political and economic power. With regard to China, American capitalists had hoped simply to replace their Japanese counterparts. The latter had concentrated eighty percent of all foreign investments in their hands by the end of the war.

American investors had practiced restraint through the entire pre-ceding history of Sino-American relations. They had not enjoyed the essential political guarantees necessary for normal operations in China. As a result, the American government now demanded from China an agreement on U.S. control of national affairs. Simultaneously, taking into account the troubled experience of Japan, the United States sought to cloak its expansionism in the guise of peaceful intentions, concern for national democratization and for China's independence as a state. Having chosen to support the most reactionary elements of the Chinese bureaucracy and landholders, headed by Chiang Kai-shek, the United States concurrently searched for the support of Chinese democratic circles including the Chinese Communist Party. After Mao Tse-tung's declaration at the seventh Party congress that he would welcome foreign investments, the United States hoped to protect its interests via a coalition government with communist participation. Consequently, American representatives served as intermediaries in negotiations between the Kuomintang and the Chinese Communist Party.

From the first days following Japan's capitulation, Washington had begun interfering in China's internal affairs, in support of Chiang Kai-shek. United States mediation clearly had the purpose of subordinating the popular democratic movement, led by the communists, to the Kuomintang. On November 15, 1945, the American government announced continuation of the Lend-Lease Act for China. With this move it hoped to stress that the United States did not consider the war in China finished. Hence, acting under the conditions of a state of war, the United States endeavored to support Chiang Kai-shek in the fight against Chinese democrats. Somewhat earlier, in September, the American high command began transferring Kuomintang armies by ship and plane from India and Yun-nan province to the Shang-hai, Nanking and Tientsin areas. By October these forces were concentrated in northern China, in position for an impending offensive against the National Liberation Army.

With this American support, the Kuomintang government violated the agreement made with the communists on October 10. On October 13, the attack began in north China, with the aim of taking over railroad and sea communications linking north China and Manchuria. (After expulsion of Japanese armies, popular democratic rule had been organized in Manchuria.) To strengthen its position, Chiang Kai-shek's government utilized the Japanese armies which had surrendered and whose disarming had been delayed for this purpose. Now they undertook to defend the most important strategic points along the railroads and at ports. Once again the Chinese people were faced by threatened civil war and foreign intervention. In these circumstances, the Chinese Communist Party offered to continue peace negotiations and to expedite a consultative political conference. The negotiations were renewed on October 21, only to be broken off again on November 17, with no positive results. Disturbed by the unfolding situation, Chinese democratic organizations launched a wide campaign for once more renewing the talks. In mid-November, on the initiative of the Democratic League, progressive organizations set up the Society for Struggle Against Civil War, which appealed to the Chinese people to demand a consultative political conference without delay. The Kuomintang made no answer to these appeals, and civil war once again engulfed China.

As the dimensions of civil war in China enlarged, the situation in Japan also changed. The national democratic forces met with successes. Despite obstacles posed by American occupation authorities and reactionary resistance, democratic ideas spread increasingly in Japan. The bastions of absolutism collapsed and conservative traditions and pseudoscientific theories began to break down. True learning began to replace them, including the science of social development and scientific understanding of the world. It became possible to reevaluate the history of the Japanese people, the sources of the state and its role in society. As Ienaga Saburo writes: "The beneficial activities of thinkers who had risen against the ruling regime won wide notice. The publication of certain books made clear the situation prevailing among the ruling classes and the mechanism of state power—the diary of Hara Kei, Harada Kuamo's memoirs, and so forth. Intellectual activities of this nature combined to create circumstances which made possible swift progress in researching modern history. This was typical of the postwar years."[9]

Political activities by democratic organizations also intensified. In answer to massive firings under the guise of rationalizing production, a mighty wave of strikes arose, culminating in a general political strike on February 1, 1947. Around five million workers and employees took part. The workers demanded overthrow of the Yoshida government, recognition of trade unions, and improvement in their material life. This strike was the first major clash after the war between Japanese workers and the united front composed of Japanese capitalism and American occupation authorities. Although the strike was crushed, it had great influence on society and helped strengthen the workers' cohesion and consciousness.

The American occupation command insisted on the resignation of the Yoshida[10] cabinet and called for new parliamentary elections. In the April 1947 balloting, Japan's democratic public demonstrated its strength. The Liberal Party lost nearly half of its former votes, declining from 12.6 million in the 1946 elections to only 6.8 million. The Socialist Party, which represented leftist forces, received 7.17 million votes, thereby gaining first place among the parties. The right socialist Katayama[11] became premier of the new Japanese government.

The course of events in Japan increasingly disturbed the American government. This became even more pronounced as the U.S. position in China deteriorated. Experience showed that the United States could not count on the support of Japanese democratic spokesmen. It could find allies only among the ruling classes. For their part, Japanese reactionary leaders sought "working agreements" with the occupation authorities and American capitalists. They hoped thereby to halt Japan's democratization. The highly placed government and court representative, Prince Takamatsu, and the emperor's advisor Hidenari Terasaki, convinced MacArthur's headquarters to take more resolute measures in the battle with the "red peril." They demanded that the Japanese Communist Party be outlawed. The Liberal Party demanded "restoration of the economy on the basis of working relationships with American capital." Satisfaction of these demands was to lay foundations for a new stage in Japan's postwar development, the restoration of monopolistic power with the help of American investments. By the end of 1947 an alliance was evolving between government circles in the United States and Japanese ruling classes. Changing international conditions in the Far East led the United States to seek the support of capitalist Japan.

CHINA IN SEARCH OF POPULAR DEMOCRACY

Having renewed the civil war, Chiang Kai-shek believed that the sole key to victory lay in the military and economic aid of the United States. In return Chiang Kai-shek's government was prepared to give American capitalists a free hand in the country. Agreements concerning commerce, finances, transportation and military affairs were concluded to implement the American-Kuomintang accommodation. American investors gained a privileged position and the government in Washington controlled China's political, economic and cultural life. The foundations were laid by the Sino-American Treaty of Friendship, Commerce, and Maritime Relations, dated November 4, 1946.[12] Under the pretext of "equality between partners to the treaty," American monopolies garnered opportunities to exploit the nationalist regime in China. China enjoyed reciprocal rights which, however, it was in no position to exercise in any practical way. Further, the American government stipulated that American companies were only obliged to pay taxes and duties in China that were no higher than those in the United States, even though Chinese merchants must pay far higher domestic rates. In other words, the advantages accorded to American enterprises in the new treaty discriminated against domestic Chinese companies as well as other foreign firms. This subordinated the Chinese economy to the interests of the United States.

The treaty of friendship, commerce and sea trade of 1946 was augmented later by a series of agreements. In December 1946, American military and civil aircraft gained free access to Chinese air space and airports. An agreement on cooperation in building a Chinese naval fleet was reached in December 1947, followed by mutual assistance pacts of October 28, 1947 and July 3, 1948, and agreement on a joint American-Chinese commission for village reconstruction (in the form of an exchange of notes) in August 1948.[13] American advisors, directed by the United States Secretary of Defense, prepared a plan for construction of "a great northwestern and southwestern road," which envisioned railroad construction in the direction of Kan-su and Hsin-chiang provinces in the northwest and through Yun-nan province toward Burma in the southwest. American concerns concluded deals with the Kuomintang administration "for the development of Kuang-tung, Kuang-hsi and Hunan provinces." These called for extracting rich deposits of tungsten, antimony, bismuth, lead, zinc, mercury and other ores. All these treaties and agreements were to establish juridical and economic foundations for American mastery in all spheres of Chinese life.

Not without cause the Chinese historian Chien Pen-li reached the conclusion that the Sino-American treaty could have the same consequences for China as the twenty-one demands forced upon China by the Japanese in 1915. He wrote: "To so shame the motherland, to sell it out as Chiang Kai-shek did, is an act that neither Yuan Shi-kai nor Wang Ching-wei dared. According to this treaty, the American imperialists acquired not only unlimited rights to control Chiang Kai-shek's economy, but unlimited control of China's politics and army as well."[14] This system, established legally by treaty, undermined China's national and social renaissance. It worked against the vital interests of both the working class and the middle class. No matter how American diplomats tried to veil political ambitions, the Chinese people clearly saw that a new threat hung over their country. New colonial enslavement faced them, in which China would be an open market for American capital and at the same time a subsidiary for raw materials for the United States. Even the Chinese reactionaries began to entertain doubts, and many Kuomintang leaders lost faith in their American allies. The Chinese Communist Party, expressing the country's national feelings, called for a coalition government composed of all the democratic parties and groups that had participated in the anti-Japanese popular front. The Party first urged the elimination of financial monopolies (both foreign and domestic) and termination of the reactionary feudal system. The bourgeois-democratic revolution must be pursued to its conclusion. In foreign policy matters, the communists and the democratic public demanded that the Kuomintang government drop its anti-Soviet course. Equal and friendly relations should be established with all peace-loving states, and the countries of Asia victimized by the Japanese should become independent democratic republics.

At first the Kuomintang armies enjoyed successes in the war, thanks to their superior arms. Despite that advantage, popular-democratic forces soon began to achieve local, then general victories. In northeastern China the National Liberation Army stopped Kuomintang advances at the headwaters of the Sungari River in mid-1946. Supplied by the Soviet Union with captured Japanese weapons, the NLA soon controlled broad areas in the northern and eastern parts of Chi-lin province, in Hei-lung Chiang and Inner Mongolia. Their domain included such important centers as Harbin, Tsitsihar and Chia-mu-ssu. In August 1946 a conference was called in Harbin, including representatives of all classes of the populace, all democratic parties, and units of the NLA. It created the central institution of popular rule in northeastern China, the Northeastern Administrative Committee.

Harbin was connected to the Soviet Union by the river Sungari and by railroads from two directions. Thus it was the chief military arsenal and economic center for the popular-democratic regions of China. Deep to the rear, in Chia-mu-ssu on the Sungari, military and political schools were organized to prepare leaders, as were army administrative services and hospitals. Revitalized railroad and river communications, both within the country and abroad, permitted the popular-democratic administration of northeastern China to set up lasting economic ties with the Soviet Union. These developed on the basis of the first commercial agreement between Soviet foreign trade organizations and the Northeastern Administrative Committee, concluded on December 21, 1946.[15] Soviet organizations also maintained extensive economic ties with authorities of Liao-tung peninsula and Hsin-chiang province.

In these territories industry, transport and banking quickly recovered. They were now the property of the people and their administration rested in the hands of popular-democratic institutions. A large-scale agrarian transformation also began when, in the fall of 1947, an All-China Land Conference took place in Harbin. It adopted "Basic Principles of Chinese Land Law" which foresaw elimination of proprietal ownership. With Soviet collaboration, the strategic and military support bases of the National Liberation Army were established in northeastern China. On September 15, 1947, Lin Piao and Lo Jung-huan launched the NLA offensive which marked the turning point in the civil war. In fifty days the National Liberation Army overran forty-two towns and the chief district defenses of the Kuomintang armies in

Chang-chun and Chi-lin provinces. Successful NLA advances from the northeast allowed other army formations to switch to the offensive in northern, northwestern and eastern China. They laid siege to strong Kuomintang garrisons in Peking, Tientsin-ching, Kalgan, Tai-yuan, Chinan and Tsingtao.

Trying to block these advances, the Kuomintang armies destroyed railroad communications, major bridges and railroad structures. A difficult situation ensued along the railroads of southern northeastern China and in north China. In June 1948, at the request of the northeastern China authorities, the Soviet Ministry of Transport assigned a large group of Soviet railroad workers and repair trains to Harbin. With Soviet supervision and supplies, 120 bridges were rebuilt in record time. These included the "Sungari II" bridge and the bridge connecting Chang-chun and Chi-lin on the Sungari river. By December 15, 1948, railroad communications were completely restored and direct railroad links opened between Harbin, Mukden and north China. Reunion of popular democratic territories in northeast, north, northwest and east China made possible rapid victories throughout the country. Pressed by the NLA armies, the Kuomintang troops either surrendered or retreated to the south in panic. The Kuomintang attempted to gain time by agreeing to "peace" talks with the Chinese Communist Party (as announced by Chiang Kai-shek in his New Year's speech on January 1, 1949).

The Kuomintang government had maintained a hostile policy toward the Soviet Union throughout the years following World War II. Now it turned to the Soviet government (as well as to the United States and England) to mediate negotiations to end the civil war. The Soviet government refused the request and expressed its belief that the Chinese people themselves would be able to determine pathways for building a democratic and peace-loving country. Speaking out, the Chinese Communist Party expressed willingness to halt the bloodshed and reach a peace agreement. The conditions of such an agreement must, however, guarantee a popular-democratic republic in China. Far-sighted Kuomintang leaders agreed to accept the terms of the Chinese Communist Party. At the negotiations held April 1-15, 1949, the Kuomintang delegation was headed by Chang Chi-chung, governor-general of Hsin-chiang province, while Chou En-lai led the communist negotiators. They worked out "The Final Corrected Project on Agreement for Internal Peace," based on the Chinese Communist Party's eight conditions.[16] The Kuomintang government led by Li Tsung-jen refused to sign the agreement, thereby disavowing the authority of its delegations.[17] In protest, the Kuomintang delegation refused to return to Nanking and remained in Peking. Renewed military operations produced the complete defeat of the Kuomintang armies and the collapse of Chiang Kai-shek's regime. The chief cities of the Yangtze valley fell in April and May, 1949; in July the National Liberation Army unleashed a conclusive offensive in south central, southeast, northwest and southwest China. As a result, by fall 1949 nearly all of continental China was cleared of Kuomintang armies, the government fleeing to Taiwan.[18]

Everywhere authority fell into the hands of popular-democratic administrations led by the communists. In a peaceful new situation the Chinese Communist Party shouldered the task of organizing the country's government and determining China's political and economic development, in keeping with the interests of the Chinese working class and prevailing conditions in the country. The past three years of civil war had necessitated changes in the postwar development plan proposed by the Seventh Congress of the Chinese Communist Party in April 1945. At that time, prior to expulsion of the Japanese and the general civil war, Mao Tse-tung had given a speech entitled "Coalition Government." He stated that "at the present stage the Chinese people cannot and therefore should not attempt to create a socialist governmental order." For a long time after liberation China would experience a unique new type of democracy differing from the Soviet Union, based on the "union of democratic classes." The latter would include not only the peasantry and the working class, but also the bourgeoisie. Mao based this conclusion on the fact that the domestic middle class had not been connected to foreign capitalist monopolies. Therefore, the bourgeoisie would join the working people in creating a new democratic government. Ignoring the antagonistic contradictions between the working class and the bourgeoisie, Mao accepted collaboration with the bourgeoisie and considered dictatorship of the proletariat unsuitable for China. He denied the leading role of the working class in a new democratic state.[19]

In reality, events in China unfolded in a manner far different from Mao Tse-tung's outline. Class antagonisms sharpened during the course of the civil war; the Chinese bourgeoisie turned against the people and quite early looked to international capitalism for support, wishing an alliance with American imperial circles. At the same time, the role of the Chinese working class expanded in direct proportion to the liberation of cities, particularly in northeastern China. Bonds with the Soviet Union multiplied and large former Japanese properties reverted to popular ownership. As class distinctions altered, and favorable international circumstances developed, the Chinese Communist Party reexamined former suppositions and statements. This became essential, for these positions had been formed when the Chinese Communist Party was isolated from industrial centers, as well as from the international communist movement. Therefore the goals and means of China's development demanded new definition.

Accordingly, the Second Plenum (Seventh Congress) of the Party Central Committee met in March, 1949 to consider the Party's tasks in final victory and postwar construction. Two points of view found expression during the deliberations to choose directions for China's further development both at home and abroad. Mao Tse-tung repeated his evaluation of the national bourgeoisie's role and reached the conclusion that it was essential to preserve "private capitalism for a rather extended period after the victory of the revolution," which "must not be subjected to overly great or overly harsh limitations." Although Mao mentioned a government sector "with a socialist character," he did not single it out from other economic sectors and made no mention of its leading role.[20] He spoke of a socialist state as a distant prospect, stressing as before that for an extended period it would be necessary to preserve a new form of democracy with a multifarious economy. At that time close economic relations existed between the Soviet Union and the popular-democratic administration. Nevertheless, Mao Tse-tung did not consider it necessary to guide the Party toward further strengthening and expansion of Sino-Soviet relations. He called on the "world anti-imperialist front headed by the Soviet Union" to work merely for "the systematic and complete elimination of imperialist forces in China." It was not to be involved at all in establishing socialism in China or in building world social concord. Insisting on a unique third way for China's development, dissimilar to either Western capitalism or the Soviet "dictatorship of the proletariat," Mao retained his plan for a coalition government. It would be based not on the dictatorship of a single ruling class, but on the union of several classes, on the "democratic dictatorship of the people," including the domestic bourgeoisie.[21]

Adherents of a second point of view suggested at the central committee plenum maintained that conditions in China already had matured sufficiently to allow the completion of the bourgeois-democratic (called "new-democratic" by Mao) stage of the revolution. It was possible to move on to the socialist stage under the leadership of the working class. This viewpoint was expressed in the resolutions of the plenum. In determining the tasks of the party the plenum did not accept Mao's assertions that the Chinese people would not be able to establish a socialist government without an extended waiting period. Rather, the plenum considered it necessary to "restore and develop production rapidly and to resist foreign imperialism in order to assure the inexorable transformation of China from an agricultural to an industrial nation, from a new-democratic state to a socialist state."[22] The Second Plenum continued to use Mao's terminology in a number of cases, guarding his prestige. Nonetheless, the plenum reached decisions which differed essentially in general direction and spirit from Mao's "third way." Now entering the phase of socialist revolution, the Chinese people, led by the Chinese Communist Party, had begun building a socialist state.

JAPAN–"THE WAY BACK"

During 1948, influenced by the popular-democratic victory in China and growing socialist and national liberation movements in other parts of the world, United States officials were constrained to reconsider their policies toward Japan. With the collapse of the Kuomintang regime in China, the United States lost its main stronghold on the Asian continent. This situation required new strategic bases in the Far East to maintain the American role in East and Southeast Asia. American government leaders believed that thanks to its geographic location and economic potential, subjugated Japan might compensate for the loss of China.

The first U.S. step to make use of Japan as a strategic base was to bolster the occupation regime. After the surrender, the United States granted its commander-in-chief in Japan all the prerogatives of supreme authority. Despite this sweeping power, the American government was not content with the developing situation in Japan. Economic and social antagonisms in the country were sharpening and internal unrest growing. The formal liquidation of the major monopolies had meant little, for they continued to exist, hindering the normal functioning of industry, transport, banking, and commerce, and maliciously disorganizing all aspects of the country's life. Economic difficulties arising in Japan forced the United States to ship foodstuffs, cotton, coal and other vital commodities to the country. The balance of trade grew greatly distorted in favor of the United States; to cover the foreign trade deficit, the Americans had to grant Japan short term commercial credits.

Table 1:   Japan's Foreign Trade 1946-1948[*]

| | EXPORT | | IMPORT | | BALANCE | |
	Total	U.S. Share	Total	U.S. Share	Total	U.S. Share
1946	103	74	306	298	-203	-224
1947	174	20	524	434	-350	-414
1948	258	16	684	441	-426	-425

*Japan Statistical Yearbook, 1950, Tokyo, 1951. In millions of dollars.

Escalating American imports could not impact importantly on Japanese economic recovery because a large part of imports consisted of consumer products or raw materials for enterprises serving the American army of occupation. Whereas democratic public opinion was calling for the nationalization of the large industrial firms which previously had belonged to the "Zaibatsu," they continued to stand idle, for the American administration would not permit their rejuvenation on a nationalized basis.[23]

At the same time the United States had no desire to absorb great financial losses in Japan by itself. The capitalist foundations were shaking and the Japanese democratic movement was gaining strength. As a result, there were insufficient guarantees for American capital that its investments would earn profits. An additional factor for Washington, particularly after the Chinese misfortune, was the importance of public support in Japan itself. This support was needed to establish a regime which would assure American control and permit Japan's transformation into an American strategic base in the Far East. The American government set about achieving this goal with the assistance of Japanese reactionaries. Even though they had been overthrown by the war, these rightists displayed continued vitality and durability in the contest with the democratic forces of Japan. Now the Japanese leaders were ready to serve American capitalism, since they counted on it to aid them in restoring their former "grandeur." Consequently the United States government made common cause with Japanese bourgeois monopolists to stabilize the Japanese economy. This new American policy, called by the Japanese the "course of return," determined the character of Japanese-American relations.

In January 1948 a public campaign took place in the United States designed to condemn the policy of "dispersal of Japanese industry." Supposedly the policy did not correspond to American strategic interests in radically altered Far Eastern circumstances. After the American public was prepared for this re-orientation in official policy, Washington took practical steps to accomplish the change. The United States military mission headed by the undersecretary of war, William H. Draper, began talks with the Japanese business world in Tokyo in March 1948. They sought restoration of the "liquidated" Zaibatsu monopolies in order that they might participate in remilitarization. In these and subsequent talks American and Japanese representatives agreed to annul the reparations imposed on Japan by the allied powers. Dismantling of enterprises was to cease, plants were to be returned to their owners, and all earlier measures designed to eliminate the giant monopolies and disperse Japanese industry were rescinded.

The Americans agreed to grant financial assistance for repairs and the expansion of industrial facilities. They promised cooperation in creating a domestic political situation to guarantee "normal" operation of major Japanese capitalist activities. For their part, the Japanese monopolies agreed to restore Japan's military and economic potential under the control and in the interests of the United States. "The healing" of the political situation had begun when, in March 1948, the cabinet of the right socialist Katayama resigned, making way for a transitional coalition cabinet led by Ashida.[24] Then the American administration, in collaboration with the Japanese authorities, unveiled an open attack on the democratic gains of the Japanese people. Blue and white collar workers in government institutions were forbidden to strike or bargain collectively. Massive arrests occurred and workers' meetings were broken up. When the Ashida cabinet was replaced by the one-party Yoshida government, an even broader offensive started against democratic rights.[25] The Yoshida cabinet gave the United States confidence that its "new policy" would be formalized by suitable intergovernmental agreements.

The actual content of this new policy was laid forth in a plan for the stabilization of the Japanese economy presented on December 10, 1948. The United States Congress allocated 1.27 billion dollars to implement the program, while MacArthur's headquarters demanded that free investment privileges be extended to foreign capital.[26] General MacArthur quite openly told the Japanese authorities that the American plan "would require the reformation of Japanese thinking and actions, intensified economizing in all facets of life, and temporary renunciation of certain privileges and freedoms inherent in a free society."[27] The first steps taken by the Yoshida government followed in April 1949, and involved a wage freeze for blue and white collar workers and an end to subsidies for unprofitable enterprises. As a result many small plants and factories closed and some 1.5 million workers and employees lost their positions. These measures led to a sharp reduction in the purchasing power of the Japanese people while cutting expenses for major monopolies. Enormous quantities of goods became available for export.

In 1949 Japan's exports nearly doubled (510 million dollars compared to 258 million in 1948). Despite the continuing growth of imports (905 million dollars compared to 648 million in 1948), the negative balance of payments was reduced from 426 million to 395 million dollars.[28] Thanks to protection and the aid of American capital, the Japanese monopolies again began to acquire power, and could hope to regain the positions lost because of the war. Still, they had to reckon with the fact that their unchecked domination of domestic affairs would encounter the resistance of the working class and progressive democratic public opinion. Moreover, to win opportunities in the outside world the monopolies must surmount many obstacles. To proceed for the moment in alliance with and under the "umbrella" of American military and financial might at home and abroad was the choice elected by ruling circles in Japan.

SUMMARY

United States imperial circles were disappointed in their hopes for the Far East. The defeat of Japan was to have removed their chief rival in the Pacific basin. The weakened positions of England and France were to have permitted the United States, without particular effort, to establish its hegemony in that part of the world. This did not happen. The United States underestimated the growing might of socialism, which was spreading to new territories and forming an independent world system. Further, the strength of the peoples of Asia was greater than expected. Freed from colonial and national dependence, they aspired to new, democratic paths of development. After World War II it became more clear in East Asia than anywhere else that a change was occurring in the balance of power. The change was not in national or racial terms, but in social and class terms. At the head of the forces of peace and democracy stood the Soviet Union, while the United States led the forces of war and capitalist exploitation.

In the immediate postwar years China proved to be the chief arena of class conflicts in East Asia. Reactionary forces led by American imperialists gave the world new confirmation of the international nature of capitalism. They ignored the intrinsic national interests of peoples in order to maintain their hold on the means of exploitation and enslave-ment. American international "solidarity," expressed in terms of war materials and direct military assistance to the Kuomintang regime, permitted the Chinese counterrevolution to unleash a long civil war, and even to achieve temporary success over the popular-democratic armies.

The course of events in China confirmed the accuracy of another of Lenin's conclusions, that victory over international capitalism would require "an international workers' alliance, their international brother-hood." The Soviet Union came to the aid of the struggling Chinese people. With its support, powerful strategic bases were built in north-eastern China. These bases allowed the popular-democratic armies to organize a strong counteroffensive, leading to a fundamental change in the fortunes of the civil war. The Chinese people and its vanguard, the Chinese Communist Party, accorded full credit to Soviet assistance as the chief factor leading to victory in the Chinese revolution.[29] Inter-national proletarian solidarity furthered the position of communist internationalists in the Chinese Communist Party at that historical moment. This unity with international workers helped to eliminate national short-sightedness and "great Han" chauvinism.[30]

The failure of the plans of the United States for expansion in China certainly did not mean that American monopolist capital abandoned its strategic plans for the Pacific, or that imperialism had turned into a "paper tiger" as Mao Tse-tung claimed.[31] In Mao's view imperialism was unable to support reactionary regimes in East Asian countries. After the Chiang Kai-shek clique fled to Taiwan, U.S. imperial circles made their headquarters in Japan, converting it into their chief strategic base in the Far East. The disarmed Japanese monopolies, at least for the moment renouncing their "special" historical mission in Asia as "the divine race of Yamato," forged an alliance with the United States against the national liberation and democratic movements of the Asian peoples.

At the end of the 1940s a new constellation had formed in the Far East. It included Chiang Kai-shek's reactionary regime on Taiwan, the Japanese monopolies, and reactionary governments in other countries which were under American control. Opposed to them were popular-democratic forces, which had posted victories in China and North Korea, and by swelling national liberation movements in other East Asian countries, in brotherly concord with the Soviet Union.

CHAPTER EIGHT

The Divergent Societies

At the beginning of the 1950s it became apparent that China and Japan were going their separate ways. In China, where the Chinese Communist Party headed the political power of the working people, new conditions appeared which allowed the completion of the bourgeois-democratic stage of the revolution and facilitated the transition to a socialist course of development. Previously the Japanese had owned or controlled heavy industry as well as main rail lines, means of communication and banks. Now these assets had become the common property of the people, forming the government sector of the national economy and playing an important part in numerous branches of the country's economy. The powerful bourgeoisie had fled continental China, while the middle and petite bourgeoisie were weak and incapable of either financial or technical direction of heavy industry. At the same time the Chinese popular government was able to utilize Soviet financial, scientific and technical aid. In this manner it was able to gain both political and economic power. The victory of the Chinese revolution produced an enormous impact in Asia, Africa and Latin America.

Japan was in a different position. Under the American occupation the Japanese people were unable to take advantage of the positive circumstances prevailing after the war. American militarists isolated Japanese democratic forces from the outside world, particularly from the world socialist system. Having sided with the Japanese bourgeoisie, the Americans created for them the essential conditions of a capitalist order. In contrast to China, the war had not destroyed the apparatus of bourgeois rule in Japan. The Japanese military and civil administration contained numerous members of the privileged intelligentsia expelled from China and the other countries they had occupied during the war. At that time they had served the monopolies or had been stockholders in commercial production companies and banks. Returning to Japan, they swelled the ranks of the bourgeoisie. The leadership of the reformed middle class parties came from these people; they filled cabinet posts and managerial positions in the resurgent monopolies. Japan's dependence on imports of raw materials and foodstuffs strengthened its rapprochement with the United States.

The democratic activities of the Japanese people continued to grow. However, deference to rightists, opportunism, and small numbers made the Socialist Party ineffective. It was not yet recovered from the grave losses suffered by the Communist Party, and was unable to find a leading position in society and to oppose the rejuvenated bourgeois monopolies. At the beginning of the 1950s Japan remained an occupied country. A bond had developed between American imperialist circles wishing to convert Japan into a strategic base, and the Japanese bourgeois monopolists who hoped to regain their lost positions with American help. Their common enemies were popular democracy and the socialist world.

CHINA'S SOCIALIST PATH

The Chinese People's Republic took form when the bourgeois-democratic revolution was not yet completed. Not all of the country's territory was liberated from the Kuomintang, which continued to enjoy American economic and military aid. Extensive foreign-owned industrial, urban and commercial banking property still existed in the country, belonging largely to English, American and French capitalists. Much Chinese territory remained the property of landlords, monasteries and commercial lenders. On the other hand, political power had shifted to the people, led by the Chinese Communist Party. The working class of the industrial northeast, Shang-hai, Tientsin, Peking and Han-kou became the main support of popular rule, first in the cities and then throughout the country. Popular-democratic administrations gradually liberated more territory from the Kuomintang, gained control of the economy and began eliminating feudal land-holding through socialization of businesses and property. Circumstances developed that speeded the transition from the bourgeois democratic stage of the revolution to the socialist stage.

Based on the decisions of the Second Plenum of the Central Committee of the Chinese Communist Party of April 1949, the first session of the Chinese National Political Consultative Council (NPCC) formed the Central People's Government on September 29, 1949.[2] The nature of the government and its aims were determined by the changed conditions and the actual relationships of political forces in the country. The NPCC recognized the leadership of the working class and its avantgarde, the Communist Party, as the essential and chief factor for building a truly national state. In the introduction to the "General Program" this was spelled out as follows: "The dictatorship of popular democracy in China will be accomplished by the state power of the Popular-Democratic United Front of the working class, the peasants, the petty bourgeoisie, the domestic bourgeoisie and other patriotic, democratic elements. It will be based on the union of workers and peasants and it will be directed by the working class."[3] Although the "General Program" of the NPCC cannot be regarded as the socialist charter of the Chinese people, it did represent a definite socialist impulse. (The popular democratic government was charged with creating "a flourishing, strong China," but not a socialist one.) Economic development received a pronounced socialist orientation inasmuch as "the popular republic's chief material base" was to be the state sector, which according to the General Program would be "socialist in character." The leading role of the working class would be assured by strengthening and expanding the socialist material base, facilitating the peaceful transition from a bourgeois democratic to a socialist revolution in China.

The Soviet Union warmly greeted the establishment of the Chinese People's Republic [CPR]. It was joined in this by all the people's democracies and progressive public opinion throughout the world. The USSR quickly replied when the Chinese Republic's president expressed his desire to establish diplomatic relations with all countries of the world. The Soviet government confirmed its agreement to diplomatic relations in a note from the foreign ministry of the USSR on October 2, 1949. A number of other nations, primarily the peoples' democracies of Asia and Eastern Europe, quickly joined the Soviet Union in recognizing the People's Republic as the "only legal government of China." A major milestone in further bolstering the CPR's political, economic and military position were the talks between its delegation in Moscow, headed by Mao Tse-tung, and the Soviet government. These conversations resulted in a Treaty of Friendship, Alliance and Mutual Aid, signed on February 14, 1950.[4] Agreement between the governments of the USSR and the CPR on granting of credits followed, and further accords were soon to come relating to the Chinese Chang-chun railroad, Port Arthur and Ta-lien, on return to the CPR government without compensation of property acquired from Japanese owners in Manchuria and of Russian military garrison buildings in Peking.

The Treaty of Friendship and Alliance guaranteed to the Chinese people that any attempted aggression by Japan or any other nation in compact with Japan would bring Soviet assistance. It expressed the aspirations of both nations for comprehensive economic collaboration on terms of equality, consideration of mutual interests and mutual respect for state sovereignty, territorial integrity and non-interference in the internal affairs of each country. The Soviet Union granted China the largest single credit ever in the history of China's relations with foreign countries (with the exception of the 500 million dollars the United States granted the Kuomintang government for military aid in 1942). The terms were extremely generous—one percent annually—a rate never previously seen in either Soviet or Chinese experience.[5] Deliveries had begun even before the agreement was signed. The Soviet Union supplied China with equipment for power stations, metallurgical and machine tool plants, mining, railroads, and the like. Other materials also arrived for rebuilding and developing China's economy, destroyed by prolonged warfare.

According to the agreement the Soviet government renounced its rights to the Chinese Northeastern Railroad, Port Arthur, and Ta-lien. This resulted from Soviet feelings of friendship and trust in the government of the Chinese People's Republic. Joint use of Port Arthur for thirty years had been a condition of the Sino-Soviet treaty of 1945; this condition was now cancelled. Rights to joint operation of the Chinese Northeastern Railroad and all railroad property "would be ceded to the CPR after conclusion of a peace treaty with Japan, but not later than the end of 1952." Soviet forces would be withdrawn from Port Arthur, and the fortifications at that naval base would be transferred to the Chinese on the same schedule as the railroad. The Soviet Union expressed willingness to aid the CPR during 1950-1952 in training the qualified specialists needed to take over operation of these enterprises and installations. The two governments agreed that the "question of Ta-lien would be reconsidered after peace was concluded with Japan" in accordance with the terms of the Crimean agreement calling for an international free port of Ta-lien.[6]

Several scientific and technical pacts followed the political and economic agreements. They called for Soviet collaboration with the Chinese. One form of cooperation was to be temporary contributions by Soviet organizations to restore and operate certain enterprises on terms of joint ownership and management. Such joint companies included Sov-Kit-Metal (Soviet-Chinese Metals), Sov-Kit-Neft (Soviet-Chinese Oil), the Soviet-Chinese Civil Aviation Company, and Sov-Kit-Sudostroy (Soviet-Chinese Shipbuilding). Another approach was to send Soviet specialists to China, or to bring Chinese to the Soviet Union for study. Military, economic, scientific and technical aid from the Soviet Union helped the Chinese People's Republic to rebuild industry rapidly. The level of production in 1949 was only half the highest level prior to liberation, a figure prevailing also in other sectors of the economy. Agriculture called for equally urgent measures inasmuch as feudal relationships still remained.

In foreign affairs new difficulties awaited the Chinese People's Republic during its very first year of existence. American imperialists, who had begun warfare against the Korean People's Democratic Republic, posed a direct military threat on the Sino-Korean border. Simultaneously the American government organized an extensive economic blockade of the CPR, aiming to sever its ties with the capitalist countries that, in 1950, provided 75 percent of China's foreign trade. American imperialist plans once again suffered bankruptcy. Fulfilling its treaty obligations, the USSR granted China a supplemental credit of about 450 million dollars, earmarked for urgent needs of the Chinese people and for re-equipping the army. The Soviet Union also endeavored to provide all products needed by the Chinese economy, while assisting China in developing its export and re-export trade.

In its early years the Chinese People's Republic faced the grave possibility of economic ruin in combination with obstacles presented by the international situation. Nonetheless, the Chinese Communist Party proved capable of inspiring the people to overcome economic and military difficulties. With brotherly aid from the Soviet Union, in a relatively short time it restored the national economy. By the end of 1952 the CPR reached and in some areas surpassed prewar industrial production totals. For example, electrical energy was 21.9 percent higher, steel 46.1 percent higher, and paper 125 percent higher than the prewar figures. Production in the state sector formed 41.5 percent of the total gross national product. During the three years since formation of the new republic, extensive agrarian reform had been carried out. Reform had reached a rural population of around 450 million people, with the exception of certain regions with national minorities, excising the material and political foundations of feudalism. This made possible the complete restoration of agricultural production and the yield of by-products to prewar levels by the end of 1952 (an increase of 48.5 percent in comparison with 1949).

Based on the experience of 1949-1952, the Party Central Committee formulated and announced in 1952 "the general line of the Chinese Communist Party for the transitional period." It defined means and practices for building socialism in China, stating: "The essence of the Party's general line during the transitional period lies in making socialist ownership of the means of production the sole economic foundation of our country and society . . . . To accomplish these goals about three five-year plans will be necessary, that is, about fifteen years. Counting from 1953, these tasks basically will be completed by 1967, during which time China can be transformed fundamentally into a great socialist state." To achieve these goals of building socialism, the Communist Party called upon the Chinese people to concentrate its efforts on building a strong, modern, socialist industry. Industrialization became the chief task of the transitional period. It would be achieved by high regard for work and by enthusiasm as well as by China's rich material resources, the generous help extended by the Soviet Union and other socialist countries, and the further strengthening and perfecting of the guiding role of the Chinese Communist Party.

After extensive national discussions, the Party's general line was accepted by the Chinese National People's Congress in September, 1954. This government program then became a part of the Chinese constitution. The introduction to the constitution makes the following statement: "The period beginning with the creation of the Chinese People's Republic and lasting until construction of a socialist society is a transitional period. The basic purposes of the state during the period of transition are the gradual socialist industrialization of the country and the gradual socialist transformation of agriculture, cottage industry, capital industry and commerce."[7] The first five-year plan was prepared on this basis for the years 1953-1957. It may be summarized as intending to create the primary base of socialism and accomplish the partial achievement of socialist agriculture, cottage industry, private manufacturing and commerce. The plan foresaw an appropriation of 76,640 billion yen (equivalent to 21,875 tons of gold) for economic and cultural projects during the period. Construction of new plants, or the reconstruction and expansion of existing ones, would require 42,740 billion. Basic industrial construction would include 695 planned structures, of which 156 would be built with Soviet aid. By the end of 1957 gross industrial output was scheduled to increase by 98.3 percent compared to 1952, and its share in the value of the gross national product to grow from 26.7 percent to 36 percent.

The plan projected slower growth rates for agriculture, where production was to increase by 23.3 percent during the five-year plan. During the first five-year plan, comprehensive development was planned for the Huang-Ho and Huai-Ho river basins. Ninety-one mechanized state farms were to be created, 194 machine-tractor stations, and thirteen major reservoirs. These installations would strengthen the base of agricultural production and pave the way for transition to large state and collective farms.

A favorable international situation contributed to the fulfillment of the first Chinese five-year plan. In mid-1953 the war in Korea came to an end. Despite American resistance, on July 21, 1954, at the Geneva conference, representatives of the USSR, England, France and other interested nations adopted a resolution calling for an end to military operations and peaceful settlement of disputes in Vietnam, Laos and Cambodia. China's peaceful foreign policy received support and sympathy from the nations of the world, particularly in Asia. The Bandung Conference of April 18-24, 1955, in which the Chinese delegation took an active role, further unified peace-loving Asian nations on the basis of the "five points" of peaceful coexistence and international relations based on equality.[8] China's friendly relations with the Soviet Union and other nations continued to strengthen and multiply. Soviet credits to China grew and reached 1816 million rubles in 1956. With Soviet technical aid the Chinese created new industrial branches: aircraft manufacture, automobile and tractor production, peaceful uses of atomic energy, and so forth. The other peoples' democracies also aided China. Poland provided chemical and food plants, Czechoslovakia shipped electrical power stations and machine tool equipment, the German Democratic Republic delivered equipment for fabricating machinery, instruments and chemicals. Between 1950 and 1957 (inclusive) China's foreign trade escalated from 4.15 billion to 10.45 billion yen, or 2.5 times. Imports were clearly industrial in nature: equipment, materials and fuel for industry increased from 83.1 percent in 1951 to 92.7 percent in 1957. Evidence of China's industrialization also appeared in the export mix: the proportion of industrial products increased from 9.3 percent to 27.5 percent in the same span. At the end of the first five-year plan, the socialist countries were accounting for seventy percent of China's trade. The industrious Chinese people contributed to this advance, exploiting the nation's vast resources in the service of the people's government. Soviet aid, along with that of other socialist countries, helped China to fulfill the basic projected goals ahead of time—in 1956. By the end of 1957 targets for industrial production as a whole had been surpassed by fifteen percent.

Together with the development of a socialist economy, Chinese culture also progressed. Marxism-Leninism found confirmation as the ideological foundation of the Chinese Communist Party. A new, people's intelligentsia appeared, and the many peoples of China joined to form a unified socialist state. Between 1949 and 1956 the number of students grew from 116,000 to 380,000; high school enrollments leaped from 1,268,000 to 5,860,000, and elementary school pupils roughly doubled from 24,390,000 to 57,700,000. The total number of books published in the same period grew from 100 million to 1.6 billion copies.

These successes in the economy, and in science and culture, were accompanied by serious and lingering problems in agriculture, manufacturing and cottage industries. The agricultural development plan was published near the end of the five-year plan and scheduled to take effect in 1956 and last for twelve years, that is, until the close of the transitional period in 1967. Major irrigation construction, virgin lands projects and agrotechnical complexes were postponed until the second and third five-year plans. During the same period a socialist transformation was expected to take place in the countryside, ending the system of cooperative farming by individual peasants. Prior to introducing the twelve-year plan, however, Mao Tse-tung suggested a fundamentally different approach to agricultural development. On July 31, 1955, he reported on cooperative agriculture at a conference of secretaries of provincial, city and district Party committees. Mao demanded that collectivization be completed by the spring of 1960, and in some provinces by the end of the current five-year plan, or in the spring of 1957. He did not relate the problem of collectivization to the problem of mechanizing agricultural production, considering that 20 to 25 years would be needed for mechanization.

The campaign for increased rural activity brought 92 percent of peasant farms into cooperatives by the middle of 1956. The methods employed in these cooperatives included simple labor cooperation and sharing of primitive implements. The many millions of peasants in cooperative farms lacked the means for efficient production on socialized land, for home crafts and private plot gardening had been disrupted. Since no major construction took place in the villages, the agricultural yield could not be increased meaningfully. Although urban industrial construction was extensive and rapid, it could not absorb the entire population freed from the villages. Meanwhile cottage industries, which previously had served as alternative employment, had not developed sufficiently. Many craftsmen and tradesmen were drawn away to industry in the cities, causing the number of workers in cottage industries actually to decline from 7,489,400 in 1952 to 6,527,700 in 1957. The problem of employment became acute and required a quick solution.

Mao Tse-tung ignored the fact that, in calling for the accelerated transformation of the village, his left deviation had caused the problem. He began an assault on the general position of the Chinese Communist Party, trying to convince the Chinese people that he was not condemning socialist construction but rather the "slave tempo" of the five-year plan and central planning itself, which supposedly "froze the initiative of the masses." Simultaneously he tried to interpret socialism in a different way. He wanted to replace science with utopia and dreams, to reject past socialist progress and equate the socialist order with a new-democratic system.[9] In short, he wanted to inject the bourgeois nationalist manner of development into socialism. In the past, Mao had taken a rightist stance in his struggle with advocates of the socialist approach, terming them left opportunists and adventurers. Now he set about attacking the socialist viewpoint from an anarchical and arch-leftist position, demanding an end to "plan clichés" and insisting on accelerated economic expansion. Mao labelled China's industrial development to this point as inadequate, and proposed that the growth target be doubled to thirty percent. As before he tried to protect the national bourgeoisie, and did not seek faster transition in industry and commerce.

Mao Tse-tung's first attacks on the general line of the Chinese Communist Party were successful. He shook the system of state planning and obtained a postponement "for reworking" the projected twelve-year agricultural development plan. Plan targets were doubled for economic construction and production in 1956. But then, by the middle of 1956, the grave consequences of Mao's breaking of the "old framework" became apparent. The leap forward in agriculture produced a negative effect on agricultural production. Meanwhile, accelerated industrial activity exhausted reserves and raw material supplies, causing production bottlenecks and imbalances between individual branches of the economy.

The deviation from the general Party program prevailed in foreign affairs as well. Mao Tse-tung and his followers began to evince a nationalistic, great power stance toward China's neighbors in Southeast Asia, where several million Chinese émigrés lived. These included major industrialists, bankers, merchants and middle class political figures who not infrequently held important posts in the economy and politics of their countries. The Peking leadership attempted to protect the Chinese moneylenders and bourgeois nationalists who were acting to prevent progressive social measures in Burma and India. Mao's government attempted to utilize the overseas Chinese as agents of subversion, subordinating the interests of the workers of those countries to great power chauvinist ideas which continued the traditional policy of the Chinese emperors. The slogan "creation of a mighty and flourishing China," to which the Chinese Communist Party had imported socialist content in the early days of the new state, now evolved into a great power instrument for resurrecting the former grandeur of the "Middle

Kingdom" (Chung Kuo) in the eyes of Asia. This tendency also appeared at home in relation to the non-Chinese nationalities, small national groups being subjected to pressure and mistrust. As the first secretary of the Party committee for Inner Mongolia, Ulanfu, complained: "The rights of cadres from national minorities are not respected when it comes to managing the affairs of their regions. All tasks are taken over by workers of Chinese national origin."[10] By administrative measures ethnic Chinese were transferred to national minority regions, while small national groups fell victim to forced assimilation.

The adventurism of Mao's course grew apparent, and dissatisfaction with it grew among party workers and intellectuals. In September 1956, the Eighth Congress of the Chinese Communist Party convened. It summed up the accomplishments of the first five-year plan, and called upon the people to press on with the general Party program, with the goal of converting China into "an advanced socialist industrial state." The congress presented broad economic targets for the second five-year plan (1958-1962), according to which the gross national product would rise by 75 percent in comparison with 1957. Industrial production would be approximately two times greater and agriculture would produce 35 percent more. The dominant feature of the second five-year plan would remain, as in the first one, full-speed development of basic heavy industry, such production to amount to fifty percent of overall industrial output as compared to 38 percent in the plan for 1957. At the same time, new importance was attributed to the expansion of light manufacturing and cottage industry.

In the new plan agriculture would receive more attention than previously, with primary emphasis on grains and industrial crops. Grain production would increase from 181 million tons in 1957 to 250 million tons in 1962. (The maximum prewar crop had been 138 million tons in 1936.) While collectivized agriculture was accorded most importance, peasant farming on private plots was encouraged on the "condition that these not affect production in cooperatives." It was also pointed out that the "blind merging of small cooperatives into large ones must be prevented in order to avoid difficulties in management and operational organization which might impact negatively on agriculture." In defining the development projected in the second five-year plan, the Chinese Communist Party pointed out the "clear tendency toward easing of tensions," that "day by day, economic construction is expanding in the great Soviet Union and in the peoples' democracies" and that the "democratic dictatorship of the people is becoming more secure in our country." The second five-year plan proclaimed the goal of "completing socialist transformation and assuring for our country the opportunity in the next three five-year plans to build a comprehensive industrial system, in order that our country will change from backward agriculture to an advanced socialist industrial society."[11]

Aid from the Soviet Union and the people's democracies was a highly appreciated factor in accomplishing the first five-year plan in China. The Eighth Party Congress pointed out the necessity of "strengthening international cooperation and expanding mutual economic, cultural and commercial bonds with the Soviet Union and the people's democracies while developing the national economy and creating a comprehensive industrial system." The point of departure should be ". . . division of labor and cooperation in the areas of economics, technology and scientific research work . . . . This would lead to accelerated development of the national economy, to a general upsurge in the economy and culture of the socialist nations, led by the Soviet Union."[12]

At the same time the Eighth Party Congress could not ignore such phenomena as growing "great Han" chauvinism,[13] oppression of small nationalities, the developing personality cult, and violation of the collegiate principle in Party leadership. The resolution of the Congress on this matter pointed out that "workers of Chinese nationality should overcome erroneous views of great Han chauvinism in all their forms." In the Party "it is unacceptable to act in ways which violate the party's political line and organizational principles, to display willfulness and to place persons above the party collective."[14]

Having created the foundations of industrialization during the first five-year plan, the Chinese People's Republic had struck out on the road to socialism. The Central Committee's report to the Eighth Party Congress stated: "In the struggle between capitalism and socialism in our country, the question of "who will dominate whom" already has been decided in favor of socialism." The second five-year plan was to guarantee China's transformation into an industrialized agrarian nation.

JAPAN'S POSTWAR DEVELOPMENT

Japan's development took place in different circumstances during this era. The American plan to restore Japan's military economic potential, called the "stabilization plan" by American officials, would create a strategic military base for the United States in the Far East.[15] The Japanese monopolies were fervent advocates of the American plan since it finally legalized their position and turned over to them the economic and political management of the country. Bourgeois nationalist circles in Japan also supported the concept, hoping to overcome the postwar crisis and accelerate Japan's re-birth on "American shoulders."

The United States entertained corresponding political plans. On General MacArthur's advice as a "keen connoisseur of Eastern psychology," the United States turned back administrative affairs to Japanese themselves. For this purpose strong Japanese police forces came into being in 1949, numbering as many as 300,000 men. In 1950 the Japanese authorities received permission for a "police reserve corps" of 75,000 men, armed with American tanks, aircraft, armored vehicles and automatic weapons. At that time MacArthur's staff correctly assumed that in the immediate future Japanese nationalism would pose no threat to U.S. interests and might prove useful against leftist forces. Accordingly, the American command raised no opposition to a variety of nationalist organizations made up, for example, of former air force pilots ("Wakabatokai"), naval officers ("Rasutonia"), "fighters for the great empire of Yamato," and fascist youth.

Japan's workers and the progressive intelligentsia did not sit idly in the face of these reactionary threats. A wave of demonstrations by workers, students and the intelligentsia swept Japan in the spring of 1950. In May metal workers declared a strike; they were joined by miners, railroad workers, textile workers, subway and movie studio employees. The strikers set forth political demands to combat American plans for aggression against the Chinese and Korean peoples and to preserve democratic freedoms. Students took an active part in the anti-American movement, demonstrating for freedom of education and opposing conversion of Japan into an American military base. Demonstrations by workers, public servants and students in Tokyo on May 20 turned into a powerful protest against the American occupation; they ended in bloody clashes with American soldiers and Japanese police. The growing leftist movement in the country found expression in the 1950 parliamentary elections. Progressive forces campaigned on platforms calling for quick completion of a peace treaty, preservation of Japan's neutrality in international conflicts, and denial of military bases on Japanese territory to foreign governments. The socialists and other leftist parties and groups won a number of additional seats in parliament.

The situation which had evolved in Japan increasingly disturbed Washington. For a new "leap" to the Asian continent, the United States required a more durable and permanent "trampoline" on the Japanese islands. In these conditions, American diplomacy searched for new forms of occupation. It was necessary to veil in some clever way the expansionist aspirations of American capitalism in order to create the impression of "equal" and "allied" relations between the United States and Japan. The United States was also interested in orienting the Japanese economy to the needs of the Korean War. With this in mind, American government officials were ready for further rapprochement with Japanese big business, which at this historical point threatened no serious competition in the Far East. In turn, Japanese capitalists were happy to warm their hands at the fire in Korea while simultaneously bolstering domestic and foreign economic and political positions with American help. Collaboration with the United States promised enormous orders and the opportunity for industrial modernization. On that foundation the capitalists might expand exports, one of the chief means of reestablishing their influence.

Contrary to the wishes and will of the Japanese people, the United States and Japan broke the peace agreement on September 8, 1951. They signed the separate San Francisco peace treaty, along with other countries dependent on the United States. Concurrently, an American-Japanese "security pact" was concluded, which amounted to a new legalized form of military alliance between the two countries.[16] The San Francisco treaty gave the United States major political advantages. It automatically disbanded the Allied institutions for monitoring the Potsdam agreements and regulations adopted by the occupation authorities. All limitations on American activities in Japan were removed. In addition the United States could now structure relations on the basis of a bilateral treaty. Further, the agreement obligated the Allies to remove their forces from Japan within ninety days of its effective date, thus restoring total sovereignty to Japan. In reality, these provisions of the treaty were bypassed by the United States: on the basis of the "security pact" America might station armed forces in Japan and maintain military bases there.

Notwithstanding massive domestic protests, Japan's rulers hastened to ratify the treaty and the "security pact." They saw in these documents a dependable guarantee for consolidating the power of the monopolies and for further limitation of the Japanese people's democratic rights. The military and political arrangement was followed by coordination of economic activities, the United States government reciprocating for Japanese military hardware by financing industrial and transportation construction and reconstruction, and supplying Japan with copious equipment and raw materials. Beyond utilizing the Japanese economy for the current needs of the Korean war, American capital investments provided the basis for continued U.S. influence in

Japan, placing as they did Japan's economy in direct dependence on American financial, technical and raw material sources. The flow of American capital to Japan as a result of the Korean war amounted to the huge sum of 2,374 million dollars from 1950-1953. This permitted Japan fully to pay for rapidly growing imports (from 974 million in 1950 to 2,410 million dollars in 1953). It was also able to create large foreign exchange reserves to cover subsequent foreign trade deficits. The following statistics covering the Japanese balance of payments during the Korean war attest to this (in millions of dollars).

	1950	1951	1952	1953	Total
Trade Balance	+127	-428	-429	-945	-1,675
Non-commercial Balance	+ 55	+167	- 81	- 58	+ 83
Special Orders and Purchases	+149	+592	+824	+809	+2,374
Balance	+331	+331	+314	-194	+ 782

The Korean war speeded concentration of capital in Japan and determined the direction of the development of Japanese industry. Large American military orders required quick, guaranteed delivery. They could be filled only by the mighty industrial and financial concerns. This circumstance ruined small and medium firms, which the trusts then swallowed. From the beginning of the Korean war until April 1953, the capital of the six largest banks grew from 751 million to 14,270 million yen. These banks effectively monopolized credit flow in the national economy and controlled the fundamental branches of Japan's industry and transportation. In 1951 alone the commission for "just and honest transactions" examined more than 1500 mergers and 722 liquidation applications for transferring property to the burgeoning giant companies.

Concentration of industry, transport and finance in the hands of the big trading companies permitted them to dominate domestic resources, extract maximum profit by exploiting the workers, and direct their funds into the most profitable and promising industries. This held true even though 62.2 percent of new capital in Japan came from abroad. The most rapid advances occurred in machine tool and instrumentation manufacture, chemicals and metals. Processing industries acquired modern high capacity equipment and enjoyed expanding domestic markets. Thus, in 1950 total employment in processing concerns reached 4,261,000 and the value of their production was 2,372 billion yen. By 1953 these figures had grown to 5,171,000 men and 5,877 billion yen, and by 1957 to 6,605,000 men and 10,457 billion yen.[17]

The technological modernization of Japanese industry stimulated a sharp increase in labor productivity. On the average each man working in a processing industry in 1950 produced goods in the value of 555,000 yen (1540 dollars). In 1953 the average was 1,130,000 yen (3100 dollars) and in 1957 it reached 1,583,000 yen (4397 dollars). At the same time real wages in processing industries (extremely low in 1950) increased by only 25.7 percent by 1953, 34.1 percent by 1955 and 49 percent by 1957. They remained markedly lower than wages in Europe.[18] Rapid growth of labor productivity and maintenance of low wage levels generated enormous excess profits for Japanese big business, and provided the chief domestic source for financing heavy industry and transport. Favorable domestic and international conditions allowed Japan at the end of the first year of the Korean war (1951) to reach the prewar level of industrial production. In 1955 that level was surpassed by 55.1 percent and in 1957 by 127 percent. Processing industries had grown by 140 percent and extracting by 47 percent.

Japanese big business had again acquired power. Cheap domestic labor and modernized production promoted favorable terms for competition in world markets. Far from being an obstacle, Japan's continuing dependence on the United States actually furthered this achievement. In 1957 Japan's foreign trade reached 7,142 million dollars as against 1,584 million dollars during the prewar years (1936). Lacking many raw materials, Japan assumed the role of the "world's factory," processing ores and materials from many Asian and American countries, including the United States. Of the total Japanese imports of 4,284 million dollars, industrial raw materials and fuels made up 2,725 million, or 63.6 percent. Meanwhile Japan's exports took on a distinctly industrial character, amounting to 2,547 million dollars of the total exports of 2,858 million, or 89.4 percent.

Japan continued to press industrial progress. To do so, it needed to import expensive industrial equipment, particularly sophisticated modern machinery. No thought was wasted on the fact that the simultaneous import of raw materials and equipment stimulated significant deficits in the country's balance of payments and exhausted its foreign exchange reserves. Special American orders and American expenditures for bases on Japanese territory continued to cover most of the deficits. During the Korean war Washington spent 824.2 million in 1952 and 809.5

million in 1953. Although both accounts declined after the war, they still averaged 574 million dollars annually between 1954-1957. Thus even after the war in Korea, the United States continued to be Japan's sole creditor, and main partner in foreign trade. Japanese-American economic relations exerted a direct impact on Japan's political life and governmental policies. The press, foreign as well as domestic, printed one-sided evaluations of Japan's policies at that time, citing only the dependency on American capital. It was not pointed out that the character of American-Japanese relations to no smaller degree corresponded to the interests of Japan's own capitalists who already had become sufficiently strong to use American arms and dollars for their own benefit, and markedly to influence U.S. policy.

The monopolists succeeded in bringing relative political stabilization to Japan. The Yoshida government remained in power for the six years between 1949-1954,[19] relying on the extreme rightist Liberal Party, which represented major financial interests and openly supported a military alliance with the United States. Liberal Party policies met determined popular opposition. The leftist movement looked to social freedoms, improvement of the workers' economic position, and establishment of equal, friendly relations with all peace-loving peoples and nations, especially the neighboring Soviet Union, the Chinese People's Republic and the Korean People's Democratic Republic. Progressive Japanese welcomed the joint USSR-China declaration on relations with Japan of October 12, 1954, which expressed Asian concerns about Japan's military and economic dependence on the United States. Such relationships "could be employed in aggressive plans foreign to the interests of the Japanese people and to the task of maintaining peace in the Far East." The USSR and China, the declaration said, were willing to develop broad commercial relations with Japan "on mutually beneficial terms," and to establish close cultural bonds.[20]

Thus the Japanese people might expect peaceful, neighborly relations with the largest countries in the world, the USSR and China. Development of mutually beneficial trade would create a lasting foundation for a peacefully flourishing economy in Japan. Pressured by leftist forces, the Democratic Party government of Premier Hatoyama, which came to power in December 1954,[21] began talks with the Soviet Union in June 1955 on normalizing relations. A joint declaration was signed when Hatoyama visited Moscow on October 19, 1956. It ended the "state of war" between the two countries and renewed diplomatic relations. The Protocol of Trade Development, signed the same day, included reciprocal "most favored nation" status, and laid the foundation for mutually beneficial trade.[22]

Normalization of Soviet-Japanese relations benefited Japan's sovereignty as an independent state and its international prestige. In addition, Japan entered the United Nations. These factors contributed positively to the consolidation of the position of Japanese leftist forces. They were not numerous enough, however, to weaken seriously the position of the reactionary leadership or to extract the nation from American financial control. Japanese big business circles stalled by resorting to social demagogy, meanwhile continuing to pursue the same political course. Japan moved ever further from the Potsdam decisions which had charted guidelines for peaceful democratic development. Japan was drawn into aggressive plans in the Far East, while supporting the powers of reaction against movements for Asian independence.

SINO-JAPANESE RELATIONS, 1956-1957

In the declaration accompanying the foundation of the Chinese People's Republic, the Chinese government expressed the wish for "diplomatic relations with any foreign government which wished to observe the principles of equality, mutual benefit and mutual respect for territorial integrity and sovereignty."[23] In accord with the general program of the People's Political Consultative Council, Chinese authorities used as a point of departure the rule that any state wanting to establish diplomatic relations must first break relations with "the Kuomintang reactionaries" who had become entrenched on Taiwan.

In those years an extensive campaign continued in Japan calling for recognition of the government of the People's Republic as the only legal government of China, and for the establishment of diplomatic relations. At the end of 1949, Japanese progressives formed the Parliamentary League for Assisting Sino-Japanese Trade. Japanese industrial and commercial leaders supported it and advocated restoring trade with China, particularly to import Manchurian coal and iron ore from Hainan. In 1950 China and Japan exchanged goods worth 58.9 million dollars, of which Japanese imports were 39.3 and exports 19.6 million dollars. Thanks to their territorial proximity, Chinese raw materials reached Japan at far lower prices than American, Australian or Indian commodities. Having inherited a ruined economy from the Kuomintang government, the People's Republic was anxious to develop trade with Japan. Chinese industry in Manchuria and occupied China had been equipped largely with Japanese products, which meant technological dependence on Japan. Thus a Japanese-Chinese rapprochement answered the needs of both nations.

The Korean war and the U.S.-Japanese security pact placed Japan under American military and economic control, effectively interrupting normal expansion of Sino-Japanese ties. The Yoshida government pursued policies which were hostile to China. Not yet a member of the United Nations, Japan agreed to abide by the embargo forced on the U.N. General Assembly by the American bloc on May 18, 1951. Further, Japan joined the "China Committee" formed by the nations of the North Atlantic Treaty Organization (with the exception of Iceland), which prepared a list of some 430 items forbidden for shipment to China. In essence, the Japanese government was moving toward cessation of trade with China, inasmuch as it agreed not to sell industrial equipment, machinery, nonferrous metals, steel or numerous other goods of interest to China.

Under American pressure the Yoshida cabinet hurled a direct political challenge at the Chinese people. Refusing to recognize the legitimate CPR government, the Japanese authorities signed a bilateral "peace treaty" with the Chiang Kai-shek government on Taiwan, thereby closing all roads to normal relations with the Chinese People's Republic. The mainland government regarded treaties and agreements made by the Japanese with the United States as acts "hostile to the Soviet Union and China." They represented a "threat to the peoples of Asia" and had the purpose of "regenerating Japanese militarism." On May 6, 1952, the Chinese foreign ministry delivered a strong protest against the "peace treaty" with the Chiang Kai-shek government.[24]

The Yoshida government's policy toward China provoked dissatisfaction in Japanese bourgeois quarters as well. Many Japanese businessmen, particularly those with no direct profit from their American "allies," did not participate in the windfalls resulting from special orders. They could not be reconciled to the loss of trade with China, particularly since China's foreign trade was quickly expanding. After the start of Korean peace talks, Japanese industrialists and merchants, fearing declining American purchases, became more anxious for expanded trade with China. These tendencies were restrained by Japan's leadership, which feared that normalized relations with the People's Republic would damage ties with the United States.

On the other hand, the Japanese government could not ignore the real economic benefits of trade with China. It was obliged to consider public demands for normal relations with China. In such circumstances, Tokyo's leaders set about seeking a compromise solution. Not without American knowledge, they decided to limit overtures to trade matters. In addition, it was determined that commerce would not be conducted through official government channels via treaties and agreements. Rather, a private system would be employed involving transactions between companies and (non-governmental) trade organizations. This formula skirted the issue of recognition of the Chinese People's Republic and permitted Japanese firms to develop trade without any obligations on the part of the Japanese government. At the same time, Japan continued to adhere to the embargo imposed by the China Committee's list of forbidden goods. It maintained official relations with the Taiwan government and refused to grant financial guarantees for Sino-Japanese commercial transactions. The Chinese government, pursuing a consistent policy of normalizing relations with Japan, agreed to commercial ties on this private basis, without deciding the question of diplomatic recognition. Even such a limited trade bond was an important step toward complete normalization of relations. China possessed a sufficiently secure international position to conduct a consistent, peaceful policy and avoid departures from its principles.

On June 1, 1952, representatives of Japanese business arrived in Peking. They signed a one year trade agreement calling for goods in the value of thirty million pounds sterling to be delivered by each side. Analogous trade agreements were signed on October 29, 1953 and May 4, 1955, the latter being extended for 1956 and 1957. The Japanese signers represented the Association for Assisting Sino-Japanese Trade Development and the Sino-Japanese Export-Import Association, which enjoyed the active support of the Parliamentary League for Assisting Sino-Japanese Trade. On the Chinese side, the agreement was signed in the name of the Committee for Promotion of International Trade. According to these trade agreements, the goods to be delivered fell into three groups on the basis of their importance to the respective national economies. The first group of Japanese products included ferrous and nonferrous metals, transport and other equipment. These were to be exchanged for Chinese iron and manganese ore, pig iron, coal and soy beans. The implementation of these agreements required that the Japanese government withdraw from the pro-American "blockade" of China, and that it legalize Sino-Japanese commerce and participation therein by government financial institutions and banks in one form or another. Even the largest Japanese firms representing individual concerns sought trade with China.

In 1955 an influential businessman, representing Japanese monopolies, visited Peking as the guest of the government. He was Kuhara Fusanosuke, and in his sojourn of two months in the People's Republic he conducted far-reaching exchanges of opinion with Chou En-lai and

Mao Tse-tung. At this very moment Mao was pursuing policies which openly contradicted those of the Chinese Communist Party's general position. He sought to change policies toward the socialist countries and to line up the nations and peoples of Asia behind China on a pan-Asian basis. Mao's statement that "only the peoples of Asia should be involved in Asian affairs" gained wide attention. As Kuhara's reports show, he and Mao talked precisely about allying China and Japan on a nationalistic, racial basis. Based on these new tendencies in Mao Tse-tung's policies, Kuhara fervently sought normalization of relations with China. Stressing Asian common interests, he recommended that the Japanese government define its position concerning the People's Republic. Mao Tse-tung endeavored to win over leftist forces in Japan with the same plan. Ignoring the obvious expansionist aims of Japan's monopolists, who were organically bound to American imperialism, and without noticing deepening social conflicts in Japanese society, Mao attempted to demonstrate the possibility of a unified front, including the powerful Japanese middle class, against the United States.

Mao's calls for reconciliation with Japan on a nationalist basis would have separated the two countries from the world democratic movement and placed them in opposition to peoples and nations of other continents. Certain rightist groups in Japan responded positively, while democratic groups saw in the Chinese People's Republic a new, popular-democratic order. It was successfully building a socialist society with the assistance of other socialist countries, a factor which possessed an important meaning for the Japanese people. In contrast, representatives of the reactionary bourgeoisie looked to China only as an ally to combat the United States and other Western nations, both capitalist and socialist, as non-Asiatic.

Kuhara's mission returned with Mao's assurances of pan-Asian solidarity with Japan. Now the adherents of normal relations with China gained a strong ally, Prime Minister Hatoyama himself. He announced his readiness to cooperate in the third Sino-Japanese trade agreement, in 1955. Ishibashi, the next prime minister,[25] was an even stronger supporter of these policies. At the end of 1956 his cabinet announced a decision to exchange unofficial commercial representatives with the People's Republic and to oversee financial negotiations in trade. In practice, however, these were empty declarations. The "blockade and embargo" policy effectively continued, and the Japanese government forbade delivery of strategic goods, thereby blocking delivery of the products most essential for China. At the initiative of the Japanese government trade talks were broken off, and actual trade turned out to be significantly less than the agreements stipulated, particularly in Japanese exports to China. (See Table 2.) Noticeable trade increases in 1956 proved to be of short duration. In subsequent years Sino-Japanese trade again declined. Japanese big business resisted changing policy toward China since such a move inevitably would weaken its "alliance" with the United States. Mao Tse-tung's nationalist advances met with sympathy but did not offer sufficient guarantees to the monopolies, which doubted Mao's dependability. These doubts increased especially after the Eighth Congress of the Chinese Communist Party in September 1956, which confirmed the general party line calling for continued socialist construction in China and further friendly relations with the USSR and other socialist states.

Table 2:
Japanese Trade with China 1950-1957 (in millions of dollars)*

	Total Trade		Japanese Exports		Japanese Imports	
	agreed	actual	agreed	actual	agreed	actual
1950	---	58.9	---	19.6	---	39.3
1951	---	27.4	---	5.8	---	21.6
1952	---	15.5	---	0.6	---	14.9
1953	168	34.2	84	4.5	84	29.7
1954	168	59.9	84	19.1	84	40.8
1955	168	109.3	84	28.5	84	80.8
1956	168	151.0	84	67.4	84	83.6
1957	168	141.0	84	60.5	84	80.5

*Source: "Nittyu boeki" (Japanese-Chinese Trade), Tokyo, 1964.

In 1957 the extreme rightist cabinet headed by Premier Kishi took over, based on the Liberal Democratic Party.[26] Kishi's government instituted a harsh policy toward China and disavowed all the promises made by preceding cabinets concerning cooperation in expanding Sino-Japanese trade. Talks dealing with the fourth trade agreement grew complicated. To please the United States, the Kishi administration openly stressed its friendly relations with the Taiwan regime of Chiang Kai-shek as the "legal" government of all China. At the beginning of 1958 Sino-Japanese relations abruptly broke off.

THE CHINESE AND JAPANESE ECONOMIES, 1949-1957

Varying conditions prevailed in China and Japan during 1949-1957. The four years preceding the formation of the Chinese People's Republic saw a devastating civil war which continued to batter an economy already demolished by the prolonged war against Japan. As a result, industrial production in 1949 was only fifty percent that of 1936, and agriculture but 75 percent. A severe shortage of technical, engineering and other specialized personnel added to the problem. During the years of Japanese occupation of the country's chief industrial region, Manchuria, Japanese enterprises had used Japanese specialists exclusively. They returned to Japan after the war. Few specialists remained at factories belonging to other foreign governments or to Kuomintang capitalists. Another circumstance affecting restoration and development of the Chinese economy was that after the communist victory, the People's Republic was compelled to maintain a large army to repel foreign aggression. The war in Korea increased this threat particularly.

These difficulties might have proved insurmountable had China remained alone. The aid of the Soviet Union and other socialist countries provided essential support. This is underscored by the official report to the First Session of the Chinese National Peoples Congress: "Acting in a spirit of friendship and mutual aid, the Soviet Union is providing enormous material, financial and scientific assistance to us.... We have noted that friendship in the preface of our constitution, bearing witness to the fact that Sino-Soviet friendship is eternal and indestructable."[27] The creative energy of the free Chinese people joined together with the brotherly help of the socialist countries, helping to overcome difficulties brought on by destruction and limited material and human resources. Within three years the economy was functioning again, and China launched an extensive plan of economic and cultural progress.

Japan enjoyed certain advantages over China. Numerous engineering, economic, financial and managerial personnel returned to the country after the war. Japan had large reserves of qualified workers to supply all key branches of industry and transport. With active American participation, the state monopoly system for directing the economy was preserved. By the start of the 1950s Japan already had regained prewar levels of industrial production. As quartermaster for the American army during the Korean war, Japan used to advantage American technical and financial might as a means of accelerated economic development. Measured by industrial growth rate, Japan moved up among the leaders of the capitalist world.

Notwithstanding Japan's advantages and its own difficulties during the years 1949-1957, China's economic growth rate surpassed Japan's (Table 3). This growth took place without distortions, according to plan.

Table 3:

Chinese and Japanese Growth Rates, 1949-1957

	People's Republic of China			Japan		
	1949	1952	1957	1949	1952	1957
National Income	100	169.7	259.7	100	185.8	302.7
Industrial Production	100	244.9	559.2	100	177.7	319.7
Agricultural Production	100	148.5	185.1	100	155.8	183.9

*Sources: (in Chinese:) *The Great Decade,* Peking, 1959; *Statistical Data on the Achievements in Economic and Cultural Construction in the Chinese People's Republic,* Peking, 1959; *Japan Statistical Year Book,* 1950, 1963.

The somewhat higher growth rate in Japan's national income for the period is explained chiefly by increased earnings for services. These include payments for maintaining American bases, and maritime earnings, and are not related to the level of production. In terms of industrial production, China's development during this era was significantly faster. At the end of the first five-year plan in 1957, China had surpassed Japan in quantities of certain industrial goods produced, as shown below.

Table 4:
Production of Basic and Industrial Goods in China and Japan,
1949-1957*

		Chinese People's Republic		Japan	
		1949	1957	1949	1957
Coal	Thous. tons	32,430	130,000	37,973	52,255
Electrical Energy	Bil. KW hrs.	4.3	19.3	41.5	81.3
Steel	Thous. tons	158	5,350	3,111	12,570
Pig Iron	Thous. tons	252	5,936	1,549	6,815
Metal-cutting Lathes	Units	1,582	28,000	6,680	34,824
Cement	Thous. tons	660	6,860	3,278	15,176
Cotton Fabrics	Mil. meters	1,890	5,050	823	3,212
Paper	Thous. tons	228	1,222	594	1,748
Salt	Thous. tons	2,985	8,277	396	869
Sugar	Thous. tons	199	864	------	1,101

*Sources: *The Great Decade,* Peking, 1959; *Japan Statistical Year Book,* 1950, 1963.

The tables illustrate how the gap between the two countries narrowed considerably in production of metal-cutting lathes, pig iron, paper, cement and certain other goods. The Chinese People's Republic continued to lag behind in electrical output. Despite extensive new electrical installations, part of which began operations during the first eight years, China was still producing less than half as much electricity as had Japan in 1949. The electrification level of the economy was a weak point in China and one of Japan's main advantages. This is particularly true when we consider that most of Japan's power was produced by hydroelectric power stations, at a significantly lower rate than for thermal electro-energy. In 1957 hydroelectric production was 56.7 billion kilowatt hours, or about seventy percent of total output.

With richer natural resources, China led Japan by a wide margin in producing many nonferrous and rare metals. In the first five-year plan, with the help of specialists from the Soviet Union and other socialist countries, a comprehensive geological survey in China discovered rich resources of ferrous, nonferrous and rare metals as well as minerals. During 1955-1957 the extraction of these minerals satisfied domestic needs and permitted China to become a major exporter of lead, tungsten, molybdenum, antimony, mercury, spodumene, beryllium, graphite, talc and quartz.

China and Japan have different situations concerning foodstuffs. China has the potential to satisfy domestic needs completely, and to become a major exporter of certain plant and animal products. Between 1949 and 1957 the production of grain, the staple food, expanded in China to 78 million tons, which was sufficient to supply the city populations and the needs of industry. These consumers took 46 million tons annually by the end of the first five-year plan. The food supply in the countryside also improved. During the years of the first five-year plan, China exported from 600,000-1,000,000 tons of rice annually, 800,000-1,000,000 tons of soy beans, 200-225,000 tons of pork, as well as vegetable oil, tea, fruits and many other products.

The Japanese production levels of grain and oil-yield crops, which are important to Chinese and Japanese diets, do not begin to satisfy the population's needs. Japan must import these products, partly from China.

Table 5:
Grain and Oil-Producing Crop Production in China and Japan
1949-1957 (mil. tons)*

	People's Republic of China		Japan	
	1949	1957	1949	1957
Grains, total	108	185	17.8	21.1
Rice	48.7	86.8	9.4	11.5
Wheat	13.8	23.6	1.3	1.3
Soy Beans	5.1	10.5	-----	0.459
Peanuts	1.26	2.6	-----	0.072

*Sources: *The Great Decade of the Chinese People's Republic. Japan Statistical Year Book, 1951,* 1963.

As in any developing socialist country, a characteristic feature of Chinese industrial development has been the steadiness and consistency of forward progress. The most significant growth in industrial production took place during the recovery period of 1950-1952, when average annual growth amounted to 34.8 percent. The years of widespread planned construction (1953-1957) required enormous capital investments to create new industry which began producing only after the plan period. In those years the growth of industrial production maintained a level of eighteen percent without particular fluctuations (although some exceptions occurred in 1956 during Mao Tse-tung's attempt at the first "great leap forward"). Japan's industrial growth was marked by extreme disproportions in the growth rate within quite broad limits. During the Korean war, growth varied between 10 and 35 percent, then sank to 6.4 percent in 1954, and 9 percent in 1955-1956. It rose again to 19 percent in 1957. These variations were even more pronounced in particular branches and types of production.

In the period being considered, China and Japan both achieved high growth rates in industrial development. Having surpassed prewar levels of production, both countries moved forward quite rapidly, even though development took place in fundamentally different socio-economic systems. The chief distinction was that Japan's expansion brought with it dependence on foreign markets, raw material sources and sales. Meanwhile China's economic independence grew from year to year. All branches of the economy developed. Along with rapid growth in processing industries, geological investigations were conducted and mineral ore extraction increased. Although this did not bring great income to the country, it created a foundation for long-term industrial progress.

The two countries also exhibited contrasting international positions. The Chinese People's Republic had become a full member of the socialist community, and its international stature as a peace-loving socialist state was generally recognized. Japan remained in political and economic dependence on the United States, and Japanese leaders bound their country's fate to reactionary military alliances created by imperialists in Asia. Objectively, a favorable situation existed for neighborly relations between China and Japan after the expulsion of Chiang Kai-shek's reactionary regime and its American protectors. For reasons beyond the control of the peoples of the two countries, these ties did not materialize. The blame lies with American imperialism. Defeated in China, American officials moved their headquarters to Japan. They violated their responsibilities to the Allies, then retarded Japan's democratization by force, while helping the Japanese monopolies consolidate their power. Extensive American financial, technical and military assistance guaranteed enormous regular orders to industry. Relying on this, Japanese big business was able to restore and increase industrial production rapidly. In turn, this assured high employment and an improved standard of living. Domestic magnates utilized the country's economic successes to neutralize and demolish the democratic movement, and to influence the petty bourgeoisie and certain classes of workers who receive their wages from the rebuilt enterprises.

During the Korean war, Japanese ruling circles catered to their American partners, causing the complete cessation of economic and other relations with China. At the same time, China's transformation and socialist construction made a powerful impact on Japanese progressives. In China they saw a worthy example for the Asian peoples. China's rapidly waxing foreign trade reminded the Japanese middle class of the capacious Chinese market, which might be lost through delay in establishing ties with it. The idea of normal ties and diplomatic recognition of China gained in popularity. Though its nature varied year by year, the desire for normalization exerted a definite influence on Japanese government policy. The trend to nationalism and Mao Tse-tung's direct expression of racist views rekindled thoughts of rapprochement on a racial foundation. A union of this kind would end dependence on the United States. This vision also revitalized former imperial aspirations. Moreover, between 1955-1956 outlooks of character attracted various members of the Japanese oligarchy.

In September 1956, the Eighth Congress of the Chinese Communist Party established a foreign policy based on the principles of socialist internationalism and equal relations with all countries, and condemned nationalist manifestations. As a result, Japan's rulers turned to a one-sided, pro-American policy in their relations with China. As the 1960s dawned Sino-Japanese relations met a dead end and were almost completely suspended.

At the end of the 1950s China entered a time of grave political and economic upheavals. These complications arose at the beginning of 1958, when Mao Tse-tung was able to replace the general program of the Chinese Communist Party with a "special," nationalist course of development. In the sixties, big business continued to consolidate its power in Japan with U.S. assistance. The Japanese-American Treaty of Mutual Cooperation and Security facilitated Japan's remilitarization and participation in aggressive blocs led by the United States. Further, the treaty opened possibilities for expansion abroad.

MAO TSE-TUNG'S "SPECIAL" NATIONALIST POLICY

Immediately following the Eighth Party Congress Mao began an attack on its decisions. It is true that in his first speeches following the congress he did not openly demand reconsideration or rejection of the second five-year plan (for 1958-1962). Mao needed to reckon with the popularity of the Party's general line and its unquestionable successes. Consequently, before announcing a break with the Party, he strove to discredit it by stressing difficulties in the process of socialist construction. In February 1957, in a speech at a meeting of the Supreme Government Council, Mao presented a veiled attack on all the major decisions of the Eighth Congress. He contrasted them to his old bourgeois nationalist conceptions of a "new democracy."

The general Party program advocated "making socialist ownership of the means of production the sole economic basis." Approximately within three five-year plans, industrialization would transform China fundamentally into "a great socialist state." Mao disagreed, declaring that this transformation would require "several decades." Consequently, different tasks would be posed than those called for by the general program. Attributing as before special qualities to the Chinese bourgeoisie, Mao asserted: "In our country, contradictions between the working class and the domestic bourgeoisie relate to contradictions within the people (that is, they are not antagonistic—M.S.). The class struggle between the working class and the domestic bourgeoisie is in general a class struggle within the people, since the domestic bourgeoisie in our country has an essentially dual nature."[1] Mao attempted to conceal his bourgeois nationalist doctrine of a "new democracy" with socialist terminology, and to attribute capitalism's laws to socialism. He said: "In a socialist society, the basic conflicts continue to be between production relationships and the work forces. These are contradictions between superstructures and the economic base."

Mao's first practical measure to violate the general line was to eliminate centrally planned development of the country's economy. He contrasted the socialist law of systematic and proportional development to the "line of the masses," based on decentralization and spontaneity. "Unified planning" should extend only to "questions of grain, natural calamities, employment, education, questions of the intelligentsia, the united front of all patriotic forces, or the question of national minorities." All other problems, Mao asserted, could be worked out and achieved by "social organizations or directly by the masses." Mao Tsetung offered the following guiding principles:

1. "Politics are the commanding force." Political reforms and socialist transformation should come without dependence on physical circumstances. Material production itself should be subordinate to the state's higher interests.

2. "Foreign rules and clichés are to be smashed" and economic development including industry is to be achieved on a popular, primitive basis, permitting the numerous peasantry to be attracted into production.

3. The state's political and economic foundation should become the village, the peasantry, since it is not "corrupted" by city culture and more completely expresses national interests.

4. Labor should not be based on material incentives but on military discipline, on a garrison regime. Military affairs are the peasants' most important duties.

5. China's former might was to be resurrected, and China was to be converted into the world's leading state; development of the country's internal life was to be subordinated to foreign policy goals.

The implementation of Mao's course began in 1958 with a new "perfecting" of the socialist transformation of the village. The decisions of the Eighth Party Congress called for further strengthening the material base of agriculture. To that end, the peasants' social and personal interests would be combined; handicrafts and garden plot output would be emphasized. In contrast to this, Mao exhorted the peasants to transform the agricultural cooperatives into "people's communes." In justification, China's leaders attributed the rich spring and summer harvest of 1958 not to favorable climatic conditions, the real cause, but to rapid completion of collectivization. They concluded that despite the backward agricultural system, transition to "people's communes" would permit even quicker increases.

When they entered "people's communes," the peasants were supposed to surrender all their property, including domestic utensils and personal effects. Instead of pay, all members of the commune would be treated and cared for equally.[2] The "people's commune" was to encompass the territory and populace of an entire rural district, regardless of social position. Around 26,000 communes were set up throughout the country, containing more than 740,000 agricultural cooperatives. The "people's commune" would include industry as well. To accomplish their industrial function, the communes were to take part in the "great leap" by creating extensive primitive and dwarf industry, primarily small blast furnaces and steel smelters. The campaign to reunite agricultural and industrial production within the framework of the "people's communes" began to spread to major industrial enterprises.[3] Military matters were among the chief tasks of the communes. Each was to provide a specified military unit organized in batallions, companies and squads. Members were to engage in training and maintaining military discipline at home and at work. Other social and administrative functions were also entrusted to the communes at the expense of local government organizations.

An enlarged session of the central committee political bureau was called by Mao in August 1958. Its resolution proclaimed that "the people's commune is the best organizational form for building socialism and gradual transition to communism. It will develop into the initial unit of the future communist society."[4] In Mao's estimation, it was not the worker but the Chinese peasant himself who possessed all the necessary qualities to become the leading element in society. The inexperience of the peasant in science and technology and his illiteracy and poverty were ideal human qualities. Mao asserted that these qualities helped the peasants to welcome revolutionary ideas. "Poverty forces one to think of changes, forces one to act, to carry on revolution. There is nothing on a piece of blank paper, but on it can be written the newest, most beautiful words, and the newest, most beautiful pictures can be drawn on it."[5]

The village was declared to be a school for reeducating the intelligentsia, workers and youth. "Work hardening" of city dwellers was an indispensable factor for "correct reeducation" in the spirit of the ideas of Mao Tse-tung. Peasants should also take the leading position in industry; "the great leap" diverted more than fifty million peasants from agricultural work to handicraft metallurgy. In this manner, peasants attracted to industry during the peak months of the "great leap forward" more than tripled the number of permanent workers. This was supposed to confirm the leading role of the village.

The "people's communes" and the "great leap forward" constituted two of the banners in Mao Tse-tung's policy of "three red banners." The third "banner" was the general program, but not that of the Chinese Communist Party which had been prepared in the first years of popular rule, confirmed by the Eighth Party Congress (in September, 1956) and successfully pursued until 1958. Mao's new line was summarized by the slogan "straining all forces to build socialism on the principle of bigger, quicker, better and cheaper." Not by chance did Mao leave out the goals of his program and the approximate period for their achievement. The new line spoke only of methods and attitudes of building socialism, expressed in rhetorical style with mellifluous hieroglyphs. Mao did not want to restrict the targets and dates of completion of his program by party decisions for such limitation was his prerogative, the prerogative of the "leader." At the same time, the new "general line" contained principles which would completely eliminate the previous program and decisions of the Eighth Party Congress. Each seemingly harmless word from Mao in practice expressed a comprehensive program of destructive actions.[6]

As in previous years, during the bourgeois democratic stage, Mao Tse-tung talked of socialism and communism as distant prospects. His concrete program for the coming years contained no elements of scientific socialism. The slogans he advanced for the people did not define the social features of the new "shape" of the country or of the ten thousand years of "happiness." Among these slogans were "Struggle stubbornly for three years and achieve change in the basic shape of most regions of the country," and "Several years of tenacious labor, ten thousand years of happiness." Mao's new political course was presented to the enlarged session of the politbureau of the Party Central Committee. Based on military experience, it foresaw the conversion of the entire country into an armed camp in which, in places, democracy would be replaced by despotic centralized power. The creative energy of the masses would be stimulated by militarization of the entire populace in the people's volunteer communes.

The employment problem became aggravated toward the end of the first five-year plan. This eased Mao's attack on the decisions of the Eighth Party Congress. His promises to solve the problem "with one sweep" attracted people throughout the country. During 1958 the system of planned government gave way to the new policy of the "three red banners," which reflected the rebellious, destructive mood of the proletarian masses and poor folk and contained no constructive program. The Chinese people were to regret the adventurism of this policy for it ruined the country during the ensuing years.

THE "THREE RED BANNERS"

Striving to inspire the masses to overcome difficulties on the way to the "great leap forward" in agriculture and industry, official Chinese publicity intentionally exaggerated production figures. Significant quantities of damaged or completely worthless goods were concealed. Recommendations and simplistic technological schemes were distributed with no scientific rationale. Under the flag of "stagnancy" and "foreign corruption," criticism was heaped on the scientific and technical intelligentsia, primarily foreign advisors, specialists and skilled workers. Primitive and backward methods of production were extolled. The Party and government press falsified data on total yields in basic branches of agriculture for 1958. These were supposed to show that in one year production had reached the targets for the entire five-year plan, through 1962. The information report of the sixth planum of the central committee (November, 1958) gave the following preliminary figures for 1958 production compared with 1957 (in millions of tons).

	1957	1958	1962 plan
Steel	5.35	11	10.5- 12
Coal	130	270	190 -210
Grain	185	375	250
Cotton	1.64	3.35	2.4

The conclusion followed that, prior to this time, China had been developing at "slave rates" and that the general Party program for an eighteen year transitional period (1949-1967) was "conservative and refuted by life." Using blatantly falsified statistics, the sixth plenum set unjustifiably high figures for 1959: steel production was to reach 18 million tons, coal—380 million, grain—525 million and (unprocessed) cotton—5 million tons. Data on such "glorious victories" and "glittering" prospects aroused general rejoicing and satisfaction, their purpose being to prove the possibility of achieving the "communist" opportionment of products "to each according to his needs." In this connection, in the "people's communes" free public dining halls were opened, with standardized and equalized rations.

Early in 1959 serious difficulties in food supply appeared as a consequence of these adventuristic experiments. The government acquisitions system was demolished. The state had received 40-45 million tons of grain each year of the first five-year plan, of which 30 million tons were purchased and 15 million collected as taxes. From the rich harvest of 1958 the state received only about 15 million tons, mainly as tax payments. Meanwhile normal grain requirements for the cities amounted to 25-30 million tons. By the middle of 1959, swine and fowl had almost completely disappeared from China,[7] and major food shortages arose. The situation was aggravated by tens of millions of peasants who had left agricultural work for blast furnace construction, planting fruit gardens and military training. Equalized distribution affected the peasants' attitude to social production and brought a drop in labor productivity. The ruinous consequences of garrison "communization" became evident by the end of 1958. Notwithstanding this, the sixth plenum of the Party Central Committee, in making some interpretive corrections as to the features and role of "people's communes," continued to assert that "on the broad horizon of the eastern part of Asia, like a rising sun, a new organization has appeared, the mighty people's commune."

Mao Tse-tung obviously wished to avoid responsibility for the failure of the "three red banners." Hence he withdrew from candidacy for the presidency of the Republic for the next term. He retained party leadership as president of the Chinese Communist Party. The sixth plenum's decisions could not avoid the rapidly approaching catastrophe in China's economy, since it was not dared openly to condemn and reject Mao's policies.

At the start of the "great leap," China maintained extensive economic, scientific and technical ties with the Soviet Union and other socialist countries. Talks had started in 1956 and 1957 on construction and supply assistance for 125 large industrial enterprises. These led to two agreements signed on August 8, 1958 and February 7, 1959. An important agreement was concluded on January 18, 1958 between the Soviet and Chinese academies of science, entitled "Joint Pursuit of Important Research in Science and Technology and Related Soviet Aid Grants to China." Large deliveries of industrial and laboratory equipment began and scientific research unfolded extensively in all branches of China's national economy.

The "great leap" brought ever greater disorder to projected industrial construction. The damage began when imported equipment designated for specific structures was scattered to various other buildings in violation of engineered installation blueprints, making the proper use of equipment impossible. Many cases of damage, destruction and machinery shut-downs resulted. Specialists from the Soviet Union and other socialist countries could not carry out their responsibilities for construction, installation and start-up operations. Numerous previously unplanned structures materialized, having neither equipment nor raw materials, nor qualified workers and specialists. This made it impossible to complete construction according to schedule, while enormous resources were tied up in unfinished buildings. Industrialization of a modern technical character was disorganized. The "small metallurgy" created at Mao Tse-tung's behest in many home blast furnaces and smelters proved to be an empty waste of resources, costing more than 4 million yuan.[8] This program was halted completely in 1959, and most of the finished blast furnaces were destroyed. In agriculture, the equalized distribution of products, lack of work incentives, irrational cultivation methods, and reduced area of cultivation, caused sharp harvest declines. The failure of the "great leap forward" in industry and agriculture radically worsened the situation in China. At the eighth plenum of the Party Central Committee in August 1959, protests were raised by a group of central committee members headed by politbureau[9] member Marshal Peng Teh-huai, a deputy premier and minister of defense. He criticized the "great leap," branding it a petty bourgeois phantasy which had cost the Chinese people dearly. Peng Teh-huai wrote the following to Mao Tse-tung:

> Petty bourgeois ardour leads us easily to commit "left" deviations. We have studied little, and paid little attention to analysis of the actual current situation . . . . We too early rejected the law of equivalency and suggested free food, calculating that there was plenty of bread. In some regions we repudiated the policy of centralized marketing, and fought for the right to eat to satiety. Without expert studies we thoughtlessly set up certain types of technology, and rashly rejected certain economic laws and scientific principles. All this comprises a type of "leftist deviation." These comrades (leftists-M.S.) believed that everything might be replaced by politics, if only politics became the commanding force. They forgot that politics as the force of leadership cannot replace concrete measures in economic work . . . . The historical experience of our party witnesses that the correction of such "leftism" generally is harder than overturning rightist conservatism.

Peng Teh-huai called for Party unity, for improving the ideological education of Party members in order that they might "draw a clear boundary between truth and falsehood."[10]

Mao Tse-tung was able to remove from Party leadership and brand as "right deviationists" those who criticized him, including Peng Teh-huai, politbureau candidate member Chang Wen-tien and several other members of the central committee. Many provincial committee secretaries also lost their positions. Nonetheless, the Party plenum could not ignore the failures of the "great leap," with the result that targets for some products were reduced: steel from 18 to 12 million tons, coal from 380 to 335 million tons, grain from 525 to 275 million tons, and cotton (fiber) from 5 to 2.3 million tons. Regarding the "people's communes," the plenum decided on a consistent policy of "greater rewards for more work." This meant a return to socialist principles for rewarding work. It was decided to reorganize the economy into "great production brigades," which in size would be about equal to the previous cooperatives.

Nonetheless, the general political impulse remained the same. The decisions of the eighth plenum reiterated the policy of the "great leap forward." The Party and the people were exhorted, "following the leadership of the party and comrade Mao Tse-tung, to overcome all difficulties and shortcomings in our work, to overcome the right opportunist drift among certain unstable elements, and to fight to fulfill the second five-year plan (1959-1962) in two years (1958-1959)."[11] No concrete program appeared for eliminating the ruinous results of the "great leap." The situation in industry deteriorated catastrophically. Lack of raw materials, ruined equipment, and disrupted management forced many enterprises either to cease operations or to operate with reduced loads and deliver poor quality goods. Agricultural difficulties also worsened. There followed a partial retreat from the "three red banners" policy including the repudiation of equalized food rations for the entire agricultural population and the restoration of garden plots. The peasants treated these half-measures with open distrust; productivity sagged sharply and the peasants refused en masse to work collectivized fields. These problems were aggravated further by unfavorable weather conditions in 1959 and 1960.

By the end of 1960 the disorganization of the national economy reached such a degree that the Party leadership demanded extraordinary and urgent measures to avoid widespread hunger. Mao's resignation from the presidency of the country and the election of Liu Shao-chi to that post was not a mere formality. Nor did it, as the sixth plenum stated, express the central committee's desire to afford Mao Tse-tung "even greater opportunity to concentrate his efforts on questions concerning the course, policy and line of the Party and government, and to free more time for work in Marxist-Leninist theory."[12] Liu Shao-chi's leadership of the country brought several developments in China's domestic life which returned the country to the general program of the Chinese Communist Party and the resolution of the first session of the Eighth Party Congress. Unfortunately, these measures in 1959 and 1960 were of a halfway nature, and did not eliminate all the ruinous consequences of Mao's "special" course. Fluctuations and vacillations resulting from the lack of unified leadership began to affect international affairs; they were particularly apparent at the Moscow Conference of Communist and Workers Parties in 1960. Anti-Leninist, schismatic proposals, presented at the outset of the conference by the Chinese Communist Party delegation, unexpectedly were withdrawn. In the name of the Chinese Party the delegation leader, Liu Shao-chi, joined in the resolution which had been prepared by conference participants.

Mao continued to influence the national affairs of China, especially in ideology and Party leadership. Starting in 1959, in violation of the Chinese constitution, Mao ceased to convoke annual sessions of the congress, avoided periodic plenums of the central committee and ignored the principle of democratic leadership.[13] The Party constitution demanded the education "of its members and the people in the spirit of internationalism, expressed in the appeal 'proletarians of all countries, unite!' " Mao's propaganda increasingly cultivated great Chinese chauvinism, racism, hatred of all things Western, and the personal dictatorship of Mao Tse-tung. In China's foreign policy, fanaticism and great Chinese chauvinism was manifested in a war psychosis relating to the border conflict with India, and in a nationalistic concern for Chinese moneylenders, bankers, merchants and planters in Indonesia.[14] Provisions of the Sino-Soviet treaty of "Friendship, Alliance and Mutual Aid" had included the obligation for each country to "consult with each other on all important international questions." Notwithstanding this provision, China began in 1958 to stage war provocations and violate the peace-loving policies of the socialist countries, to reject agreements and curtail economic, scientific-technical and cultural ties.[15] Concurrently the Chinese leadership actively sought partners and allies in the capitalist world. The great Chinese nationalist aspirations of Mao Tse-tung increasingly shaped the foreign policy of the Chinese People's Republic.

STRENGTHENING THE "GREAT LEAP FORWARD"

The ninth plenum of the Party Central Committee took place in January 1961 and adopted a resolution "On the Conference of Representatives of Communist and Workers' Parties in Moscow."[16] The resolution voiced "satisfaction with the work of the Chinese delegation, headed by Liu Shao-chi" and "fully approved the 'Declaration and Appeal' to the peoples of all the world." The Party Central Committee repeated that "the urgent tasks . . . are protection of peace throughout the world, achievement of peaceful coexistence and peaceful competition between countries with differing social systems, and avoidance of a new world war which is being sought by the imperialists." The plenum was constrained to adopt urgent measures concerning China's economic problems, proclaiming a policy of "standardizing, augmenting and heightening." This meant suspension of work on all unfinished structures, cessation of new building, and closing enterprises which lacked sufficient raw materials and qualified personnel. Industry was directed to supply the needs of agriculture, bringing renovation of many enterprises, then fulfill the needs of the population and develop heavy industry. First place thus was assigned to agriculture. As the plenum's resolutions stated, "agriculture is the basis of the national economy. The entire Party and the whole nation should employ all means to develop agriculture and grain production." Hunger in the cities and food shortages in the villages compelled pragmatism in agriculture. The main effort was to increase grain harvests, the restoration of industrial crops such as raw silk, tea, fiber crops, tung oil, citrus fruits and others, being reserved for the future.

Although "regulatory" measures generated significant declines in industrial production (as much as fifty percent compared to 1959), they promoted a limited return to orderliness and efficiency. Such regulations had been necessary for the "great leap" policy and displayed an openly contrived and temporary character. Nonetheless, Mao's supporters attempted to establish them as long range Party policy in order to discredit industrialization and convince the people of its unprofitability for China. The press published letters from "people's communes" with demands for return of land taken by industrial enterprises. Calculations were fabricated to illustrate the advantages of using the land for agriculture and not for industry. A new campaign spread through the country aiming to discredit equipment imported from socialist countries, and to curtail commercial, scientific and technical ties with those countries.

At the tenth plenum of the Central Committee in September 1962, the dispute within the Party flared again. Healthy forces inside the Party demanded a return to socialist forms of economic management, and they received extensive support from the Chinese people. Questions dealing with national economic planning were discussed at sessions of the Chinese National People's Congress in March and April, 1962, and in December 1964. Several resolutions sought to return garden plots, about five percent of total communal land area, to the peasants, and to exempt them from taxes were they to till newly opened or deserted land such as roadsides, hill slopes and ravines. Private farming would stress the breeding of pigs and domestic fowl, handicrafts would be favored and peasant markets reopened. While limited, these partial corrections to Mao's domestic economic policy nevertheless favorably affected the Chinese economy. Harvests (particularly vegetables) from garden plots augmented growing yields on the collective lands of "great production brigades," adding to an enlarged general harvest. Meanwhile, the production of goods by industry swelled as well, the provisioning of cities improved, and commerce livened noticeably.

The Chinese press again began to print articles on long-term economic planning. A Central Committee decision called for the expansion and strengthening of the Chinese State Planning Commission. Other signs appeared indicating the growth of healthy, socialist forces in the Party. At the Chinese National People's Congress (first session, third convening) in December 1964, the government reported several factors which characterized the state of the economy. It was noted that agricultural production in the three years 1962-1964 had reached a level "comparable to harvests in past years." It was projected that "in total yields of grain, cotton, tobacco, sugar cane, and also of pigs and small horned stock, that is, the most important branches of farming and animal husbandry, the levels of 1957, the last year of the first five-year plan, would be surpassed (in 1964—M.S.)." This report further stated that "China's gross industrial production in 1964 would grow over 1963 by fifteen percent and more; it would significantly surpass the 1957 level." For the first time in five years a general plan for development of the Chinese economy existed. It predicted "growth of gross agricultural production by about five percent over 1964" and expansion of gross industrial production approximately by eleven percent over 1964." The plan for 1965 aimed at "completing the unfinished tasks of regulating the national economy and preparing for fulfillment of the third five-year plan, which would start in 1965." Management of the national economy would join centralized direction with broad mass movements and, it was noted, it was essential to "adopt and utilize domestically all the best found in the experience and technology of foreign countries."

Another situation was taking shape in ideology and foreign policy. Circumstances inside the Party after the ninth and tenth plenums of the Central Committee, which had expressed serious opposition to Mao's policies, hampered adherence to the "ideas" of the "leader." It appeared that his will prevailed in these policy spheres. Mao's initial step to bolster his influence was to displace the Party Central Committee in foreign policy and internal party matters. After the tenth plenum he discontinued Central Committee plenums, Party conferences and meetings. The dominant role of the army, and not the Party, echoed throughout all ideological propaganda. Several watchwords gained wide currency, among them "study the army's example," "imitate Premier Lei Feng in devotion to Mao Tse-tung," "give your life for Mao," and so forth. Such slogans strangled internationalist political and educational work in the Chinese Communist Party and lent a great Chinese nationalist and militarist tinge to all ideological propaganda.

With the Party Central Committee isolated from leadership, and relying on the army, Mao urged several policies: In ideology to annul the decisions of the Eighth Party Congress, according to which "in its activities the Chinese Communist Party should be guided by Marxism-Leninism," and instead confirm "the ideas of Mao" as the sole ideological teaching; in matters of policy to strive for the transformation of China into a leading world center especially in relation to Asia, Africa and Latin America; in economics to militarize the national economy. This impulse in Mao's politics inexorably led to strained relations with the socialist countries, with Marxist-Leninist communist parties, and eventually with the countries of Asia, Africa and Latin America. Mao began to break away from the international communist movement by rejecting the decisions of the Moscow conferences of 1957 and 1960, reached with the Chinese Communist Party's participation.

Repudiating the Marxist-Leninist class analysis of the modern era and denying the historic role of the working class, Mao Tse-tung held forth his own interpretation and evaluation of world forces, based on geographic and nationalist principles. He ignored the obvious fact that the principal force opposing imperialism comprised the socialist countries, primarily the Soviet Union. In Mao's words, "the chief zone of the storms of world revolution will be the broad regions of Asia, Africa and Latin America," and "the working classes of socialist and capitalist countries should . . . resolutely support revolutionary actions there, and regard the cause of liberation as their own most dependable support and in their own direct interests."[17]

Mao Tse-tung's anti-Marxist evaluation of the contemporary world originated in his misunderstanding of the economic essence of imperialism as a product of the monopolistic stage in the development of capital. As V.I. Lenin wrote, "the rivalry of several large states aspiring to hegemony is essential."[18] Mao equated imperialism with the expansionist policies of individual states, and found such qualities only in the

United States, which was aspiring to "create an empire unheard of in this world." All other imperialist governments–the Federal Republic of Germany, England, France and Japan–Mao relegated to the "intermediate zone, lying between the United States and the socialist camp."[19] Mao asserted that America's primary goal was to control the nations of the intermediate zone, and to choke the revolution of oppressed peoples and nations therein. Only thereafter would the United States strive to eliminate the socialist nations. Ignoring the basic contradictions between the modern socialist and capitalist systems, Mao admitted to no distinctions in relations with socialist and capitalist countries of the "intermediate zone." The events of the last decade show that he went even further. Mao's group curtailed political and economic ties with the socialist countries while expanding trade and other intercourse with the "intermediate countries" of the capitalist world.

At first Mao Tse-tung's group tried to conceal the diminution of economic, scientific and technological ties with the socialist countries. Though they advocated "reliance on our own strength," supposedly leading to reduction of foreign trade and other forms of economic ties with other states, the followers of Mao Tse-tung were exposed in their deceit. Democratic forces throughout the world learned that Mao's approach was being applied exclusively against the socialist countries. (China's foreign trade with the capitalist countries grew from 1,207 million dollars in 1959 to 2,494 million dollars in 1965, while that with the socialist states fell from 2,550 to 1,108 million dollars in the same period.) Mao's supporters threw off their masks to display brazen provocations, groundless quibbling and malicious violation of treaty obligations while insistently seeking to reduce relations with the socialist countries to a minimum.

Mao Tse-tung began to view the socialist countries, especially the Soviet Union, as the chief obstacles to his hegemonial ambitions. As a result Mao set about weakening the world socialist system, both by fostering schism and by provoking clashes with the other countries, not excluding atomic warfare. His design was to isolate the Soviet Union and European socialist countries from developing countries in Africa, Asia and Latin America, and from the national liberation movements of the peoples of those continents. To accomplish their policies Mao's disciples recruited numerous agents from the Chinese middle class living in the developing countries. They also courted individual leaders in these nations. Mao's associates exploited conferences, symposiums and meetings of Asian and African representatives to fan racial enmity and to gather a group of countries around China. Thereupon, first in Asia, China would become established as the leading political force. To promote an alliance of East Asian countries, Mao proposed an independent intergovernmental organization to counter the United Nations which, eventually, would be called upon to unite all the peoples of Asia and Africa. An important part in these plans was assigned to Indonesia, whose former president, Sukarno, reacted positively. Indonesia's departure from the United Nations was one of the first practical steps. China and Indonesia were to be linked by agreements in finances, economics, commerce, aviation, and the like. Meanwhile pro-Chinese agents, largely overseas Chinese[20] holding key positions in Indonesia's commerce and finances, were to assure China's leadership in the new "axis."

The struggle for mastery in Asia is further illustrated by the ambitions of Mao Tse-tung's government in relation to Burma, its attempts to weaken India in Southeast Asia and to ignite armed conflict between India and Pakistan. Under the pretext of "safeguarding" the twelve million Chinese emigrants in Southeast Asian countries, Mao's supporters declared that interference in the internal affairs of these nations was China's "legal right." But by the end of 1965 China's internal and international affairs had turned against Mao Tse-tung. In those spheres where partisans of the Eighth Party Congress had overcome Mao's "special" nationalist course (for example, in the economy), the country had progressed and quickly healed wounds inflicted by the experimentation. By contrast, where Mao's course was followed without restraint, as in foreign relations, the Chinese government and the Chinese Communist Party had lost prestige. Normal ties with socialist countries and communist parties had been ruined, and the country and the Party driven into isolation.

THE "CULTURAL REVOLUTION"

Foreign policy failures and the violation of basic constitutional and programmatic principles introduced serious dissatisfaction among Chinese communists, the creative intelligentsia and the working people at large. The unrest was reflected in scholarly articles, in journalism and in artistic work.[21] Open protests grew against Mao's widening dictatorship, and against the nationalist policy of China in Tibet, Inner Mongolia, Hsin-chiang province and other regions. The Chinese government announced a return to long range central economic planning. Beginning in 1966 the third five-year plan, interrupted by the "great leap forward," once again was implemented. This step offered confirmation of the desires of many government and Party leaders for a return to socialist methods of economic management, and signalled the final abandonment of the bankrupt theory of "progress by leaps" and voluntary methods of operation. Thus even while the 72-year old "leader" was still alive, his "ideas" were discredited and his removal from power was being prepared.[22]

Mao Tse-tung attacked his opponents with determination. The "cultural revolution," as it was called, erupted in China with the primary aim of imposing Mao's ideas by force. The purpose of the cultural revolution was to establish the infallibility of Mao's authority and on that foundation to build a dictatorship of the "leader's" personal power. Mao expected to crush the opposition quite easily and turn the country down a "unique" path of development. Rather than risking reliance on Party organizations, trade unions or even youth organizations, he brought unorganized students into the struggle, calling them "red guards"—Hun Wei Ping. Their rebellious demonstrations, and those of the "Jao Fang" proletarians, were supposed to paralyze the activities of Party and government institutions and impose capitulation on Mao's opponents.

Mao believed that this capitulation should take place at the eleventh plenum of the Party Central Committee, called for August 1966. Materials published in the Chinese press on the results of the plenum, as well as subsequent events, indicate that the plenum was unable to accomplish this task. For this reason therefore, during the plenum Mao decided to "open fire on the headquarters" in attacking official institutions and leaders such as Liu Shao-chi and Teng Hsiao-ping. The Party leadership and lower-echelon organizations did not support him and the red guards lacked sufficient strength. Thereupon Mao's group brought the army into the struggle and dispersed Party, government and union organizations. At the beginning of 1967, Mao started to set up so-called "revolutionary committees." A meeting of his supporters took place eighteen months after the start of the campaign to form revolutionary committees. Although it was called the "twelfth plenum of the Party Central Committee," only forty of the 174 members and candidate members of the Central Committee of the Chinese Communist Party attended. It proclaimed that the "magnificent and decisive" victory of the "cultural revolution" had eliminated constitutional organs of popular authority and charter institutions of the Chinese Communist Party. In their place 29 revolutionary committees assumed authority in all provinces, urban centers and autonomous regions of China. In this manner Mao attempted to create the illusion of broad Party support for his arbitrary actions, and to legalize usurpation of popular authority by Mao's revolutionary committees. These were composed of people who during the cultural revolution had been unquestioning executors of the "leader's" will, regardless of their party and social affiliations. The leading role in the "revcoms" fell to army representatives, who participated directly in administration and various other public activities.

As the "revcoms" were substituted for democratic government and party offices, Mao's associates met widespread resistance. The workers of such large cities as Shang-hai, Wu-han, and Canton, rose in opposition together with peasants, national minorities and army units. There were risings in Wu-han, Nanking and other places. However, the opposition forces did not have organizations covering the entire country. By early 1969, after three years of the "cultural revolution," the Maoists gained the upper hand with army aid and generally stabilized Mao Tse-tung's personal rule. Mao's successes resulted from ten years of systematic sabotage of normal Party functioning. Under "cult of the leader" conditions, all charter and policy principles of the Chinese Communist Party were eliminated. Party ties with the world communist movement were severed, and feelings of proletarian solidarity were choked. Under Mao's pressure the Party leadership discarded the Marxist-Leninist approach to domestic and international events.

Having disrupted the Party, Mao might divert the working class from active political life and cut away its role as society's vanguard. Starting in 1960, this goal was accomplished by closing enterprises, suspending construction and transferring populations from cities to the countryside. During the cultural revolution, the Maoists strove to split the ranks of the workers by turning unskilled workers, chiefly young people, against worker organizations. The so-called "Jao Fang," uniting mainly unqualified and poorly paid young workers, waged an extensive campaign for lower wages and abolition of progressive-rate and piecework compansation. This campaign, called the "battle with bourgeois economism," stirred the master workers to obstinate resistance. Strikes and stoppages occurred in many Chinese cities, to be brutally crushed by the army. The popularized slogan "both workers and peasants" furthered the stratification of the working class. It demanded that a person be simultaneously a worker and a peasant, systematically alternating work in the city with work in the countryside. Since the Maoists preferred the village, it is perfectly clear that the call "both workers and peasants" was meant to teach peasant ideology to the workers, including nationalism, esteem for the "father-leader" and the like. The massive migrations to the countryside which began in 1968, "for training as peasants," represented an auxiliary method of disorganizing the already small industrial proletariat.

Although the "cultural revolution" was not widespread in the villages, its influence was strongly felt on local government, in relations between the peasantry and government authorities, and between peasants and administrations of "people's communes." The peasants were urged to compete with the "Ta-chai people's commune," that is, to operate with local resources instead of relying on government assistance. This converted the village into a tributary of government, surrendering most of its production without compensation even though the Chinese village could not increase agricultural yields with the limited resources at its disposal.

The system of controlling cooperative agriculture by "people's commune" management of large regions in effect separated commune administration from the peasant producers. At the same time, a significant part of the peasants' collective property and output fell into the hands of the commune managements. In other words, property was estranged from the collective owners. This separation increased particularly after introduction of military control in the "people's communes," which in essence had been converted into institutions of extra-economic coercion. Moreover, Mao's group attempted to stratify the peasants and arouse a spurious "class conflict." Ten to twelve years after the completion of agricultural collectivization, when social control of land and the means of production had been attained, committees of "the poor and lower middle class" began to form in the communes. They were under army control and opposed the remaining cooperative peasantry. This artificial "class struggle" was cited to justify the presence of military force.

Government authority in China lost its popular-democratic nature under the Maoists. The entire social superstructure ceased to promote socialism. Serving Mao's personal dictatorship, it formed a military bureaucracy, subordinating China's domestic development to great-power ambitions abroad. The character and the goals of society changed fundamentally as a result. The twelfth plenum announced that the Party's chief goal was "decisively, finally, cleanly and thoroughly to destroy the American imperialists" and "contemporary revisionism." To this end Mao's group assigned to the country the task of completely mobilizing the people and converting China into a "unified armed camp." The aim of public activity should not be the betterment of the physical and spiritual life of the people, nor the realization of socialist and communist ideals. Rather, it was the creation of a mighty China capable of guaranteeing the expansion and consolidation "of the ideas of Mao Tse-tung" in the international arena. Mao proclaimed that the basic principle of socialist production, "to each according to his work," supposedly caused the "bourgeoisation" of workers and other elements of the urban populace. The struggle against "bourgeois economism," or production stimulated through incentives, was regarded as a class struggle and worker "economism" must be firmly counteracted.

The Maoists destroyed systematic management of the national economy, replacing it with military control. Long-range planning ceased as did the construction of large complexes of metallurgy and machine building. Mining and geological work slowed, and all major investments were shunted into arms and industry, including atomic development. The prevailing policy called for a maximum "squeezing of the juice" out of a backward, undeveloped economy. In major non-military types of industrial production, China's advancement was retarded by at least eight to ten years. During the two years of the "cultural revolution" (1967-1968) industrial production declined by about ten to fifteen percent. (See Table 6) The "cultural revolution" damaged metallurgy, especially with China losing its world markets as a major exporter of tungsten, molybdenum, beryllium, spodemene concentrates, lead, antimony, mercury and other nonferrous and rare metals. For many ferrous metals, particularly ordinary steel, China was forced to import from Japan, West Germany and other capitalist nations. Arms production functioned in different circumstances. In the years of the "cultural revolution" armaments enjoyed careful protection from the vandalism of the red guards and the workers, allowing its development to continue. Raw materials came mainly from the capitalist nations: imports amounted to 5.2 billion dollars in the five years 1965-1969 (Japan provided 1.4 billion, and West Germany 675 million dollars of the total.)

In 1965 China's agriculture achieved 1957 levels only in basic crops and in hog raising. Results lagged significantly behind targets for 1962, and even more so for 1965 (see Table 7). The years of the cultural revolution halted progress in agriculture, which stagnated at the level of the last years of the first five-year plan 1956-1957, although China's population during the intervening twelve years grew by at least 90-100 million people. From an exporter of edible grains China had become one of the leading importers in the world. Beginning in 1962, China annually imported 4-6 million tons of grain from Australia, Canada, Argentina and France. The state of crisis in China's agriculture was not caused solely by the upheavals connected directly to the "great leap forward" and the "cultural revolution." Even more to blame was the curtailment

Table 6. Production of Basic Types of Industrial Goods in China, 1957-1969

		1957	1959*	1962 Actual (Est)**	Second Five Year Plan	1965 Actual (Est)**	1965 Plan***	1967 Actual (Est)**	1967 Plan***	1969 Actual (Est)*	1969 Plan***
Coal	Mil tons	130.0	335.0	200	190-200	225.0	300.0	170	400.0	210	525.0
Electrical Energy	Bil KWH	19.3	41.0	25	40- 43	55.0	63.0	50-55	120.0	60-65	180.0
Steel	Mil tons	5.4	12.0	6-7	10.5-12	11.5	20.4	9-10	30.0	12-13	43.0
Pig Iron	Mil tons	-----	13.5	7-8	--------	13.5	20.0	11-12	30.0	14-15	43.0
Cement	Mil tons	6.0	12.3	5-6	12.5-14.5	12.5	18.0	10-11	21.5	12-13	25.0
Metal Lathes	Thousands	28.0	70.0	30	60 -65	40.0	85.0	35	102.0	40-45	112.0
Cotton Fabric	Mil meters	5.0	7.5	5-6	9.4-10.4	6.3	13.3	60	16.2	6.5-7.0	18.0
Edible Veg. Oil	Mil tons	1.1	1.4	0.7-0.8	3.1-3.2	1.1	4.2	1.2	5.0	1.3	5.5

*Steel and pig iron do not include cottage manufacture.

**The estimates for 1965, 1967 and 1969 were calculated on the basis of figures given in "Report of the Government of the Chinese People's Republic" (*Informational Bulletin* of the New China News Agency, January 1, 1965), and communications in the Chinese press. These figures have been published in part in the Soviet Union. See *Kommunist*, August 1967, No. 12; *Voprosy ekonomiki* (Questions of Economics), 1969, No. 6, and *Izvestia*, April 27, 1970.

***The provisional plans for 1965, 1967 and 1969 were calculated on the basis of standard plan figures for 1962, accepted by the eighth plenum of the Chinese Communist Party for the second five year plan. Allowance was made for approximate planned increases in coal, steel, pig iron, cement and electrical energy at the rate of fifteen percent, in metal-cutting lathes, cotton fabric and edible oils, at the rate of ten percent annually.

Table 7. Basic Types of Agricultural Production and Livestock in China, 1957-1969

		1957	1959	1962		1965		1967		1969	
				Actual	Planned	Actual (Est)*	Planned **	Actual (Est)*	Planned **	Actual (Est)*	Planned
Grain (Sweet Potatoes)	Mil tons	185.0	195.0	160-170	250.0	185.0	290.0	190.0	320.0	200.0	340.0
Cotton (fiber)	Mil tons	1.6	1.8	0.9	2.4	1.6	3.0	1.4	3.6	1.5	3.8
Soy Beans	Mil tons	10.1	12.0	7-8	12.2	9-10	14.0	9.0	15.0	10.0	16.0
Hogs	Mil head	150.0	75.0	110-120	250.0	150.0	340.0	140.0	410.0	150.0	460.0

*Estimates for 1965, 1967 and 1969 calculated on the basis of data given in the "Report of the Government of the People's Republic of China" (Informational Bulletin of the New China News Agency, January 1, 1965), and the Chinese press. In the USSR these statistics have been published in part. See Kommunist, 1967, No. 12; Voprosy ekonomiki (Questions of Economics), 1969, No. 6; Izvestiia, April 27, 1970.

**The provisional plans for 1965, 1967 and 1969 have been calculated on the basis of the standard plan figures for 1962, which were adopted by the Chinese Communist Party Congress for the second five year plan, with inclusion of averaged planned increases in grain, cotton and soy bean production at five percent and of hog production at ten percent annually.

of the government's aid to vitally essential land management projects. The three chief problems of China's agriculture—limited land, low yields, and climatic disasters—remained unsolved.

From the beginning of the 20th century until 1950 the tilled land remained at about the same level, around 100 million hectares. Only in 1956-1957 did it grow, reaching about 110-112 million hectares. On the other hand, Chinese economists calculate that with advanced land development procedures the tillable area might be increased to 220-225 million hectares, or approximately double the current figure. The first twelve-year plan for the development of the Chinese economy projected reclamation of thirty million hectares of virgin lands, largely in China's northwestern, northeastern and northern regions. The results of the first five-year plan demonstrated that China could increase crop frequency and thereby expand the country's cultivated land. Thus, whereas during the 1930's the crop rotation coefficient reached 120 percent of tillable land, in 1952 it climbed to 130 percent and in 1956-1957 it reached 142 percent.

Grain yields hovered at a low level in comparison to other countries. The twelve-year plan for agricultural development projected an increase in grain yield from the 1955 level of 11.2 hundredweight/hectare to 30 in wheat, and in rice from 30 to 60 hundredweight/hectare. Crop yield increases were to be achieved by greater use of fertilizer, and expansion of irrigation from 26 million hectares in 1955 to 60 million in 1967. Chemical fertilizers were to be utilized for the most part, their production to be expanded to 5-6 million tons in 1962 and 15 million tons in 1967. Several measures were planned for land development and for combatting natural disasters, requiring large government investment. Agrotechnical improvements were tied to new hydroelectrical systems on the Huang-Ho and in the Huai Ho basin (called with good cause China's "river of woe"), in the "Great Lakes" district and in many other regions. All of this enormous construction was vital to the further advance of agriculture. During "the great leap forward" construction had been interrupted and then suspended. All attempts by Mao Tse-tung's group to solve agriculture's problems "with the enthusiasm of the masses" came to naught. The limited local resources of the "people's communes" proved insufficient when combined with backward, primitive technology. These methods proved successful only in maintaining the previous level of agricultural production. In the face of rapidly growing population, supply declined relentlessly.

The introduction in 1968 to military supervision in industrial and agricultural management halted declines and even brought a slight upward movement. This was particularly true when all government, social and political administration fell into "revolutionary committee" (military) hands. While this reversed some of the anarchy spawned by the "cultural revolution," the militarization of the economy, founded on intimidation and a ban on material incentives, succeeded only temporarily in stabilizing the economy. In the prevailing situation in China, nationalized industrial and agricultural production lost its underlying socialist character. There was no opportunity to display the advantages of the socialist economic system. Socialism in China was distorted and its very existence was threatened. At the Ninth Congress of the Chinese Communist Party in Peking in April 1969, Mao offered no positive development program. As before, he concentrated on the struggle against the general Party line and the decisions of the Eighth Congress, held in September 1956. The Maoists repudiated earlier Party decisions under the banner of struggle with "Liu Shao-chi's acquiescent and revisionist line." For their part, Liu Shao-chi and some other leaders condemned Mao's faction in, for example, "A Hundred Statements of Liu Shao-chi Against the Ideas of Mao Tse-tung," and "Down With the Blood-sucking Treachery of Po Yi-po." These statements made clear that the crimes of these persons amounted to dedication to the general Party line and the decisions of the Eighth Congress.

The Chinese People's Republic thus lived in the thrall of the military bureaucratic apparatus of Mao Tse-tung. It was therefore the sole nation in the world socialist system which had ceased to advance. With its economic ties to the socialist countries broken, China from year to year escalated its dependence on the capitalist world. (See Table 8)

Hence, while in 1959 more than two thirds of China's foreign trade was with the socialist countries, in 1969 the share of those countries dropped to one quarter. Gross trade with the capitalist nations correspondingly grew from 32 percent to 75 percent. The qualitative changes in China's foreign trade are concealed by quantitative ones. Satisfaction of China's needs for imported equipment and materials today is determined by alliances, by imperialist blocs and by their quotas and "lists of allowed items." The foreign trade of the Chinese People's Republic consequently grew dependent on the capitalist world.

JAPAN'S FOREIGN AND DOMESTIC POLICIES

Attitudes toward the Japanese-American "security pact" [Treaty of Mutual Cooperation and Security] determined the policies of influential segments of Japanese society and should have governed the short-term

Table 8. China's Foreign Trade*

	1950		1959		1965		1966		1968		1969	
Total Trade	1254	100%	3752	100%	3602	100%	3952	100%	3475	100%	3600	100%
Socialist Countries	325	26	2555	68	1108	30.7	1072	27	865	24.9	895	24.9
Capitalist Countries	929	74	1202	32	2494	69.3	2880	73	2610	75.1	2705	75.1

*Source: *Kommunist*, 1967, No. 12; *Izvestiya*, April 27, 1969. Amounts in millions of rubles.

development of economic life. Democratic public opinion saw in the one-sided and pro-American "security pact" the danger of renascent Japanese militarism and Japan's participation in American-incited wars of aggression. The treaty was appraised as an insult to national honor and as a violation of constitutional and democratic rights. It also furthered the consolidation of the power of big business. The contest to annul the treaty coincided with Japan's struggle to achieve democratic methods of development and equitable relations with all nations, particularly those of the world socialist system.

Toward the end of the 1950s, opposition to the "security pact" began to root among the ruling liberal democrats. Japanese monopolies no longer needed the assistance of American capital to stabilize their country's internal economy and to solidify political control. Japan now possessed a first class industry and exerted noteworthy influence in world markets. According to the terms of the security pact, Japan received merely a guarantee of "security" in compensation for all the services provided to the United States. There was no provision for participation in formulating and executing American strategy in the Far East. Some leaders of the Liberal Democratic Party believed that the time had come to end dependence on America and to regain complete sovereignty and independence in foreign affairs. This group within the liberal bourgeoisie was prepared even to support certain anti-American demands raised the country's leftists.

Foreign minister Fujiyama belonged to this group.[23] Carrying out the wishes of some bourgeois monopolist circles, he promised that in discussions of treaty revisions he would obtain equality and a ban on atomic weapons in Japan.[24] As it turned out, the right wing was the more influential group in the Liberal Democratic Party, particularly after Premier Kishi Nobosuke's victory in the elections of May, 1958.[25] Kishi's group believed that "alliance" with the United States would continue to benefit Japan as long as the fundamental strategic territories of Southeast Asia were under American control either indirectly or through SEATO. Japan's interests included South Korea, the Philippines, Taiwan, South Vietnam, and Thailand. As a Japanese author, Noguchi Yuichiro, wrote: "It was in this connection that the plan appeared to penetrate Southeast Asia on the shoulders of the U.S."[26] The governing group merely sought the reexamination of individual articles of the pact while preserving the alliance with the United States. Reconsideration of the security pact met with "understanding" even in official American quarters. The United States was interested in defining more precisely the legal status of certain American special rights. Further, the new document would be signed by a Japanese government of the 1960s, which economically and politically differed by far from that of 1951. The United States also hoped somehow to regulate Japan's activities in foreign markets, where they were rivalling the operations of American companies. Leaders in Washington were also disturbed by Japan's relations with China, particularly after the "China Committee" decided to abolish those restrictions on trade with China not applicable to other socialist countries. This took effect after January 1, 1958.

Prior to the beginning of official Japanese-American talks, the American ambassador, MacArthur, suggested three possible variants for a future treaty: agreement on leasing bases to the United States on Japanese territory; a "corrected" version of the 1951 treaty; and a treaty for "mutual defense." The first two variants would not alter any principles of Japanese-American relations since they would be based on the old treaty. Another approach to relations was presented by the third variant. The topic of talks would not be simply unilateral "security" for Japan as an American base, but would call for Japan's participation in "mutual defense." In other words, Japan would become enmeshed in American aggressive policies in the Far East. This would violate the very foundations of the postwar Japanese constitution. Thus it represented a direct challenge to democratic public opinion in Japan.

Foreign minister Fujiyama guided the government toward the second variant. He pointed to the dangers for Japan in taking on responsibilities for "mutual defense." Also, as Fukusuma Shingo wrote, "he took positions designed to gain popularity in the country."[27] Fujiyama's proposal did not correspond to the views of the Liberal Democratic Party leadership. Kishi's cabinet aimed rather to bring Japan's financial might into the international arena, and to take active part in American policies in the Far East. Guided by these considerations, the Japanese administration agreed to accept the third variant as the basis for talks. Premier Kishi himself led the delegation which went to the United States where on January 19, 1960, the Treaty of Mutual Cooperation and Security was signed.[28] The treaty signatories defined their aims as "common interest in supporting international peace and security in the Far East." In making common cause with the United States, Japan's government agreed to support American intervention in Korea and Vietnam, and to favor Chiang Kai-shek's Taiwan regime. Article III of the treaty stipulated the obligations relating to "resistance to armed attack." It foresaw that the signatories would collaborate with each other by "unceasing self-help and mutual assistance." That is, they would jointly carry out punitive measures in neighboring Asian countries. To pay for equal partnership in imperial expansion in the Far East, the Japanese government confirmed its agreement to grant the United States "the right of its army, air force and naval forces to services and territories in Japan." (Article VI).

During the final stage of negotiations, Article II was added. Although unforeseen in the initial proposal, it turned out to be one of the key points of the treaty in that it called for economic cooperation. Neither country might continue to ignore their rivalry for international markets, which complicated the alliance. Therefore the two powers assumed the responsibility for "striving to eliminate conflicts in international economic policies and to strengthen economic cooperation." Japanese officials hoped that Article II would provide the basis for attracting American capital into large-scale cooperative ventures in Southeast Asia. Screening themselves with the flag of the United Nations, the United States and Japan set the new treaty to last "until such time as measures undertaken by the United Nations would take effect. These would satisfactorily assure preservation of international peace and security in the vicinity of Japan."

The treaty granted to each country the right, "after it had been in effect for ten years, to inform the other country of its intention to withdraw from the treaty." In such an eventuality, the leaders of each country might base their policy on the principles of the first Japanese-American treaty. The new treaty allowed Japan to bolster the political and economic dominance of big business and to veer the country toward renewed militarism and foreign expansion. The treaty made Japan a participant in American imperial policies and an ally of all the reactionary puppet regimes of Asia. The treaty was rejected by the majority of the Japanese people, and its revocation became the rallying cry of the Japanese left during the 1960s.

THE RISE OF THE JAPANESE ECONOMY

At the end of the 1950s Japan enjoyed a new wave of economic prosperity. It rapidly overtook developed European nations not only in growth rate but in absolute quantities of industrial production. When the sixties began Japan was in fifth spot in industrial output, behind the United States, the USSR, West Germany and England. By 1968 it had gained third place, led only by the United States and the Soviet Union. In terms of per capita income Japan still remained behind France, England, West Germany and especially the United States. This was explained by the continuing low productivity of Japanese labor (27 percent in comparison with the United States in 1967). Japan lagged behind other capitalist nations in investment of national product: Japan-47.8 percent, the United States-63.5 percent, France-63 percent, England-60.6 percent, and West Germany-60.2 percent. But at the same time Japan led those countries considerably in increasing the national product: Japan-40.7 percent, the United States-16.5 percent, West Germany-30.2 percent, England-30.2 percent, and France-29.4 percent. This permitted Japan to expand its economy at particularly high rates. Whereas, prior to World War II, the annual growth rate of Japan's gross national product had been 4-5 percent, in 1955-1968 it reached ten percent (in real terms). A notably rapid growth occurred in such branches of industry as steel production, pig iron, automobiles, chemical products and electrical appliances. Japan's national product growth occurred exclusively through industrial progress, for agriculture's share decreased noticeably and amounted to but ten percent of the total sum. An economy based on agriculture and light industry before the war, Japan was transformed into a highly developed industrial state.

Gains in industrial production resulted from an adept utilization of an exceptionally favorable market position. Japanese economists, wishing to characterize the present stage in the country's economic development, speak of a "second discovery of Japan" following the "industrial revolution under the Meiji." This terminology makes the point that, as during the 1870s and 1880s, Japan modernized its industrial structure by using the latest Western technological achievements. Although in general scientific sophistication Japan lagged far behind the world's advanced nations, it occupied the first rank in practical application of the latest accomplishments of world science and technology. Japan has been a major importer of technology for the past fifteen years, including acquisition and utilization of foreign patents, licenses, and various scientific and technical information. Meanwhile Japan's technological exports were minor. The use of foreign patents and licenses was especially significant for the manufacture of electronics, petrochemicals, electro-energy, large-scale electrical equipment and complex machinery. In Noguchi Yuichiro's words, "the bulk of the equipment which insured rapid industrial development was borrowed from other countries."[29] This policy enabled Japan to catch up with advanced Western nations by the early 1960s and in some types of products to surpass them.

The Japanese government uncovered sources of foreign capital to pay for industrial equipment and technological imports. Rapidly growing exports served as the primary source for foreign exchange. Foreign credits and direct investments also contributed significantly to the Japanese economy. From 1950 to April 1969 the total of loans and credits received from external sources amounted to $5,146,500,000. In addition, foreign exchange income of 1908 million dollars for the same period originated in commercial transactions, acquisition of stocks in Japanese enterprises and from Japanese owners of foreign stocks.[30] The United States continued to be Japan's chief creditor. Much American capital was attracted through special orders involving Japanese products needed by the American military. The value of special orders for the years 1959-1968 grew by 2.8 times, climbing from 471 million in 1959 to 1250 million dollars in 1968. Furthermore, the Japanese government stimulated the flow of foreign capital by direct industrial investments and credits. The data below, for November 1959, shows that Japanese banks established higher annual interest rates than available in the United States and western Europe to attract foreign capital.

Japan 6.94%
The United States, West Germany, England and France . 4.0
Holland 3.5
Belgium 3.25

Consequently, Japan became a more favorable capital market than the United States and western European countries.[31]

Japan's domestic capital was important in assuring high rates of industrial development. The rapid increase of gross national product, from 15,499 billion yen in 1960 to 51,092 billion yen in 1968, yielded an increase in capital accumulation from 33.7 percent to 38.6 percent. In absolute terms this meant a jump from 5,233 billion yen to 19,705 billion yen. In these conditions the monopoly banks, the primary financiers, were able to support a vast new industrial expansion. This was a very vital factor in speeding industrial development. Japanese companies might meet their capital needs by using only 30-35 percent domestic resources and drawing the remainder (65-70 percent) from the sale of securities (about 15 percent) and bank credits. This system of financing raised unproductive interest expenses yet, because of favorable trade balances, it permitted profitable operations and produced seemingly limitless credits to finance rapidly growing production.

Table 9 Basic Industrial Production in Japan
1959-1968*

		1959	1960	1964	1968
Steel	Mil tons	16.6	22.1	39.8	66.9
Pig Iron	Mil tons	9.4	11.9	23.8	46.6
Metal Lathes	Thousands	47.8	80.1	131.1	184.3
Light Automobiles	Thousands	78.6	165.1	579.7	2,056.0
Radios	Thousands	10,025.0	12,851.0	24,370.0	30,189.0
Television Sets	Thousands**	2,872.0	3,578.0	5,273.0	9,140.0
Steel vessels	Units	826	1,148.0	1,657.0	1,955.0
	Thous Tons	1,827.0	1,759.0	4,079.0	7,999.0
Fabrics	Thous Sq Meters	5,163.0	6,182.0	6,311.0	6,639.0
Cotton	Thous Sq Meters	2,757.0	3,222.0	2,965.0	2,744.0
Synthetics	Thous Sq Meters	120.7	270.6	762.1	1,408.0
Paper	Thous Tons	3,828.0	4,513.0	7,367.0	9,957.0
Cement	Thous Tons	. . . . . .	22,537.0	. . . .	47,160.0

*"Monthly Statistics of Japan," July 1969, No. 97.

**The Russian text has "millions" as the unit of measure here, but this seems clearly erroneous.

Growth of industrial production value was as follows (in billions of yen):

	1959	1964	1968
Total Value	3,587.1	8,508.2	15,349.2
Processing Manufacture	2,826.9	6,674.4	12,096.1
Mining	193.8	223.9	277.6
Construction	566.4	1,609.9	2,975.5

Japan's industrial expansion owed much to the progressive concentration of ownership by a few giant monopolies. Of 530,000 companies, 527 held 50 percent of all business stocks, 60 percent of manufacturing facilities and 44 percent of total net profit. On the other hand, the number of employees of these companies did not exceed 18 percent of the overall total. In seeking profits, the monopolies emphasized products promising high returns, which caused extreme imbalance in the economy and magnified reliance on foreign raw materials and sales. Whereas the index of industrial production value (with 1960 equal to 100) rose by 66.2 percent in 1964 and by 175 percent in 1968, mining rose only 9.5 percent in 1964 and 13.7 percent in 1968.

It became essential to eliminate obstacles to attracting private capital for expansion of electrical energy. Electricity was the foundation of all other branches of industry, yet investments in it produced only half as much profit as those in processing industries. The Japanese authorities let major monopolies run this branch of the economy, while the government itself operated inefficient electrical plants and absorbed their deficits. In 1951 the territory of Japan was divided into nine regions, called the "nine kingdoms" by the Japanese,[32] and each was turned over to a specific corporation. These corporations transferred a significant share of production expenses (energy losses in the grid, transformer costs, and maintenance) to the small consumer, thereby reducing their own costs. Data of the Consultative Committee on Questions of Electrical Energy indicate that the cost of a kilowatt hour of electricity was 12.1 yen to the small consumer, but only 3.85 yen to large users.

The aggregate measures taken to promote primarily monopolistic capital further consolidated the big business economic mastery. Japan's companies managed to reduce the personal consumption share of the national product from 57 percent in 1960 to 55 percent in 1964 and to 52 percent in 1968, thereby increasing the exploitation of hired labor. Nonetheless, with rapidly growing industrial production, the value of marketed consumer goods continued to rise from 8,823 billion yen in 1960 to 15,944 billion yen in 1964 and 26,666 billion yen in 1968.[33] Personal consumption contributed to the expansion of domestic markets and thereby created favorable conditions for industrial growth. However, despite economic successes in many branches of the national economy, technological backwardness continued, particularly in agriculture. In this sector labor productivity remained low. During the last ten to fifteen years it averaged but 28.2 percent of that in manufacturing. Consequently, agriculture became unprofitable. Because farming did not assure a minimum standard of living to the peasant family, about eighty percent of the peasants engaged in seasonal labor in other branches of the economy. To avoid complete disruption of agricultural production, the Japanese government was forced to establish higher official prices for grain and vegetable oil crops, and to limit their import. Artificial price increases for rice amounted to 98.4 percent from 1960 to 1968. This eased the situation for the most prosperous peasants, but it also inflated the cost of food. From 1960 to 1965 the annual increase in retail prices for consumer goods, led by agricultural products, was 6.2 percent, and in 1966-1968, 4.8 percent.[34] With extremely limited peasant income and small land holdings, agricultural mechanization was practically impossible. Japan's agriculture represented a unique colony of the capitalistic city, offering cheap labor to the Japanese monopolies and enabling them to compete successfully in world markets.

Japan's second and no less acute economic and social problem is tied to its numerous tiny and middle-sized enterprises. (See Table 10). Despite rapid economic centralization, small and medium-sized businesses grew in numbers. They accounted for half of all manufacturing, and continue to play the chief role in assuring employment for the populace. However, the wages of workers at small and middle-size manufacturing plants were but 60-70 percent of those of workers in large enterprises.[35] Presumably the number of small and middle-size enterprises will continue to increase, but productivity and wages, even with modernization will continue to lag behind those at larger companies.[36] For the period 1965-1968, general industrial productivity grew by 49.6 percent, and in manufacturing by 50.5 percent. Under pressure from the working class, big business was obliged to raise wages. Yet, because of rising retail prices, the increases amounted to but 23.2 percent and 27.4 percent, or only half the value gained by the monopolies due to growing productivity. Since, according to official statistics, consumer goods, fuel, housing and services rose in price by 15 percent, it is evident that real purchasing power increased by only 8-12 percent. Furthermore, official data show that many categories of workers do not enjoy the fruits even of this progress, despite the rapid growth of the economy. As sociologist Ioji Watanuki writes, "workers at medium-sized and small businesses, day laborers, small merchants, mothers and the children of working families have not enjoyed the benefits of rapid economic growth."[37] The Japanese monopolies retained about ninety percent of the value added in 1966-1970, thanks to the intensification of labor. At the same time, big business has enjoyed bumper success in economic expansion abroad and in competition in world markets.

JAPAN'S FOREIGN TRADE AND CAPITAL EXPORT

During the years 1958 to 1969, Japan moved ahead rapidly in foreign commerce. This is apparent from the following data (expressed in millions of dollars):[38]

Table 10. The Structure of Japanese Manufacturing*

	1956			1966		
	Light	Heavy	Total	Light	Heavy	Total
Enterprises	350,105(100)	83,268(100)	433,373(100)	477,629(100)	147,203(100)	594,832(100)
Small and Med. (to 299 workers)	349,144(99.7)	82,299(98.8)	431,443(99.6)	446,041(99.6)	145,171(98.6)	591,212(99.4)
Large	961(0.3)	969(1.2)	1,930(0.4)	1,588(0.4)	2,032(1.4)	3,620(0.6)
Workers**	3,699(100)	2,349(100)	6,048(100)	5,653(100)	4,639(100)	10,292(100)
Small and Med.**	3,066(82.9)	1,306(55.6)	4,372(72.3)	4,647(82.2)	2,530(54.5)	7,177(69.7)
Large**	633(17.1)	1,043(44.4)	1,676(27.7)	1,006(17.8)	2,109(45.5)	3,115(30.3)
Production***	4,436.6(100)	4,437.5(100)	8,837.1(100)	14,908.5(100)	19,561.9(100)	34,470.4(100)
Small and Med.***	3,029.8(68.3)	1,660.3(37.4)	4,690.1(52.9)	10,541.7(70.7)	6,983.9(35.7)	17,525.6(50.8)
Large***	1,406.8(31.7)	2,777.2(62.6)	4,183.0(47.1)	4,366.8(29.3)	12,578.0(64.3)	16,944.8(49.2)

*Source: *"Economic Survey of Japan, 1968-1969,"* p. 153.

** Thousand

***Billion Yen

YEAR	EXPORT	IMPORT	TOTAL	BALANCE
1958	2,877	3,033	5,910	− 156
1960	4,055	4,491	8,546	− 436
1962	4,916	5,637	10,533	− 721
1964	6,673	7,938	14,611	−1,265
1965	8,452	8,169	16,621	+ 283
1966	9,776	9,523	19,299	+ 253
1967	10,442	11,663	22,105	−1,221
1968	12,972	12,987	25,959	− 15
1969	15,990	15,024	31,014	+ 966

At the end of the 1960s Japan eliminated its negative balance of trade. Including the significant non-commercial receipts from freight, foreign investments and American special orders, financial surpluses formed, allowing Japan to enter the international market as a creditor.

Japan's industrialization was reflected in the structure of its exports. In 1969 the share of industrial goods shipped abroad reached 90 percent, higher than that of the United States (65 percent), France (70 percent), or England (83 percent), and at nearly the same level as West Germany (89 percent) and Switzerland (92 percent). The character of industrial exports also experienced a basic change. Prior to World War II, the bulk of Japan's exports consisted of textiles (52 percent in 1934-1936). In 1969, heavy manufacturing provided 65 percent of the total; machines and instruments accounted for 40 percent, and metals and metal products for 18.1 percent. Light manufacturing contributed 27.2 percent, of which 14.1 percent were textiles. Japan's imports consist chiefly of industrial raw materials (70 percent in 1969), industrial products and foodstuffs. The economy's needs for raw materials and commodities are largely satisfied by imports, particularly of such items as cotton, wool, bauxite, nickel, phosphates, rubber, and copra, all of which are 100 percent imported. Imports also supply 98 percent of oil, 95 percent of iron ore, 85 percent of copper ore, 80 percent of salt, and 76 percent of wheat.

The leading partners in Japan's foreign trade are the United States and the countries of Southeast Asia. In 1969 the American share was 31 percent (4,958 million dollars) of Japan's exports, and 27.3 percent (4,090 million dollars) of imports. The respective figures for the countries of Southeast Asia were 28.7 percent (4,317 million dollars), and 15.8 percent (2,374 million dollars). These regions play an important role in Japan's foreign trade not only in terms of total exchange, but as the chief sources of foreign currency, permitting Japan to balance deficits in trade with the Middle East (for oil, cotton and other goods), Latin America, and Australia. Although trade with the socialist countries grew somewhat in the 1960s, it still amounted to a relatively insignificant part of Japan's foreign trade totals. In 1969 the socialist countries' share was 4.3 percent (695 million dollars) of Japan's export and 6.1 percent (920 million dollars) of its imports. In total trade, the Soviet Union held first place among the socialist countries, with 730 million dollars; China followed with 625 million dollars. In Japanese exports, China leads with 391 million dollars, and the USSR is second with 268 million. The development of trade with the socialist countries, which could become major partners, remains one of Japan's future tasks.

Analysis of the trade structure and its geographical directions permits certain conclusions about foreign trade policy. As a country lacking industrial and agricultural raw materials, Japan is dependent on sources abroad. Therefore, it must develop foreign commerce. Limitations on imports relate only to luxury items, alcoholic beverages and tobacco products, along with some other secondary products. These limitations are not protectionist, but are explained solely by considerations of foreign exchange. Raw material imports are accelerated, even if they affect the interests of domestic mining concerns. This is an expression of the traditional Japanese policy which seeks to conserve domestic resources for extraordinary circumstances such as war or embargoes by source countries. Importing also assures cheaper raw materials for domestic manufacturers. Japan is forced to meet the fierce competition of the Western countries. Thanks to low official prices (at times at "dumping" levels), Japanese exporters not only penetrate the markets of the industrially developed nations of Europe and America, but even force out domestic products of those countries. The further growth of Japan's exports at the rates of the past decade will invite sharper rivalries for markets. Such considerations require Japanese big business to seek new types of economic expansion. In conjunction with the development of a larger export product-mix, the export of capital is proposed as the chief foreign trade innovation for the coming decade.

Japan possesses large and rapidly escalating reserves of foreign exchange. At the end of 1969 these totalled 3,496 million dollars, and should reach four billion dollars by the end of 1970, permitting a capital export program in 1969. Japanese officials plan to emphasize long-term industrial credits and direct investments in the economies of developing nations and other countries. In this connection the Japanese bourgeois press considers that major Japanese investments are "generally desired" by Asian and other countries. Proposals of the Ministry of Economics to the Japanese government call for capital exports approaching four percent of the gross national product by 1974. This compares to 2.2 percent in 1968. According to projections of the Japanese Institute for Research in Capital Investments, Japan's GNP by 1971 will be 200 billion, and by 1975 it will reach 350 billion dollars. This would provide 6 billion and 14 billion dollars respectively in those years, bringing Japan's total foreign investments to 40-50 billion dollars.

Because Japan is a world power in economics, the directors of its big business believe that Japan should exercise a potent influence on the domestic industrial production of other nations, including those of Europe and America. Analysis of Japan's investments reveals that the largest share has entered the capitalist countries for participation in modern industrial plants, or into banking and trade. In 1968, of 1,562 million dollars invested abroad, only 229 million dollars went to Asian countries, chiefly South Korea and Taiwan. Investments in Southeast Asia and Oceania (largely Indonesia) were 43 million dollars. The chief market for Japanese capital remains the United States (494 million dollars, or 31.6 percent), and Central and South America (345 million, or 22.1 percent).[39]

Recently, capital flow to the developing nations gradually has grown. Companies have been established to exploit resources and for industrial production in Australia and countries of Asia and Africa. Even at this date, however, the Japanese monopolies do not want to consider the interests of the developing countries of Asia, Africa and other continents. These lands are prepared to accept Japan's economic and technological cooperation, but not to the detriment of their economic independence and industrial progress. Japan's rulers labor to convert their country into a single world factory, at least for the countries of Asia. They imagine that capital export in the coming decade will bind the economies of developing nations to industrial Japan, and assure its leading regional role.

JAPANESE MILITARIZATION

The Japanese bourgeois press offers two theses in predicting developments for the coming decade. Both justify the need for Japan to adopt the leading role in Asia. In the first place, American involvement is declining and England has withdrawn from the region. Secondly, there is a flowering communist peril from China and even the Soviet Union, particularly because of the supposed vacuum in East and Southeast Asia as the United States and England depart. Such conclusions are also featured in addresses by leaders of the ruling Liberal Democratic Party, and were echoed in the official Japanese-American communique concluding the Nixon-Sato meeting in November 1969.[40] That communique violated the Japanese constitution in that Japan accepted military responsibilities to defend not only Japanese territory, but also South Korea and Taiwan. Further, the Japanese interpretation of defense reaches beyond its own territory or territory defined as "vitally important to the defense of Japan itself" to include preventive military action against a potential foe.[41] Therefore, under the guise of preparations for "self-defense," Japanese authorities are instituting an extensive program of open and secret militarization. Japanese papers publish data on the "fourth plan for strengthening the armed forces," and write of the need for "speeding development of defense industry and increasing exports of Japanese weapons to the countries of Southeast Asia."[42] The head of the Office of National Defense, Nakasone Yasuhiro, explained the fourth defense plan, to be implemented beginning in 1972. It stands in contrast to the second and third plans in which the arming of Japan's self-defense forces took place "in the framework of complete dependence on American forces." The fourth plan required "lesser dependence of Japan's defense on American armed forces," and allowed Japanese armed forces to be sent abroad "to maintain peace."[43] A leading manufacturer, "Mitsubishi," was transformed into a gigantic military arsenal, developing modern weapons, and Japanese newspapers reported plans for expansion of the Mitsubishi firm into atomic industry.[44] Foreign newspapers reported that the Japanese budget for 1968 allocated some 6.5 billion dollars for modernization of the armed forces, namely creation of rocket units and military aviation.[45]

The militarization of the country presented but one aspect of the program. Japan's rulers made attempts to revive the "spirit of the emperor" and the great-power, racist ideas of elitism and the divine origin of the nation of Yamato. Rapid economic expansion allowed big business to conceal sharp social conflicts. Still, the entire Japanese economic success stemmed chiefly from the defeat of Japanese militarism as well as from favorable international circumstances, including the Korean and Vietnam wars. Yet various officials attributed economic progress to the superiority of the state monopoly system and the special qualities of the Japanese nation. Celebration of Japan's might and the inflamation of extreme nationalism increasingly characterized official Japanese publicity. Consequently, the struggle in Japanese society presently revolves around the paramount national problem of guaranteeing the further development of the country and the well-being of society. Should Japan develop as a peace-loving democratic state, allowing the entire Japanese people to enjoy the benefits of a prosperous society? Or, rather should the chief priority of Japanese policies be expansion abroad, complete with the required centralized and militarized economy governed by experienced monopolies, as the sole sustenance of the "great empire of Yamato"?

Japan's post-war experience supports the demand of democratic public opinion for a peaceful and neutral policy. Despite the lack of natural resources and rapidly growing population (from 75.8 million in 1946 to 101.4 million in 1968), Japan was able to develop at unusually rapid rates. Although military trade and U.S. financial and technical assistance helped, an important factor was the peaceful coexistence among various social systems. Advances in the Japanese standard of living brought significant expansion of domestic markets, which absorbed most Japanese industrial products. However, at the present historical moment, realistic conditions for fundamental social transformation do not exist in Japan. Transition to the higher level of social development represented by socialism is not possible. Nevertheless, forces do exist capable of maintaining the country on a peaceful course, blocking the road to militarism and thereby safeguarding the Japanese people from a terrible catastrophe. In Japan the antagonism between elements of society has long endured, assuring that in the immediate future the progressive democratic movement will achieve but partial victories. Still, Japan's future is directly linked to improved ties between socialism and democracy, and opposition to the forces of imperialism and militarism.

SINO-JAPANESE RELATIONS, 1958-1969

Thoroughgoing changes occurred in Sino-Japanese affairs in 1958. Both the representatives of the left and the powerful bourgeoisie in Japan appealed for normal relations with China. The fourth Sino-Japanese nongovernmental trade agreement was signed in March 1958. The Japanese delegation was headed by the parliamentary deputy Ikedo Masanosuke of the Liberal Democratic Party. The terms included commercial representation in Tokyo and Peking, obviously with the sanction of the Japanese government. A few days before the agreement was signed, in February, 1958, the Chinese foreign trade agency and the Yawata steel foundry of Japan signed a substantial barter contract to exchange Japanese steel for Chinese bituminous coal, iron ore and other goods. The bipartite deliveries specified in this agreement amounted to ten billion yen for the first year and 100 billion yen in the last year of the contract. The leaders of the Chinese People's Republic hoped to utilize Japanese public opinion, which they overestimated, to force the Japanese government into inter-governmental talks, which would result in official diplomatic relations. Guided by these purposes, the Chinese commerical mission which arrived in Tokyo in accordance with the non-governmental trade agreement, attempted to make use of the official flag as a means of according the delegation legitimacy as an official organization. Finding this unacceptable, the Japanese government, contrary to international legal practice, protested the actions of the Chinese trade delegation. Then, not without the knowledge of official authorities, young hooligans tore the flag of the Chinese People's Republic off the building of the trade mission in Nagasaki, and defiled it.

The Kishi government assumed a hostile stance in other matters as well concerning the Chinese People's Republic. Notwithstanding statements by previous Japanese premiers—Hatoyama and Ikeda— of Japan's willingness to cooperate in trade relations, the Kishi government refused to grant official bank guarantees for Japanese commercial transactions, in China. For this reason the Chinese government abrogated the fourth trade agreement and the steel foundry contracts with Yawata as well, and recalled China's trade mission to Peking. New complexities now infested Sino-Japanese relations, followed by attempts to find ways out of the difficulties. In October 1959 talks were held in Peking between delegations of the Chinese Communist Party, including Liu Shao-chi, Chou En-lai, and others, and of the Japanese Communist Party made up of Nosaka Sanzo, Hakamada Satomi, Kurahara Korehito, Ishima Ichiro and Iwama Masao. A joint communique dated October 20, 1959 evaluated the international situation and Japan's domestic outlooks, and defined the positions of both parties concerning these problems.[46] The communique stated:

At the present time the countries of the socialist camp, headed by the Soviet Union, are conducting economic and cultural construction at rapid rates. The movement for national independence, democracy and freedom in Asia, Africa and Latin America continues to grow. . . . It is in these circumstances that the peaceful policies of the socialist camp receive increasingly fervent support. . . . Thanks to the peaceful policies of the socialist camp, the aggressive activities of the imperialist bloc and its cold war policy will continue to suffer defeat in the future.

The two parties declared their complete support for Soviet proposals for lessening international tension, for an end to the cold war, and for peaceful coexistence between countries with differing social systems. The communique called attention to the fact that, "in the Far East, American imperialists and their stooges, the Japanese reactionaries, endeavor still to revitalize Japanese militarism and wish to revise the Japanese-American security pact in order to strengthen their dominion and plunder of the Japanese people, and to strengthen the unconcealed military alliance directed against China and the Soviet Union. In the name of the Japanese Communist Party, the Japanese delegation stated: "The path of the Japanese people is the path of peace, independence, democracy and neutrality. This means that in foreign affairs the complete independence of the Japanese people is essential to destroy the military alliances concluded with foreign governments, and to establish relations of peace and friendship with all countries." The Chinese Party representatives in turn assured the Japanese communists that the "basic course of China's foreign policy lay in the conscientious, unswerving and precise observance of the five principles of peaceful coexistence," and that the Chinese Communist Party wholly and completely supports the "just position of the Japanese Communist Party and has limitless respect for the heroic struggle of the Communist Party and the people of Japan." Both delegations declared that the "peoples and communist parties of China and Japan, together with the peoples of all countries, would make an even larger contribution to the struggle for peace in the Far East and throughout the world, for securing the independence of all countries, and for developing the cause of democracy and social progress."

In this document the two communist parties reached the only correct conclusion, making use of scientific, Marxist analysis of the social situation in Japan and internationally. Their conclusion indicated that reactionaries were united by class rather than by racial affinities. The alliance of Japanese and American monopolies was directed against the working people of Japan and the socialist countries—the USSR and the Chinese People's Republic. The struggle for democracy and social progress for the Japanese and Chinese peoples should be carried on in cooperation with the peoples of all countries. The stand of the Chinese and Japanese communist parties evoked broad support and sympathy in world democratic circles. Nevertheless, circumstances in Japan and China did not permit these progressive views to become government policies guiding relations between the two countries.

In Japan such a policy was prevented by monopolistic capital, which continued to strengthen its position with American assistance. Japanese business leaders regarded the mainland Chinese as class enemies posing an obstacle to their plans for international expansion. They believed that for the moment capitalist Japan would be better off to maintain its alliance with the United States. In keeping with the terms of the recent American-Japanese treaty for "mutual cooperation and security," Japan must limit its ties with China to trade. No political or diplomatic recognition should be extended to the Chinese People's Republic, for this would bring no economic benefits to Japan.[47]

The situation in China also had changed, where Mao Tse-tung's group had concentrated leadership in its hands. Discarding the general party line, the Maoists had begun a radical reappraisal of the country's entire foreign policy, including relations with Japan. The communique of the Chinese and Japanese communist parties did not suit Mao. In rejecting a scientific, Marxist-Leninist analysis of the world situation, Mao declared that the fundamental clashes in the world should take place between the peoples of Asia and Africa, on one side, and the peoples of Europe and America, on the other. In other words, not a class but a racial premise was advanced, and from this Mao drew the conclusion that Japan should not remain neutral as the two parties had declared. It should become China's ally because the peoples of China and Japan belonged to one and the same race and were close in culture, style of life and traditions. Mao and his partisan's extolled nationalism and racism as the foundation of international relations. Whereas the Japanese communists called on Japanese people to combat American imperialism and the domestic monopolies alike, Mao's group wished to focus the struggle against American imperialism and the small number of highly placed persons closely linked to the United States. The battle of the working people against monopolies was postponed. The Maoists particularly demonstrated their racist foreign policy with respect to the Soviet Union. Feigning "understanding" and sympathy with the Japanese revanchists who sought the reexamination of the World War II settlements, the Chinese coterie willingly supported Japanese territorial pretensions. Making common cause with them, Mao's partisans themselves claimed "rights" to the ancient lands of peoples of the Soviet Union.[48]

Mao Tse-tung's nationalist ideas found "understanding" and support in Japan chiefly among the revanchist group. This company comprised the most militant representatives of the capital monopolies, who were prepared to accept a pan-Asiatic alliance and who naturally realized that such an alliance would be led by Mao Tse-tung or some other Asian "ally." Nonetheless, they would have been completely satisfied by an alliance with Mao's nationalistic China, which was adopting an anti-Soviet stance. The association might be employed to weaken Western rivals, including the United States. And, as the ruler of China, Mao suited them since he had retarded the country's progress through his management of the government and his adventuristic experiments in the "great leap forward" and other revolutionary upheavals. Consequently, prosperous Japan saw new opportunities for leadership in East Asia.

Certain Japanese businessmen sought rapprochement with China from purely financial considerations, entertaining no far-reaching political plans. Inasmuch as China's economic relations with the Soviet Union and the East European socialist countries had been curtailed, Japanese import-export companies did not wish to miss the opportunity of supplanting them in China's trade. They demanded that their government revise its official China policy, not restrict Sino-Japanese trade, and allow Japanese capital to participate in China's industrialization. Beginning in 1962 numerous unofficial Japanese delegations visited the Chinese People's Republic. The delegations were headed by prestigious Liberal Democratic Party leaders, who were members of parliament. In high-level meetings these Japanese missions reached the same conclusion about growing nationalist tendencies in Chinese policies and Mao's insistent wish for cooperation with Japan on a racial basis. The influential liberal-democrat Hayato Ikeda, after his return from Peking in 1964, reported: "In China they have a feeling of kinship and closeness to the Asian nations. Nationalism has transcended ideology. Does not the Sino-Soviet dispute express this?"[49] Racial affinity as an ideological basis for Sino-Japanese friendship found adherents in Japanese leftist circles as well. The influence of Mao Tse-tung enlarged among leaders of the Japanese socialist party, who advocated normal relations and pan-Asian unity against the European nations. In January 1959 a meeting of business groups took place in Tokyo. Kajuo Suzuki, president of the Society for Sino-Japanese Trade Collaboration and one of the leaders of the Socialist Party of Japan, urged ". . . as a countermeasure against western European countries, settlement of relations with Southeast Asian countries, including communist China, and the calling of an Asian economic conference, including communist China, to consider countermeasures for the development of Asian trade."[50]

Loyal Japanese disciples of Mao accepted at face value his appeal to follow the Chinese way. They preached extreme nationalism and racism under concealment of bold slogans for "the solidarity of the nations of Asia," and "the struggle against American and European imperialism." They urged the Japanese people to break their ties to the world community and to destroy the workers' solidarity, achieved in the battle with international imperialism. But these declarations offered nothing to the people as a whole, who demanded normal ties with the Chinese People's Republic. The democratic Japanese public wanted to regard China as a peace-loving country working to achieve socialism and clinging to the principles of freedom and equality between peoples and nations, mutual respect for sovereignty, territorial integrity, and noninterference in the internal affairs of others. Guided by these principles, Japanese workers continued to advocate recognition of the Chinese People's Republic as the only legitimate and representative organ of the Chinese people. Nevertheless, the official Japanese government policy remained unchanged. It reflected the interests of the most influential persons among the liberal-democrats. While Japan's leaders wished to preserve their alliance wtih the United States, they equally were prepared to develop trade with China even though it would increase China's economic potential. As before, the Japanese government refused to supply China with sophisticated, highly productive equipment and strategic materials, and it prohibited loans or financial guarantees to Chinese organizations on long-term agreements. In essence, trade with mainland China was limited to secondary products of little interest.

In these complex circumstances occurred the first trade talks since the break in relations in 1958. Although high level representatives of the two countries participated, the conversations were of a non-governmental character. In September 1962, the prominent liberal-democrat and member of parliament, Kenjo Matsumura, visited China for extensive discussions with Premier Chou En-lai and Foreign Minister Chen Yi; he was also received by Mao Tse-tung. Their concluding statement read: "Both sides are unanimous in finding it essential gradually and diligently to achieve normalization of relations between the two countries, including political and economic relations."[51] To pursue this agreement in principle, the former minister of trade and industry and member of parliament from the Liberal Democratic Party, Tatsunosuke Takasaki, journeyed to Peking on October 28, 1962. He was accompanied by numerous commercial and industrial representatives from the Association for the Development of Foreign Trade. The talks ended with the signing, on November 9, 1962, of a memorandum "On Developing Private Trade Between Japan and China." The principal signers were Takasaki and Liao Chen-chi, president of the Chinese Committee for Solidarity with the Countries of Asia and Africa. Trade conditions were outlined for a five-year period, from 1963 to 1967, setting the annual total exchange at 36 million pounds sterling (100 million dollars).

To make it practical to achieve this trade volume, offices opened in Peking (the "Takasaki Trade Office") and in Tokyo (the "Liao Chen-chi Trade Office"). Provisions of the agreement were to be fulfilled on the basis of long-term barter. The Japanese agreed to deliver rolled steel (including high-quality categories), chemical fertilizers, agricultural machinery, operative equipment and other goods. The Chinese were to provide coal, iron ore, soy beans, corn, salt and lead. Besides the trade established by this memorandum, commercial operations were to be expanded through so-called friendly firms, recommended by the Association for Cooperation in Developing Sino-Japanese Trade and the Association for International Trade, as well as the Chinese-Japanese Friendship Society. Japanese "friendly firms" were to provide most of the trade (see Table 11). While the total value of commercial exchange was increased, the trade structure as such did not differ essentially from that stipulated in the memorandum.

Table 11.
Sino-Japanese Trade 1963-1965 (millions of dollars)[52]

	1963	1964	1965
Total Trade Exchange	137	310	469
Per Liao-Takasaki memorandum	64	114	182
Through "friendly firms"	73	196	287
Japanese Export Total	62	153	245
Per Liao-Takasaki memorandum	37	69	90
Through "friendly firms"	25	84	155
Japanese Import Total	75	157	225
Per Liao-Takasaki memorandum	28	45	93
Through "friendly firms"	47	112	132

Despite the interest of Japanese firms in exporting marine equipment and other wares, the Japanese government continued to block delivery of such products to China "for strategic considerations." For example, in the fall of 1964 Chinese foreign trade organizations purchased a 12,500 ton freighter from the Japanese "Hitachi Zosen" firm, and complete equipment for a vinylon plant costing more than 25 million dollars from the "Nichibo" company. Terms called for payment over five years. Yet in April 1965 the Japanese government refused to permit the Japanese Import-Export Bank to finance these transactions for the Japanese firms. To a certain extent, this official position was a concession to Chiang Kai-shek's Taiwan regime. The Japanese government had agreed to prohibit official institutions, including the Import-Export Bank, from non-governmental trade with the Chinese People's Republic. Meanwhile, Japan actively was promoting economic relations with Taiwan. Their combined trade for 1950-1963 significantly exceeded that between Japan and the People's Republic, and only in 1964 was it slightly less. (In 1964 total trade with Taiwan was 279 million, and with the mainland, 310 million dollars.) In April 1965 a large loan of 150 million dollars was granted Taiwan on relatively liberal terms, thus underlining Japan's special interest in developing the economy of that strategically important island.[53]

The Japanese government also demonstrated its loyalty to Taiwan in political affairs. In May 1965, Tokyo announced the release of the "Provisional Government of the Taiwan Republic." After eighteen years in Japan, its head Liao Wen-yi returned to Taiwan to "participate in the anti-communist battle" under the leadership of Chiang Kai-shek. This benevolent attitude toward the Taiwan regime proved clearly that Japan's projected policies toward China did not neglect Chiang Kai-shek's nationalist forces, which in suitable circumstances could be mobilized. Following the United States in this question, Japan stubbornly insisted on Taiwan's right to represent China in the United Nations. Japan also leaned toward the "creation of two Chinas" in order to separate Taiwan from the Chinese mainland, calculating that, sooner or later, it would be able to bring that "independent" island into the Japanese empire.

Meanwhile Japan collaborated extensively with Taiwan in the political and military blocs created by the Americans. The Japanese government and the "government" of Taiwan were among the first organizers of the new and aggressive ASPAC alliance (the Asian-Pacific Council), created under American auspices and including Japan, Taiwan, Thailand, the Philippines, South Vietnam, South Korea, New Zealand, Australia and Malaysia. At the same time, the Japanese leaders did not want openly to alienate the Chinese People's Republic. Beginning in 1965 they again sought ways to revive ties. In January of that year a large group from the Liberal-Democratic Party formed the "Society for the Study of Asian and African Problems," which included as members such adherents of rapprochement with mainland China as Utsunomia Tokuma, Kawasaki Hidezi, and Matsumura Kenjo, the society's advisor. The society also included former foreign minister Fujiyama, supporters of former foreign minister Miki, and others. The society appealed to the

Japanese government to initiate improved relations with Asian nations, primarily in East Asia. Members of the society labored to convince officials that the Chinese People's Republic was not a communist country, and that it might join with Japan in stabilizing the nations of Asia. Matsumura Kenjo, upon his return from China in 1966 (at the height of the "cultural revolution") made the following statement:

> They say that China is a communist country. Is that assertion completely true? In China they are as attentive to Buddhism as if it were the state religion. Yet that contradicts materialism. Further, take the realm of economics. In it there remain those whom it is acceptable to call capitalists. Take education. The greatest efforts there are directed to heighten patriotic, and in the final analysis, nationalistic, great-Han attitudes.[54] Doesn't true communism overcome national differences and state borders? If these circumstances are considered, then what indeed represents the attributes of communism in China? Regardless of all this, at the present time in Japan the views of many peoples in positions of authority are too narrow. Should not they, in a spirit of patriotism and patriotic aspirations, open their eyes wider and take into account what is happening in the world?[55]

Matsumura realistically interpreted developments occurring in China's domestic and foreign affairs. Anti-Sovietism, the struggle with Marxist-Leninist parties in the international communist movement, renunciation of the common struggle of socialist countries and the world's progressive forces against American aggression—all these factors convinced Japanese nationalists and revanchists that Peking's leaders merely resorted to "leftist" phraseology and anti-imperialist slogans for propaganda purposes. In the antagonism between socialism and imperialism, they held a neutral position and, seen objectively, they were aiding the imperialist camp.[56] China's deepening estrangement from the socialist countries and its weakened influence in East Asian countries could not help but be reflected in the official Japanese position. This was especially so after the abortive putsch by Mao Tse-tung's supporters in Indonesia and the attempt to touch off an India-Pakistan conflict. The Liberal Democratic Party leadership actively sought new approaches to the problem of China. The Society for the Study of Asian and African Problems became an important political center counting among its members the closest colleagues of Premier Sato (Kuno Tiuji and others). A new policy for China resulted, its main distinction being that Japan should not link China to matters concerning its "alliance" with the United States. It was recommended that the Japanese government manage its affairs independently of the United States, and that it serve also as a mediator of Sino-American relations, thereby possibly regaining the leading role in Far Eastern affairs. The Japanese authorities did not conceal the fact that improved ties with the Chinese People's Republic were contingent on changed policies by Mao's leadership, particularly after the "cultural revolution." The joint communique of the meeting of President Johnson and Premier Sato in Washington, November 14-15, 1967,[57] expressed the conviction that "communist" China would finally retreat from its "implacable" position and strive to live peacefully "in the international community."

For its part, the Chinese leadership continually altered its foreign policy. In 1966 the Maoists broke ties with the Japanese Communist Party, launched a blatant slander campaign against it, and expelled Japanese Party representatives from Peking, along with correspondents for the communist newspaper "Akahata." Chinese foreign trade organizations severed ties with the Japanese "friendly firms" which represented leftist organizations and progressive circles in the Japanese business world, and representatives of three such firms were sent home from Peking in 1966. These firms, "Haga," "Mutsumi" and "Sanshin," had been pioneers in Japan's trade with the Chinese People's Republic. Some Maoists tried to provoke a split in the Japanese Communist Party and to disrupt activities of the Japanese-Chinese Society and other binational organizations. Adopting the methods of the "cultural revolution," the Japanese Maoists turned to reliance on classless elements and Chinese emigrants subsidized by Peking. They organized provocations, diversions and attacks on Japanese communists, trying by threats and blackmail to "spread the ideas of Mao," to assert the authority of "the leader of the nations of Asia."

Meanwhile, Mao's clique associated increasingly with Japan's monopolies. In May 1966 a delegation headed by Matsumura visited China.[58] The delegation also included Matsumoto Shunichi, an advisor to the foreign minister of Japan. Matsumura conducted talks with the Chinese government on numerous Sino-Japanese and international problems. They agreed in principle to extend the "Liao-Takasaki" trade agreement, which was to expire in 1967. They also discussed direct air links between the two countries, exchange of scientific and technical information, Sino-American and Sino-Soviet relations, the war in Vietnam, and other matters. In August and September 1966, a group of parliamentary members from the Liberal Democratic Party went to China, led by former foreign minister Kosaka Jentaro. Among the group was the former chief of the Japanese defense administration, Masumi Esaki. Besides questions of mutual interest, the delegation set conditions for Japan's mediation in normalizing Sino-American relations. Later, the head of the Japanese delegation asserted that, in the course of these talks, no objection was raised to Japanese mediation, and the Chinese leaders viewed this purpose "with understanding." After returning from China in November 1966, Kosaka visited the United States.

At the beginning of 1968, negotiations once more got underway in Peking on Sino-Japanese affairs. The non-official Japanese mission, led by parliament members Furui Yoshimi and Tagawa Seiichi, signed a new one-year trade agreement. Within the framework of the "Liao-Takasaki" memorandum, it called for reductions in deliveries of Chinese goods, primarily foodstuffs such as soy beans, rice and like commodities. The published communique also touched upon general policy questions. The representatives agreed (the Japanese delegation in the form of demands to be presented to their government) to three political principles: Japan would not pursue policies hostile to China; Japan would not be a part of any plot to create two Chinas; there would be no obstacles from the Japanese side in normalizing Sino-Japanese relations or applying the principle of the inseparability of politics and economics.

Important political principles were thus included in the communique. Their content went directly against official Japanese government policy, thereby displaying the heightened aspirations of leaders of the Liberal Democratic Party for radically different policies toward the Chinese People's Republic. The fact that the Japanese government did not protest these views, so divergent from its own, demonstrated that it too was ready for new approaches to the Chinese problem. Nonetheless, as Premier Sato stated several times, Japan "was still interested in its alliance with the United States." Consequently, any compromise with China should not jeopardize the Japanese-American alliance, and the Japanese government continued strictly to limit the schedule of products available for delivery to China. These limitations applied to high-grade steel, equipment and other strategic materials. But, at the same time, the authorities promoted trade in secondary goods and, notwithstanding the significant curtailment of trade between the countries in 1967-1968 because of disruptions stemming from the "cultural revolution," Japanese firms maintained their export levels in the China trade. In 1969 the value of general trade even increased, as indicated by the following data (in millions of dollars):[59]

	1966	1967	1968	1969
Total Trade	621	557	550	626
Japanese Export to the CPR	315	288	326	391
Japanese Import from the CPR	306	269	224	235

Then, at the end of 1969, fundamental changes occurred in Japan's official policies regarding China. The ninth congress of the Chinese Communist Party (in April 1969) saw Mao Tse-tung's leadership take new directions. Under the guise of arch-revolutionary slogans about "the world revolution," the Maoists openly repudiated the Party's general line, calculated to build socialism in China. An anti-Soviet foreign policy and the harrassment of the world socialist system gained precedence. With tacit American approval,[60] Japanese leaders decided the time had come to end the boycott of the Chinese People's Republic and, accordingly, in December 1969 the Japanese government officially called for talks. Premier Sato declared: "If communist China wishes to begin inter-governmental contacts with Japan to lessen tension in the Far East and improve Japan's relations with communist China, the government would welcome such a proposal and would give it positive consideration."[61]

Accompanying Sato's address the foreign minister, Kiichi Aichi, suggested two hypotheses under consideration by the Japanese government in determining new policy to China: 1) Following the disorders of the "cultural revolution" the Chinese People's Republic was practising a diplomacy designed to smooth international relations; 2) It was expected that at the end of 1969 or early in 1970 diplomatic contacts between the United States and mainland China would be renewed for, as the Nixon-Sato communique stated American and Japanese relations with the Chinese People's Republic were to improve.[62] Tokyo assumed that the braking of China's progress by the "great leap forward" and the "cultural revolution," and China's weakened international situation due to strained ties with the socialist countries, would make Peking's leaders more pliable and compliant. In the immediate future China would not seriously rival Japanese goods and capital. Therefore, political concessions such as diplomatic recognition and United Nations membership for the Chinese People's Republic would be a small price for an alliance in the forthcoming struggle for the mastery of Asia.

For Mao Tse-tung the improvement of relations with Japan was becoming essential. Japan held first place in mainland China's trade with capitalist countries, about twenty percent of total trade. At the Canton fairs and in trade through Hong Kong, the fundamental channels to the Western world, Japanese firms dominated. They assisted Chinese foreign trade organizations in circumventing controls by the United States and other governments, helping China to obtain high-grade steel, alloys, electronic instrumentation and sophisticated equipment, such as that needed for China's atomic industry. For their part, the Maoists sought Japanese support for the racist "ideas of Mao," and in the name of a racist political alliance they were prepared to make extensive economic concessions, even to permit Japanese investments in China's industry and transport. This was the more acceptable given the existing state of the Chinese economy and its catastrophic lag behind Japan, which weakened China's positions as Asia's leading nation. (See Table 12).

Table 12.
The Economy of the Chinese People's Republic and Japan
1958-1969[63]

		China (est.)		Japan	
National		1958	1969	1958	1969
Income	Bil dollars	---	65.5	32.0	131.7
Steel	Mil tons	8.0	13.0	12.1	82.2
Pig Iron	Mil tons	9.5	15.0	7.4	58.3
Electrical					
Energy	Bil kwh	27.5	65.0	83.1	250.0
Coal	Mil tons	270.0	225.0	49.7	44.8
Metal Lathes	Thousands	35.0	45.0	32.7	231.4
Automobiles	Thousands	30.0	50.0	180.0	6490.0
Cotton Fabric	Mil Sq Meters	6.0	7.0	2.6	2.8
Grain	Mil tons	210.0	195.0	15.6	14.7
Rice	Mil tons	110.0	100.0	12.0	14.0

Given the existing state of the two economies, China had become an involuntary consumer of Japanese equipment and other industrial commodities, and a supplier of raw materials. The product structure of Sino-Japanese trade exchange in recent years convincingly exhibited this undesirable and inequitable trend for China, one which scarcely may be expected to change in the near future. Nonetheless, because of lagging Chinese industrialization, trade expansion even on the existing basis is in the interests of both countries. This is especially true if the Japanese government continues to relax restrictions on the export of modern equipment to China. Continuing talks and suggested compromises by both parties indicate a willingness to consider radical solutions. In seeking compromise, both governments are striving to minimize disagreements, while leaving fundamental questions which separate them for future solutions. They hope that time will help to remove obstacles to Sino-Japanese friendship.

The present leaders of the Chinese People's Republic apparently believe that the very fact of Japan's economic rise and its foreign trade expansion inexorably will evoke a clash with the United States. Confirmation of this thesis is found in the sharpening "textile war" between Japanese and American producers. Consequently, Peking's criticism of Japanese government leaders is concentrated on the single theme of the Japanese-American alliance. The Sino-Japanese trade talks led to a communique, published in Peking on April 19, 1970, which produces the conclusion that the Chinese assign the entire blame for the state of Sino-Japanese affairs to the "pro-American policies of the Sato government."[64] Peking's leaders ignore the class character of the Japanese monopolies, which race to expand not because of their alliance with the United States, but in keeping with the inherent laws of imperialism. The Maoists see no hindrances to links with the Japanese monopolies except the dissolution of Japan's alliance with the United States.

On the other hand, Japanese officials view with sympathy Peking's thesis of the "inferiority and dependence" of Japanese policies. It gives them cause to seek an alliance on nationalist and racial foundations and to embrace again their earlier doctrine of creating an alliance (a "co-prosperity sphere") of Asian nations under Japan's aegis. It is certain that Japan will not seek solution to the problem of China through honest, equal and mutually beneficial friendship with the Chinese people and assistance in overcoming economic backwardness. Japanese monopolists would like to see China weak and isolated from the socialist countries, and unable to prevent Japan's mastery in Asia. Thus, while at the beginning of the 1970s basic changes occurred in the domestic and foreign positions of China and Japan, the relations between them remained unsettled, and were limited mainly to trade. While trade exchange expanded somewhat toward the end of the 1960s, it remained far from its real potential and unsatisfactory in serving the interests of the two countries in mutual ties.

China experienced major upheavals during the decade of the 1960s and the period of the "great leap forward" and the "cultural revolution," and was weakened politically and economically. The curtailment of relations with the socialist countries brought international isolation and retarded economic development while, during the same period Japan achieved significant economic progress, becoming the third mightiest industrial power in the world. Tokyo's international importance, particularly in East and Southeast Asia, grew noticeably. Comparatively, changing and differing domestic and international circumstances generated an imbalance in real economic development levels unfavorable to

China. During the decade following the establishment of the Chinese People's Republic, China maintained extensive ties with the socialist countries and relied on scientific and technical cooperation with them, and experienced average annual rates of industrial development which were higher than those of Japan. Yet during the 1960s the Chinese People's Republic became greatly weakened in comparison to economically mighty Japan, according to all economic indicators. Mao Tsetung's administration issued loud propaganda about the triumphs of the "cultural revolution" and the transformation of China into the third "atomic state." However, this did not reflect the actual situation of the country, particularly in comparison with Japan. Japanese revanchists manipulated this propaganda to frighten their people "with the threat of China" and thus to justify remilitarization, the growth in military potential which included atomic rockets, and confirmation of Japan's leading role in Asia.

Understandably, the future in the Far East depends not only on the relative strength of China and Japan. Doubtless it will be determined by the balance between the real world powers—socialism and imperialism—in that region. Nevertheless, it is equally indisputable that the standing of China and Japan and their relations with each other will also play important parts in the fates of the peoples of Asia.

CONCLUSIONS

The history of East Asia's leading states, China and Japan, serves as brilliant confirmation of the materialist teaching of the primacy of material production in forming nations, states, culture and ideology among peoples of various world races. It demonstrates that, in the final reckoning, "the determining moment of history is production and reproduction of life itself."[1] Broad territories of East and Southeast Asia, both on the continent and on the Asian islands, settled chiefly by the Mongoloid race, witnessed fierce clashes during various historical periods. Such conflicts caused the decline of some and the ascension of other, stronger peoples who enjoyed some material advantage or more perfected military organization.

The Chinese state proved particularly durable. Despite severe upheavals and temporary loss of national independence, it endured and was able, in ancient times and in the Middle Ages, to take precedence among East Asian peoples. Enjoying favorable climate and soil conditions, China's civilization was based on settled populations engaged in varied agriculture. The wars of Asia, accompanied by vast migrations, involved the Chinese people as well, and the resulting commingling with other peoples enriched both material and intellectual life. The basic sources of backwardness and retarded development in the Japanese islands included isolation from and hostility to, until the sixth to seventh centuries of our era, the vital sources of ancient civilization and world historical events occurring on the Asian continent. The more powerful Chinese state did not conquer the Japanese islands and include them in the Han, Tang or Ming empires. This is not explained by any special feeling of benevolence on the part of the Chinese emperors. China's history demonstrates its need constantly to preserve its own existence in cruel struggles against strong nomadic states. Even during the greatest territorial conquests of the Han and Tang dynasties, danger never ceased to confront mainland China. On the heels of victories came defeats, and foreign rulers sat on the thrones of China, content to overlook the Japanese islands, which held no real economic or military significance for China.

China found no success when it attempted to penetrate Japan during the Mongolian Yuan dynasty in the second half of the 13th century, or to establish a protectorate during the Ming dynasty at the beginning of the 15th century. Feudal Japan now possessed nearly balanced forces with China, and was capable of defending its statehood and independence. As commercial capital grew stronger in Japan, the country began to expand from its islands and to establish footholds in Korea. Over several centuries Korea suffered through clashes between China and Japan, culminating in the first major Sino-Japanese war in 1894-1895, which laid the foundation for Japan's imperial expansion into China. It was during this period that Japanese imperialists first suggested the idea of "racial kinship" with the peoples of China as a mask to conceal its struggle for China using the slogan "the security of the peoples of the yellow race." Japan's racist propaganda initially enjoyed a certain success with the Chinese public. Even after the Sino-Japanese war some Chinese leaders, including Sun Yat-sen, retained illusions that the racially similar Japan would come to China's aid, sheltering it from Western colonialism and cooperating in its economic and political development.

Two more decades were needed before significant elements of Chinese society including the middle class intelligentsia, would understand that Japanese imperialism was just like any other imperialism. The bourgeois Japanese monopolies were guided by class interests and not racial ones. In terms of avarice and cruelty they were not inferior to their rivals, and in some ways even surpassed them; the "21 demands" presented by the Japanese government to China as an ultimatum in 1915 finally revealed the full scope of Japan's plans of conquest.[2] From this moment on anti-Japanese sentiment became an integral part of the Chinese people's struggle against imperialism. Then, during the 1930s imperial Japan reached the borders of China and inflicted aggression directly on the Chinese people. No longer could the appeal of "protection of the related race" deceive the Chinese, nor were Japanese imperial circles hesitant in discarding it. In order to neutralize their Western rivals for the moment, and even gain their cooperation, they declared the Chinese people to be "inferior" and the Chinese rulers "incapable" of dealing with the prevailing "chaos" and eliminating the "red peril." At that point Japan assumed the burden of establishing "a new order" in China and guaranteeing the "interests" of the imperial powers.

As disagreements with their imperial rivals flowered, especially with the United States and England, and a clash with them grew unavoidable, Japanese officials resurrected their rallying cry of "protecting the peoples of the yellow race from white imperialism." There followed the Japanese proclamations of the "Greater East Asia Co-Prosperity

Sphere" guided by the "divine" empire of Yamato. Then, during the years of Japanese occupation, the peoples of East and Southeast Asia, particularly China, experienced colonial enslavement and learned at first hand the "concern" of imperial Japan "for the fate of the peoples of the yellow race," and of Japan's "civilizing" role among the "unorganized" Asian peoples. World War II and the international events following it served to convince the peoples of the world that in the struggle for national independence and freedom in society the oppressed peoples and nations must first combat the forces of imperialism and their domestic, reactionary adherents. Success depends on rallying the inner strengths of working people and on solidarity with the world socialist system. The help and cooperation of the world socialist system is the chief guarantee of victory for the antagonistic forces of the modern world are divided along class rather than racial lines.

In the general and established socio-historical process reactionary and imperialistic forces hinder progressive development even though their determining role in contemporary society is undermined and they still maintain powerful entrenchments in world economics. This factor, unfortunately, makes it impossible to label them as "paper tigers." The imperialists strive to utilize their resources fully, and in several regions of the world they are taking the offensive. East and Southeast Asia have been the most active arenas for world imperialism in recent decades. The losses suffered by the United States, the leading imperialist nation, compelled a regrouping to seek new reserves and to transfer the role of "world gendarme" from the Americans to other world powers. The recent arrangement between President Nixon and Premier Sato (of November 1969) should be regarded in exactly this light,[3] for it allows Japanese leaders to claim primacy in East and Southeast Asia. The solidarity of the United States and Japan in their recent joint actions will continue for the moment but, because of the basic laws of capitalism, there is the likelihood of intensifying conflicts between them. Two provocative tendencies already have appeared in Japan's foreign policies, the first being the continuation of the alliance with the United States and its attendant benefits for Japan's monopolies, and the second being the preparation for assumption of the leading role in East and Southeast Asia and the transformation of Japan into the region's foremost power.

To accomplish these foreign policy goals, Tokyo's rulers continue to concentrate their attention on the paramount task of expanding their economic and military potential. They have learned the lessons of the lost war; economic infirmity, which the Japanese imperialists offset by military force, was one of the outstanding reasons for the failure of Japan's plans for expansion. To eliminate this shortcoming and create a durable economic base with technologically advanced industry and a corresponding level of military might—such are the compelling ambitions of Japanese monopolies.

Although they remain in the second echelon maintained by the American aggressors, Japan's rulers calculate that time is on their side. They believe that American positions in Asia are decaying, and they hope for substantial concessions from the United States before serious conflicts erupt. Japan's leadership still seeks support on the Asian continent in accomplishing its second and supreme goal, that of "taking a place in the world commensurate with its status as the third industrial power of the world." It is perfectly understood that alliances with the puppet regimes of South Korea and Taiwan do not strengthen Japan particularly. Among the nations of Asia, Japan's best ally would be China. But only a bourgeois nationalist China could agree to an alliance with Japanese monopolists, an alliance that could be created on a racial basis within the framework of a new "East Asia Co-Prosperity Sphere." However, Japanese ambitions for primacy must be repressed for the time being. Japanese big business believes, meanwhile, that the weakening of ties between the Chinese People's Republic and the Soviet Union and other socialist countries has slowed China's economic progress. China has fallen far behind Japan and urgently needs Japan's economic, scientific and technical cooperation. Japan's leaders further believe that nationalist and racist attitudes dominate socialist principles in Mao's policies, and that today's Chinese leaders see but one obstacle to normal relations with Japan, namely the Japanese alliance with the United States. Otherwise the Maoists are prepared to cooperate with Japan on all other problems, including the anti-Soviet territorial demands of the Japanese revanchists.

The position adopted by Mao Tse-tung's group provides cause for such conclusions. Mao's repeated statements and those of his partisans confirm their aspiration to establish links with Japan based on the policy of "Asia for Asians." Guided by the principle that "command is the essence of politics," Mao wishes to establish China's influence, together with "the ideas of Mao Tse-tung," and therefore in certain circumstances he can afford to compromise and allow to Japan leadership in Asian economic life. All the same, there exist other elements in China who would offer Japan political and economic compromises, and recognize Japan's political-economic authority in Asia within a pan-Asiatic union. It is this group which hopes to restore capitalism in China. A Sino-Japanese alliance of this kind would deny the vital interests of the Chinese people, and undermine the gains won in the long battle against Japanese imperialism and the reactionary Kuomintang. Furthermore, such a partnership would violate the interests of all Asian peoples, particularly those of the socialist countries, and would aggravate international tensions in the Far East. An alliance of such character is impractical because of the existence of conditions hostile to it and because it is self-contradictory. However, despite the obvious theoretical and political defects of regional, racial alliances, attempts to form them sometimes persist. In certain historical situations accords of this kind can last for limited periods, to the detriment of the socialist and democratic world.

Counteracting these plans is the victory of the popular revolution in China. With the cooperation of the socialist countries, the primary material basis for socialism has been created there. This affords the Chinese people the opportunity to embark on the socialist path of development and to build relations with other countries, including Japan, on principles of equality and independence. The solution of the problem of China's socialist industrialization will certainly require expansion of economic ties with advanced industrial countries, and in this Japan is certain to have an important place. Sino-Japanese trade and other forms of economic interchange (investments, credits, etc.) can provide a solid basis for neighborly relations. Of course, such a beneficial direction in Sino-Japanese relations will appear only if Japan demonstrates good will. Beneficial ties must begin with equality and regard for the interests of both nations. The progressive Japanese public desires a peace-loving and neutral country. China and the other socialist countries would open to such a Japan a large market for its industrial goods and for capital investments, and become a source for the most valuable raw materials and many other commodities. Socialist industrial development would help Japan's exports. A long-lasting and durable international division of labor is possible between China and Japan, considering their varying resources, qualified labor forces and production capabilities. Equally bright prospects for cooperation exist in the arts and sciences, whose fruits would be enriched thanks to some similarities in language, culture and daily life. This opportunity can become a reality if their societies properly influence the public policies of both states, and if such policies correspond to the fundamental interests of the peoples of China and Japan. Another crucial factor remains the regional balance between the modern world powers of socialism and imperialism.

NOTES

CHAPTER ONE

1. Fan Wen-lan, *Drevnaia istoriia Kitaia (Ancient History of China)* (Moscow, 1958), pp. 23-27. (Author) Fan Wen-lan, a famous Chinese communist historian, is frequently cited by the author. See Albert Feuerwerker and S. Cheng, *Chinese Communist Studies of Modern Chinese History* (Harvard University Press, 1951).

2. Sladkovsky with other scholars names the period after the chronicles *Chun-chiu (Spring and Autumn Annals)*, which present a terse account of major events in the years 722-481 B.C., centering on the court of the state of Lu. See Edwin O. Reischauer and John K. Fairbank, *East Asia: the Great Tradition* (Boston, 1960), pp. 66-68 (hereafter cited as *East Asia—Tradition*).

3. Nan-yueh included the territory of the modern provinces of Kuan-tung and Kuan-hsi.

4. During Chin Shih Huang-ti's rule, separate sections of the wall along the border were joined to form the Great Wall of China, stretching from the Yellow Sea to the border of modern Hsin-chiang province, a distance of nearly 5,000 kilometers. (Author)

5. *Shih-ching (The Book of Songs)* is an ancient miscellany containing 305 songs and poems of the 11th-7th centuries B.C., the selection and editing of which is attributed to Confucius. *Shu-ching (Historical Documents)* comprise the second of Confucius's five books, and are devoted to governmental affairs. (Author)

6. *Ocherki istorii Kitaia do opiumnykh voin (Survey of China's History to the Opium Wars)* (Moscow, 1959), p. 58. (Author)

7. Hawks Pott, *Ocherk istorii Kitaia (Survey of China's History)* (Peking, 1914), p. 36. (Author) No information could be found on the author or an English edition of this work.

8. This population decrease is inferred on the basis of the Historical Chronicles. See *Ocherki istorii Kitaia do opiumnykh voin*, p. 69. (Author)

9. See *East Asia—Tradition*, pp. 111-113, for a sketch of Ssu-ma Chien's adventurous life and monumental writings.

10. *Ocherki istorii Kitaia do opiumnykh voin*, p. 85. (Author)

11. *Ocherki istorii Kitaia do opiumnykh voin*, p. 86. (Author) A *ching* as a unit of land measure amounts to roughly 15.13 acres, with some regional variations.

12. The Great Plain of China, also called the Yellow or North China Plain, extends from the Huang Ho (Yellow River) in the north to the Yangtze delta in the south, forming a key agricultural area.

13. *Ocherki istorii Kitaia do opiumnykh voin*, p. 191. (Author)

14. The land measure *mou* varies from region to region, but usually about 6.6 mou equal one acre.

15. *Ocherki istorii Kitaia do opiumnykh voin*, p. 210. (Author) The Tang ruler Li Shih-min was posthumously granted the title Tai Tsung, or Grand Ancestor. Hence he is sometimes referred to as Tan Tai Tsung. See *East Asia—Tradition*, p. 155. The terms Eastern and Western Khanate, and Arabian Caliphate, refer to the Turkish and Moslem states which existed during this historical period.

16. Khan Mocho was a Turkish leader who seemed destined to establish a new unified Turkish empire until he was murdered in 717 A.D. Thereafter his empire collapsed. See *Encyclopedia Britannica; Macropaedia,* Vol. 4, 325.

17. N.I. Konrad, *Zapad i vostok (The West and the East)* (Moscow, 1966), p. 128. (Author)

18. On the Sino-Japanese exchange of missions, see Tsunoda Ryusaku and L. Carrington Goodrichs, "Japan in the Chinese Dynastic Histories," *Perkins Asiatic Monograph,* No. 2, 1951. (Author) Sladkovsky calls the Japanese empress both Himiko and Pimiko.

19. The Japanese historian Yoshi Kuno remarks that the dispatch of this mission to China was a major event for Japan for the following reasons: the mission was the first international contact with China made by the Japanese emperor; the first communication to China written in Japan was sent along with the mission; and the term "emperor" was used for the first time in referring to the rulers of China and Japan. The letter marked the first time events in Japan and China had been described correctly and in a balanced manner. See Yoshi S. Kuno, *Japanese Expansion on the Asiatic Continent* (Washington, 1967), pp. 15-16. (Author)

20. Ito Nobuo et al., *Nihon bijutsushi (A History of Japanese Art),* Tokyo, 1959. (Author)

21. Cited in Ienaga Saburo, *Nihon bunkashi (A History of Japanese Culture)* (Tokyo, 1967), p. 205. (Author)

22. Matsumoto Yoshio, *Nihon bunkashi (A History of Japanese Culture)* Tokyo, 1967. (Author)

23. Gunji Masakatsu, *Yaponskii teatr Kabuki (The Japanese Kabuki Theater)* (Moscow, 1969), pp. 32-33.

24. The Soviet scholar Ya. B. Radul-Zatulovsky states that while *A Thousand Hieroglyphs* was prepared for Wu Ti in the third century, it was not known widely until the sixth, and could not have reached Japan until then. On the other hand, the dispatch of a Japanese mission for study in China in 609 A.D. confirms knowledge of Confucianism in Japan by that time. See Ya. B. Radul-Zatulovsky, *Konfutsianstvo i ego rasprostranenie v Yaponii (Confucianism and its Spread in Japan)* (Moscow-Leningrad, 1947), pp. 189-221. (Author)

25. The concepts of duty to one's benevolent superior and to one's society, then to one's family, form an important part of the Samurai mentality. See *East Asia—Tradition,* p. 618.

26. See Mitsudo Inoue, *Introduction to Japanese History Before the Meiji Restoration* (Tokyo, 1962), p. 31. (Author) *Kojiki,* or the *Record of Ancient Things,* according to its translator Donald L. Philippi, is a basic source for the origins of Japan. Philippi's translation of *Kojiki* was published by Princeton University Press in 1969. *Nihongi* is a chronicle of Japan from the earliest times to 697 A.D., translated by W.A. Aston and published by Charles E. Tuttle Company, Rutland, Vermont, 1972. Both works were published in collaboration with Tokyo University Press.

27. Sladkovsky gives no page citations for his quotes from Nakamura Hajima's book.

28. Three basic dogmas of Buddhism are: Humans exist in darkness and temptation in relation to the true essence of the world, pure understanding of Buddha; One must free himself from worldly desires and strive for a state of Nirvana, the condition of complete harmony with the surrounding world; and finally, Man will be able to achieve the transformation into Buddha himself. (Author)

29. The author does not name the single powerful family seeking primacy; presumably he is referring to the Soga family. See John Whitney Hall, *Japan from Prehistory to Modern Times* (New York, 1970), p. 42 ff.

30. Buddhism has two directions, the Hinayana (small chariot) found in southern India, Ceylon, Burma and Thailand, and the Mahayana (great chariot) of northern India, China, Mongolia, Korea and Japan. The Mahayana believes that enlightenment can be attained by acceptance of the dogma of the nonexistence of all matter, and by transmitting this wisdom to others for their "salvation." See Radul-Zatulovsky, *Konfutsianstvo.* (Author)

31. Bodhisattva is the sainthood to which a Buddhist monk aspires. On the combination of Buddhism and Confucianism, see Ryusaka Tsunoda, *Sources of the Japanese Tradition* (New York, 1958), p. 131.

CHAPTER TWO

1. The unit of measure *liang* indicated an ounce of silver, while *ching* here refers to the brick-like compressed form in which tea was traded.

2. Wang An-shih was called by the emperor to be prime minister in 1069 A.D. He established a special commission to carry out governmental reforms. (Author)

3. The White Lotus society predicted a future in which darkness would give way to light (ming) and a new emperor would be born to establish the Ming dynasty. (Author)

4. Nanking became the capital with the establishment of the Ming dynasty; in 1403 the third Ming emperor moved his capital back to what is now Peking. (Author)

5. Timur the Lame, or Tamerlane, expanded the Mongolian empire from his capital at Samarkand in all directions. He had plans for conquests in China when he died in 1405. See *East Asia—Tradition*, pp. 325-326. Kokand was a khanate in present-day Uzbekistan, or the Uzbek SSR.

6. *Ocherki istorii Kitaia do opiumnykh voin*, p. 469. (Author)

7. In the provinces of Ssu-chuan and Hu-pei, another peasant rebel leader, Chang Hsian-chung, formed a separate state with the same name. (Author)

8. The "eight-bannered army" was composed chiefly of Manchurians and Mongols, although Chinese who showed their loyalty to the Manchurian throne were accepted into it. All members of the army were regarded as Manchurians regardless of their origin. See Fan Wen-lan, *Novaia istoriia Kitaia (Modern History of China)* (Moscow, 1955), pp. 15-16. (Author)

9. *Ocherki istorii Kitaia do opiumnykh voin*, p. 544. (Author)

10. The Nerchinsk and Kiakhta treaties, with other diplomatic notes of the period, can be found in Mark Mancall, *Russia and China, Their Diplomatic Relations to 1728* (Cambridge, Mass., 1971), pp. 280-310.

11. *Ocherki istorii Kitaia do opiumnykh voin*, p. 549. (Author) The Kazakhs as in the past inhabit Kazakhstan, now a republic of the USSR.

12. Although the resident was technically a diplomatic agent, he had the force of Chin armies behind him. Hence he effectively ruled Tibet at this time.

13. Toward the end of the Ming dynasty, China's population decreased from 52 million to 19 million. In the same period cultivated land area declined from 701 million to 549 million mou. (Author) Roughly 6.6 mou equal one acre.

14. The emperor's court instituted the demeaning diplomatic ceremony known

as the "kowtow" in the seventh century. Newly-arrived foreign ambassadors were required to practice their performance before court dignitaries, then, on their knees, make nine bows to the ground and, finally, crawl on their knees to the emperor. (Author)

15. Quoted from an official message from Chien Lung to King George II of England in 1793. *Ocherki istorii Kitaia do opiumnykh voin*, p. 562. (Author)

16. Marx and Engels, "Revoliutsiia v Kitae i Evrope (The Revolution in China and Europe)," *Sochineniia (Works)*, 2nd ed., Vol. 9, 100 (Russian edition). (Author)

17. This period is also called the Heian period, after the former name of the modern city of Kyoto.

18. The Shogun, or military governor, wielded most of the power in this and other periods of Japanese history. See *East Asia—Tradition*, p. 535.

19. Hani Goro, *Istoriia yaponskogo naroda (A History of the Japanese People)* (Moscow, 1957), p. 51. (Author)

20. Mitsudo Inoue, *Introduction to Japanese History before the Meiji Restoration*, pp. 63-64.

21. Acquaintance with firearms came about when a Portuguese pirate ship crashed on Japanese shores and three pirates, with weapons, were rescued. (Author)

22. Mitsudo Inoue, *Introduction to Japanese History*, pp. 80-81. (Author)

23. The Dutch were excluded from the bans because they had assisted the bakufu (headquarters of the Shogunate) in crushing a Catholic rebellion. In addition, Japanese authorities did not consider anyone but the Catholics to be Christians. See Yoshi Kuno, *Japanese Expansion on the Asiatic Continent*, Vol. 2, 317. (Author)

24. Fujimura Toru, *Kindai keizai-no tenkai (An Economic History of Japan in Modern Times)* (Tokyo, 1956), p. 54. (Author)

25. The Dutch were permitted to reside only on the island of Deshima, which was connected to Nagasaki by a bridge. Except for certain Buddhist monks, nobody was allowed to visit the island, nor were the Dutch allowed on the shore without special visas. Dutch vessels were allowed to enter the port of Nagasaki once annually, in June or July, and to remain until September. See Yoshi Kuno, *Japanese Expansion on the Asiatic Continent*, Vol. 2, 317-318. (Author)

26. The word *Rampo* is the Japanese word for the Dutch style of medicine.

27. Kaibo Seiryo, who wrote in the early years of the nineteenth century, remarked on the senselessness of rewarding children for devotion to their ancestors, and on the parasitic life style of the Samurai. He advocated positive contributions to the state in practical ways, such as introducing new plants or building vessels. See Ienaga Saburo, *Nihon bunkashi (History of Japanese Culture)*, p. 225. (Author)

28. The Shogunate reacted forcefully to this threat by executing or exiling the aristocrats who had advocated restoration of imperial power. (Author)

29. A hectare, the metric measurement of land surface, equals 2.471 acres.

30. Emperor Cheng Tsu demanded that the Shogun create an army to combat piracy, issue laws and enforce them against the pirates. This Japanese service to the Chinese throne would be "highly valued and noted in the chronicles, to be respected by posterity." Such steps were to be undertaken "with respect, immediately, and effectively." Shogun Yoshimoto replied that "the Mongols had twice sent their fleets to impose their will on Japan, and those fleets had counted in the

thousands, yet they had ended up on the bottom of the sea. Japan needs no moats or great walls; we are ready to meet your armies (sent to enforce such a decree) in the proper way." The Shogun did not receive later envoys from Cheng Tsu, instead expelling them from Japan. See Yoshi Kuni, *Japanese Expansion*, Vol. 1, 178-179. (Author)

CHAPTER THREE

1. In March 1839, the newly-arrived Chin chief commissar in Canton issued an order calling for confiscation of all opium supplies held by foreign firms. Further importation was forbidden under penalty of death. Subsequent events led to the actual beginning of hostilities. (Author)

2. The Nanking treaty is contained in *Major Peace Treaties of Modern History, 1648-1967* (New York, 1967), pp. 1059-1064. Hereafter cited as *Major Peace Treaties*. Only page numbers will be given since the four volumes are paginated consecutively.

3. The Mandarins were officials who constituted the upper level of the Chinese bureaucracy. Along with the court itself, they controlled the country.

4. Marx and Engels, "Pervyi mezhdunarodnyi obzor (The First International Survey)," *Sochineniia (Works)* Russian edition, Vol. 7, 233. (Author)

5. Hua Kang, *Istoriia revoliutsionnoi voiny taipinskogo gosudarstva (The History of the Revolutionary War of the Tai Ping State)* (Moscow, 1952), p. 268. (Author)

6. Ibid., p. 280. The Tai Ping government went on to say that all goods except opium would be allowed free importation, and that commerce among nations should be conducted in an orderly and open way. (Author)

7. The Tientsin treaties are found in *Major Peace Treaties*, pp. 1065-1080.

8. In early 1862 a military force including French, English and American troops was garrisoned in the foreign settlements of Shanghai. England, France and the United States also supplied Chin armies with modern weapons and military supplies. (Author)

9. Marx and Engels, "Pervyi mezhdunarodnyi obzor," *Sochineniia*, 2nd ed., Vol. 7, 234. (Author)

10. The term "thick-heads" is the author's designation for the group of tradition-oriented leaders around the court of Empress Tzu Hsi. They instigated the Boxer movement but were themselves a more exclusive group. The institution of elite Manchurian military organizations known as "banner armies" dates back to the mid-17th century. It performed civil administrative as well as military tasks. See Wolfram Eberhard, *A History of China* (University of California Press, 1968) pp. 268-269.

11. Fan Wen-lan, *Novaia istoriia Kitaia*, p. 307. (Author)

12. As one adherent of the "thick-heads" and a close relative of the emperor put it: "(The foreign aggressors) will certainly come. But even if they do, there is no need to fear them. It will be impossible to prevent them from making war. But if there is war, we should not be disturbed. After the war we can conclude a peace agreement and thus avoid further conflicts." Quoted from Fan Wen-lan, *Novaia istoriia Kitaia*, p. 326. (Author)

13. Ibid., p. 302. (Author)

14. Ibid., p. 305. (Author)

15. The Kuomintang party was the successor to Sun Yat-sen's party, with a more popular direction and greater stress on land reform. The original philosophy, which could accommodate the admission of communists including Mao Tse-tung, gradually evolved in a more conservative direction as social forces in revolutionary China became more sharply defined. Finally, the Kuomintang became the party of Chiang Kai-shek.

16. The *liang* is equivalent to one ounce of silver.

17. The *yuan* and the exchange *tael* fluctuated greatly in value.

18. Fan Wen-lan, *Novaia istoriia Kitaia,* p. 324. (Author)

19. The Shogunate, it will be remembered, was the military power center of Japan for many centuries.

20. The treaty signed by Admiral Perry and the Japanese can be found in W.M. Malloy, *Treaties, Conventions, International Acts, Protocols and Agreements between the United States of America and Other Powers* (Washington, 1910), Vol. 1, 996 ff.

21. The Japanese-British treaty of 1902 can be found in *British and Foreign State Papers,* Vol. 83.

22. Ienaga Saburo, *Nihon bunkashi (History of Japanese Culture),* p. 244. (Author)

23. On the traditional Japanese education, see Herbert Passin, *Society and Education in Japan* (New York, 1965), p. 3 ff.

24. Ando Yoshio, "The Foundation of Japanese Heavy Industry" in *The Modernization of Japan* (Tokyo, 1966), Vol. 1, 38. (Author)

25. The Tokugawa family held power through the Shogunate for hundreds of years.

26. Natural or subsistence farming provides for the entire needs of the farm household and produces nothing for the market. Semi-natural farming might produce small amounts for local markets, or trade off certain tasks within a small group of peasants—shoemaking, cloth weaving or the like. Neither manner of farming produced large amounts for urban consumption.

27. V.I. Lenin, "Imperializm i raskol sotsializma (Imperialism and the Schism of Socialism)" in *Polnoe sobranie sochinenii (Complete Works),* Vol. 3, 174. (Author)

28. The Sino-Japanese treaty of 1871 can be found in *Treaties, Conventions . . . between China and Foreign States* (Shanghai, 1917), Vol. 2, 508.

29. The Shimonoseki peace treaty between the Emperor of Japan and the Emperor of China is in *Major Peace Treaties,* pp. 1101-1110.

CHAPTER FOUR

1. See Note 12, Chapter 3. (Author)

2. Quoted in Fan Wen-lan, *Novaia istoriia Kitaia,* p. 457. (Author)

3. Ibid., pp. 456-465. (Author)

4. S.L. Tikhvinsky, *Dvizhenie za reformu v Kitae i Kan Yu-vei (The Reform Movement in China and Kang Yo-wei)* (Moscow, 1959), pp. 223-224. (Author)

5. Ibid., p. 465. (Author)

6. No more precise identification of the English consul Karles could be found.

7. Fan Wen-lan, *Novaia istoriia Kitaia,* p. 465. (Author)

8. Carrying out the terms of the Russo-Chinese treaty of alliance of 22 May

1896, tsarist Russia signed a convention with China calling for transfer to Russia of Port Arthur and Ta-lien, along with rights to construct a railroad through Manchuria. France and Germany gained similar rights in other regions. (Author) The English text is found in *American Journal of International Law,* Supplement 4, p. 289.

9. Sladkovsky apparently means Marshal Yamagata Aritomo.

10. The value of exchange taels and of the yuan fluctuated considerably during this period due to internal instability and China's international position.

11. The text of the Boxer Protocol is in *Major Peace Treaties,* pp. 1135-1143.

12. Japanese attempts to set up an occupational regime in Korea led to widespread anti-Japanese demonstrations there. In 1896 the Korean king managed to escape from Japanese supervision and to hide in the Russian embassy. The king renounced the agreements forced on him by the Japanese; on 14 May 1896 Russia and Japan agreed (in the Waeber-Komura Agreement) to joint advisory roles in Korea. (Author) For the English text of the agreement see *American Journal of International Law,* Supplement 1, p. 215.

13. E.D. Grimm, *Sbornik dogovorov i drugikh dokumentov po istorii mezhdunarodnykh otnoshenii na Dal'nem Vostoke (A Collection of Treaties and Other Documents on the History of International Relations in the Far East)* (Moscow, 1927), p. 130. (Author) Hereafter Grimm, *Sbornik dogovorov.* The English text is in William W. Rockhill, *Treaties and Conventions with or Concerning China and Korea, 1894-1904* (Washington, 1904), p. 181.

14. Sun Yat-sen, *Izbrannye proizvedeniia (Selected Works)* (Peking, 1956), Vol. 1, 164. (Author) The author uses this edition as his basic source for the writings of Sun Yat-sen.

15. The agreement referred to here was negotiated by American statesman Elihu Root and Japanese minister Takahira Kogoro. It is found in *Treaties, Conventions, International Acts, Protocols and Agreements Between the United States of America and Other Powers, 1707-1909* (Washington: GPO, 1910), pp. 1045-1047.

16. The author cites no source for this agreement. A preliminary version is found in Russian in Grimm, *Sbornik dogovorov,* pp. 168-170; the English text of the public agreement is in *United States Foreign Relations* (1907), No. 2, p. 765.

17. The statistics are from G.F. Remer, *Foreign Investments in China* (New York, 1933), pp. 429, 438. (Author)

18. V.I. Lenin "Goriuchii material v mirovoi politike (Fuel in World Politics)," *Polnoe sobranie sochinenii,* Vol. 17, 179. (Author)

19. Sun Yat-sen, *Izbrannyi proizvedeniia,* Vol, 1, 69. (Author)

20. Ibid., p. 75. (Author) "Han" refers to the venerated ancient dynasty which ruled China 220 B.C.-206 A.D. Allusion to it connotates the past glories of China.

21. V.I. Lenin, "Demokratiia i narodnichestvo v Kitae (Democracy and Populism in China)," *Polnoe sobranie sochinenii,* Vol. 21, 404. (Author)

22. See Note 10. Mixed companies were financed with capital from the home country and a foreign nation, which generally sought to have full control of the company.

23. The revolution led by Sun Yat-sen is usually called the Hsing Chung-hui revolution. The author uses a Russian variant Hsing-hai. See John K. Fairbank, Edwin O. Reischauer and Albert M. Craig, *East Asia, the Modern Transformation* (Harvard University Press, 1973), p. 635. Hereafter *East Asia-Transformation.*

24. According to conditions of the secret convention negotiated by Sazonov

and Motono, dated 25 July 1912, Russia agreed to "recognize and preserve special Japanese interests in the part of Inner Mongolia located east of meridian 116° 27'. See Grimm, *Sbornik dogovorov*, p. 180. (Author)

25. The Anglo-Japanese treaty of 13 June 1911 is found in *British and Foreign State Papers*, Vol. 1, 133. *The Index of British Treaties* dates it 13 July.

26. Sun Yat-sen, *Izbrannye proizvedeniia*, Vol. 1, 184. (Author)

27. Ibid., p. 183. (Author)

28. Ibid., pp. 85-93. (Author)

29. V.I. Lenin, "Otstalaia Evropa i peredovaia Aziia (Backward Europe and Advanced Asia)," *Polnoe sobranie sochinenii*, Vol. 23, 167. (Author) The mathematics here may be in error, since the quoted discount rate would have resulted in a return of 225 million for only 193.5 million rubles delivered to China.

30. Sun Chao-jen was formerly Sun Yat-sen's deputy in the United League and one of the leaders of the Kuomintang, Sun's democratic party. Sun Chao-jen was murdered on 21 March 1913. (Author)

31. Quoted in T. Efimov, *Ocherki po novoi i noveishei istorii Kitaia (Survey of Modern and Recent Chinese History)* (Moscow, 1951), pp. 184-185. (Author)

32. Cited in T.E. La Farque, *China and the World War* (London, 1937), p. 75. (Author)

33. These notes are found in Grimm, *Sbornik dogovorov*, pp. 192-194. (Author) Included also in MacMurray, *Treaties and Agreements with and Concerning China, 1894-1919* (New York, 1921), Vol. 2, 1394-1396.

34. General Terauchi formed a non-partisan cabinet which lasted some two years during 1916-1918 before giving way to party government led by Hara Kei. See *East Asia-Transformation*, pp. 562, 571.

35. Data from V. Maslenikov, *Kitai (China)* (Moscow, 1946), p. 175. (Author)

36. After the United States entered the war against Germany, American diplomacy, supported by England and France, pressed China to enter the war. On 14 August 1917 China declared war on Germany. (Author)

37. See Sun Yat-sen, *Izbrannye proizvedeniia*, Vol. 1, 188-191, for this and the following quotations. (Author)

38. Georgi V. Chicherin (1872-1936) was a Soviet diplomat and government minister.

39. Quoted in *Bol'shevik* (1950), No. 19, pp. 46-48. (Author)

40. Quoted in *Mezhdunarodnye otnosheniia na Dal'nem Vostoke (International Relations in the Far East)* (Moscow, 1951), p. 327. (Author)

41. Hara Kei (1856-1921) was the first premier of commoner background; his cabinet held power from 1918 to 1921. See *East Asia-Transformation* (pp. 571 ff) for further details on his career. Tanaka Giichi (1863-1929) served Hara as war minister and allegedly authored the Tanaka Memorial, a master plan for Japanese conquest of Asia. See Masao Maruyama, *Thought and Behavior in Modern Japanese Politics* (London, 1969), p. 388. Hereafter *Thought and Behavior*.

42. The nine-power treaty which concluded the Washington Conference is found in *League of Nations Treaty Series* (Vol. 25, 196) and in most other diplomatic collections.

43. Sun Yat-sen, *Izbrannye proizvedeniia*, Vol. 2, 482. (Author)

44. The Sino-Soviet accord "On General Principles for Regulating Questions Between the USSR and the Chinese Republic," is found in *League of Nations Treaty Series*, Vol. 37, 175 ff.

45. Marshal V.K. Bluecher, alias Galen (1889-1938), served with Soviet forces

in Manchuria 1927-1933, then rose to a leading position in the Soviet army. Mikhail M. Borodin (1884-1951) was a Party agent who worked closely with Bluecher. See Max Beloff, *The Foreign Policy of the Soviet Union 1929-1941* (Oxford, 1947), pp. 211-213. A good biographical sketch of Borodin is in *Encyclopaedia Britannica—Micropaedia,* Vol. 2, 171. Bluecher is succinctly described in *Encyclopaedia Britannica—Macropaedia,* Vol. 3, 371.

CHAPTER FIVE

1. The Manifesto is quoted from Sun Yat-sen *Izbrannye proizvedeniia (Selected Works),* Vol. 2, 521 ff. (Author) The English text is found in San Min Chu Yi, *The Three Principles of the People* (Institute of Pacific Relations:Shanghai, 1927).

2. Ibid., pp. 865-869. (Author)

3. Ibid., pp. 897-898. (Author)

4. The "paper tiger" group was composed of the merchant bourgeoisie which enjoyed the support of England. It attempted an uprising against the Canton government in 1924, which was crushed with the aid of workers, peasants, and cadets from the Whampoa academy. Here and in the text below, Chiang Kai-shek's government and its institutions are designated "nationalist."

5. Shidehara Kijuro was Japan's foreign minister in the 1920s. His name is attached prominently to general government policies of the period. See *East Asia-Transformation,* pp. 571 and *Thought and Behavior,* p. 384.

6. On Tanaka Giichi, see Note 41, Chapter Four.

7. On Borodin and Bluecher, see Note 45, Chapter Four.

8. The Sino-American treaty of 25 July 1928 is found in Malloy, *Treaties, Conventions* (cited in Note 20, Chapter Three), Vol. 4, 4020-4024.

9. Wakatsuki Reijiro, a liberal who was Prime Minister 1926-1927 and in 1931. See *East Asia-Transformation,* pp. 573-587, et passim.

10. The Russian source of the Tanaka Memorial is *Istoriia voiny na Tikhom okeane (History of the War in the Pacific Ocean)* (Moscow, 1957), Vol. 1, 337-353. (Author) Tanaka's policy toward China was announced in the *New York Times,* 23 April 1927, section 4, p. 3. Controversy concerning it continued for years thereafter. The text of the Tanaka Memorial is in *The Puppet State of "Manchukuo,"* (China United Press: Shanghai, 1935), pp. 204-238.

11. The Sino-Japanese treaty in effect at the time gave Japan the same advantages as other major foreign powers.

12. Hamaguchi Osachi (1870-1931) was a leader of the liberal Minsei To Party from its formation in 1927 until his death in 1931 (after an assassination attempt on him in 1930). See *Thought and Behavior,* p. 358.

13. Cited in *Sovetsko-kitaiskii konflikt 1929 (The Soviet-Chinese Conflict of 1929)* (Moscow, 1930), p. 28. (Author)

14. Pu Yi (1906-1967) had a varied career, being emperor (at the age of two) after the death of Kuang-hsu and Empress Tzu Hsi. After the liberal revolution, he was retired on a pension of four million Chinese dollars, later leaving the forbidden city for the diplomatic quarter of Peking, where he became involved with Japanese plans for "restoration" of Manchu rule under Japan's tutelage. Following the communist revolution and incarceration until 1959, he served in several innocuous capacities in China until his death in 1967. (Author) Note based also on *East Asia-Transformation,* pp. 587-708, et passim.

15. The Lytton Commission was appointed by the League of Nations to investigate the Japanese invasion of Manchuria in 1931. It was headed by the Second Earl of Lytton.

16. For the Portsmouth Treaty of 1905, see *Major Peace Treaties*, pp. 1149-1155.

17. For the Soviet-Japanese Convention of 1925, see Grimm, *Sbornik dogovorov*, pp. 213-218. (Author) The English text is in *League of Nations Treaty Series*, Vol. 34, 46-53.

18. Inukai Tsuyoshi is considered the last of the "party cabinet" leaders. He was assassinated in 1932. See *East Asia-Transformation*, pp. 581, 587.

19. Admiral Saito Makoto is considered a moderate. See *East Asia-Transformation*, p. 588.

20. Quoted in the *Manchukuo Year Book* (1942), p. 762. (Author)

21. Pu Yi, *The First Half of My Life* (in Chinese) (Peking, 1964), p. 292. (Author)

22. *Manchukuo Year Book* (1942), pp. 843-845. (Author)

23. Ibid., p. 801. (Author)

24. The Agreement in Tangku of May 31, 1933 is found in Westel W. Willoughby, *The Sino-Japanese Controversy and the League of Nations* (Baltimore, 1935), pp. 507-508. (Author)

25. Hirota Koki (1879-1948) a rightist government leader who was hanged after WW II as a war criminal. See *Thought and Behavior*, p. 360.

26. Pu Yi, *The First Half of My Life* (in Chinese), p. 276. (Author)

27. *China Year Book* (Shanghai, 1934), pp. 725-726. (Author)

28. *Materialy protsessa glavnykh yaponskikh voennykh prestupnikov* (Materials from the Trial of the Chief Japanese War Criminals), pp. 2726-2728, 9551-9553. (Author)

29. The traditions of the Samurai and its code of moral discipline, known as bushido, formed an important part of the myth of Japanese supremacy.

30. The Anti-Comintern Pact signed by Germany and Japan against the Soviet Union on November 25, 1936 is found in *English and Foreign State Papers*, Vol. 140, 529.

31. *Materialy protsessa*, p. 5936. (Author)

32. Hayashi Senjuro (1876-1942), served as Japan's war minister and as prime minister from February to June 1937. See *Thought and Behavior*, p. 359.

33. Konoe Fumimaro (1891-1945) was the descendant of the Fujiwara family which ruled Japan during the Heian period. His political development followed a classic pattern of liberalism (and even socialism), gradually turning further and further to the right. He served as prime minister several times, and was suspected of war crimes when he committed suicide by poison in 1945. See *Thought and Behavior*, p. 368.

34. The Brussels Conference included the participants in the Washington Conference of 1921-22, excepting Japan, and with the addition of the USSR. The Chinese proposal (supported by the USSR) for economic sanctions against Japan was rejected; the American and English delegations called on the Soviet Union to begin direct military actions against Japan, since the Sino-Japanese conflict was near the Soviet border. (Author)

35. K.V. Kukushkin, *Antiiaponskii front v Kitae* (The Anti-Japanese Front in China) in *Komintern i vostok* (The Comintern and the East) (Moscow, 1969), pp. 350-354. (Author)

36. Ibid., p. 354. (Author)

37. The Chun-yang Agency was the central Nationalist press agency.

38. The Sino-Soviet non-aggression pact of 21 August 1937 is found in *League of Nations Treaty Series,* Vol. 181, 101-105.

39. Hiranuma Kiichiro (1867-1952) was prominent in Japanese politics during the period 1923-1941. Convicted as a war criminal, he died in prison. See *Thought and Behavior,* p. 360.

40. Article 1 of the Triple Alliance Pact stipulated that Japan "recognizes and respects the leadership of Germany and Italy in creating a new order in Europe." Article 3 referred to mutual support by the signatory states "by all political, economic and military means." Since Germany had a non-aggression pact with the USSR, the Triple Alliance Pact formally excepted relations with the USSR from pact provisions. (Author)

41. *Istoriia voiny na Tikhom okeane (History of the War in the Pacific Ocean),* (Moscow, 1958), Vol. III, 366.

42. The treaty text is presented in Russian in *Istoriia voiny na Tikhom okeane,* Vol. III, 368-371. (Author) The text is found in English in *Contemporary Japan,* Vol. 10 (1941), pp. 131-138.

43. Nomura Tichisaburo (1 877-   ) was foreign minister prior to appointment as ambassador to the United States in December 1940. After the war he staunchly advocated Japanese rearmament. See *Thought and Behavior,* pp. 379-380.

44. Tojo Hideki (1 884-1948), Japan's prime minister during World War II, was virtually a dictator. He rose through the military to serve as war minister in the second and third Konoe cabinets, and became prime minister just before the beginning of the war, retaining the post of war minister. He was found guilty of war crimes and hanged in 1948. See *Thought and Behavior,* p. 389.

CHAPTER SIX

1. Barbarossa was the code name for Hitler's plan to conquer the Soviet Union. The name comes from the medieval Frederick Barbarossa, a German ruler who held the title of Holy Roman Emperor and died while on his way to the Third Crusade.

2. The Khalkhyn Gol incident involved Japanese probing of the border between Manchuria and Mongolia, leading to a major battle in 1939. See *East Asia-Transformation,* p. 792.

3. The Soviet-Japanese pact is found in the *American Journal of International Law,* Vol. 35 (Documents), p. 171.

4. M. Yu. Roginsky, S. Ya. Rozenblit, *Mezhdunarodnyi protsess glavnykh yaponskikh voennykh prestupnikov (The International Trial of the Principal Japanese War Criminals)* (Moscow-Leningrad, 1950), p. 243.

5. At that time Japan was conducting negotiations with the United States supposedly intended to settle the points of dispute.

6. The text of the Tripartite Pact of 11 December 1941 is found in *International Legislation,* VIII, No. 610, pp. 635 ff.

7. A.M. Dubinsky, *Osvoboditel'naia missiia Sovetskogo Soyuza na Dal'nem Vostoke (The Liberating Mission of the Soviet Union in the Far East)* (Moscow, 1966), p. 342. (Author)

8. *Japan Times Advertiser,* February 1, 1942. (Author)

9. The "Three A" movement led by Samsudin proclaimed the special mission

of Japan, its unique qualities, and its destiny as the "light of Asia," the "director of Asia" and the "protector of Asia." (Author)

10. Sukarno (1901-1970) became the principal leader of the movement for Indonesia's independence and was proclaimed the country's president when it achieved nationhood in 1949. Eventually his leftist sentiments encouraged the abortive communist takeover of 1965, and gradually he was removed from power. On his rise to power, see *East Asia-Transformation*, pp. 771-778, and *Encyclopedia Britannica, Macropaedia*, Vol. 17, 783-784.

11. To establish the new order in Indochina, the Japanese employed the French administrative apparatus of the Vichy governor-general, Admiral Decoux. (Author)

12. Aung San began his political career as secretary of the Burmese Student Union in 1936, and continued his activities until he was assassinated in 1947. See *East Asia-Transformation*, pp. 749, 772-775.

13. The Burmese leader Ba Maw was part of the group which sought in late 1930 to restore the ancient Burman kingdom. In 1942, in reaction to previous French colonial rule, he headed the puppet Japanese government of Burma. See *East Asia-Transformation*, pp. 748-749, 772.

14. The text of the original Anti-Comintern Pact between Germany and Japan is found in *British and Foreign State Papers*, Vol. 140, 529. Manchukuo's admission to the pact is shown in *British and Foreign State Papers*, Vol. 143, 502.

15. At a festive banquet arranged by War Minister Ho Ying-chin to mark the departure of German diplomats from Chungking, Ho Ying-chin expressed his faith in the victory of Germany and Japan and called for post-war cooperation when fascist Germany approached the borders of China. (After Germany recognized the government of Wang Ching-wei, the Chungking government was forced to break diplomatic relations with Germany.) (Author)

16. Here and elsewhere the word "liberated" indicates areas held by the communists.

17. Elliott Roosevelt, *Ego glazami (As He Saw It)* (Moscow, 1947), p. 69. (Author)

18. The Sino-American agreement is found in *The China White Paper, August 1949* (Stanford, 1967), pp. 514-519. The date of the agreement is not 11 November 1943, but 11 January 1943, according to the above source.

19. The Atlantic Charter declaration is found in *League of Nations Treaty Series*, pp. 204, 384.

20. *Mainichi*, 31 July 1943. (Author)

21. *Contemporary Japan*, Vol. 12, (Nos. 1-3) January-March 1943. (Author)

22. *Japan Yearbook* (1944-1945), p. 173. (Author)

23. Ibid., p. 71. (Author)

24. In his article "Thoughts on Preserving the Integrity of China" (1903), Sun Yat-sen called upon Japan to help China protect itself from attempts by nations of the "white race" to violate the territorial integrity of China. The basis of his plea was that "China is a country which is bound to Japan by a common historical fate and by strategic position. China and Japan possess a mutual race and a mutual culture." (See S.L. Tikhvinsky, *Sun Yat-sen* (Moscow, 1964), p. 65. In 1924 Sun Yat-sen wrote: "Our internal political tasks are to overthrow the militarists and completely free the oppressed people; our foreign policy should be the struggle against imperial aggression and union with all nations of the world oppressed by imperialism in order to achieve liberation through joint assistance and common efforts." Sun Yat-sen, *Izbrannye proizvedeniia (Selected Works)*, p. 414. (Author)

25. *The Japan Yearbook,* (1944-1945), p. 174. (Author)

26. Loc. cit. (Author)

27. On 4 June 1943, the former president of the Indian National Congress, Subhas Chandra Bos, arrived in Japan. He formed a provisional government for India, declaring his "only goal to be to drive the British out of India, even if it is necessary for that to employ the aid of the devil or any other force on earth." See V.S. Rudnev, *Ocherki noveishei istorii Malaii (Survey of the Recent History of Malaya)* (Moscow, 1959), p. 47. (Author)

28. *The Japan Yearbook,* (1944-1945), p. 789. (Author)

29. *Kuo-min Kung-pao (People's Public Journal)* (newspaper), 29 September 1942. (Author)

30. *Vneshnaia politika Sovetskogo Soiuza v period Otechestvennoi voiny (The Foreign Policy of the Soviet Union During the Fatherland War),* Vol. 1, 414-415. (Author)

31. In the Cairo Declaration, the United States, England and China indicated that the aim of the war was to "deprive Japan of all the islands in the Pacific Ocean which it had captured or occupied since the beginning of World War I, while all territories taken from China, such as Manchuria, Formosa and the Pescadores Islands, were to be returned to the Chinese Republic . . . . The three allies, in concert with those members of the United Nations who were in a state of war with Japan, would continue serious and lasting operations to bring about the unconditional surrender of Japan. Quoted from *Izvestiia* (newspaper), 3 December 1943. (Author)

32. The text of the agreement signed at Yalta is found in the *American Journal of International Law,* Supplement 39, p. 103; or in *British and Foreign State Papers,* Vol. 148, 88.

33. At the beginning of 1944 Admiral Nimitz, commander-in-chief of the American fleet in the Pacific Ocean, recognized the necessity of amphibious landings in China to establish beachheads for operations against Japan. See M.S. Steward, "Victory Lies in China," *The Nation,* Vol. 158, No. 9 (26 February 1944), p. 242. (Author)

34. Henry L. Stimson and MacGeorge Bundy, *On Active Service in Peace and War* (New York), pp. 618, 619. (Author)

35. Harry S. Truman, *Memoirs* (New York, 1955), I, 314. (Author)

36. Isolated clashes between the Eighth National Liberation Army and Kuomintang troops in July of 1945 led to pitched battles, and the major Chinese newspaper *Ta-kung-pao* on 3 August 1945 stated: "The civil war in China already has begun." See A.M. Dubinsky, *Osvoboditel'naia missiia Sovetskogo Soiuza na Dal'nem Vostoke (The Liberating Mission of the Soviet Union in the Far East)* (Moscow, 1966), p. 522. (Author)

37. The Crimea Declaration is found in *British and Foreign State Papers,* 148,88; or in *Documents on American Foreign Policy (1944-1945),* VII, 355.

38. See Inoue Kiyoshi et al., *Istoriia sovremennoi Yaponii (History of Modern Japan)* (Moscow, 1955), p. 264. (Author)

39. A.M. Dubinsky, *Osvoboditel'naia missiia Sovetskogo Soyuza na Dal'nem Vostoke,* p. 558. (Author)

40. *Chich-fang jih-pao (Liberation Press),* 13 August 1945. See also Peng Ming, *Istoriia kitaisko-sovetskoi druzhby (The History of Sino-Soviet Friendship)* (Moscow, 1959), p. 228. (Author) *Chinese Communist Studies in Modern Chinese History,* p. 46.

41. R. Malinovsky, M. Zakharov et al., *Final (The Finale)* (Moscow, 1966) p. 310. Despite the historical facts, apologists of American imperialism attempt to explain the quick end of the war in Japan not by participation of the Soviet Union and its rapid destruction of Japan's best forces on the Asian continent, but by the effect of the atomic bombs dropped by the Americans on Hiroshima (6 August) and Nagasaki (9 August). In reality, the destruction of those peaceful cities, which lacked even the least role in the defense of Japan, could not have brought a turning point in the war. They did not affect Japan's military potential in any way. At the time of the atomic attacks the American command knew of the impending Soviet attack on the Kuan-tung army, and government officials in the United States recognized that this would decide the outcome of the war. For example, former Secretary of State (Edward) Stettinius in his book *Roosevelt and the Russians* (New York, 1947), attributed special importance to the Kuan-tung army and held that "if Russia does not enter the war and engage that army in battle, it is impossible to count on the success of an invasion of the Japanese Islands." (Author)

CHAPTER SEVEN

1. *Tegeran, Yalta, Potsdam. Sobrnik dokumentov (Teheran, Yalta, Potsdam. A Collection of Documents)* (Moscow, 1967), pp. 54-55. (Author) The English text is in *British and Foreign State Papers,* Vol. 148, 19. See also Robert Beitzell, *Tehran Yalta Potsdam. The Soviet Protocols* (Gulf Breeze, FL: Academic International Press, 1970).

2. The communique of the Cairo Conference is found in *Foreign Relations. The Conferences at Cairo and Teheran, 1943* (1961), p. 448; or in *Basic Documents of American Foreign Policy,* Document 13, p. 22.

3. The Teheran Declaration is found in *British and Foreign State Papers,* 148, 19.

4. The declaration contained the following six conditions: 1. The legality of popularly elected governments and forces was to be recognized in liberated regions. 2. The Eighth and Fourth Armies were to determine in their regions the manner in which Japanese forces would capitulate. 3. Punishment for traitors and disbanding of the puppet armies would be determined. 4. There would be just and rational reorganization of the armies. 5. The legal status of all parties and groups would be recognized. 6. A conference would be called without delay, including all parties and groups, to decide questions connected with the establishment of a democratic coalition government. See *Ocherki istorii Kitaia v noveishee vremia (Survey of the Recent History of China)* (Moscow, 1959), pp. 382-383. (Author)

5. Printed in *Chich-fang jih-pao,* 12 October 1945. (Author) On the three national principles expounded by Sun Yat-sen, see p. 261 above.

6. The English text of the Potsdam declaration is found in the *American Journal of International Law,* supplement 39, p. 245; or in *British and Foreign State Papers,* Vol. 145, 852.

7. *Basic Initial Post-Surrender Directive to the Supreme Commander for the Allied Powers for the Occupation and Control of Japan,* 1945. (Author)

8. For the complete text of the Japanese constitution of 1946, see Amos J. Peaslee, *Constitutions of Nations,* Vol. 2, 518-533.

9. Ienaga Saburo, *Nihon bunkashi (History of Japanese Culture),* p. 259.

(Author) Hara Kei was an important leader of the early Japanese party Seiyukai. See *East Asia-Transformation,* pp. 571-574. Harada Kumao was the personal secretary of Prince Saionji Kimmochi, who held power both as prime minister and indirectly as an important advisor of the emperor. On Harada, see *Thought and Behavior,* p. 358.

10. Yoshida Shigeru (1878-1967) actually led several cabinets between 1946 and 1954. See *Thought and Behavior,* pp. 393, 397.

11. Katayama Tetsu (1887-) was Japan's only prime minister from the Socialist Party, holding office May 1947-June 1948. See *Thought and Behavior,* pp. 365-366.

12. The text of the Sino-American Treaty on Friendship, Commerce and Maritime Relations of 4 November 1946 is found in *U.S. Department of State Treaties and Other International Acts Series,* No. 1871.

13. The agreements between China and the United States of 1947 and 1948 are found in *Treaties and Other International Acts Series,* No. 1687; and *United States Treaties and Other International Agreements,* Vol. 3 (1952), Part 4, p. 5469.

14. Tsin Pen-li, *Istoriia ekonomicheskoi agressii amerikanskogo imperializma v Kitae (The History of Economic Aggression by American Imperialism in China)* (Moscow, 1951), p. 103. (Author)

15. Soviet trade with the popular democratic regions of Northeastern China amounted to 93 million rubles in 1947, to 151 million in 1948 and to 205 million rubles in 1949 (with the ruble at an exchange rate of .9 per dollar). The USSR sent oil products, automobiles, industrial equipment, metals, medical supplies, fabrics, sugar, cotton, rubber and paper, and other items. China supplied grain, vegetable oils, meat and bristles to the Soviet Union. Several mixed Sino-Soviet companies were established on the Liao-tung peninsula. As Chinese specialists gained production skills, the Soviet partners in these companies transferred their rights to local Chinese organizations and the companies became purely Chinese. Similarly, trade with Hsin-chiang province rose from 10.5 million rubles in 1946, to 16 million in 1949. Soviet specialists assisted in geological explorations for non-ferrous metals and oil, and helped to organize the processing of the raw materials which were discovered. See *Leninskaia politika v otnoshenii Kitaia (Leninist Policy Toward China),* pp. 130-136. (Author)

16. On 14 January 1949 the Chinese Communist Party presented eight conditions for a peace agreement with the Kuomintang. They included punishment of war criminals, annulment of the constitution proclaimed by the Kuomintang on 25 December 1946, revocation of other laws of the Kuomintang, restructuring of Kuomintang armies along democratic lines, confiscation of bureaucratic capital, agrarian reform, annulment of traitorous agreements, and the calling of a conference for political consultation which would exclude reactionary elements, and would aim to create a democratic coalition government. Published in *Chien Ko-ming Chin-hsin tao-ti (Bring the Revolution to an End)* (Chang-chun, 1949), pp. 18-23. (Author)

17. On 21 January 1949 Chiang Kai-shek announced his retirement and the transfer of the duties of head of the government to Li Tsung-jen. (Author)

18. Complete liberation of southern and southwestern regions of China came only after the proclamation of the Chinese People's Republic on 1 October 1949, and some regions were still contested until the middle of 1950. (Author)

19. Mao Tse-tung wrote: "These various demands and contradictions (between

the working class and the bourgeoisie—M.S.) can be resolved, and then all these classes together can create a political order, an economy and a culture for the new democracy." In the Russian edition of Mao's works published in 1953, the editorial committee of the Central Committee of the Chinese Communist Party made fundamental changes in the text, thereby correcting Mao's bourgeois-nationalistic views. Such changes were also made in other articles written by Mao Tse-tung. See Mao Tse-tung *Izbrannye proizvedeniia (Selected Works)* (Moscow, 1953), Vol. 3, 201-372, and Vol. 4, 495-472. (Author)

20. Mao stated: "The national bourgeoisie of China and its representatives either take part or preserve neutrality in the popular democratic revolutionary struggle to the degree that they submit to oppression or limitations from imperialism, feudalism, and bureaucratic capital. For that reason, and because China's economy remains backward still, for a rather long time after the victory of the revolution it will be necessary to utilize the activities of private capital in the interests of developing the national economy both in urban and rural areas. We should also make use of the slogan of Sun Yat-sen on restricting capital . . . . In no case should extremely great and severe limitations be placed on the private capital sector of the economy; it must retain the opportunity to exist and develop within the framework of the economic policies and the plan of the people's republic. Mao Tse-tung, *Izbrannye proizvedeniia (Selected Works)* (Peking, 1964), Vol. 4, 448. (Author)

21. It is worthy of note that the report to the Second Plenum of the Central Committee of the Chinese Communist Party (VII Session) was published abroad only in 1964, when Mao Tse-tung already had proclaimed publicly the anti-Soviet direction to be taken in foreign policy, and the struggle to be waged against the resolutions of the Eighth Party Congress concerning socialist construction in China. As in 1953, the editors in Peking changed Mao's original statements before their publication abroad, adding such phrases as "under the direction of the working class," "the leading role of the working class," "building of socialism," and so forth. (Author)

22. The following excerpt was published by the Chinese Party Central Committee in December 1953, from the resolutions of the Second Plenum of 1949: "Despite the fact that China's modern industry contributes but ten percent of the total national product, it is still highly concentrated. The largest and most important capital investments are in the hands of imperialists and their servants among the Chinese bureaucratic bourgeoisie. To confiscate that capital for the proletariat of the people's republic means to give the people's republic the opportunity to take the vital arteries of the country's economy into its hands, and to turn them into the leading segment of the national economy. That segment of the economy will then have a socialist, rather than a capitalist character." (Author)

23. The term *zaibatsu* refers to the traditional powerful trading companies which developed in Japan in the 19th and 20th centuries, concentrating enormous capital in private hands, frequently with government-granted privileges. These early conglomerates controlled the Japanese economy to an extreme degree. See *East Asia-Transformation*, pp. 505-511. (Author)

24. Ashida's cabinet contained seven representatives of the Democratic Party, led by Ashida himself as prime minister. The Socialist Party had the ministerial post of deputy prime minister, held by the right-wing socialist Nishio, and seven secondary ministerial posts, while the Party of Collaboration received two ministerial posts. (Author)

25. Yoshida Shigeru (1878-1967) served in the foreign ministry before the war. He opposed the militarists and was out of office during the war, but played an important post-war role, heading five cabinets until his retirement in 1954. See *Thought and Behavior*, p. 393.

26. *Documents Concerning the Allied Occupation of Japan*, Vol. 13, 101.

27. Ibid., p. 27.

28. *Japan Statistical Yearbook, 1963* (Tokyo, 1964), p. 253. (Author)

29. Mao Tse-tung, *Izbrannye proizvedeniia (Selected Works)*, Vol. 4, 508.

30. The flourishing of China during the Han dynasty (206 B.C.-220 A.D.) has caused that era and its greatness to be cited as the model for Chinese renaissance and glory in subsequent periods.

31. Mao Tse-tung, op. cit., Vol. 4, 118.

CHAPTER EIGHT

1. The Japanese Communist Party was vigorously persecuted during the late 1940s and the chief leaders were banned from activities by MacArthur in May 1950. (Author)

2. The Political Consultative Council was established at the end of 1945 on the basis of the agreement of 10 October 1945 between the Chinese Communist Party and the Kuomintang. In reality, the council accomplished nothing and its activity was paralyzed by the Kuomintang. The new National Political Consultative Council did not include reactionary classes or their parties. It met in Peking 21-30 September 1949 and adopted several statutes relating to organization of the Chinese People's Republic. See *Obrazovanie Kitaiskoi Narodnoi Respubliki. Dokumenty i materialy (Establishment of the Chinese People's Republic. Documents and Materials)* (Moscow, 1950), pp. 13-54. (Author)

3. Ibid., p. 30. (Author)

4. The text of the agreement is found in the *American Journal of International Law*, Vol. 44 (1950), No. 3, Documents, p. 83.

5. According to the agreement, the credits were to be retired in the amount of 300 million dollars by the Chinese government in equal installments over a period of ten years beginning on 31 December 1954, by deliveries of Chinese goods at world prices, delivery of gold, or payment in American dollars. See *Obrazovanie Kitaiskoi Narodnoi Respubliki. Dokumenty i materialy,* pp. 119-121. (Author)

6. Point 2, Part 8 of the Crimean agreement of 1945 foresaw an "international free port at Ta-lien with guarantees for the special interests of the Soviet Union in that port, and renewal of the lease at Port Arthur as a naval base of the USSR." *Vneshnaia politika SSSR. Sbornik dokumentov (Foreign Policy of the USSR. A Collection of Documents)* (Moscow, 1947), Vol. 5, 537-538. (Author) See *A Decade of American Foreign Policy. Basic Documents,* Document 16, p. 27 ff.

7. Announcement of the party line was prepared by the Department of Agitation and Propaganda of the Central Committee of the Chinese Communist Party, and published in December 1953 as *Theses for Study and Propaganda of the General Line of the Party in the Transition Period* (Peking, 1953). (Author)

8. The five principles proclaimed by the Bandung Conference were mutual respect for territorial integrity and sovereignty, non-aggression, non-interference in domestic affairs, equality and mutually beneficial relations, and peaceful coexistence. (Author) The English text is in G. Wint, ed., *Asia: A Handbook* (New York, 1955), p. 798.

9. "New-democratic" is the author's term for Mao's class approach which pragmatically included the working class and the bourgeoisie. Here the author intimates that this "revision" is philosophically unacceptable.

10. *Materialy VIII Vsekitaiskogo s'ezda KPK (Materials of the Eighth All-China Congress of the Chinese Communist Party)* (Peking, 1956), Vol. 2, 68. (Author)

11. For discussion and materials consult *Materialy VIII Vsekitaiskogo s'ezda KPK*, pp. 117, 237-238, and 239. (Author)

12. Ibid., p. 265-266. (Author)

13. See Note 13, Chapter Nine. (Author)

14. *Materialy VIII Vsekitaiskogo s'ezda KPK*, Vol. 1, 143. (Author)

15. The plan is also known as the "Dodge plan," for Joseph M. Dodge, a banker from Chicago who visited Japan at the beginning of 1949 as the representative of American financial circles. Under Dodge's direction, the Japanese national budget for 1949-1950 was reworked, reducing expenditures on social needs and increasing taxes. See *Ocherki noveishei istorii Yaponii (Survey of Recent Japanese History)*, p. 322. (Author)

16. The text of the San Francisco treaty is found in *Major Peace Treaties of Modern History*, pp. 2641-2656. The Japanese-American security pact is printed in George R. Packard, *Protest in Tokyo. The Security Crisis of 1960* ((Princeton, N.J., 1966), pp. 355-357) which offers a comprehensive discussion of this and other Japanese-American agreements.

17. *Japan Statistical Yearbook, 1963* (1964), pp. 154-157. (Author)

18. According to statistics in the Japanese journal *Oriental Economist* of January 1972, in 1958 the average wages of an American worker were more than eight times those of a Japanese worker, while an English worker received three times as much and a worker in West Germany received two and a half times as much. Even with correction for higher labor productivity and lower prices in Japan, real income for the Japanese worker was three to four times less that of an American worker, two times less than an English worker, and one and a half to two times less than a West German worker. (Author)

19. See Note 25, Chapter Seven, on Yoshida Shigeru. (Author)

20. The declaration of China and the Soviet Union on relations with Japan, dated 12 October 1954, is found in English in *United Nations Treaty Series*, Vol. 226, 70.

21. Hatoyama Ichiro, the leader of this cabinet, was a conservative who as minister of education in 1933 had dismissed liberals from Kyoto University. See *East Asia-Transformation*, pp. 594, 837.

22. The Soviet-Japanese declaration and Protocol of Trade Development of 19 October 1956 is found in *United Nations Treaty Series*, Vol. 263, 119-127.

23. *Obrazovanie Kitaiskoi Narodnoi Respubliki. Dokumenty i materialy (Formation of the Chinese People's Republic. Documents and Materials)*, p. 66. (Author)

24. The Peace agreement of 28 April 1952 between Japan and the Chinese government on Taiwan is found in *United Nations Treaty Series*, Vol. 138, 3.

25. Ishibashi Tanzan (1884-) led the Japanese government briefly in 1956. Ishibashi Tanzan's health failed and he was forced to resign in February 1957. See Packard, *Protest in Tokyo*, p. 7 et passim.

26. Kishi Nobosuke was a minister in the Tojo cabinet which declared war on the United States. He lead the government as prime minister, 1957-1970.

27. From the report on governmental activities made by Chou En-lai on 23 September 1954. See *Obrazovanie Kitaiskoi Narodnoi Respubliki. Dokumenty i materialy*, p. 132. (Author)

CHAPTER NINE

1. The quotations and the program here and below are found in *Narodnyi Kitai (People's China)* (1957), No. 13, Prilozhenie (Supplement). (Author)

2. The model constitution of the commune Wei-shin called for a system of food supply in which all members, regardless of the number of workers in the family, would receive food products in proportion to the number of family members and corresponding to established government standards of nutritional needs. See *Dvizhenie za sozdanie narodnykh kommun v Kitae (The Movement for Creating Popular Communes in China)* (Peking, 1958), p. 79. (Author)

3. In September 1958 Mao Tse-tung visited one of the largest metallurgical plants in the country at Wu-han. Its blast furnace had been built during the "great leap forward." Mao issued an order to combine the Wu-han metallurgical complex and nearby agricultural regions into a unified "people's commune." *Pravda*, 30 September 1958. (Author)

4. *Dvizhenie za sozdanie narodnykh kommun v Kitae*, p. 9. (Author)

5. *Vtoraia sessiia VIII Vsekitaiskogo s'ezda KPK (Second Session of the VIII National Congress of the CPC)* (Peking, 1958), p. 66. (Author)

6. "Bigger" expressed the unsatisfactory construction measures of the first five-year plan; "quicker" referred to the slavish tempos of the first and second five-year plans; "better" expressed the notion that until the present construction was done poorly, using inferior materials of the socialist countries; "cheaper" meant the abolition of expensive large-scale industrial construction and expensive scientific and technical aid from the socialist countries. (Author)

7. In China swine and domestic fowl are usually estimated on the basis of the number of peasant households. There are in the country about 120 million families, of which some ten million are Moslems and other nationalities which do not raise pigs. Toward the end of the first five-year plan, each family was estimated to have one pig and 20 birds, while an additional 30-40 million swine were held in the public sector. (Author)

8. Near the end of 1958 a multitude of dwarf blast furnaces appeared on the fringes of cities and villages, creating at night the impression of an enormous torchlight parade. Every "people's commune" was to have its own furnaces, made of adobe. However, they produced iron with a sulphur content of no less than four percent. Since a content of no more than 0.2-0.4 percent sulphur is required, this iron was unsuitable for industrial use. Yet 60-90 million workers were occupied in this "small metallurgy." (Author)

9. The politbureau in both Chinese and Soviet organization is the highest level of party leadership. See Donald W. Treadgold, *Soviet and Chinese Communism Similarities and Differences* (Seattle, 1967), pp. 58-61, 95-96.

10. *Chung-kuo (China)* (Hong Kong, 1968), No. 48. (Author)

11. *Dokumenty VIII plenuma TsK KPK VIII sozyva (Documents of the Eighth Plenum of the Central Committee of the Chinese Communist Party, Eighth Session)* (Peking, 1959), pp. 4-5, 20. (Author)

12. *Materialy VI plenuma TsK KPK VIII sozyva*, pp. 1-2. (Author)

13. According to the constitution, the mandate of the All-China Congress of the Chinese Communist Party lasted five years, and annual meetings of the congress were to be held. (*Materialy VIII s'ezda KPK*, Vol. 1, 157.) Party plenums were to be called at least twice annually (ibid., p. 158). Actually the first meeting following the eighth plenum took place only in January 1961, a year and a half later. (Author)

14. The first armed clashes on the Sino-Indian border took place in mid-1959. Despite pleas from the Soviet government and many Asian states for a peaceful settlement, Chinese propaganda inflamed hatred of India. Major armed conflicts occurred in 1962. In Indonesia, governmental economic reforms affected Chinese merchants and moneylenders. The Chinese embassy in Djakarta came to their assistance, thus interfering in the internal affairs of the country and bringing protests from the government and the public of Indonesia. (Author)

15. The Sino-Soviet Treaty of Friendship, Alliance and Mutual Assistance is found in *United Nations Treaty Series*, Vol. 226, 5.

16. See *Informatsionnyi biulleten agentstva Sin'khua (The Information Bulletin of the New China Agency)*, 22 January 1961, pp. 3-4. (Author)

17. *Otvet TsK KPK na pis'mo TsK KPSS ot 30 marta 1963 g. (Reply of the Central Committee of the Chinese Communist Party to the Letter of the Central Committee of the Communist Party of the Soviet Union of 30 March 1963)* (Peking, 1963), pp. 13, 15. (Author)

18. V.I. Lenin, "Imperializm, kak vysshaia stadiia kapitalizma (Imperialism as the Highest Stage of Capitalism)," *Polnoe sobranie sochinenii (Complete Works)*, Vol. 27, 389. (Author)

19. *Otvet TsK KPK na pis'mo TsK KPSS ot 30 marta 1963 g.*, pp. 11-12. (Author)

20. The overseas Chinese are those ethnically Chinese inhabitants of other nations, especially in Asia but also in Africa and elsewhere. They have maintained unusually strong ties with the homeland in comparison to other emigres, for long periods.

21. For example, the writer Tung To in his "Notes from Three Villages" and "Evening Discussions at the Foot of Yang-shan" stated that one should "study the government" which is "stronger than us," "unite with it" and "rejoice, when a friend is stronger than you," for he who "thinks highly of himself and shoves away his teacher with a kick after his first successes, will learn nothing." These statements were correctly understood by the Maoists to be a defense of friendship with the Soviet Union, and a rejection of anti-Sovietism. Quoted from I.M. Nadeyev, *"Kul'turnaia revoliutsiia" i sud'ba kitaiskoi literatury (The "Cultural Revolution" and the Fate of Chinese Literature)* (Moscow, 1969), p. 109. (Author)

22. From the end of 1964 to May 1965, Mao Tse-tung did not appear publicly, nor did he meet with any officials. Rumors spread that he was seriously ill, and possible successors were discussed, including Liu Shao-chi. (Author)

23. Fujiyama Aichiro served as Japan's foreign minister 1957-1962. On his role in Japanese-American agreements, see Packard, *Protest in Tokyo*, p. 7 et passim.

24. *Yapono-amerikanskii "Dogovor bezopasnosti" (The Japanese-American "Security Pact")* (Moscow, 1962), p. 18. (Author)

25. On Kishi Nobosuke, see Note 26, Chapter Eight. (Author)

26. *Yapono-amerikanskii "Dogover bezopasnosti,"* p. 49. (Author)

27. Ibid., p. 19. (Author)

28. The text of the Japanese-American Treaty of Mutual Cooperation and Security is found in *Documents of American Foreign Relations, 1960*, pp. 425-431.

29. According to data of the Japanese government's Bureau of Economic Planning, the Japanese GNP in 1968 was 141.9 billion dollars, while that of the German Federal Republic was 132.2 billion, of France-117.6 billion, and of England 87.3 billion dollars. Per capita income was (in dollars): in the United States

$3543, in France $1644, in England $1583, in the German Federal Republic $1567, and in Japan $1100. See *Economic Survey of Japan, 1968-1969* (Tokyo, 1969), p. 83. (Author)

30. *East-West Trade Bulletin* (Tokyo, 1969), p. 6. Other important sources for the economic statistics quoted here are: *Monthly Statistics of Japan*, No. 97, July 1969; and *Economic Survey of Japan, 1968-1969*, pp. 83, 144-165. (Author)

31. The departure of domestic capital, largely to Japan, forced the government of the United States to impose limitations. In July 1963, President Kennedy announced a special "equalizing" tax of fifteen percent on the purchase of foreign stocks, and a graduated tax of 2.75 to 15 percent on credits granted abroad, depending on the term of the loan. Japanese Foreign Minister Ohira went to the United States to request an exemption for Japan or other special dispensations, but these were refused and the tax became effective in September 1964. (Author)

32. The regions and the capital involved were as follows: Tokyo, 120 billion yen; Kansai, 66.6 billion yen; Chubu, 81 billion yen; Tohoku, 30 billion yen; Kyushu, 40.5 billion yen; Chugoku, 24.6 billion yen; Shikoku, 12 billion yen; Hokuriku, 27 billion yen; Hokaido, 25 billion yen. See *Novoe litso yaponskoi promyshlennosti (The New Face of Japanese Industry)* (Moscow, 1967), p. 106. (Author)

33. *Monthly Statistics of Japan, 1969*, No. 97, p. 117. (Author)

34. *Economic Survey of Japan, 1968-1969*, pp. 144-147, 165. (Author)

35. *Economic Picture of Japan* (Tokyo, 1968), p. 52. (Author)

36. In 1956-1966 the growth of labor productivity in small enterprises ranged from 37 percent (between 1956 and 1961) to 45 percent (1961-1966), in comparison to the increase in labor productivity at large enterprises. See *Economic Survey of Japan, 1968-1969*, p. 155. (Author)

37. Joje Watanuki, *The Future of Japanese Politics* (Tokyo, 1969), p. 9. (Author)

38. *Economic Statistics* (Japanese), 1970, No. 6. (Author)

39. For further information on these economic developments, see *Japan Times*, 1 January 1970, and *East-West Trade Bulletin*, October 1969, p. 3. (Author)

40. The Nixon-Sato communique of November 1969 is found in *The New York Times*, 22 November 1969, Section 14, p. 4. Prime Minister Sato Eisaku became Japan's premier in 1964, and resigned in 1972.

41. In the opinion of Professor Taoko Rioichi of Kyoto University, a country in defending itself has the right "independently to determine the degree of danger and to utilize measures which contradict international law in order to protect its interests from threatened attack or presumed attack." Taoko Rioichi, *The Right of Self-Defense in International Law* (Tokyo, 1969), p. 60. (Author)

42. See *Sankei Shimbun*, 29 May 1969, and *Mainichi*, 20 May 1969. (Author)

43. *Mainichi Daily News*, 22 March 1970. At the meeting of the budget committee of the upper chamber of the parliament on 1 April 1970, Nakasone Yasuhiro declared that he would present a resolution to change the law forbidding dispatch of Japanese forces abroad, and would insist on legalization of such dispatch of defensive forces abroad for peaceful purposes. (Author)

44. *Japan Times*, 23 November 1969. (Author)

45. *Sunday Times* (London), 14 January 1968. (Author)

46. The communique of the Japanese and Chinese communist parties was published in *Jen-min jih-pao (People's Daily News)*, 21 October 1959. (Author)

47. U.S. State Department officials insisted on this argument, and in August 1958 sent a "Memorandum on Non-Recognition of the Chinese People's Republic"

to American embassies. It stated that recognition of the CPR would bring no economic benefits, and cited the example of England, which had recognized the CPR without any subsequent increase in trade. At the same time Germany and Japan had been developing trade without diplomatic relations. The conclusion made was that trade and diplomatic recognition of the People's Republic should not be linked. (Author)

48. On 17 January 1965 in a conversation with the Japanese parliamentary deputy, Utsunomia Tokuma, Chinese Deputy Premier Chen Yi stated that the Chinese People's Republic already advocated return of the Kurile Islands to Japan, and that "the USSR had taken some 1.5 million square kilometers of China's territory." *Asahi* (newspaper), 18 January 1965. (Author)

49. *Toyo keizai (East Asia Monthly)*, 1964, No. 3154. (Author)

50. *Asahi*, 16 January 1959. (Author)

51. *Informatsionnyi biulleten' agentstva Sin'khua (The Information Bulletin of the New China Agency)*, 21 September 1962, No. 1043, p. 1. (Author)

52. The author gives no source for these statistics.

53. The Taipeh press wrote: "In the past Japan possessed a major economic base on Taiwan. At that time Japan's economic influence extended to all branches of the island's economy, so that Taiwan's economy gradually came into Japanese hands. The credits which are intended for the development of Taiwan's economy either directly or indirectly will increase Japan's influence on Taiwan's economy." *Huan-jan jih-pao*, 9 May 1965. (Author)

54. See Note 30, Chapter Seven. (Author)

55. *Toyo keizai*, 1966, No. 3316, p. 55. (Author)

56. In an interview of Mao Tse-tung by Edward Snow, published in the French magazine *Nouveau Candide* (11-18 February 1965), Mao made the following comment on the possibility of war between China and the United States over Vietnam: "War would occur only if American armies entered China. . . . China's armies will not engage in a war beyond the borders of their own territory. That is clear. The Chinese will fight only if the Americans attack them. That is also clear." (Author)

57. The Johnson-Sato communique is found in *The New York Times*, 16 November 1967, Section 3, p. 1. (Author)

58. On Matsumura, see above, p. 237. (Author)

59. *East-West Trade*, 1 March 1970, pp. 10-14. (Author)

60. The Nixon-Sato communique of 22 November 1969 states: "The President and the Prime Minister share the hope that communist China will support greater cooperation and consultation in international matters." *The New York Times*, 22 November 1969, Section 14, p. 4. (Author)

61. *Japan Times*, 14 December 1969. (Author)

62. Loc. cit. (Author)

63. The author gives no source for these statistics.

64. It is interesting to note that Premier Sato was not insulted when the sum of Peking's accusations amounted to his adherence to the Japanese-American alliance. In the Japanese Council of Advisors on 20 April 1970, Sato announced that even before the departure of the Japanese delegation for Peking, "he had expected that he would be subjected to harsh criticism by the Chinese." Nonetheless he was convinced "that the entire problem of China could be settled in the 1970s." (Author) The Sino-Japanese communique of 19 April 1970 was discussed in *The New York Times*, 19, 21, 30 April 1970.

CONCLUSION

1. Karl Marx and Friedrich Engels, "Proizkhozhdenie sem'i, chastnoi sobstvennosti i gosudarstva (The Origin of the Family, Private Property and the State)," *Sochineniia (Works),* Vol. 2. (Author)

2. The full text of Japan's 21 demands is found in Henry Chung, *The Oriental Policy of the United States* (New York, 1970), pp. 271-276.

3. The agreement between President Nixon and Premier Sato is given in the communique published in *The New York Times,* 22 November 1969, Section 14, p. 4.